The Mahatma Misunderstood

The Mahatma Misunderstood

The Politics and Forms of Literary Nationalism in India

SNEHAL SHINGAVI

Anthem Press
An imprint of Wimbledon Publishing Company
www.anthempress.com

This edition first published in UK and USA 2014
by ANTHEM PRESS
75–76 Blackfriars Road, London SE1 8HA, UK
or PO Box 9779, London SW19 7ZG, UK
and
244 Madison Ave. #116, New York, NY 10016, USA

First published in hardback by Anthem Press in 2013

Copyright © Snehal Shingavi 2014

The author asserts the moral right to be identified as the author of this work.

All rights reserved. Without limiting the rights under copyright reserved above, no part of this publication may be reproduced, stored or introduced into a retrieval system, or transmitted, in any form or by any means (electronic, mechanical, photocopying, recording or otherwise), without the prior written permission of both the copyright owner and the above publisher of this book.

British Library Cataloguing-in-Publication Data
A catalogue record for this book is available from the British Library.

Library of Congress Cataloging-in-Publication Data
The Library of Congress has catalogued the hardcover edition as follows:
Shingavi, Snehal.
 The Mahatma misunderstood : the politics and forms of literary nationalism in India / Snehal Shingavi.
  pages cm
 Includes bibliographical references and index.
 ISBN 978-0-85728-511-9 (hardcover : alk. paper)
 1. Indic fiction–History and criticism. 2. Gandhi, Mahatma, 1869–1948–In literature. 3. National characteristics, East Indian, in literature. I. Title.
 PK5423.S55 2013
 891'.1–dc23
     2012047560

ISBN-13: 978 1 78308 329 9 (Pbk)
ISBN-10: 1 78308 329 8 (Pbk)

Cover image © Maureen Jameson

This title is also available as an ebook.

CONTENTS

Acknowledgments		vii
Introduction		1
Chapter 1	The Mahatma as Proof: The Nationalist Origins of the Historiography of Indian Writing in English	13
Chapter 2	"The Mahatma didn't say so, but ...": Mulk Raj Anand's *Untouchable* and the Sympathies of Middle-Class Nationalists	29
Chapter 3	"The Mahatma may be all wrong about politics, but ...": Raja Rao's *Kanthapura* and the Religious Imagination of the Indian, Secular, Nationalist Middle Class	59
Chapter 4	The Missing Mahatma: Ahmed Ali and the Aesthetics of Muslim Anticolonialism	105
Chapter 5	The Grammar of the Gandhians: Jayaprakash Narayan and the Figure of Gandhi	155
Chapter 6	The Mahatma Misunderstood: The Arrested Development of the Nationalist Dialectic	175
Conclusion	Dangerous Solidarities	193
Notes		204
Bibliography		209
Index		223

ACKNOWLEDGMENTS

First and foremost, this dissertation would have been impossible without the support of my parents, Ashok and Ujwal, and my brother, Preetam, who had the patience to suffer through an unnecessarily long detour in my life. There are neither sufficient words nor gestures to demonstrate just how grateful I am for all of the things that they have done for me over the years.

I am also greatly indebted to the intellectual support, advice, and mentorship provided to me by Abdul Jan Mohamed, Vasudha Dalmia, and Gautam Premnath, as well as Priya Joshi and Marcial Gonzalez. Abdul Jan Mohamed stood up for me in ways that can never be repaid, at times when no one else would. Vasudha Dalmia opened more doors for me than I ever knew could be opened; to her I especially credit my love for Premchand and the world of Hindi literature. Gautam Premnath and Marcial Gonzalez are model scholar-activists whose examples I strive to follow. Priya Joshi introduced me to the world of Indian Writing in English and I have not turned back since.

Countless instructors, mentors, and advisors aided me in this process. David Lloyd, Chris Nealon, Steven Goldsmith, Richard Halpern, Eric Falci, Munis Faruqui, Adnan Malik, Stephen Best, Anne-Lise Francois, Richard Hutson, Michael Rubinstein, and Muhammad Warsi have all contributed my development. Not enough can be said about Donna Jones, Lyn Hejinian, and Susan Schweik, all of whom shaped my thinking about the discipline of literature and provided more help and generosity than I had right to ask for. I have to thank especially Janet Adelman who made it possible to survive through and thrive while teaching "The Politics and Poetics of Palestinian Resistance"; the class would not have been possible without the incredibly principled position she took.

There were also friends made during the process, all of whom are reflected in some ways throughout this dissertation. Connie You, Helga Erickson, Michael Farry, June Yoshi, Joseph Nugent, Emily Anderson, and Kimberly Johnson deserve much credit for putting up with some of the worst expressions of my ideas earliest and for being friends through some of the most trying times of graduate school. Ruth Jennison provided me with my first serious model of Marxist theory and practice and is responsible for turning me into an activist. Christine Hong never had a shortage of encouraging words, seeing design in my chaos.

Siddharth Patel, always supportive, has heard more complaints about the process of writing than humanly tolerable and more iterations of the various arguments than reasonable. Ajay Satpute has been my friend for too long for me to be able to summarize his role in my thinking in a few words. Sarah Wolf, kindred spirit, lent eyes, ears, shoulders and heart throughout the entire process of writing this dissertation. Dana Blanchard pushed me when I had run out of steam. Debates with Michael Smith made my time at Berkeley exciting. Philip Gasper made me believe that scholars had something meaningful to offer activists.

Several activists in the Bay Area have provided camaraderie, engagement, and energy: Elizabeth Terzakis, John Patel, Jean Woolsey, Jessie Muldoon, Kathryn Lybarger, Steven Damewood, John Green, Alessandro Tinonga, John Gallagher, George and Poly Vouros, Michelle Simon, Adrienne Johnstone, Amanda Maystead, Anna Matschke, Derek Wright, Ragina Johnson, Rachel Odes, Crystal Bybee, Scott Johnson, Todd Chretien, Katrina Storey, Jeff Martin, Andrew Libson, Brian Belknap, Brian Cruz, and Jeremy Tully. The work that this dissertation represents pales in comparison to the work that they do, tirelessly and without recompense. Participating in the Students for Justice in Palestine fully made me a radical, and the friends made there will always be credited with the central theme of this dissertation (that nationalism can be redeemable). I am grateful as well for time spent with the United Students Against Sweatshops, the Campaign to End the Death Penalty, the Berkeley Stop the War Coalition, the Campus Antiwar Network, the Association of Graduate Student Employees (AGSE/UAW local 2865), and the Friends of South Asia.

I am thankful for the support of the faculty and staff in the University of Mary Washington's English, Linguistics and Communications Department, who were encouraging through my time in Virginia: Constance Smith, Gary Richards, Maya Mathur, James Harding, Collin Rafferty, Marie McCallister, Teresa Kennedy, Claudia Emerson, Chris Foss, Mara Scanlon, and Antonio Barrenechea.

Finally, several people at the University of Texas, Austin, offered invaluable feedback on various pieces in this book. My colleagues in the English department—JK Barret, Matt Cohen, Elizabeth Cullingford, Rasha Diab, Barbara Harlow, Neville Hoad, Justin Hodgson, Heather Houser, Coleman Hutchison, Martin Kevorkian, David and Donna Kornhaber, Julia Lee, Lindsay Reckson, and Matt Richardson—were incredibly generous with their support and their time. Friends in the Center of Asian American Studies and the South Asia Institute—Madeline Hsu, Naomi Paik, Eric Tang, Sharmila Rudrappa, Nhi Lieu, Kamran Asdar Ali, Kamala Visweswaran, Heather Hindman, Kaushik Ghose, Shanti Kumar, Rupert Snell, Akbar Hyder, Kathryn Hansen, Carla Petievich, Gail Minault, Itty Ibrahim—offered me fantastic feedback on later stages of the work. There are undoubtedly people whom I have overlooked.

An early version of Chapter 1 appeared in *Nationalist Ideology and the Historiography of Literature in South Asia* (Social Science Press, 2010). A section of Chapter 4 appeared in *The Two Sided Canvas: Perspectives on Ahmed Ali* (Oxford University Press, 2013). I am grateful to both publishers for permission to reproduce versions of these pieces here.

This dissertation bears the impress of the ideas and encouragement provided by many of the people I have listed above. The errors in the project that follow, it bears underlining, are my own.

INTRODUCTION

In 1938, Raja Rao (1908–2006) published his short story "The Cow of the Barricades," a revisiting of the themes taken up in his most famous novel, *Kanthapura* (1938), where Rao describes the effects of Gandhian politics on a small village in Uttar Kanara. Rao had for a long time been a commentator and writer on contemporary developments in India for English language audiences, and the story was picked up in the New York–based journal, *Asia and the Americas*. In the short, imagistic and fabular narrative, life in an unnamed village is made difficult by the violent repression of Indian National Congress–led boycott activities by Indian soldiers "from Peshawar and Pindi" who are working for "the red man's Government" (Rao 1947, 177). When workers at a nearby mill decide to help, they immediately come into conflict with the president of the local Congress committee, a Gandhian named "the Master," who characteristically recommends a nonviolent strategy for resistance. The workers want to build a barricade in order to fend off the coming attack:

> But the Master said again, "No, there shall be no battle, brothers." But the workmen said again, "It is not with, 'I love you, I love you,' that you can change the grinding heart of this government," and they brought picks and scythes and a few Mohammedans brought their swords and one or two stole rifles from the mansions, and there was a regular fighting army ready to fall on the red man's men. (Rao 1947, 179)

On the day of the battle, Gauri, a universally beloved white cow who visited the village only on Tuesdays and only to nibble at the hair of the Master ("There was only one other person whose hair she had nibbled – she had nibbled at the hair of the Mahatma"), climbs on top of the barricades. The workers on one side worry that the presence of the cow will draw the villagers out onto the battlefield where they will be vulnerable to gunfire, but the soldiers on the other side are so moved by the presence of the cow that they decide to join forces with the villagers instead! In response, "their chief, the red man, saw this and fired a shot. It went through Gauri's head, and she fell a vehicle of God among lowly men." Despite the movement coming to an end temporarily in mourning for the death of the Gandhian cow, the villagers are confident that Gauri "will be reborn when India sorrows again before She is free." The story ends aphoristically, "Therefore it is said, 'The Mahatma may be all wrong about politics, but he is right about the fullness of love in all creatures – the speechful and the mute'" (Rao 1947, 181–2).

The story is allegorically dense with possibility and hope, which cannot be drowned in the blood of colonial repression against the various *swadeshi* campaigns that were a part of the movements for independence. Villagers had, after all, fought against the seizure of their land when they had refused to pay taxes during the Civil Disobedience movement (1930–34), as Gandhi had asked them to do. Running through the story is a reflection of the dynamics of these protests and a wishful thinking about the next round of agitation, already felt to be around the corner. The story, crucially, relies on a particular class-based analysis – a Socialist analysis to be precise – of the village and the nearby industrial locales, of the various elements of Indian society (workers, peasants and soldiers) coming together across communal divisions behind the metonym of the Mahatma (the cow on the barricades), a scenario that never really happens in historical record, though it was clearly the hope of much of the left-leaning intelligentsia in colonial India. Still, the debates between the workers and the Master about nonviolence are resolved in favor of the workers who are convinced that there needs to be a final confrontation with the colonial soldiers, but even that never happens; Gauri's death seems to dissipate all antagonism in favor of a resolution that recedes into the horizon. What is stunning about the ending, though, is neither the conclusion of a deferred but imminent (albeit vague) solution nor the undeterred confidence in the coming of independence but the resolution of the relationship between Gandhi and the movement in the village. All the ideas of Gandhi that one might associate with the historical figure in the fight against British colonial rule in India are abandoned in favor of a vision of Gandhi reduced to the one thing about which he was correct: "the fullness of love in all creatures." Like Gauri, then, the Mahatma "was no doubt a fervent soul who had sought the paths of this world to be born a sage in the next, for [he] was so compassionate and true" (Rao 1947, 175). Like Gauri, the Mahatma's sacrifices inspired even as his politics were ignored.

The story seems to be a kind of allegory, too, for the period between the Civil Disobedience movement and the Quit India movement (1940–42), in which many on the Left in India saw their moment to seize a decisive advantage from the Congress's failure to deliver anything but the most piecemeal of reforms in their negotiations with the British Raj. This was the period when the Congress Socialist Party and the Communist Party of India attempted to unite and enter into the Indian National Congress in order to steer it in a more radical direction. The hope of many leftist intellectuals was that their ability to offer more radical demands to the people – land redistribution, abolition of caste, freedom for minorities and women – would clarify the limits of Gandhian strategies and provide opportunities for the masses to go beyond the paternalistic and limited package of reforms that Gandhi offered. There are more traces of that sentiment in this story than there are of a natural fealty to Gandhian methods of discipline, asceticism, quietude and patience. The story grates against Gandhian techniques for liberation, especially since the nonviolence of the cow cannot, as the workers predict, pierce the heart of the "red man" even if it can unite all Indians against British colonial rule. Gandhi is at best, then, when he is like Gauri, a symbol rather than an actual participant, a rallying cry rather an ethical arbiter or political leader. Rather than being the source of nationalist struggle against the British, the Mahatma is transformed into a spiritual being, whose sacrifices allow the people to continue struggling. But the sheer audacity of the phrase ("the mahatma may be all wrong about politics, but …"), its perfect sweep across all Gandhian thought, to disavow and then reclaim him in alternate gestures, is at such odds with what we have come to expect from the Indian nationalist writing of the 1930s and 1940s. This is no longer literature written under the long shadow of the Mahatma, but rather fiction that imagines itself existing in the moment at which the Mahatma is about to be eclipsed, when more radical futures are on the horizon. Gandhism is about to be undone – wishfully anticipating post-Gandhism, even before the moment of independence!

Most critics of Rao's fiction have avoided this story in particular, even in discussions of stories from the same collection. This is in part because it frustrates the way that Rao is generally understood in the nationalist canon as a "Gandhian." Part of the reason for this is that Rao's reputation has been solidified by his earlier and far more popular novel, *Kanthapura* (which appears to endorse fully Gandhian methods of mobilization), as well as his later novels (in which he moves decidedly towards more spiritual and less overtly political themes, a move that would have placed him solidly in the camp of postindependence Gandhians in India). Because the Gandhian novelist and the post-Gandhian short story writer do not seem to share a common lineage, the latter's reputation is abandoned in favor of the former. No biography of Rao notices any sharp change in his politics between 1930 and 1947, nor do most critics detect any sharp divergence from his putatively Gandhian nationalist politics, even though Rao likely participated in violent campaigns against the British during that time (Naik 1982b). So important is the need to underline the singularity of the Gandhian vision of the independent nation that all divergences from that vision are ignored, undervalued, or completely discounted. This has the dual effect of misreading the political context of the literary output of the period and misunderstanding the aesthetic intervention that was being made by writers at the time.

The starting propositions when reading the fiction of late-colonial India appear to be that most of the literature agreed with Gandhi, that it was nationalist in orientation (as opposed to Socialist), and that it supported the movement for Indian independence and therefore the independent India as imagined by the Congress. But this picture emerges for two reasons, both of which are hidden by the common Gandhian interpretation. First, most studies of Indian fiction are hamstrung by their almost total reliance on the Indian novel in English, at the expense of other anglophone forms (poetry, short fiction, the essay) and, more importantly, the literary output in the several vernacular (also called *bhasha*) languages. Without access to these other materials, without a necessarily comparativist disposition, it is easy to mistake the reliance on Gandhi in the novel for ideological agreement. In fact, the presumption in most literary historiography to prioritize the novel as opposed to the short story, or to read fiction of this period in isolation from the writer's entire output, has generally led to a distorted understanding of the intellectual currents that animated the literary production of the period. If, following Edward Said and Benedict Anderson, we see the novel as growing up alongside the twin developments of empire and nationalism, then it is clear why the novel has received so much attention as the genre par excellence of nationalist thought (Anderson 1983). But in order to fully read the novelistic production of the period, to understand its form as well as its content, we would be remiss to understand the novel outside of its intellectual context. For instance, Mulk Raj Anand's interventions in *Untouchable* (1935) build upon his earlier attempts at representing the politics of colonialism in his essays and his long (unpublished) *Confession* (Anand, 1992). Similarly, the aesthetic strategies that Ahmed Ali deploys in *Twilight in Delhi* (1945) cannot be understood without also understanding his participation in the *Angare* (1932) project, a collection of Urdu short stories, and his debates with collaborators over the long history of Urdu literature (Mahmud 1996). Raja Rao's translational novel *Kanthapura* becomes recognizable as a formal conceit when it is placed next to his Kannada fiction, which is much more preoccupied with the relation between religion and sexism than it is with nationalism, as such. What should be clear, even from this early reading of "The Cow of the Barricades," is that allegiance to Gandhi was provisional and contingent at best and that the novel cannot be relied upon to tell the whole story of the coming of the nation-state.

The second reason for the dominance of the Gandhian reading has to do with the ideological shift that takes place within the careers of the writers from the 1930s and 1940s after independence. All of the thinkers in this study were either close to or actively involved in the activist campaigns of the Socialist and Communist movements in India. Anand and Ali were around the Communist Party of India and when its activists entered and then later took over the Progressive Writers' Movement. Raja Rao joined a Trotskyist political cell while in Europe and then returned to India and participated in agitations. Jayaprakash (J. P.) Narayan and Manabendranath (M. N.) Roy were leading figures in the Socialist and Communist parties, respectively. Kamaladevi Chattopadhyay was perhaps the most important feminist Socialist of her time but is almost exclusively remembered as the Mahatma's lieutenant during the famous Salt March. But after independence, they all underwent a process of deradicalization (what the Italian Socialist thinker Antonio Gramsci called "transformism") and more or less abandoned their explicit commitments to radical redistribution of wealth in favor of the more euphemistic social justice. Anand became a supporter of Nehruvian patterns of economic planning in India; Rao, through novels like *Comrade Kirilov* (1976), turned his back on his more radical past; and Ali was so thoroughly betrayed by the experience of partition, which left him unable to return to his ancestral home in Delhi for the rest of his life, that he did not contest his exclusion from the canon of Indian writing in English. In fact, the period under consideration and the writers chosen for inclusion in this study represent a unique moment in the political history of nationalist agitation in India when more radical political possibilities seemed genuinely to be on offer. It was a period that was not to be repeated, a period whose failure produced a retreat politically and ideologically in each of the writers and thinkers under consideration in this study. Narayan, as I show, even gave up on the prospect of Socialist revolution in India in favor of reformist, nonviolent politics after his disillusionment with both independence and the Soviet experiment. Roy, a Communist activist, was killed before he could have a more measurable influence on radical thought in the subcontinent.

Understanding these processes in literary and intellectual history makes the problem of the Mahatma's influence more, not less, important to understand. If, after all, the Mahatma is wrong about politics and the changes that are desired are far to the left of his ideals, then why do literary and political figures continue to demonstrate a residual allegiance to him? What is it about the figure of Gandhi that warrants critique and yet compels a loving endorsement? How is that writers like

Rao – a secular, Westernized, middle-class, English-educated, occasionally socialist thinker – came to define the literary and thematic questions in their prose through the religious, anti-Western, peasant-centered, antimodernist figure of the Mahatma? And does the presence of the Mahatma ultimately doom these novels to reproduce thematically the problems produced historically by Gandhian mobilizations? This double gesture, a movement of critique and collaboration, characterizes almost all of the so-called "Gandhian fiction" written in English during the period immediately leading up to India's independence in 1947. The more carefully this literature is examined, the more complicated this relationship to Gandhi becomes. In fact, because the literature was written primarily for British audiences but dealt with the problems of speaking to illiterate or monolingual, non-English-speaking groups in India – untouchables, peasants, women, Muslims – it seems to rely on the Mahatma even more than it needs to. After all, more so than any other figure in the nationalist pantheon, Gandhi comes to represent what is authentically Indian, what is genuinely populist and what – drawing out masses everywhere he goes – no novelist or other politician was ever able to do in the 1930s.

The Mahatma Misunderstood studies the relationship between novelistic production in late-colonial India and nationalist agitation led by the Congress by examining the process by which novelists who were critically engaged with Gandhian nationalism – who saw both the potentials and the pitfalls of Gandhian political strategies – came to be seen as the Mahatma's standard-bearers rather than his staunch opposition. In doing so, the book challenges the orthodoxy in postcolonial and subaltern studies, which contends that nationalists use independence to bring to power a bourgeois elite, whose version of events erases the unevenness of minority experiences and demands in favor of simplified, majoritarian citizenship (what Benedict Anderson refers to in another context as "homogeneous empty time"). If, as the dominant narrative contends, these novelists relied on Gandhian charisma as the protective halo in which they hid their critiques of empire, they did so at their own peril, as Gandhian ideas necessarily resulted in the antiminoritarian project of independent India. Rather, *The Mahatma Misunderstood* demonstrates that nationalist fiction (and by extension the nationalist political movement) was marked from the beginning by a deep ambivalence about the relevance of nationalist agitation and mainstream nationalist politics for minorities in colonial India, and sought to recast anticolonial politics through novelistic debates with the spokesman for Indian nationalism, Mohandas Karamchand Gandhi. In doing so, this book articulates a recuperative theory of nationalism in India in order to move thinking about nationalism beyond the current impasse produced by postcolonial theory in an era of transnational capitalism that too frequently forgets, underestimates, or represses the national in the transnational. By examining how formative Indian intellectuals from the 1930s and 1940s dealt with nationalism's "others" – untouchables, women, Muslims – this book demonstrates that nationalism was a contested and antagonistic field of debate in which the ultimate dominance of the bourgeois nationalist faction was not a given outcome of independence.

The picture that emerges, then, is of two kinds of misunderstanding of the Mahatma that coincide with the consolidation of official Indian nationalism after independence.

First, the category of "Gandhian" novel, which emerges as part of the nationalist canon, is shown to be structured around a misreading of the postindependence ideas about Gandhi for the pre-independence fluidity and contradictoriness of Gandhian politics. After his assassination and the development of what one critic has called the "cult of the Mahatma," it has become more difficult to appreciate nuanced debates with Gandhi in favor of seeing all political debates being resolved in Gandhian aspirations for the nation-state. This is particularly the case in the anglophone literature of the 1930s and 1940s where the deep footprints of the Mahatma are unmistakable. Critics have noticed the long speech given by Gandhi in Anand's *Untouchable*, ignoring the techno-modernist (and anti-Gandhian) solution to untouchability, as proof of the novel's endorsement of Gandhi. Rao's *Kanthapura* becomes a kind of Gandhian allegory despite the fact that the novel attempts to experiment with radical secularization as the outcome of mass agitation. Ali's *Twilight in Delhi* becomes a casualty of certain Hindu-centric assumptions about the Mahatma, as the Muslim household at the center of the novel seems to be apolitical even though the novelist was perhaps the most Gandhian of his contemporaries. By tracking the development of the novelistic idea of "Gandhi" against representations of the Mahatma in short fiction and fiction in the Indian vernacular languages, *The Mahatma Misunderstood* shows that Gandhi was strategically deployed in the anglophone novels produced by the radical wing of the intelligentsia.

The second misunderstanding of the Mahatma has to do with theoretical understandings of nationalism and the relationship between nationalism in its anticolonial phase and in its state-building phase. The tendency in postcolonial and subaltern studies has been to see statist nationalism as the necessary development of anticolonial nationalism, and therefore to challenge the radical, democratic claims of nationalism as alibis for majoritarian politics.[1] In this formulation, the deployment of ideas of "the nation" is not seen as the language of solidarity with minorities and women but as Eurocentric, elite and derivative discourses that are designed to shore up the progressive credentials of the state. Postcolonial theorists, for instance, tend to see in Gandhian ideas the bait-and-switch formula of nationalist appropriation: democratic ideas are put forward in the lead-up to independence and then foreclosed by those very same ideas after independence. Novelists who are now described as Gandhian tend, then, to be accused of committing the same political errors as Gandhian nationalism and are dismissed as Eurocentric and derivative, as elite, as majoritarian, as replicating the problems of colonialism and as being fundamentally incapable of warding off the problems posed by newer transnational circuits of power and exchange. As a consequence, postcolonial criticism tends to find all independence movements complicit in the failure of nationalism to deliver on its promises after decolonization. More importantly, it all but ignores the role played by the organized Left on the development of nationalist thought and radical politics that might have gone beyond the horizon of the nationalists.

The picture presented in *The Mahatma Misunderstood*, on the other hand, shows that statist nationalism actually requires the silencing and elimination of more radical variants of nationalism that exist alongside its bourgeois cousin. This claim is predicated on new directions in the studies of nationalist agitation in India, like Vinayak Chaturvedi's excellent *Peasant Pasts*, in which he argues, "there was no agreement on the direction of nationalism, let alone any other form of politics" in colonial India (2007, 227). What Chaturvedi shows through a detailed reading of the Patidar–Dharala conflict in Gujarat and the Gandhian agitation that followed is how low-caste peasants articulated their own demands for liberation under discourses that they inherited both from the nationalists and previous peasant kings, so that they emerge in the early part of the twentieth century as important actors and thinkers in their own right. Chaturvedi's contribution, along with those of other Indian historians, undoes the account of nationalism produced primarily by the Subaltern Studies group, in which peasant and minority interests were ruthlessly subordinated to those of the bourgeois elite, despite the heroic resistance of the former and the radical posturing of the latter. What Chaturvedi is describing, though, can be generalized to the rest of the transformed world of late-colonial India, in which all kinds of actors were entering into politics, as the nationalists were scrambling to try to both appease and contain these new demands. Peasants were joined by urban workers, the low castes, women, Muslims and other minorities in demanding their rights in the new democratic dispensation of a free India. The victory of the nationalists in the Congress for leadership of these new movements was not a foregone conclusion.

But in addition to Chaturvedi, this book also draws upon new thinking about nationalism in literary criticism from the group of critics who have been dubbed a part of the "materialist turn": Neil Lazarus, Benita Parry, Laura Chrisman, Timothy Brennan, Priyamvada Gopal, Pranav Jani and Helen Scott. Through their forceful contributions to the field of postcolonial scholarship, it is possible to think anew about the contradictions of bourgeois nationalist liberation struggles and to uncover the emancipatory and the majoritarian, statist projects as parallel processes. As Pranav Jani elegantly shows in his new book, *Decentering Rushdie*, the danger of the "linguistic turn" in literary studies is how much it flattens out the picture of literary history; in its place, Jani offers up a strategy of deep attention to "the dynamic and dialectical interplay between historical contexts and literary forms, between class positions and cosmopolitan identity, between general orientations and specific ideologies as they develop over time" (2010, 9). By following Jani's procedure, this book attempts to situate the writers of late-colonial India in a more complicated relationship to a variety of intellectual, political, historical and social dynamics than simply in relationship to the gravitational pull exercised by the Mahatma. Nationalism becomes restored as a political contest between antagonists competing for different interpretations of "the nation," rather than a linguistic or philosophical error that dooms all opposers of empire to reproducing its crimes. In fact, one of the features of the "linguistic turn" has been to raise the text as the premier site of ideological contest, which has the effect of making uses of the word "nation" more or less synonymous with the "nation-state" in its deployment by nationalists. Late-colonial novelists themselves drew upon and modified mainstream nationalism to suit their own purposes; as a result, formal readings of their narratives demonstrate the possibility of understanding nationalism as a field of ideological diversity, a diversity that was large enough to encompass ideas that would be at odds with most understandings of Indian nationalist politics.

For instance, Anand was invested in a transnational "humanism" more than a territorialized "nationalism," which would be the outcome of learning how to feel anew; Ali was eerily prescient about the dangers of Hindu chauvinism in *Twilight in Delhi*, despite still being an anticolonial novelist; and Rao endorsed a dialectical formula in which Gandhian ideas would be mobilized in order to undo themselves, with nationalism moving easily into a Socialist internationalism. Despite Gandhi's heavy presence as the dominant figure in, influence on and theme of the novels of the period, late-colonial, anglophone novelists both critically engaged with and strategically appropriated the ideas of Gandhi and the Congress in order to deal with the more enduring problems that official nationalism either refused to confront or was unable to solve: caste-based chauvinism, sexism, religious orthodoxy and Brahminical privilege, concentration of wealth and land, and communalism. The composite picture, then, is one of the many faces of the nation, the many directions and deployments of nationalism, before it becomes the nation-state. Formal readings of these late-colonial texts reveal a picture of literary nationalism as marked not by its easy dissolution into the nationalist mainstream but by its halting navigation and redirection of the contradictory aspirations of official nationalism.

This study has eschewed certain terms that have become the mainstay of postcolonial criticism – terms like "hybridity," "identity," "representation" – and has instead chosen to understand the terms deployed in the fiction and writing of the period provisionally. As a result, what postcolonial studies has preferred to understand as "hybrid" and "cosmopolitan" are here unpacked as ideological maneuvers, so the emphasis is on terms like "contradiction," "influence," and "intervention." Especially because this book deals with writers who are looking down at their social inferiors (in most instances) and representing them in their fiction, the approach of most postcolonial critics has been to see in these strategies of representation only repressive postures. But what that approach overlooks is the way that certain politics of representation were articulated as challenges to other dominant politics of representation, so that sensitive portrayals of minorities, even when dripping with paternalism, contained within them the germ of a radically democratic worldview, even if the terms of that ideology could not be fully worked out in advance of its real development in the world. This approach builds on the intervention of critics like Neil Lazarus, whose masterful book *The Postcolonial Unconscious*, offers this corrective to postcolonial studies:

> The struggle *over representations* [in postcolonial studies] gave way to the struggle *against representation* itself, on the ground that the desire to speak *for*, *of*, or even *about* others was always shadowed by a secretly authoritarian aspiration [...] the vast majority of "postcolonial" literary writings point us in a quite different direction, towards the idea not of "fundamental alienness" but of deep-seated affinity and community, across and athwart the "international division of labor." (2011, 19)

As opposed to postcolonial readings of the politics of representation, this approach has the benefit of forcing a more rigorous investigation into the meaning of all gestures of solidarity, as containing both authoritarian and democratic possibilities in them, requiring a more sensitive reading of form than can be handled at the level of language.

Because this approach builds on much work that is critical of postcolonial studies as such, it also takes a rather unique form, shuttling back and forth between readings of political campaigns, courtroom scenes, literary debates, jailhouse interviews, political speeches and long passages from the texts in question. The reliance on an eclectic range of sources and materials has been necessary to unsettle the dominant way that theory has displaced history in determining sources of meaning. It has also been necessary to unsettle the way that more orthodox Marxist accounts of the relationship between form and content have been used to occlude the ways that imaginative writing unsettles and re-establishes its own interpretive agenda. For instance, while there is much to be admired about Aijaz Ahmad's *In Theory* (1994), and much of this book owes a debt to his important contributions to South Asian literary history, his deployment of class fails to accommodate the radical gestures of writers like (early) Salman Rushdie or Arundhati Roy, and their formal experiments are easily reducible in his formulations to their class-derived politics. This book attempts to show instead that all middle-class politics are cleft by contradictory influences and that only a careful attention to historical processes and ideological formations can reveal how certain forms get grafted onto their respective contents.

But this book is not only designed as an intervention into Anglo-American postcolonial studies. A postindependence nationalist reading strategy in India has reached the same conclusion as the postcolonial critic but inverted it: finding virtue in early anglophone Indian writers where the other sees vice. Chapter 1, "The Mahatma as Proof" charts the history of how writing from the 1930s and 1940s was rediscovered when the appropriateness of English for an independent India was being debated in the 1960s and 1970s, when the Indian constitution mandated a shift away from English as the official state language. New political constituencies sought to couch their defense of the Indian-ness of English by showing the Gandhian-ness of Indian writing in English of the 1930s and 1940s, and thereby produced a homology between the Indian nation, Gandhi and novels about Gandhi written in English. This misreading of late-colonial novels was the result of the language debates in the 1950s and 1960s, in which professors of English were attempting simultaneously to construct a canon of Indian writing in English and demonstrate the viability of English as a national and nationalist language. In the course of this debate, nationalist anglophone writers came to be the mascots for English's nationalist potential, since these writers were able to make the case for nationalism in the idiom of the colonizer. At the same time, that argument rested on the presence of Gandhi (as a character, as a topic of conversation, as a trope) in this fiction, since his assassination had left him (more or less) the undisputed father of the nation. As a result, ideological conformity with Gandhian nationalism was highlighted at the expense of political critique. The nationalist reading of this fiction then tended to take postindependence statist (and Gandhian) virtues and read them back into the fiction of the 1930s and 1940s, even when these novels explicitly and formally critiqued Gandhian political ideas.

Chapters 2, 3 and 4 deal with individual novelists – Mulk Raj Anand, Raja Rao and Ahmed Ali – by reading their chief novels of the period in relation to their other prose. In fact, rather than being the natural heirs to Gandhian thought, these members of the English-educated middle class were in many ways the least likely candidates to be spokespeople for the Mahatma, as their modern, secular and progressive ideas came into direct conflict with Gandhi's valorization of the peasant past, his deployment of religious idioms, and his unwillingness to challenge Hindu orthodoxy at its core. Their interest in minorities who were being underserved by both nationalism and the Raj led them to experiments in novelistic forms, primarily by adapting vernacular literary traditions to the novel (e.g. the verse epic, *harikatha*, *sthalapurana*, *ghazal* and *shehrashob*), in an attempt both to democratize the subject of the novel and create new patterns of readerly ethics. Ali's adaptation of the patronized shehrashob for the patronless world of post-Mutiny Delhi, for instance, made it possible to link up the emotional universe of the orthodox, putatively apolitical Muslim with the world of nationalist struggle without secularizing the former. The resulting picture of middle-class nationalism is one of deep contradiction: enthusiasm over the unity of nationalist opposition to empire and, simultaneously, a nagging suspicion that nationalism could not or would not be able to resolve the problems that this unity papered over.

Rereading the early novels of Anand, Rao and Ali (more or less considered the "founding fathers" of Indian writing in English), *The Mahatma Misunderstood* demonstrates that nationalism also comprised a series of gestures (ethical humanist, primitivist, progressive, antichauvinist, cosmopolitan, feminist, traditionalist) that enabled a (semi-) durable kind of solidarity between the middle class and its others (peasants, women, untouchables) and made the project of a unitary nation secondary to the production of anticolonial political coalitions. Late-colonial writers turned to some of Gandhi's contemporaries (e.g. Bhimrao Ambedkar, Gangarao Deshpande, J. P. Narayan, M. N. Roy and Kamaladevi Chattopadhyay) and used the terms of their critiques to find solutions to problems that the Congress was either explicitly unwilling or unconsciously unable to solve: middle-class and upper-caste privileges and prerogatives, Eurocentrism and Anglophilia, religious and national chauvinisms, and sexist worldviews. More broadly, this book contends that all gestures of solidarity (nationalist or otherwise) are syntactically and rhetorically identical to gestures of opportunism and cooptation, and that the reading of these moments in nationalist writing cannot and should not, therefore, be assumed to be reducible to defenses of the postindependence state and official nationalist politics. By disarticulating nationalism into its component parts, *The Mahatma Misunderstood* aims to reorient postcolonial studies by refiguring nationalism as useful politics in the contemporary moment.

The theoretical organization of this monograph is primarily Gramscian, an approach developed in comparison to Partha Chatterjee's reading of Gramsci in his famous text, *Nationalist Thought and the Colonial World: A Derivative Discourse* (1986). Chapters 5 and 6 demonstrate how the decline of any substantial leftist opposition to Gandhi and the Congress meant that most radical intellectual thought underwent a process that Gramsci called "transformism," the absorption and conservatization of leftist thinking to be brought in line with the success of the nationalist consolidation of power. Narayan always knew that a radical revolution would be necessary, but he thought that the coming to power of the bourgeoisie would be signaled by the defeat of Gandhi's heir, Nehru, and not his victory over the Congress leadership. As a result, Narayan repeatedly deferred the need to organize more radical constituencies to shift the direction of nationalist politics. Roy, on the other hand, was a more substantial critic of Gandhi but felt that the processes that Gandhi was unleashing would automatically outstrip the Mahatma's careful and deliberate control. A careful reading of his speeches reveals the ways that this "natural" leapfrogging over the Mahatma was troped as metalepsis in not only Narayan's and Roy's writings but in the writings of most of the leftist thinkers of the period. The inability to prepare for a final confrontation with the nationalist bourgeoisie produced a long period of demoralization, more commonly understood as postcolonial dissatisfaction, which still lingers today.

There are two consequences to this process. The first explains the periodization of this inquiry; the period between 1920 and 1940 was perhaps the last time that an organized Left mounted a substantial challenge to the political ideas of the Congress in the lead up to independence. The decline of the Left and its absorption into the Congress, a process that is traced through the figures of Narayan and Roy, meant that the possibility of a more radical transformation of Indian society against a Gandhian–Nehruvian state also declined. The readings that are uncovered of the novels of the 1930s and 1940s are symptomatic of this process. The second is that the romantic figure of Gandhi has, after his death, absorbed and defanged all of the antistatist politics (save the Maoists) in postindependence India. The decline of confrontational, anti-imperial politics in the contemporary moment is also a consequence of the hegemony of the idea of the Mahatma over activism today. By recovering the Mahatma as the site of a misunderstanding about what the nation-state meant and how it could be transformed, this monograph hopes to play a small part in the revival of radical currents that are organizing wherever the banner of the Mahatma is raised.

Chapter 1

THE MAHATMA AS PROOF: THE NATIONALIST ORIGINS OF THE HISTORIOGRAPHY OF INDIAN WRITING IN ENGLISH

It is perhaps easy enough to understand why anglophone Indian novels of the 1930s and 1940s are called Gandhian novels. Aside from the long shadow that Gandhi casts on all aspects of late-colonial India, the literature of the period also bears heavy traces of the Mahatma. Mulk Raj Anand's *Untouchable* not only includes a long speech by Gandhi as its climax, the entire novel was rewritten after a conversation with Gandhi. Moorthy, the main character in Raja Rao's *Kanthapura*, is affectionately called the "Little Mountain," a reference to the fact that he is the local lieutenant of the Mahatma, whom the villagers have dubbed the "Big Mountain." The other novels of the period, like Bhabhani Bhattacharya's *So Many Hungers* (1947) and R. K. Narayan's *Swami and Friends* (1935), involved Gandhian-style agitations and Congress rallies. The cumulative effect has been to see the literary period in the era immediately preceding independence, as one critic has described it, as the "Gandhian whirlwind."

But there is a problem with this historiographical procedure: none of the novelists in question would have called themselves Gandhian. Anand was a social democrat, uncomfortable with Gandhian ideas about religion; Rao disagreed with many of Gandhi's ideas about women and politics, joining up with Trotskyist groups in the early 1930s; and Ali, probably the closest politically to Gandhi of all of the writers of the period, was never involved in nationalist politics but is left out of the canon altogether, partly because he is a Muslim and partly because he ended up in Pakistan after partition. Any critical account of this literature, then, has to begin by asking the question: what makes a text Gandhian and how much Gandhi does one need before a novel becomes a mouthpiece for Gandhian politics?

The story, however, is complicated by the fact that Gandhi and late-colonial anglophone writing are connected by a critical misreading. The Gandhi of the 1930s and 1940s was a symbol that meant something quite different from the idea of Gandhi that developed after independence, his assassination and the partition of the country. The cult of the Mahatma that was invoked by the Indian nation (sometimes reverentially, sometimes cynically) meant – at least throughout the 1960s and 1970s – that Gandhi (now dubbed the father of the nation) became a more concrete symbol than he would have been otherwise. As Claude Markovits has elegantly argued:

> One of the greatest paradoxes in relation to Gandhi is the contrast between the diversity of perceptions of him in his lifetime and the very limited range of iconic representations retained of him by posterity. In his lifetime, Gandhi had been perceived successively and simultaneously as a Bolshevik, a fanatic, a trouble-maker, a hypocrite, an eccentric, a reactionary, a revolutionary, a saint, a renouncer, a messiah, an avatar. He was likened both to Lenin and to Jesus Christ, indicating the wide scope of representations. After his death, two views of him have become dominant: in India he is remembered as the father of the nation, outside India he is remembered as an apostle of nonviolence. (Markovits 2004, 13)

The critical deployment of the term "Gandhian" in the phrase "Gandhian novel" itself occludes the real political, cultural and religious debates that were happening with the Mahatma and over his very body.

By the 1970s, a consensus had developed about the origins and interpretations of the Indian novel in English. This national consensus consisted of the following propositions: while there may have been vernacular traditions, British masters and early experiments, the Indian novel in English really came into its own in the 1930s; the 1930s were an important break in the periodization of the novel since it was clear that the novel's concern was now nationalism and it seemed to bear the imprint and influence of Gandhi, as opposed to the earlier novels of the nineteenth century, which tended to have a more personal and limited view; the Indian novelist in English was preoccupied with the representation of India in its entirety, usually for a European readership; and its most important practitioners were Anand, Narayan and Rao, though Bhattacharya, Desani and Singh could be added without much controversy (Riemenschneider 2005). By themselves these propositions are hardly controversial, but the reason that these propositions and not others (e.g. the diasporic origins of the novel in English, the continuities between vernacular literature and English literature, the effect of publishing and patronage trends in England on the rise of certain Indian authors, or the influences of regional ideologies or local political movements or intellectual developments in Europe) came to dominate had as much to do with the history and form of these novels as it had to do with the needs of academic circles and a wing of the Indian ruling class to make the case for the national utility of English in the 1960s and 1970s. Novels in English could do what none of the vernacular literatures could: namely, suture together a geographically and linguistically disparate readership in its identity as Indian, and therefore they had to be preserved as part of the national heritage. As a result, the national consensus triumphantly contended, the Indian novel in English came into its own as the twin of the newly independent Indian nation-state, bearing all of the marks of a bright future:

> It is no mere coincidence that there came a sudden flowering of Indian fiction in English in the 1930's – a period during which the star of Gandhiji attained its meridian on the Indian horizon. Under the leadership of Gandhiji, the Indian freedom-struggle already more than a generation old, became so thoroughly democratized that the

freedom-consciousness percolated, for the first time, to the very grass-roots of Indian society, and revitalized it to the core. It is possible to see a close connection between this and the rise of the Indian novel in English. Fiction, of all literary forms, is most vitally concerned with social conditions and values, and at this time, Indian society, galvanized into a new social and political awareness, was bound to seek creative expressions for its new consciousness and the novel has, in all ages, been a handy instrument for this purpose. The "Three Musketeers" of Indian fiction in English – Mulk Raj Anand, Raja Rao and R. K. Narayan started writing during the 1930's, and the first of the novels of the first two demonstrate the Gandhian impact convincingly. (Jussawalla 1985, 158–9)

The terms that then came to define this approach to the novels of the 1930s and 1940s were "Indian," "nationalist," and "Gandhian" (as opposed to say "Punjabi," "modern," "secular," "Nehruvian," "diasporic," "imagist," "Socialist-realist," "translational," or "experimental"), since these were unproblematic virtues in the newly independent nation. By the 1980s and 1990s, however, once critical opinion had shifted with respect to the value of "nationalism" and Gandhism (and with the growing national disillusionment with the Congress, the rise of viable and powerful separatist movements in India, and the growing support for the Naxalites on a number of college and university campuses), readings of these novels were merely inverted. The global attention on Salman Rushdie and his claims about the primacy of English only served to bring this development into sharper relief by giving it a formal – as opposed to a political – aspect. But instead of reorganizing the historiography of the Indian novel in English, the postcolonial, feminist and minority readings of these same novels found vice where there had previously been virtue. The novels of the 1930s and 1940s tended to be seen as allied to a variant of Congress politics and the agendas of its leaders, principally Gandhi. They continued to be perceived as homogenizing or flattening out the differences in the Indian nation in favor of a mythical national unity, which could only serve to stamp out the rights and identities of minorities. The novels were seen as products of limited, chauvinistic and elitist worldviews, all of which were directly related to the novels' ideological proximity to nationalism. This essay seeks to map out how the terms of this historiography came to dominate the critical vocabulary and some of the problems that continue to plague such a historiographical consensus.

By the late 1970s and early 1980s, the canon of Indian writing in English had become fairly well established in Indian universities. Courses on Indian writing in English were now a part of most major university curricula at both the graduate and undergraduate level. A small industry of graduate dissertations and book-length studies of Indian writing in English was produced in the 1970s in order to cement the formation of the Indian English canon and to accredit instructors in the new field. The crowning feature of this development was the Sahitya Akademi's publication of M. K. Naik's *A History of Indian English Literature* to fill the glaring absence of "a systematic, comprehensive and critical history of this literature, clearly defining its nature and scope, adopting proper periodization and relating writers and school firmly to changing socio-political conditions" (1982a, v).

There may have been some early disagreements as to the exact genealogy and composition of the canon, but these were more or less resolved by the time that Rushdie became an international celebrity and Indian writing in English was thrust into the global marketplace. As new debates about the character of Indian writing emerged in the 1980s and 1990s – between those who advocated English as the only important Indian literary language and those who saw it as a bastardization and exoticization of more developed vernacular literary traditions – understandings of the intellectual, political and aesthetic preoccupations of the canon were mapped out. The new controversies were important to both the understanding of the terrain of Indian writing and the defense of the intellectual and literary output of the subcontinent, but in many ways they masked a deeper and more salient contradiction in Indian writing in English and, in fact, may have been symptomatic of this problem. For if the question of which language was to represent India in the global literary marketplace had resonance, it was because India had just barely survived a fissiparous debate about the national language, which was resolved not by the parties agreeing to the three-language compromise but by the needs of the nation-state in wedding its population to supporting the troops in the coming war with China.

Part of the reason that Indian writing in English was so well suited for this ideological role had to do with its origins, beginning as it did with some early experiments in prose and poetry in the nineteenth century – with figures like Raja Rammohan Roy, Henry Derozio and Toru Dutt – and continuing through the early nationalist, political writings of members of the Congress, which secured for it a relationship to the nationalist pantheon. Despite the variety of thinkers and attitudes that might have been involved in early nineteenth-century publications (though new research has argued that the origins extend back even further), Indian writing in English really began to become interesting, the critical consensus stressed, around the 1930s when, under the influence of Mahatma Gandhi, literary practitioners began their first mature ventures into the Indian novel in English. Anand's *Untouchable*, Narayan's *Swami and Friends* and Rao's *Kanthapura* – now lauded as the three foundational texts of the canon – were understood to represent a radical break from the "old Macaulayan amplitude and richness of phrasing and weight of miscellaneous learning" that had characterized the previous generations of writers (Iyengar 1962a, 272). These three novelists were held up as markers for a new kind of English: an Indian English prose, which was capable of moving beyond a crass mimicry of the British intelligentsia and was able to offer a uniquely Indian contribution to the cosmopolitan world of English letters. Moreover, since each novel bore the clear imprint of the Mahatma – Gandhi appeared as a character or a clear theme in each of the novels – then it certainly had to be a confident Gandhian nationalism to inaugurate the kinds of radical formal developments that these texts evinced. Consider, for instance, the defense of this literary history given by Naik, one of the leading figures in establishing the canon for Indian writing in English:

> By 1930, Indian English literature was more than a century old; and yet, curiously enough, it had not yet produced a single novelist with substantial output. And then came a sudden flowering when the Gandhian age (1920–1947) had perhaps reached its highest

point of glory during the Civil Disobedience Movement of the "thirties." It is possible to see the connection here, if one remembers that by this decade the nationalist upsurge had stirred the whole country to the roots to a degree and on a scale unprecedented earlier, making it acutely conscious of its present and its past and filling it with new hopes for the future. A society compelled into self-awareness like this provides a fertile soil for fiction and it is no accident that three major Indian English novelists – viz., Mulk Raj Anand, R. K. Narayan and Raja Rao began their career [sic] during this phase. It was, in fact, during this period that Indian English fiction discovered some of its most significant themes. (1984, 103–4)

Now, whether or not these writers actually represented a stylistic break with the past is beyond the scope of this chapter. What is of interest here is how nationalism under Gandhi was credited with making the kinds of changes in style, rhythm, syntax and form of which Anand, Narayan and Rao were seen as merely symptomatic. In fact, the seismic political event that was the Noncooperation movement (1920–22) could not but have found its aftershocks in the imaginative prose of Indian writers, the argument goes, since what it discovers in the prose is Gandhian. Little reference is then made to either the political ideas of these novelists (on the off chance that they might have differed from Gandhi's) or to the novels themselves, since the argument was nicely tautological. Having been born under the sign of Gandhi, novelists were bound to reproduce their indebtedness to him. Gandhi's relevance to the genesis of this new literary style or to the political direction of these novels was based more on the needs of the postindependence Indian state and university than on the real proximity of these writers to a Gandhian worldview. The anxiety about English-language instruction in the new Indian university required a consciously aggressive rereading of these texts to demonstrate the nationalist contributions that could be made in English, and that by reading back through the needs of the postindependence Indian state we can begin to uncover a different legacy of engagement between literature and nationalism, which begins to shatter certain notions of nationalist movements and their automatic and unmediated influence on the middle class.

In 1962, while making the case for reading literature with an eye towards both Western and Indian classical (Sanskritic) critical traditions, K. R. S. Iyengar, then the doyen of criticism of English literature in India and vice-chancellor of Andhra University, produced a polemic about the role of the artist in a modern, independent India:

The man of letters in independent India, whether he writes in English or in one of the modern Indian languages, has a part to play in projecting before the people a vision of the unity as well as the variety, the variety that is held together by the unity, of India. A Hindi or a Bengali or a Tamil writer, while reflecting accurately the contours of his particular linguistic area, has also, and perhaps even more emphatically, to stress the undying elements in Indian culture. It is thus necessary for our writers to conceive their works simultaneously in diverse planes of reality so that the lesser may not hide the greater, nor the greater quite obliterate the lesser. In recent years preposterous theories were propounded to prove that the worse was the better reason, and the country was in consequence cleft in two. Siren voices are even now occasionally raised to bewitch us into perpetrating the cultural atomization of the Indian Union. There is no doubt that our men of letters – not the least those who write in English – can organize the best insurance against all such attempts. [...] Even Indo-Anglian literature, though being appareled in a seemingly alien garb, is at its best Indian to the core, being (in C. R. Reddy's words) "a modern facet of that glory which, commencing from the Vedas, has continued to spread its mellow light, now with greater and now with lesser brilliance under the inexorable vicissitudes of time and history, ever increasingly up to the present time of Tagore, Iqbal and Aurobindo Ghose, and bids fair to expand with our and our humanity's expanding future." Literature in India, in the future as in the past, should function as a mystic bond of union between the individual and the State, the provincial unit and the national aggregate. (Iyengar 1962b, 243)

These new Indian "men of letters" were responsible for doing two things primarily: binding the "undying elements of Indian culture" to the present in order to resist the impulse of modernity (and perhaps global cosmopolitanism) and tying the particular, regional expressions of artistic creativity to the needs of the newly emerging nation-state. The contradictions of such a maneuver are clear, it seems, even to Iyengar, as he has to formulate and reformulate the project in an odd rhetorical stutter ("a vision of the unity as well as the variety, the variety that is held together by the unity, of India"), a strange redundancy that perhaps betrays another anxiety ("a mystic bond of union") and the use of metaphysics as a metaphor for the challenges of India's linguistic diversity ("conceive their works simultaneously in diverse planes of reality"). But there is little doubt that Iyengar reflected a genuine hope for this emerging class of thinkers and artists. A newly independent nation would need to find some way of expressing its traditions and particularities, even as it became modern and general, especially if it was to have any hope of succeeding. And since an Indian spirit could seamlessly speak in classical Sanskrit as well as modern Bengali, Urdu and Farsi (in C. R. Reddy's list), there was no reason to presume that the new nation could not find a voice in each of its fifteen hundred linguistic registers. Oscillating back and forth between languages and a modern Indian identity, these "men of letters," no matter what language they spoke, held out the best possibility to train and nurture a sober, political, democratic populace. The nation only awaited its bards and their critic-patrons.

But Iyengar had clear stakes in the language these "men of letters" would speak, at least to one another. He had sat on the English Review Committee, appointed by the University Grants Commission in 1960, to evaluate the quality and character of English education in India and to make recommendations for its improvement. Composed of five English professors (G. C. Bannerjee, V. K. Gokak, C. D. Narasimhaiah, A. G. Stock and K. R. S. Iyengar – all of whom produced textbooks that would be used for university instruction) and two commissioners (S. Mathai and P. J. Philip), the commission was tasked with, among other things, "re-organising the M.A. course in English to provide for an intensive study of the language as a tool of knowledge rather than as literature" (University Grants Commission 1965, 4). While the commission recommended that "Every student should have taken a paper on the English Language at some stage before he obtains the

M.A. degree in English," the commission also recommended requiring "two optional papers e.g., Shakespeare, American literature, Indian writing in English, etc." (University Grants Commission 1965, 36–7). The report itself is rather unremarkable, concluding, as it does, that English education in India was not nearly as advanced as it needed to be to serve the interests of the developing nation. But what is of interest is the intersection of the commission's finding with the debates about language and literature that had been percolating in India since independence. It was necessary to shore up the credentials and quality of English instruction and education in India at precisely the time when its utility to the new nation was about to expire. Perhaps even more remarkable would be the consolidation of the category of "Indian writing in English" as a discipline of study for university graduates, perhaps for the first time here in any official state document.

The timing of Iyengar's polemic – a mere three years before the Indian constitution would have to be revised to establish a new national language to replace English – gave rise to its content; literature and criticism were being directed to perform a role slightly more mundane than the Arnoldian characters from which Iyengar clearly drew his inspiration (Arnold 2006). Here, artists and critics stand as the best – and perhaps last – line of defense protecting the union in the face of growing movements towards "cultural atomization." For all of its longevity amidst the "inexorable vicissitudes of time and history," Indian unity was tenuous, and the intellectual elites of the country knew it. Debates begun under British occupation about the need for separate constituencies had empowered minority organizations to demand autonomy and unique representation in order to prevent the tyranny of the majority; first Muslims, then untouchables, women, Christians and Sikhs began to mobilize lobbies to demand that the British Raj negotiate directly with them instead of their Congress interlocutors. This became the bête noire of the Congress, which saw these separate electorates as strategies designed to "divide and rule" India by pitting various communities against one another and by undermining its position as the sole voice for Indians. The Congress's opposition to the separate electorates and its unwillingness to forge meaningful political alliances to remedy minority grievances hardened the beliefs of some who felt that a high-caste, Hindu nation could never successfully represent them: as Muslims, as untouchables, as non-Hindi speakers. After independence, minority demands were articulated by calling for secession from the Indian state. Pakistan had already successfully won its separation from India on the basis that there were two nations on the subcontinent, one Hindu and one Muslim, that each deserved their own state. And now there was a real fear that there were not two but hundreds of nations who could claim that their political identities and cultural rights were being trammeled under the weight of an imagined national unity.

The risks were not slight, even if they were exaggerated. The opening salvos of the language wars were fired early, after the report of the Linguistic Provinces Commission was published in 1948, which threatened the aspirations of new linguistic states like Andhra, Kerala, Karnataka and Maharashtra by concluding that "the first and last need of India at the present moment is that it should be made a nation. Everything which helps the growth of nationalism has to go forward, and everything which throws obstacles in its way has to be rejected [...]. We have applied this test to linguistic provinces also, and judged by this test, in our opinion, they fail and cannot be supported" (Windmiller 1954, 299).

Protests were not long in coming: in 1951, Swami Sitaram and several of his followers undertook (and then called off at the request of Vinoba Bhave) a Gandhian "fast to death," demanding the creation of an Andhra state to defend the rights of Telugu speakers in a Tamil state; in 1952, Potti Sriramulu fasted for 56 days to demand an Andhra state and died, setting off a wave of protests and riots; in 1953, several Andhra legislators resigned from their posts in Madras (Windmiller 1954, 300–304). The central government was ultimately pressured into passing the Andhra State Bill (1953) and creating a new Telugu-speaking state and into quickly moving towards organizing the States Reorganization Commission, which would recommend the creation of new states on linguistic lines (Ramaswamy 1956). And as the arguments for linguistic representation and particularism increased, it was not hard to imagine that the Indian nation could disintegrate from the inside out.

The genuine fear of those, like Iyengar, who were watching the language controversy develop, was that the Indian nation was not nearly elastic enough a concept to contain the national ambitions of the various linguistic states and that the result would be the production of several mini-Pakistans (the country was "cleft in two"). Each of the new linguistic states was a product of well-organized lobbies that advocated for the distinction of their regional culture and the irreducibility of their linguistic history (Karat 1974). And even though the new linguistic states were established within the borders of an Indian nation, it was not impossible to believe that the arguments of distinction and irreducibility would lead inevitably to the demand for another partition (Ramaswamy 1956). As a consequence, the solution of some critics, not unlike their American and British counterparts in the nineteenth century, was to locate a stable basis for nationalism in literature and criticism (in whatever language, but Iyengar's preference for English is palpable and not inconsequential) onto which the nation could stamp its imprint (Williams 1962). Forward-thinking "men of letters" were needed to develop a literature and a critical method that could inaugurate a national literature, sensitive to historical differences, but with an eye towards unity and the future. This was the Nehruvian secular slogan ("unity in diversity") marshaled to do the work that politicians and religious leaders had been unable to: establish a "mystic bond of union between the individual and the State" that could couple, permanently though not rigidly, the citizen to the political center.

There were, though, a number of problems in such a strategy, not the least of which was its unsatisfactory appeal to those with legitimate grievances against the Indian state (for instance, Kashmiris seeking an independent nation or the people of Telangana who refused to be integrated into the Indian state) and the fact that the existence of more than fifteen hundred recognized languages in the 1961 Census of India meant that this national "man of letters" would have to be cloned at least a number of times.[1] But the problems that Iyengar was describing were indeed serious. As soon as the Indian constitution was written, debates began about how a linguistically polyphonous India would ever cohere. A newly independent India had to learn to speak a new language, or more precisely, to speak to each other and be understood. As early as 1949, during the Constituent Assembly's debates about the official language, discussions would come to a grinding halt with linguistic minorities fearing the consolidation of "Hindi imperialism." Sumathi Ramaswamy describes the tragedy and comedy of these fraught discussions best: "The Assembly's proceedings broke down over several members' insistence that they would only speak in their 'mother tongue', much to the dismay of the majority who had no way of understanding what was being said. Members, especially from the South, frequently complained when chaste Hindi speakers took the floor. And every now and then, we read about members engaging each other in heated debate even while pleading mutual incomprehension" (1999, 353–4). This complicated mix of opportunism, nationalism and egalitarianism was quickly coming to a head: local elites demanded rights for their constituencies as a way to shore up their own access to power at the center, which, once secured, required the exact opposite approach to the language question; while the center, in the hopes of securing the allegiance of some powerful state groups, afforded rights selectively, generating only more demands for linguistic and political autonomy. The two realistic candidates for a national language, Hindi and English, mobilized extraordinary lobbies and instituted frighteningly intense protest.

National leaders knew that efforts toward manufacturing a monolingual nation-state would predictably be met with serious resistance, especially in those regions where people did not speak the language of the center. But linguistic diversity, argued North Indian Congress members, was a threat to national unity and central planning, representing a throwback to parochialism and the looming crisis of regional secessionism, and therefore could not be tolerated (King 1997). The project of squaring the linguistic circle may have been doomed from the beginning, especially in the country that colonialism and nationalism imagined into unity, but if there were going to be a viable state, it would need a national language to facilitate the integration of peoples from all over South Asia into a democratic polity and to ward off the "fissiparous tendencies" that were making themselves felt (Sonntag 2003, 62). To these tendencies could also be added the political mobilizations of the "Angrezi Hatao Andolan" launched by Rammanohar Lohia – a North Indian anti-Congress Socialist who was more interested in "banishing English" than in the establishment of Hindi as the national language and who was to turn eventually to electoral alliances with Hindi nationalism and Hindu revivalism – and the Jana Sangh – which began its own agitation in 1963 to abolish not only official English but public English as well, and went so far as to organize gangs to tear down street signs written in English (Sathyamurthy 1998).

English, while perhaps being the logical choice for a national language, as it had made all-India conversations possible in the Congress during British rule, was hardly an option for a nation whose new identity was based on a common struggle against British occupation and Western imperialism (Shah 1968). After all, there had been much discussion before independence about national languages before independence to color the direction of the postindependence debate: Gandhi had written and spoken in favor of Hindustani, the Congress had passed resolutions in favor of shifting away from English, and the Motilal Nehru Report (1928) had recommended Hindi as the most suitable national language (Sarkar 1989, 261–5). This nationalist pedigree gave substantial weight to the arguments for Hindi, and the secular arguments for the language (national unity) became indistinguishable from the orthodox, conservative ones ("Hindu, Hindi, Hindustan"). So, the Congress, pressured by a Hindu revivalist wing and new communal forces, settled on a Sanskritized Hindi as the new official, but not national, language of India and set about to dismantle the infrastructure of English-based governance, much to the chagrin of Nehru and the modernizers who saw English as the mechanism to decommunalize Indian politics and allow India to enter the world of international commerce (Brown 2003, 113–16). Article 343 of the Constitution of India (1950) had called for a fifteen-year time limit for English to be replaced by Hindi in the Devanagari script, and inadvertently (though not unforeseeably) inaugurated a series of heated debates about the status of languages, education, nationalism and minorities in a newly freed nation.[2]

One of the first steps in dismantling the English-speaking infrastructure involved rewriting the highly competitive Union Public Services Commission examination in Hindi in 1965. Tamil-speaking students grew increasingly convinced that this was a maneuver designed to prevent their access to highly lucrative civil service jobs. Buoyed by an increasingly influential Dravida Munnetra Kazhagam (DMK) party, students and teachers protested: a Madras State Anti-Hindi Conference was organized in 1965; the DMK defied the ban on protests on Republic Day in 1965 and declared it a "Day of Mourning" for the loss of English; and two student supporters of the DMK burned themselves to death in protest of Hindi (Forrester 1966, 24–5). The inability to contain the growing protests ultimately resulted in the legislative compromises of the States Reorganization Act (1956), the Official Languages Act (1963) and finally the amended Official Languages Act (1967). No national language was finally to emerge, but English as a language was to become deeply politicized throughout India.[3] This was, after all, only a political compromise; the social forces that had given rise to the anti-English and the anti-Hindi tendencies had not disappeared. Partly because of the legislative compromises, but also because of the new national focus on the central government created by the death of the Prime Minister and the conflict with Pakistan, the language issue was sidestepped but not completely resolved. The states would have their vernaculars; the center would speak Hindi and English; but the anxieties about and the challenges against the nationalist credentials of English speakers would continue.[4]

It is in the context of this unresolved debate that Iyengar's polemic about the national "men of letters" becomes meaningful. The uneasiness of the political compromises meant that English continued to be tainted by its colonial heritage and Hindi by its northern chauvinism; and instead of bringing the nation linguistically closer together, the dividing lines seemed to be drawn even sharper. And Iyengar was concerned with not only the ability of the nation to survive intact, but with the future of its institutions of higher education as well. The "three-language formula" posed tremendous problems for university educators and administrators who were now faced with the daunting task of reorganizing their curricula and attempting to make instruction in the regional languages meaningful. Several would agree with Iyengar's protests:

> But one thing, perhaps, is possible. Let the text-books still be in English, let the English technical terms continue, let even the medium of examination be English. Let the teacher not hesitate, if he finds it convenient, to mingle English and the regional language to facilitate comprehension. Let the regional language be used on a functional basis, and not as an exercise in sentiment or purism, or as part of a campaign against English.

A campaign against English in the field of higher education can only be a campaign against higher education itself. (1968, 43)

Iyengar himself was deeply suspicious of the arguments for tinkering with the established medium of instruction, seeing behind them the political maneuverings of North Indian political opportunists: "If the regional languages alone are to be the media of instruction and examination, what is to take the place of English as 'link-language'? It cannot be that we are deliberately planning for chaos. Or can it really be, as Rajaji [C. Rajagopalachari] suggests, that 'behind the screen of chaos is the Machiavellian hope that Hindi will fill the vacuum and take the place of English [...] and become the sole medium of instruction in the universities and be enthroned as the language of the elite in India'?" (1968, 44). Opponents of English, in Iyengar's mind, were disingenuous, placing political advancement over national progress: "[Replacing English] can only be a desperate leap in the dark. Let us not break up the nation's higher intellectual life" (44). And here, Iyengar was doing more than sounding the alarms of the impending destruction of ivory towers; he was consciously inserting himself into the debate about Indian development and progress. English, of course, represented not only the success or failure of higher education but, as the debates about the national language were demonstrating, English was also bound up in any strategy for national growth. A number of politicians and intellectuals had contributed to the debate, and the defense of English was relatively uniform along a few simple lines. English was scientific and commercial, while Hindi was inflexibly and awkwardly backward looking (Aiyar 1968). English could be global and cosmopolitan, while Hindi was necessarily parochial (Rajagopalachari 1960). English could be spoken by people all over India, while Hindi was the monopoly of the north (Menon 1968). The debate was, in fact, so uniform that advocates for English felt little to no anxiety in proclaiming that a number of the pamphlets produced in the course of the debate borrowed wholesale from one another.

But there was one important residual anxiety that remained. Even if English were to demonstrate its superiority to Hindi by virtue of its modern, scientific and commercial prowess, Hindi would always have one advantage: it was not a colonial language. Whatever else it could offer the Indian nation, English was severely debilitating for a nation that had only recently escaped the yoke of British rule. Iyengar's solution to this problem was to argue that since Indians had contributed to the development of English letters, it was quickly becoming a native tongue: "Nor must we forget that English has become for us more or less and Indian language and literature. Some of our greatest men and women have achieved triumphant self-expression in English, and added significant new dimensions to English literature" (1970, 300). And this would be the political and intellectual means by which literature would get wrapped up in the debates about language and how the hand-me-downs of the master would be dyed anew in patriotic colors. If Indians could produce good writing in English, if there were novels and poems of quality and merit written by Indians in English, then English could still be salvaged as a medium for Indians to communicate and grow. Moreover, Iyengar argued, that would be sufficient to shore English up from the charges of the *Hindi-vadis* (campaigners for Hindi) and secure the benefits of English to the Indian state: "It would be folly therefore if we still sought, through chauvinistic or other coercive means, to treat English as something utterly alien, as something useless or even inimical to higher education in India, or as something that will serve us otherwise than in prompting and preserving the unity of India and raising its prestige and power in the comity of nations" (300).

Others would adopt this argument and amplify its terms. Since nationalists spoke and wrote in English, and since nationalist literature was produced in English, English was not merely an Indian language but a nationalist language as well:

> Let it not be forgotten that the best work of the Indian National Congress has been done in English; that the Constitution has been drafted in English and is yet to be translated into understandable Hindi; that Sarojini Naidu spoke and wrote patriotic lyrics in English; that savants like Aurobindo and Radhakrishnan have thought out systems of philosophy in English; that Vivekananda's works revitalizing Hinduism, were all in English. With these great examples before us, let not any Indian think that patriotism can be the monopoly only of those that can lisp in Hindi or a regional language. (Wadia 1954, 140–41)

The nationalist pantheon was culled for English-speaking members and their contributions to the nation would now be made to stand in for the credentials of English in a kind of political tautology. And this made the case for English language instruction all the easier. English was no longer merely the language of colonial oppression; it would now be framed as the language of international opportunity and liberal, secular thought, but most of all as an explicitly all-Indian, nationalist language (National Council of Educational Research and Training 1963). The decoupling of language from literature would appease those who wanted the scientific and commercial advantages of English without feeling beholden to European values, while the broadening out of English to include commonwealth literatures would extend political decolonization to the canon.[5] English was being made into a uniquely pragmatic national discipline: its anticolonial credentials were being uncovered; its utility in securing access to markets was praised; and its secular virtues were held up as unique solutions to the problems of communalism, parochialism and social backwardness (Ram 1983). English education was transformed into a nationally significant project, alongside the introduction of Indian writing in English as part of the official curriculum in Indian universities, a curriculum that would have to be born into an extraordinarily politicized linguistic space (Shah 1968). University professors committed to an English-language education or at the very least the continuation of English as a subject found themselves having to defend the uses of English in an independent nation.

In response, a whole series of academic studies were produced in the 1960s and 1970s to defend not only the study of English as an Indian language but also the quality (read Indian-ness) of Indian fiction and poetry in English. Universities, especially (though not exclusively) in South India, churned out a series of rather quick and undertheorized accounts, largely plot summaries, of the Indian writing in English that had already been produced, as a way of justifying its continuing utility in Indian academia. Artists who wrote in English were called on to write and give talks about the ways that English could speak to specifically Indian questions. Raja Rao's introduction to *Kanthapura*, which famously argued, "English is not really an alien language to us," was reprinted scores of times (Rao 1963). Publishing houses and periodicals began to cultivate a uniquely modern, national sensibility by creating a new reading public that would seek its news, culture and commodities in English print.

But there was one more problem that remained in trying to make the case for reading Indian English-language novels as opposed to, say, Shakespeare, Jane Austen, or Matthew Arnold. For you could defend the study of English as pragmatic, but you could not then justify the study of Indian novels in English or what came to be called "Indian English," the inferior "babu-speak" of the natives. Indian English would always have the taint of mimicry and inferiority, the vulgar babble of the indigenes, incapable of sounding beautiful let alone intelligent. Consider, for instance, C. D. Narasimhaiah's (one of Iyengar's colleagues on the English Review Committee) account of Indian studies in English in South India:

> *Kanthapura* was prescribed in a South Indian university for undergraduate study in 1964. The award of a prize for *The Serpent and the Rope* in 1963 by the Sahitya Akademi at Delhi as the best novel in English by an Indian for the preceding three years, one assumed, had helped to make Raja Rao respectable and part of the establishment. But no, for before long those responsible found themselves to be the target of a vicious campaign to compel the university to withdraw *Kanthapura* from the prescriptions because, ostensibly, it was obscene, and because it was written in Indian English. Letters were written to the press, resolutions were passed by interested English teacher's associations in some colleges demanding the prescription of Jane Austen's *Pride and Prejudice* in place of *Kanthapura*, and the executive council of the University directed that the Academic Council take steps to withdraw the prescription. [...] Fortunately the vice-chancellor upheld the prescription because it was not good to break healthy academic conventions. (Narasimhaiah 1973, 76–7)[6]

And in response to this new argument that if English was to be taught, it was to be the king-emperor's English, novels from the 1930s and 1940s – which had been all but ignored when they were written originally – were rediscovered and paraded as exemplars of a successful nationalist idiom. Not only because they were written in the heady days of the Indian struggle for independence, but because they could be mined for a nationalist English, an English that was clearly in the service of the nation, and could perhaps be the basis for a literary criticism in which Indian English could also produce something of aesthetic merit. *Kanthapura*, *Untouchable* and *Swami and Friends* would have to be dusted off and brought back to the center of a national debate, despite having been forgotten long ago.

But the nationalist credentials of these texts would have to be established. Iyengar laid the groundwork for a disciplinary study of Indian writing in English through a number of books designed to introduce college students to the mine of writing that had already been produced in South Asia. His two short studies, *Indo-Anglian Literature* (1943) and *The Indian Contribution to English Literature in English* (1945), make no reference to anything like

"Gandhian literature," save an oblique reference to a commemorative volume marking Gandhi's birthday (Iyengar 1945, 289). But the two later volumes, *Indian Writing in English* (1963) and the revised *Indian Writing in English* (1973), have entire chapters dedicated to "Gandhi Literature," the first focusing on more doctrinaire discussions of Gandhi's politics and thoughts, and the second more thoroughly discussing Gandhi's impact on the novels of the era. And, more specifically, Gandhi was transformed from being merely an influence on the general cultural milieu of a nationalist India and a competent polemicist in English to becoming a specific forebear to the entire project of Indian writing in English:

> Although no great scholar, Gandhi knew very well the Old Testament in English, and his writing in English had accordingly a simplicity, pointedness and clarity that was in refreshing contrast to the heaviness often characteristic of earlier Indian writing. Thanks to the Gandhian example, Indian writing in English became recognizably functional. Gone were the old Macaulayan amplitude and richness of phrasing and weight of miscellaneous learning. [...] Indian writing and speaking in English since the Gandhian revolution has tended to be wisely utilitarian, cultivating the virtues of clarity and directness and brevity rather than eloquence and elaboration and exuberance. (Iyengar 1962a, 272–3)

Gandhi's political innovations are then cleanly coupled to stylistic innovations in English, and the utility of English for a Gandhian India is proven by metonymy. Gandhi's English would be proof that his earlier polemics against English were tactical, not philosophical, so Gandhi would become the way that these novelists were indigenized. And Gandhi's contribution to the development and study of Indian writing in English was nothing short of miraculous:

> So profoundly did Gandhi impinge on the Indian consciousness that no writer [...] could have found it possible to be involved in the creative process without Gandhi's entering it overtly or obliquely. For what was India, what was Asia (indeed, to a historian with a true sense of values, what was the world?) of the first half of this century minus Gandhi? [...] [It] was Gandhi that broke the shackles all round. It was he that broke the cumbrous, Victorian periods which had enslaved the Indian writer like his counterpart in England; it is he who broke the word and freed the thought, and broke the thought and freed the thing and made us speak like men who had something to say, and not exhort like Gods or rant like demons. (Narasimhaiah 1967, 53–4)

Gandhi's English was actually anticolonial, metaphorically smashing the enslaving idiom of a heavy, Victorian English. Few critics were as explicit as Gobinda Sarma, who, in his 1979 dissertation "Nationalism in Indo Anglian Fiction," penned the following justification for marrying English novels with Indian (read Gandhian) nationalism: "Once I can show that Indo-Anglian fiction is nationalistic in spirit, all doubts about its not being Indian in spirit would be dispelled, and all prejudices against it will vanish. And once this happens in [the] case of fiction – the biggest branch of Indo-Anglian literature – the readers should be able to study other branches of this literature with an open mind" (1990, 13). In order to justify the study of English, Indian literary criticism was reading novels pragmatically. The perceived artistic inadequacies of an inferior English was compensated for with a healthy Gandhian supplement; as long as these novelists were nationalists, they were worth study.

But once the Indian credentials of English had been established, it seems, it became all too easy to read the case backwards. Once Gandhi's English was sufficiently nationalist, then his influence could be read back into every significant work in English produced by an Indian. For instance:

> Indian English literature of the Gandhian age was inevitably influenced by these epoch-making developments [the freedom movement] in Indian life. A highly significant feature is the sudden flowering of the novel during the 'thirties, when the Gandhian movement perhaps at its strongest. It is possible to see the connection here if one remembers that by this decade, the nationalist upsurge had stirred the entire Indian society to the roots to a degree and on a scale unprecedented earlier, making it acutely conscious of the pressure of the present in all fields of national life; and it is out of this consciousness that fiction, in Lionel Trilling's words, "for our time the most effective agent of the moral imagination," emerges. Fiction, as Hazlitt puts it, is constituted of "the very web and texture of society as it really exists" and hence finds a fertile soil in a society in ferment. The work of K. S. Venkataramani, Mulk Raj Anand and Raja Rao would not perhaps have been possible had the miracle that was Gandhi not occurred during this period. In fact, it was during this age that Indian English fiction discovered some of its most compelling themes: the ordeal of the freedom struggle, East-West relationship, the communal problem and the plight of the untouchables, the landless poor, the down-trodden, the economically exploited and the oppressed. (Naik 1982a, 118)

Even if the connections to Gandhi were subconscious, they were inevitable and formative. Indian writing in English, therefore, could not help but write itself as Gandhian. And as a result of attempting to prove its nationalist credentials, "Indian writing in English" came for the critics to mean "Indian nationalist writing in English." The towering figure of the Mahatma made it all the more likely that literary and political debates with Gandhi would be overshadowed by his dominant presence. Seeing the Mahatma made it all the more impossible to understand much else.

The discipline that was forged, in many ways, to be a weapon in the national language wars now bears permanent scars. It was no longer necessary to investigate a writer's politics or intellectual history or even to examine the allegorical, thematic, or formal countercurrents at work in his or her writing; writers from the 1930s and 1940s were made to bear the weight of the nation because they spoke of and about Gandhi. Rao, Anand and Narayan were, of course, the big three, but others would round out the list: Venkataramani, Bhattacharya, Nagarajan, Ghose and Singh. Others were excluded from the canon because they were either impenetrably apolitical (like G. V. Desani's *All About H. Hatterr* (1948)) or perhaps because they fell on the opposite side of new borders and hence made the case for nationalism harder (like Ahmed Ali's *Twilight in Delhi*). But from the beginning the discipline has been politicized even as it has formed a consensus: today, the patrons and the critics of Indian writing in English agree that it is a cleanly nationalist genre. A re-examination of that legacy would open new possibilities in the understanding of both literary nationalism (as a space in which critiques of nationalist politics might press official movements in new directions) as well as the intellectual history of nationalism (as a fraught contest between intellectuals dissatisfied with official political strategies). This new engagement with literary nationalism is all the more important now that colonialism and empire have asserted themselves more aggressively in the world today.

Chapter 2

"THE MAHATMA DIDN'T SAY SO, BUT …": MULK RAJ ANAND'S *UNTOUCHABLE* AND THE SYMPATHIES OF MIDDLE-CLASS NATIONALISTS

The fires of sunset were blazing on the Western horizon. As Bakha looked at the magnificent orb of terrible brightness glowing on the margin of the sky, he felt a burning sensation within him. His face, which had paled and contracted with thoughts a moment ago, reddened in a curious conflict of despair. He didn't know what to do, where to go. He seemed to have been smothered by the misery, the anguish of the morning's memories. He stood for a while where he had landed from the tree, his head bent, as if he were tired and broken. Then the last words of the Mahatma's speech seemed to resound in his ears: "May God give you the strength to work out your soul's salvation to the end." "What did that mean?" Bakha asked himself. The Mahatma's face appeared before him enigmatic, ubiquitous. There was no answer to be found in it. Yet there was a queer kind of strength to be derived from it. Bakha recollected the words of the speech. (Anand 1940, 156)

These words open the final scene of Mulk Raj Anand's *Untouchable*. Bakha, the young untouchable sweeper, puzzles over the contradictory responses he has to his harrowing day (comprising multiple fights with and humiliations from caste Hindus) and the confusing excitement he feels from having heard the Mahatma speak at a rally against untouchability. Gandhi's prayer, though, is impenetrably dense for Bakha, who resolves the problem of the "enigmatic, ubiquitous" face of the Mahatma by thinking about the equally opaque "queer kind of strength" that produces, perhaps, the "burning sensation" within him. Gandhi's politics are not only strange, they also appear unpalatable: "Did he mean, then, that I should go on scavenging? […] But I shall never be able to leave the latrines" (156–7). Already, then, Bakha's political critique of and his personal affection for Gandhi are at odds with one another; Bakha's aspirations and desire for freedom run in the opposite direction to Gandhi's notions of occupation-by-birth, his idiosyncratic understanding of *varnashrama dharma*, which would permanently wed Bakha to the profession he hates. But Bakha cannot reject Gandhi, either, in part because of the trials of his day, which are condensed renderings of a geographically vast and historically long legacy of untouchable oppression ("an endless age of woe and suffering" (1940, 49)): lack of access to education and wells, restrictions on temple entry, payment in spoiled food, fraud by merchants, urban mob violence, sexual abuse, niggardly responses to acts of heroism, denial of medical treatment, unsanitary living conditions, verbal humiliation and the threat of conversion to a benign but irrelevant Christianity.[1] Gandhi propels but cannot steer Bakha, who cannot understand "where to go." What Gandhi can do, even as he dissolves into hollow politics, is make Bakha aware that untouchability is not a permanent affliction; even though "there was no answer to be found" in Gandhi's face, Gandhi can open up possibilities.

This is not the only critique-and-compromise with Gandhi that takes place in the novel. Initially excited by Gandhi, a "strange man [who] seemed to have the genius that could, by a single dramatic act, rally multi-coloured, multi-tongued India to himself," as soon as the mass prayer begins, Bakha's attention begins to flag (Anand 1940, 145). Then, when the Mahatma begins to explain why he decided to take what was later called his "Epic Fast" against the Communal Award of 1932 (in which separate electorates were awarded to untouchables by the British rulers), "Bakha didn't understand these words. He was restless. He hoped that the Mahatma wouldn't go on speaking of things he [Bakha] couldn't understand" (146). He becomes excited again when the Mahatma speaks about untouchability and his desire to be reborn an untouchable, but is frustrated when he blames untouchables for their own degraded condition: "But now, now the Mahatma is blaming us, Bakha felt. 'That's not fair!' He wanted to forget the last passages he heard" (148). The transparent, legible contradictions in the Mahatma's politics on caste provoke a confused reaction in Bakha. The only solution Bakha has, then, is to edit his speech to his own liking, to generate his own version of the Mahatma for himself.

Bakha emerges, at the end of the novel, not as the blind follower of the Mahatma's charismatic leadership, but as a critical supporter of the Mahatma's aspirations to abolish untouchability; after all, Bakha is astute enough to figure out that the Mahatma is not interested in the abolition of caste as such, simply the elimination of the stigma associated with caste. This reluctance to root out caste in its entirety sparked one of the most salient critiques of Gandhian attitudes made by Bhimrao Ambedkar, perhaps the most important untouchable leader in colonial India. Nor is Bakha mystified by the Mahatma's quaint religiosity, most of which Bakha finds boring, but he recognizes in Gandhi something that he cannot manufacture by himself. After encountering nothing but caste-based barriers throughout the course of the day, the possibility of a casteless unity, even an imagined one, thrills Bakha to "the very marrow of his bone": "He was in the midst of a humanity which included him in its folds and yet debarred him from entering into a sentient, living, quivering contact with it. Gandhi united him with them, in the mind, because Gandhi was in everybody's mind, including Bakha's" (Anand 1940, 138). In a world that is still cleft by caste, Gandhi becomes the closest analog to a genuine solidarity that Bakha can imagine.

But is the community that Bakha imagined the same as the nation that Gandhi wanted to bring into existence? And do all the circuits of solidarity between the caste Hindu and the outcaste end in the breaker of Gandhian nationalism, even though central aspects of Gandhian nationalism have been explicitly critiqued? Or perhaps it is a Nehruvian nationalism that captures Bakha's fascination? The other option that is given to Bakha in the closing sequence of the novel is the "flush system," a thinly veiled synecdoche for the entire suite of innovations that are the dispensation of an Indian modernity now more closely associated with Jawaharlal Nehru and the "Five Year Plans," which pushed forward Indian industrialization and land reform in the early years after independence. As the Gandhian rally comes to a close, a debate breaks out between a "fair-complexioned Muhammadan dressed in the most smartly-cut European suit" (named R. N. Bashir, but to complete the reference to Muhammad Ali Jinnah, fashioned with a "monocle in his left eye") and a "young man with a delicate feline face [...] dressed in flowing Indian robes like a poet's" (anticommunally named Iqbal Nath Sarshar, and a combination of three writers: Muhammad Iqbal, Ratan Nath Sarshar and Rabindranath Tagore). Bashir's initial dissatisfaction with Gandhian antimodernity ("He is in the fourth century B.C. with his *swadeshi* and his spinning wheel") is resolved in favor of the poet's ecstatic declaration of the power of India's "race-consciousness," which will allow India to "go the whole hog with regards to machines while [the British] fumble their way with the steam engine" (153).

The problem with any procedure that attempts to unpack the ideological content of this novel is that any reading can only be anachronistic in its attempt to name and define the nationalism that this novel endorses, especially at a time in history when there was more political advantage in eliding the differences with Gandhi than in staking out in opposition. In the novel, for instance, there are traces of other nationalists as well: Narayan, Ambedkar, Tagore, Ananda Coomaraswamy and even Anand's own idiosyncratic democratic humanism peek out from the pages of the novel. The problem for most critics of the novel (and most critics of nationalism in general) is that nationalism is generally seen as a singular political movement culminating in the establishment of a putatively majoritarian, bourgeois nation-state. But as the final pages of the novel show, nationalism itself is anxious about the ways in which it will be understood and implemented. If, as the novel imagines, Jinnah, Nehru and Gandhi all walk "homeward" with Bakha into the sunset, no reader of the novel after 1947 can take that position seriously, not the least because of the aftermath of partition but also because of the persistence of antiuntouchable chauvinism. How, the novel now invites us to ask, do we understand the process by which seemingly contradictory and mutually exclusive sets of ideas about the Indian nation-state coexist in a political movement? What separates the India of 1935 from the India of 1947 and after?

The Politics of Untouchability in Late-Colonial India

There are at the core of *Untouchable* two contradictions that dictate both the form and the content of the slim novel. The first is inherited from political debates taking place in and around nationalist circles in India in the 1930s before the signing of the Poona Pact (1932). Because the Congress and its most vocal leaders were only willing to offer slow-paced and largely symbolic solutions to problem of untouchability, advocates for its abolition appeared to these nationalists to be collaborators with the British when they argued for greater reform; the Congress, by corollary, was seen by radical untouchable political organizations as sacrificing abolition for the project of "national unity" and as a greater threat to the project of abolition than the British Empire, which these organizations argued had no ideological attachment to the ideas of caste and untouchability.

This situation was driving an ever larger wedge between the leading figures of both camps, usually represented by Mohandas Karamchand Gandhi and Bhimrao Ramji Ambedkar respectively, and was generally leading to the conclusion that independence and abolition moved in opposite directions. Anand's solution to the seeming incompatibility of nationalist and untouchable politics – the technological humanism advocated by Iqbal Nath Sarshar in the final pages of the novel – required a formal shift in literary strategy to overcome this heated political debate about who could represent untouchables. Because Anand's political alternative, while extant in the ranks of the Congress Left, was relatively unpopular and since the political camps in the untouchability debates were already well defined, both realism and allegory could more easily be exposed as partisan propaganda and therefore would be inadequate to produce the emotional (and therefore ideological) effect a novel like *Untouchable* required to suture together two seemingly opposed political worldviews. *Untouchable* needs to imagine it is capable of convincing both wings of the possibility of a joint project for national liberation and abolition of untouchability, even if neither read the novel.

Ideologically, Anand's political solution would necessitate, on the one hand, a novelistic form that could guarantee the production of "authentic" untouchables (who could, almost paradoxically, convey their absolute alienation) who desired real social improvement – as opposed to cartoon supporters of the Congress that were "content with their lot" (Anand 1940, 10) – and on the other, a manipulation of the forms of allegory and realism to create a national imagination that could successfully incorporate the demands of its disparate members and was genuine about overcoming its caste chauvinism. This is a project, in Anand's mind, of genuine cross-caste solidarity: by stitching together the demands of untouchables and the popular aspirations for a free nation, Anand attempts to demonstrate the utility of the humanist critique of religion, tradition and empire for a more successful nationalist and untouchable politics (Anand 1992, 9). *Untouchable* accomplishes this task formally; the psychological realism and novelistic structure that Anand borrows from British modernism allows him to produce an untouchable who is alienated to his core, while the national allegory that the novel gestures towards (though Anand claims not to be interested in such symbolic maneuvers) allows Anand to marry this project for social upheaval with the task of national liberation through the flexibility of the concluding term of his novel: "race-consciousness" (153).

But this particular resolution to the first problem opens up another contradiction, also inherited from the nationalist politics of the 1930s and one that the novel cannot overcome; namely, the humanist rhetoric of cross-caste solidarity was both a banner for the abolition of caste as well as a potential veneer with which bourgeois nationalists could perpetually defer demands for caste abolition. The formal techniques that the novel deployed could only produce temporary moments of solidarity; without real changes in the lot of untouchables in India, these moments of literary solidarity could only be read as opportunism, as alibis for a majoritarian nationalism that ignored, appropriated, or consciously suppressed minority demands. The idea that national liberation could secure modern flush sanitation (and thus complete the disintegration of caste that the British had begun) was simultaneously a real goal of the radical intelligentsia as well as a cheap shimmer of a promise that would secure untouchable loyalty in the movement for national independence, and which could later be abandoned or ignored. Anand's formal choices replicated this problem: the psychologically realist untouchable of the novel has both a genuine pathos that leads towards meaningful alliances as well as outlining the ideal (i.e. appropriated and ventriloquized) untouchable poster child for Congress party politicians; the national allegory of the modern untouchable who moves towards technology and freedom is both the narrative of genuine liberationist politics as well as the ideological form of yoking untouchable politics to the nationalist wagon. And because this project relied on an anticolonial humanism, the logic of the untouchable's revolt against the world necessarily involved a return to some imagined, ideal Indian nature that the untouchable inherited but was socially prohibited from realizing; the day-in-the-life form that Anand develops and inherits from the modernist British novel fits this problem particularly well as it moves simultaneously in the direction of a radical alienation of the subject and in the direction of a more global allegory of history and development. So at every instant, the logic of the novel turns on both the unique psychology of Bakha's reaction to the world as well as drawing upon a constructed national and racial past that can authenticate both national liberation and untouchable freedom.

Both of these maneuvers carry the risk of subordinating the abolition of caste-based chauvinism to national liberation, and as a result critics have not been incorrect to criticize Anand for the alignment of his novel with the Congress's failures to deliver on untouchable reform. But these critics have failed to see that the nationalist ideological dead end is in every instance the same as the ideological road to a real solidarity between the radical intelligentsia and the disenfranchised. The fact that anticolonialism could give rise – even temporarily – to strategies that would overcome the problems that nationalism encountered with respect to the question of minorities demonstrates that the conclusion of nationalist politics is a contingent, political outcome, not an inevitable, philosophical (or linguistic) one; the very fact of the technological solution to the problem of caste-based discrimination is evidence that the nationalist bourgeoisie felt at least some need to reach out to the low caste. The ultimate failure of the nation-state to deliver on these promises is not isomorphic with the aspirations and hopes of the people who were offering these promises, even as they run on seemingly parallel tracks. These contradictory strains of nationalism (liberationist and opportunist) have always been alive in nationalist politics and nationalist novels, but it requires a more formal reading of *Untouchable* to uncover these contradictions, and a more sensitive account of the political and literary possibilities available in the 1930s to show that the project of nationalism was not at all points doomed to producing the particular version of the Indian state that developed in 1947 and immediately after. The fact of a novel like Anand's shows that anticolonialism had both an elitist and a populist wing; and because the radical intelligentsia was incapable of producing broader political changes in Indian nationalism, its attempt at solidarity now appears to be the blueprint for a politics of appropriation. But this was not the result of an ideological failure of anticolonial projects as such, but a historical and political failure that was contingent on broader developments than the merely discursive formations of which literature was a part. The preservation of the novel as an index of the possibility of real solidarity is necessary in understanding its formal choices as well as the political climate of novelistic production in the 1930s.

Anand and Gandhi

Untouchable has long been aligned with Gandhi's program for the uplift of untouchables, not only because Gandhi was a prominent advocate for untouchable rights but also because, as Gandhi had personally inspired Anand to reexamine the question of untouchability, Anand himself has often credited Gandhi for the genesis of the novel.[2] His long confessional, *The Bubble*, details his early study of Gandhi's thought on the question of untouchability as well as his initial meetings with Gandhi (Anand 1984).[3] Anand described Gandhi's effect on the novel in a short essay written some sixty years later: "One day, I read an article in *Young India*, by Gandhiji, describing how he met Uka, a sweeper boy, and finding him with torn clothes and hungry, took him into his ashram. This narrative was simple, austere and seemed to me more truthful than my artificially concocted novel *Untouchable*. I told Irene this. And, in a sudden fit of revulsion against my existence, in elitist Bloomsbury, I decided to go and see the old man" (Anand 1995, 25). The trip to India to visit Gandhi was also a move "away from the Bloomsbury literary consciousness to the neo-literary worlds, whose denizens have always been considered 'vulgar' and unfit for respectable worlds" (28). Ultimately, Gandhi's impact was immense on the final product. Some six hundred pages, we are told, were edited down to one hundred and fifty and the novel was completely reorganized:

> In retrospect, I feel that, under the tutelage of the Mahatma, who did not pretend to be an artist, I was able to exorcise all those self-conscious literary elements which I had woven into the narrative in anticipation of what the critics might approve of. He thought that the paragraphs of high-sounding words, in which I had tried to unite miscellaneous elements, in what was essentially a walk through the small town of my hero, must go. Also, the old man suggested the removal of my deliberate attempts at melodramatic contrasts of the comic and tragic motifs, through which the spontaneous feelings, moods and lurking chaos in the soul of Bakha, had been somewhat suppressed. And the Mahatma asked for the deflation of those clever tricks, which had made the expression of concrete detail into a deliberate effort at style. (Anand 1992, 11)

For Anand, Gandhi represented a stylistic and formal innovation in his novel, not a political purification of the ideas within. Gandhi's intervention into Anand's novel has little to do with his specific ideas about caste or about the Congress, but more to do with the strategies for representing untouchables and for accurately reproducing the texture of their emotional world. The novel is unmistakably concerned with the lives and struggles of India's untouchables, but the influence of Gandhi, Anand suggests, changes the register of any literary representation of untouchables.

Little remains of the original manuscript, save a few sentences that are preserved in Anand's later essays, and these give a sense of the range of changes that Gandhi helped to initiate in Anand's prose:

> I have so far used the language of the mocking bird indeed. I read my garbled, gargantuan rhetorical prose: "He saw giant masses of black bodies, stinking by the foulairtake of each

ignoble creature, herdedinchains, to enter the doors of hells, held ajar by the horned doots of Yama, himself in Yab-Yam embrace with yami, sweating the oil of sweat, above the blood that oozed from flesh lacerated by whips, fear-stricken at being pushed into the ocean of filth, which exuded the smell of death," etc. Bathos! With the smell of Christian hell about it! And the fall! Infected by the neurosis of after the expulsion from the Garden of Eden! (Anand 1984, 527)

Anand's revulsion with the Christian character of his borrowed modernism finds something important in Gandhi's preference for representations of untouchables in a realistic mode. In his probably inaccurate *Little Plays of Mahatma Gandhi*, Anand recalls the conversation that took place between Gandhi and Krishan Chander Azad, Anand's alter ego:

Gandhi: Mocking bird with a vengeance! Such big big words! You don't know, that Harijans sigh, moan, groan and say a few words! They never talk in such big words! You want to make them into Dr. Johnsons!

K. C. Azad: (Humbled) I have been following the method of James Joyce. Stream of consciousness of characters! He has coined a new language. With puns! Satirical words! Joined words! Poetic phrases! ... I thought if I also use big words, and make puns, English people will think I have mastered the English language ...

Gandhi: I thought the same in London! Then an English friend, a Quaker, told me to write simply. I began to translate into English from Gujarati. Why don't you write in your language?

K. C. Azad: I have no language. My mother tongue is Punjabi. But the Sarkar has appointed English and Urdu as court languages! ... Except Bhai Vir Singh and Dhani Ram Chatrath Poets! Few of us write in Punjabi. The only novel writer is Nanak Singh. There are no publishers in Punjabi or Urdu. Even Dr. Muhammad Iqbal writes in Urdu and Persian not in Punjabi! No one can earn a living as a writer in Punjabi. In English – my novel may get published in London ...

Gandhi: Acha! Write in any language that comes to hand. But say what Harijans say! And the poor say! Translate their speech literally. Don't use "Thees" and "Thous!" Above all you must be sincere! Truthful! Write of life as it really is! ... Of the poor! Few writers have written about the poor! Only Sarat Babu! And Prem Chand! – I hear! (Anand 1991, 22–3)

Anand's problem – that Indian writers get little attention in the vernacular languages – produces another problem: the inadequacy of certain English styles to capture the topical material of Anand's novel.[4] Gandhi's exemplars, Sarat Chandra Chatterjee and Dhanpat Rai Srivastav (Premchand), stand out in this dialogue as alternative, realist poles to the literary embellishments of a modernist Joyce. Joycean modernism here fails to capture the reality and worldview of the untouchable, whose speech, Gandhi argues with characteristic paternalism, is limited to being able to "sigh, moan, groan and say a few words." The literary pyrotechnics of European modernism outstrip the actual linguistic developments of real untouchables, at least as Gandhi and Anand see them. So the debate about language and style turns back to the question of representational politics; Anand seems to absorb from Gandhi a terminology of authenticity from this exchange: sincerity, literalness, simplicity and truth. The problem, rather than an adherence to Gandhian dogma about caste, here, is that novelistic untouchables needed to be translated accurately.

But the formal changes in the novel also seem to make Gandhi and his specific political intervention into constitutional reform and untouchable uplift much more prominent by exclusively foregrounding him (Niranjan 1979). In the final pages of *Untouchable*, Bakha is told that Gandhi "is not speaking about *swadeshi*, or on civil disobedience [...]. The government has allowed him out of gaol only if he will keep strictly within the limits of his propaganda for harijans (men of God, as Gandhi chooses to call the Untouchables), for the removal of untouchability" (Anand, 1940, 141). The political moment of this leg of Gandhi's campaign against untouchability (1932–33) follows the failure of the second Round Table Conference (1931) and the Poona Pact signed at Yeravda Jail under the pressure of Gandhi's Epic Fast, both of which had been necessitated by a heightened critical pitch in the debates about untouchable representation in formal politics in the new constitutional government (Ray 1996). The appearance of Gandhi's speech in the final pages of the novel has often been read as the product of Anand's endorsement of Gandhi's often-paternalistic strategies with respect to untouchables as well as the Congress plan for the independent Indian nation.[5] The text of Gandhi's speech was lifted from a *Young India* reprint of a similar speech that Gandhi gave as part of this tour, during which Gandhi made no small mention of his problems with the British constitutional reforms despite legal injunctions to the contrary:

> I have emerged [...] from the ordeal of a penance undertaken for a cause which is as dear to me as life itself. The British Government sought to pursue a policy of divide and rule in giving to our brethren of the depressed classes separate electorates in the Councils that will be created under the new constitution. I do not believe that the bureaucracy is sincere in its efforts to elaborate the new constitution. But it is one of the conditions under which I have been released from gaol that I shall not carry on any propaganda against the government. So I shall not refer to that matter. I shall only speak about the so-called "Untouchables," whom the government tried to alienate from Hinduism by giving them a separate legal and political status. (Anand 1940, 146)

Gandhi's speech lays out the basic contours of his position at the Round Table Conference and the reasons for his unwillingness to compromise with Ambedkar on the question of separate electorates. First, separate electorates, which would have reserved certain seats for untouchables in the councils and only allowed untouchables to vote for them, were part of a "divide and rule" strategy, through which the British could hope to use the untouchable cause as a stick with which to beat the Congress's claims to represent the entire nation. Second, separate electorates would make it impossible for there to be any rapprochement between Hinduism and the untouchables by creating an irreparable breach between them, consolidated by "a separate legal and political status." And finally, separate electorates would ensure the longevity of untouchability as opposed to enabling the move towards abolition, as political power would now depend on its perpetuation.[6]

Gandhi's interpretation of the debates about separate electorates was representative of a growing majority of the Congress, who believed that the proposed constitutional separation of untouchables from Hindus into separate voting blocs would make national liberation incomparably more difficult.[7] This conclusion was largely the result of the Congress's experiences in the wake of the Morley–Minto and Montagu–Chelmsford reforms and the political legacy of the Muslim League, in which the question of minorities in India was used to establish both adversaries to the Congress as well as to secure the ideological architecture of the British claim that only they could rule so wide and disparate a nation as India.[8] The creation of separate electorates for Muslims had already produced a vocal constituency of Muslim elites who were dependent on – and therefore allied to – British patronage, and who repeatedly undermined the Congress's demands for responsible government and *swaraj*. Gandhi's fear had been that the creation of separate electorates for untouchables would merely reproduce the pattern of the Muslim League and produce another antagonist in the project for national liberation (Arnold 2001b, 201). This was also the expressed strategy of the British Empire, which had, through the zero-sum game of census-based political representation, demonstrated both its ideological commitment to a nonunitary India and to the exploitation of caste and communal hierarchies in order to prevent the formation of any unified movement (Chandra 1979). The official position of the British continued to be the one expressed by Sir John Strachey: "There is not, and never was an India, or even any country of India. [...] That men of the Punjab, Bengal, the North-West Provinces and Madras, should ever feel that they belong to one great Indian nation, is impossible" (Sarkar 1989, 2). Regional differences then gave way to differences of religion and then caste distinctions; as long as the Congress could not solve the problem of poor Muslims and exploited untouchables, the British could claim that their rule was a necessary defense of minorities in India. Ramsay MacDonald could in fact offer up the Communal Award (1932) with the belief that he was the sole defender of minority rights (Menon 1995).

But Gandhi's solution to this real problem of British rule masked other political debates created by the Congress's strategy. While preserving the idea of national liberation seemed to require defending the idea of a unified India, it also threatened to empty the minorities problem of all content and sacrifice minority demands in the interests of a purported unity. First, as long as the Congress was unable to put forward immediate, meaningful solutions to the minorities question, its appeals for slow-paced reform would sound like alibis for chauvinism, which the British happily exploited to their advantage to preserve their rhetorical position as the only liberal modernizers in India. And the more Gandhi insisted that he alone spoke for the Indian nation, the more he alienated genuine leaders of minorities, especially Ambedkar, from the project of independence. Ambedkar had already indicated his willingness to abandon independence in favor of strategic alliances with the British, since independence might risk a caste-Hindu majority and the perpetual discrimination of untouchables: "No caste Hindu, once he occupies a position of influence, would allow a member of the Depressed Classes, to rise in the social or economic scale but, on the contrary would aim to stabilize his condition as a hewer of wood and drawer of water. We have more to hope from the British officer who, free from communal or caste bias, unfettered by any wicked tradition, is quick to respond to the prompting of his conscience and the dictates of humanity" (Jaffrelot 2005, 92). Incidentally, the Ambedkarite position finds itself in the novel in Bakha's instinctive preference for British military attire and the modern freedom it symbolizes. In the two narratives that were developing around constitutional reform, independence and abolition, though not philosophically mutually exclusive, were becoming politically opposed, since members of each camp had repeatedly professed their support for the demands of the other.

Gandhi, though, was unwilling to admit another difficulty that was also at the root of the Congress's inability to press for the reforms demanded by the minorities. In particular, the Congress contained both elements that were principally opposed to caste-based chauvinism and those that were unwilling to implement the necessary reforms to eliminate untouchability (i.e. temple entry, opening roads, increased access to wells and schools, economic development and the abolition of caste). This was further complicated by the fears that had grown up in orthodox circles that untouchables were being converted to Christianity, Islam and Sikhism, thus undermining the electoral power of Hindus and the number of seats that would be allocated to them. The Congress's inability to put forward any reasonable constructive program towards caste abolition was the direct result of the competing interests that had collected under its umbrella. For one thing, the caste chauvinism of the Brahminical right wing of the Congress – represented notably by Madan Mohan Malaviya and the Hindu Mahasabha – made it impossible for the Congress to adopt more radical solutions to caste discrimination, even after the removal of untouchability was made a formal part of its constitution.[9] The orthodox right wing was able consistently to channel this sentiment into social service programs rather than political empowerment and to delay and defer political action on immediate questions like access to roads, schools, wells and temples. And Gandhi's refusal to call for the abolition of caste altogether provided the right wing of the Congress with sufficient cover for their more chauvinist ideas.[10]

But no less important were the positions taken by the Congress's moderate and left wings: Gandhi's paternalist solution offered the untouchables temporary moral relief but left *varnashrama* and caste prerogatives relatively intact, while the left wing's economic determinism, which argued that nationalism would lift all economic boats, had no specific plan for the untouchable future (Brown 1989, 266). Even though the moderates and the Left were convinced that caste-based discrimination had to be ended and had themselves engaged in social activism to that end, neither had a coherent plan that it could implement and neither was willing to open a rift with the orthodox right wing to defend the principle of equality (Sarkar 1989). More importantly, none of them were able to convince substantial numbers of untouchable political activists that their plan could produce the desired end. Necessarily, this vacillation in the Congress reduced a number of their measures to symbolic proposals and began to establish a pattern of sacrificing the demand of abolition to the needs of national unity: by 1932, the Anti-Untouchability League had been taken over by the Hindu Mahasabha, renamed the Harijan Sevak Sangh, and had its political content emptied; two legislative attempts (led by Ranga Iyer and Subbarayan) to abolish untouchability failed to get necessary support and failed to call for the abolition of caste, thus preserving caste hierarchies that amounted to the same thing as untouchability; Gandhi even began to hedge on important temple entry *satyagrahas* (Jaffrelot 2005). Congress members and their allies organized parallel institutions to Ambedkar's (like the All-India Depressed Classes Association) in a conscious attempt to undermine his autonomous movement and to return untouchables to the Hindu–Congress fold.[11] The most radical of the proposals offered up by the Congress ended up being Gandhi's compromise in the Poona Pact, though the outcome of this electoral reform neither satisfied Ambedkar nor solved the still extant problem of untouchability (Mandala 1999). In the best instances, the Congress's strategy for the alleviation of caste discrimination deferred the solution into the intolerably distant future. In the worst instances, the plan put into play ideologies and forces that would benefit from the longevity of caste and caste-based associations while disarming any meaningful opposition. As a result, demands for the abolition of caste risked wrecking the fragile coalition comprising the Congress and were, therefore, too high a price to pay for the majority of its members.

Anand shared many of the Congress's opinions about the political debates that had emerged with respect to constitutional reform and devolution. In 1942, he published his epistolary defense of the Congress in *Letters on India*, with regard to its positions on independence and negotiations with the British. In it, the argument that he advances is barely distinguishable from Gandhi's and the majority of the Congress moderates:

> This curt rejection of the advances of Congress, together with the emphasis on various communities and interests, would have been enough to confirm the suspicions of nationalist India, so often had the difficulties between the Indian National Congress and the Muslim and other minorities been used to withhold self-governing institutions. I have told you that Congress is a political body, with a membership of all kinds of Indians, Hindus, Muhammadans, Sikhs, Christians, Parsis, etc., without any religious or sectarian aims. As such it must be distinguished from the two primarily religious bodies, the Hindu Mahasabha and the Muslim League. These two, though they profess political aims, are, in fact, obscurantist, sectarian bodies which have been constantly used by reactionary and vested interests as counterpoise against Congress. In this regard, the British Government has been specially anxious to use the Muslim League, under Mr. Jinnah, an eminent lawyer, largely supported by the big landlords and capitalists of Northern India, as a stick to beat the Congress with. But as the Muslim League has never published its membership figures, and there are actually more Muslims in the Congress, the British Government's encouragement of its disruptionist demand for a separate Muslim state, called Pakistan, in the north of India is known to all reasonable people as a mischievous tactic to divide India and keep it in subjection. (5)

Anand's position with respect to the minorities question is amalgamative: the national party contains minorities and is qualified to represent them. This position shares, as well, a deep suspicion of separate representation both as an avenue towards collaborationist politics and as an irresponsible method of advocating for minorities by recognizing groups with unmeasured influence. That Muslims and Hindus might have had genuine grievances that the Congress was unable or unwilling to address does not seem to factor into Anand's account here, as any attempt to undermine national unity is read as a throwback to confessional closed-mindedness. Consequently, Anand concludes by advocating for the national politics of the Congress and its exclusive negotiating rights for the Indian people.

Anand was committed to the idea of an anticolonial politics that could produce dramatic changes in the life and culture of India. His alignment of religious conservatism with British imperialism meant that in all places he saw the hand of one behind the political moves of the other. As a result, in some places, Anand's explanation of the political debates sounds even more feverish than the conservative elements in the Congress:

> These communal or separate electorates were the most vicious thing in the election procedure and were deeply resented by the people of India. According to the scheme all the seats in both the Federal and Provincial Legislatures were distributed among several vaguely defined religious, denominational and other electoral groups so that there were special seats for Sikhs, Muhammadans, "Europeans," "landholders," women, etc., each group forming an electorate by itself and returning a fixed number of representatives. The eleven such groups who were to return representatives to the Federal Assembly were obviously intended to prevent the formation of a clear majority for any party or principle in the Legislature, and sabotage its functioning from the start. (1942, 134)

In Anand's view, separate electorates would make it impossible for national unity to emerge and would make it impossible to negotiate with the British in any meaningful way. The possibility of a confident, mature coalition politics seems to have been a too-distant horizon to take seriously, and the legitimate grievances of minorities in any representational scheme without a full franchise were sidelined.

But in many important ways, Anand's position on untouchability differs from Gandhi's and the Congress. Anand had recognized early on the failure of Gandhi's political strategy to offer up a more radical rejection of the foundations of caste: "Only [Gandhi] did not give up his belief in Sanatani Hindu faith in spite of his campaign against untouchability. And his acceptance of caste as a part of the Hindu faith militated always against his humanistic tendencies and limited his appeal to the secularists. His assertion that all the Varnas are Shudras, and the Brahmins should do leatherwork, is only a concession to reformism, though he wanted a revolutionary breakthrough from the organized Hinduism to a new casteless Hinduism" (1967, 24). Gandhi's position is problematic for Anand, who holds on to the belief that one had to break with caste and Hinduism in order to reach a casteless world: "There are many other contrarieties in his thinking. On the one hand he campaigns against untouchability; on the other hand he wishes to retain the outcastes in joint electorates with the caste Hindus and goes on a fast against separate electorates. Again he reveres the Hindu majority and their rites, with a bias which makes him refuse thirty percent representation to the Muslims in the legislatures after the second Round Table Conference" (26). So while Gandhi's disposition towards caste fit nicely with Anand's humanism in terms of its spirit, Anand's actual program for uplift would differ substantially from Gandhi's. Perhaps, for this reason, the central character of Anand's novel, Bakha, remains unimpressed with the strategy on offer from Gandhi. As Anand's narrator describes, "Bakha didn't understand these words. He was restless. He hoped that the Mahatma wouldn't go on speaking of things he [Bakha] couldn't understand" (146). Ironically, Gandhi's critique of Anand's language has become Anand's critique of Gandhi's.

In many ways, this contradictory relationship to Gandhi's position and the position of the Congress characterized the mood of the politically engaged intellectuals of the 1930s:

> Despite the complexity and deep ambiguity of Untouchable identity over a period of centuries, what became a conventional account of them emerged under the spur of British imperium in the years between 1870 and 1930. By about 1930 all the major political protagonists, Gandhi included, were prepared to agree that Untouchables were both a distinctive and an oppressed segment of the Indian population. This agreement was the basis upon which a huge machinery of institutional privilege was erected so as to right the historic wrongs. But the consensus masked powerful differences as to the distinctiveness of the Untouchables, and these differences were progressively articulated in later years. (Mendelsohn and Vicziany 1998, 14)

This climate of deferred engagement gave rise in the late 1920s to Ambedkar's oppositional electoral reform strategy. Initially seeking alliances with the Congress and then with other minority organizations, Ambedkar had by the 1920s broken with the Congress and abandoned its nationalism in favor of open alliances with the British, whom he believed had no interest in preserving caste and whose liberal imperial rule might offer the necessary legal reforms to do away with caste discrimination all together, and for political representation of untouchables by untouchables (Ambedkar 1990). In 1928, he even met with the controversially composed Simon Commission, which convinced Ambedkar of the need for separate electorates for the untouchables and of the possibility of working with the British to enforce untouchable rights, which led to his vocal debates with Gandhi at the second Round Table Conference. The hope for Ambedkar had been that electoral guarantees at the center would require coalition politics to develop in any new political formation and ensure that untouchables had at least a negative veto and therefore some political voice in the legislature. That this required participating consciously with the British's strategy of undermining the Congress, while problematic, was acceptable to Ambedkar, even though it left unresolved the question of whether the British would be willing to make radical changes to the caste structure in India and whether electoral reform would, as Gandhi argued, strengthen caste identity and thereby defer caste abolition from the other side (Mathew 1991).

Caste and Colonial Modernity

Some fifty years after the publication of *Untouchable*, Anand wrote the preface to a new edition of Ambedkar's controversial *Annihilation of Caste*. While designed to commemorate the centenary of Ambedkar's birth, Anand also used his introduction as a way to explain the debates that had emerged about untouchability before Indian independence and, perhaps, to dust off his credentials for the cause of abolition. But what is important here is how steeped the Anand of the 1930s was in the debate that had been opened up by the Round Table Conferences and the Poona Pact, and the positions that had crystallized in their wake. Anand makes it clear that the positions that Gandhi advocated were undoubtedly reformist and thoroughly wedded to the very tradition that abolition had in its sights, while Ambedkar's position was derived from a more radically transformative and oppositional space. Anand does not hesitate to point out, for instance, that "Mahatma Gandhi, who himself stood for the abolition of untouchability, objected to the castigation of the fourfold Hindu Varnashram," and that Ambedkar was perhaps the sole true voice of India's most oppressed (1990, 9). But Anand's own position is much more qualified:

> I had the privilege to know Dr. B. R. Ambedkar from the late twenties onwards. He criticized me for accepting Gandhiji in the role of liberator of untouchables, in spite of the Mahatma's allegiance to Hindu Varnashram. I accepted his rebuke and did argue with the Mahatma, who justified his stand by asserting the need of unity of people of all persuasion in the interest of the political struggle against British Imperialist attempts to divide Indians through separate electorates. In fact, so strongly did he believe in unity of all sections of Indians that he "fasted unto death" against the proposal of separate electorates for the scheduled castes. (1990, 9–10)

Anand, here, positions himself between both camps. While recognizing Ambedkar's criticism of Gandhi's reliance on caste, Anand continues to defend Gandhi's position, though with qualifications. In other places, his criticisms of Gandhi and his support for Ambedkar's approach are much more pronounced:

Mahadev Desai: Hindu Dharma has done many good things.
K. C. Azad: There is no Hinduism without caste. Say the heads of Muths established by Shankara! God established the Varna Ashram – the four castes!
Gandhi: Caste was necessary in the Vedic Period. It was according to duties to be performed.
K. C. Azad: Dr. Ambedkar, the leader of the untouchables, says: there can be no Varna Ashram today. Ambedkar is a Shudra but has become a Barrister at law! You are a Vaishya but have also become a Barrister! And Mahatma!
Gandhi: Ambedkar wants separate electorates for Harijans. Like Jinnah for Muslims. We must keep together in the struggle for freedom. Some good things in our old Dharma! Lok Sangraha! (1991, 29)

Anand's apparent political equivocation presents an interpretive problem for those who would like to align him neatly with either Gandhi or his adversaries. Anand is not, like Gandhi, committed to national unity at all costs, even when he sees the danger of the separate electorates; his rage seems in places equally directed against Hinduism as much as against British imperialism, and in this instance, the compromise with orthodoxy suggested by Gandhi was not a serious option that Anand pursued. But at the same time, there is no break with Gandhi or open espousal of Ambedkar's politics or the clear charting of a course to an independent politics – and all of this makes reading his novel as national allegory more than a little difficult. The idiosyncrasies of this political worldview threaten to make the imagining of a coherent nationalist or anticolonial project impossible, especially if his resolution to the problem of caste was left this vague. Equally satisfied by Gandhi and Ambedkar, Anand's position on caste resists an easy reduction into the various defined camps.

Perhaps even more startling is the fact that, unlike the rest of the Congress Left, with which Anand is probably most easily placed, Anand stands out as one of the few who concerned himself with the question of caste and untouchability and not merely economic reform. Neither the Congress Left nor the Congress Socialist Party (established in 1934) had by the time of Anand's novel composed any important elaboration of the problems of caste and their strategies to reform or abolish it (Sarkar 1989). Nehru, in both his *The Discovery of India* (1946) and *An Autobiography* (1936), deplored the existence of untouchability, but he was not unique in his view that caste, while odious, was not the central problem facing an occupied India (Brown 2003). Anand was charting new ideological territory, as a real program of economic uplift and social reorganization had not been fully articulated by the left-wing Congress leadership. In this respect, Ambedkar was perhaps a more useful guide; his writings on caste demonstrate a full reformist program. But Ambedkar's sabbatical from the debates with Gandhi after 1932 and his inability to organize an effective challenge to either the Congress or the British meant that his ideas were not on offer in the same way as Gandhi's.

To this problem must be added the confusion caused and possibilities created by British involvement in questions of caste identity in India. The changes that were taking place to caste and caste-based identities had been accelerating by the time of the 1931 census, which aggravated already tense communal relationships as religious organizations lobbied for the inclusion of untouchables in their ranks. A number of administrative changes to colonial rule and practice – the development of caste categories in the census, the formation of caste-based fractions in the army, and the proposition of separate electorates based on caste – as well as the new experience of social vulnerability produced by industrialization and urbanization, had simultaneously increased the importance of caste in the lives of most Indians, as the ideology of colonial modernity threatened, perhaps impossibly, to erase caste altogether.[12] If, on the one hand, caste was seen to be the defining feature of a traditional and stagnating Indian society, and thus a justification for the modernizing influence of British rule, caste and caste divisions were also hardening on a new basis as a consequence of that very rule. The production of a census that aimed at precise enumeration of a caste hierarchy produced an array of petitions and an ideology that has been called "Sanskritization," organized on the basis of appeals to the hierarchy to validate claims of upward mobility on the basis of personal uplift and reform. Caste-based organizations began to spring up throughout the country and movements for the uplift of castes took hold in a number of states. In Tamil Nadu and Maharashtra, political parties were formed around caste identities, and discussions in the two Round Table Conferences promised a new politicization of caste and the entry of lower castes into official political power. Upper caste partisans were also quick to seize on the new opportunities posed by colonial rule – not least because they had been the earliest recipients of British patronage – to ensure that they could monopolize the distribution of new rights and privileges to their benefit. But the British were not above reproducing caste-based occupations; urban sanitation workers were exclusively recruited from the ranks of untouchables under colonial authority. Rather than simply ending caste, colonial modernity was reshaping and perpetuating it – producing new oppressions alongside new freedoms as well as retaining some features of old – all the while claiming for itself a singularly liberationist legacy.

For instance, the British engaged in a whole series of urban restructuring projects, designed to modernize Indian cities. Bulashah would be typical of the North Indian town redrawn in the wake of the 1857 Mutiny and the attendant anxieties of its recurrence; streets could be made wider and whole sections of the town torn down to accommodate easier surveillance, but the development of modern urban technologies, especially sanitation, were usually left unsolved by the British administrations before they were hastily handed off to native municipal governments.[13] In the newly designed North Indian urbanscape, the cantonments would be kept separate from the city, to protect the colonial military from the inevitable infectious outbreaks that would overwhelm Indian towns. Secluded in such colonial enclaves, the British attempted to inoculate themselves from the inhospitable biological environment of the native cities (Arnold 1993, 274–80). The failure to prevent the outbreak of "Asiatic cholera" had already convinced the British that their presence near crowded cities with poor sanitation in North India was already precarious. It became necessary to develop the power of institutions like the Delhi Municipal Committee and other local municipal bodies, which could bring (before the establishment of dyarchy) public sanitation under the control of the British. But the need for a regime of sanitation was bound up with both British ideologies about modernity as well as an understanding of Indian backwardness; native resistance to modern sanitation was proof both of British enlightenment and of the need for continued occupation:

> In 1888, Dufferin ordered a general inquiry on the question of sanitation and hygiene in the social consciousness of the natives. One official reported that "to the masses of the people, sanitation is foolishness." The people, he argued, are uneducated, even "inoculated by time and habit." What was the point, it was urged by the majority opinion, of wasting effort on a people whose innate social conservatism prevented them from enjoying the benefits of anything new, that is anything modern? No doubt, William Crooke argued from Azamgarh, "the time will come when they will comprehend the laws of hygiene, just as at some time or other they will get rid of the abject superstition which leads them now, where they will learn to treat their women properly, to discontinue infant marriage, and emerge from the comparative barbarism in which they are plunged at present." (Prashad 2001, 124)

As a consequence, the British could have it both ways: they could both insist on sanitation and delay its implementation. M. D. Dadabhoy called this policy towards untouchables and sanitation "benevolent indifference," but it had elements that the nationalist could critique without being overly cynical (Mendelsohn and Vicziany 1998, 26). The natives, after all, were not ready and that meant that old practices could coexist alongside new city plans; British interventions into the urban landscape complicated the problem by disrupting traditional patterns of waste management and consolidating caste occupations (Prashad 2000). The opening lines of Anand's novel are inflected with this sense of a colonial modernity that degenerates rather than improves the lot of the untouchables:

> The outcastes' colony was a group of mud-walled houses that clustered together in two rows, under the shadow both of the town and the cantonment, but outside their boundaries and separate from them. There lived the scavengers, the leather-workers, the washermen, the barbers, the water-carriers, the grass-cutters and other outcastes from Hindu society. A brook ran near the lane, once with crystal-clear water, now soiled by the dirt and filth of the public latrines situated about it, the odour of the hides and skins of dead carcasses left to dry on its banks, the dung of donkeys, sheep, horses, cows and buffaloes heaped up to be made into fuel cakes, and the biting, choking, pungent fumes that oozed from its sides. The absence of a drainage system had, through the rains of various seasons, made of the quarter a marsh which gave out the most offensive stink. And altogether the ramparts of human and animal refuse that lay on the outskirts of this little colony, and the ugliness, the squalor and the misery which lay within it, made it an "uncongenial" place to live in. (1940, 9)

Flanked by a caste-based urban economy and a military-colonial administration, the untouchable quarters in Bulashah accumulate the worst of both worlds. The "absence of a drainage system" can, it must be mentioned, only be recognized by a narrator who understands the failed promise of the colonial modernity, one who later reminds us that there are holes in the streets of Bulashah, "where, thanks to the inefficiency of the Municipal Committee, the pavement should have been but was not" (Anand 1940, 41). The growth of a colonial town does not solve the problem of untouchability; it complicates it by exposing its artificiality, its "uncongeniality." And British modernity is doubly disappointing: first, in its failure to implement promised changes; and second, in raising expectations of a different present. The untouchable quarter is "uncongenial" precisely because alternatives were extant. Solutions to the problem of the untouchability that persists in colonial urban spaces would require more radical changes than those offered up by British.

Anand and the Ethics of Solidarity

The choices facing the radical intellectual, then, were to make sense of the political positions on offer – Gandhi's religious reformism, Ambedkar's identity politics, or British imperialism – and chart out a different course from each of these. That Anand is unsatisfied with the various dominant ideas is reflected in the choices made throughout the novel: Gandhi's sympathy, not his ideas, attracts Bakha; Ambedkar is all but absent from the novelistic imagination, referenced only obliquely by the monocled,

Western-attired character at the end of the novel; and Bakha's attraction to British modernity disappears in the final swadeshi bonfire. Bakha's dissatisfaction with the choices before him runs parallel to Anand's own. This more radical position was articulated in his autobiographical essay, *Apology for Heroism*:

> But I did not let my imagination blind me to the fact that my hatred of Imperialism was bound up also with my disgust for the cruelty and hypocrisy of Indian feudal life, with its castes, creeds, dead habits and customs, and its restrictive religious rites and practices. I was one of many groping young men of my generation who had begun to question everything in our background, to look away from the big houses and to feel the misery of the inert, disease-ridden, underfed, illiterate people about us. The more authority humiliated us and insulted our intelligence by suppressing books and ideas, the more hungrily we devoured knowledge of the outside world, the more avidly we sought to contact others in Europe and Asia who we knew were thinking like us. And whether our dearest friends and nearest relations liked it or not, whether the Sarkar tortured us or talked to us persuasively, we had set our hearts on our liberation and those of other oppressed peoples, whoever they were, wherever they were and of whatever shape, size, and colour. (1946, 53–4)

This political move – an appreciation of the problems of the underclass and low caste as part of the project of anticolonialism – is at the heart of the formal choices in the novel. Anand and the other "groping young men of his generation" formed a section of the radical middle class that saw the discrimination faced by other oppressed groups as a reflection of the chauvinism and censorship that they encountered. Imperialism and Hindu orthodoxy, having run their course together, had driven the middle class to seek out collaborators in "other oppressed peoples." This is a politics of internationalism and intercaste solidarity that would push the limits of the official politics of Indian nationalism. But it would also establish, for Anand, a kind of emotional and intellectual parallel that could be used to explain how the middle class could find in the untouchable a key to the ambitions of both.

Anand's descriptions of the process of writing *Untouchable* are bound up in this pattern of seeing in the untouchable a pattern for the evolution of the radical intellectual. There were larger problems that the middle class had not thus far solved: it was too tied to tradition and superstition; it had not successfully manufactured its own revolt against either empire or orthodoxy; and it had not felt itself a part of the larger changes that were taking place in India. As a result, the evolution of an untouchable capable of revolt, one who moves from "his deep-rooted sense of inferiority and docile acceptance of the laws of fate" (Anand 1940, 83) to the subject capable of revolutionary action, could serve as the model for a middle class searching for its own language of feeling, solidarity, politics and art:

> I felt that, apart from the exuberance of my own egoism in the *Confession*, I had been trying to be truthful in Gandhi's way. But I had not so far faced our weaknesses. Our inability to revolt. Even the courage to call a spade a spade, as the English do.

Unless I could become a revolutionary, I would not be able to free myself from the corrosions behind the façade of the Hindu in me and have a vision of the free life. [...] If we want to be free we must see that life is not only for personal salvation, but to live in and through others as the revolutionaries lived. I must take out the portion about the sweeper-boy Bakha from the confessional and write about him as a new kind of hero of India, a failure against the twiceborn, but one who makes the effort to come up from the labyrinths. I must create a hero, beyond the weak-kneed me. My nerves tingled at the inspiration which had just come. The clatter and talk of the café compelled me to look away. And I wondered if, in the first instance, I could change myself, before changing others. (Anand 1984, 337)

The charge of appropriating the untouchable for other political ends is already placed at the forefront of Anand's description of his own project. The writer as revolutionary must "live in and through others," all the while making of them models of "a new kind of hero of India." But the impulse behind the appropriative move is also a move towards a different ethics, one in which appropriation changes both the writer and the untouchable. The untouchable's evolution would allow the radical intellectual to experience the world anew and develop a challenge, internally, to his own ideas about what counts as genuine liberation for both. The failure of the untouchable to revolt is in all instances the failure of the radical intelligentsia to feel and understand life correctly, "the failure of the spontaneous revolts" (Ram 1983, 17). The untouchable's social position, for Anand, places him in the position of being able to understand "things below their outer history": each act of rebellion immediately brings him into conflict with both Hindu orthodoxy and British imperialism.

This was, though, a fantasy; the alliance between the untouchable and the radical intelligentsia had not been fully completed. That Anand was attempting to address this rift in the novel is fairly straightforward, as the final pages of the book are devoted to a hasty summary of the terms of the alliance against the British. But this alliance automatically poses the problem that this chapter began with, one that I believe Anand is less conscious of and one that both animates the emotional intensity of the climactic scene and has been the source of the charge most often leveled at Anand: namely, that strategies for solidarity are in every instance identical to the strategies for appropriation, insofar as they rely on the existence of a continued alliance between orthodoxy and empire. In order to make the nationalist project meaningful to the untouchable, Anand has to imagine the conditions that would make the nationalists willing to offer, and the untouchable willing to accept, a joint program, one that risks putting the untouchable demands second and thus threatens to ignore demands for the abolition of caste. The radical solution that Anand poses requires winning national liberation as a prelude to the introduction of a technologically egalitarian sanitation regime, which ends the logic of untouchability (i.e. ends contact with "night soil" and the "pollution" at the heart of untouchability). And the problem is that without a complete overhaul of the organizations and ideologies that composed nationalism in India, there would be no organic priority to the untouchable problem. Susie Tharu's description of the opportunist potential of Anand's novel is perhaps the clearest: "What is it, we need to ask, in [Anand's] liberal nationalism – which we have tended to characterize as modern, or progressive – that keeps the untouchable working patiently while an enlightened administration attends to the resolution of his problem: the water-closet. How does a writer of Anand's stature become accomplice to a programme in which the oppressed, waiting for civilization to be brought to them, continue to be a source of cheap but proud labour?" (Tharu 1986, 61–2) Despite unfairly characterizing Anand's nationalism as "liberal," Tharu's conclusion is that Anand is in fact an unwitting accomplice in the nationalist ploy to deceive the lower castes with its humanist rhetoric, and in detecting that potential (and most prominently Anand's endorsement of Gandhi over Ambedkar as an index of that potential) she is not mistaken. Anand's humanism is also too broad, despite its Marxist and Socialist tints, not to provide cover for opportunism, especially given his political affinity to Jawaharlal Nehru and the Congress Left. Any untouchable who courts compromises with the Congress would be held up as the exemplary untouchable, sacrificing his own personal liberation for a national one. Without making too much of an example of Tharu's claim, it is also possible to see a historical error in her otherwise compelling reading of the failure of *Untouchable*'s politics. For Tharu, after all, it matters little that nationalism made its alliance with liberal imperialism in the 1940s, after the victory of the Labour Party in the Parliamentary elections and the publication of Anand's novel, an alliance that nationalism could not have predicted in the aftermath of the repression of the Civil Disobedience movement in the 1930s. The political milieu of the 1930s that was interested in caste abolition was forcing itself to ask much more radical questions than ones that could be answered fully by the nationalists.

Vijay Prashad's analysis of the effects of urban modernity on both sanitation and caste chauvinism makes sense of Tharu's critique, but only from the position of a postcolonial dissatisfaction with nationalist technocracy:

> The sanitation question in a capitalist state is framed by the nexus between technology and capital. The limit for the development of capitalist modernity (i.e. as bourgeois thought's self-image) is not something extraneous, something ancient or outside, but it is itself its limit. In other words, the limit of capitalist modernity is its constituents: the social nexus between technology and capital. Within this framework, one that relied upon the sweepers at the same time as it reviled them, the Dalits will find no emancipation. Technology is not a neutral thing, since it is imbedded within the social relations that produce and use it. The emancipation of the Dalits cannot come by technology alone, but also through the rearrangement of the social relations. (2001, 155)

Prashad's argument, that changes in the means of production don't necessarily upend societal relationships, seems to get at the heart of Anand's oversight. Still, Anand's enthusiastic embrace of technological development as a precursor for a social revolution that would do away with caste is not born out of a need to preserve middle-class leadership of nationalism, by using technology as a substitute for untouchable self-determination. Rather, Anand's error was in not being able to predict the limits to the kind of social transformation that technological development could induce. At the same time, Anand did not believe that technological improvements in India could come about without a massive change in the kinds of people who populated India: "It is possible that this generation and the next, in Europe as well as in Asia, will have to fight to preserve the relevant past culture in the period of chaos that stretched before us. And that we shall have to build a new culture on the fragments of decency and civilization which we may save. That is a task which will require all the energy, intelligence and devotion of men." Here, Anand's concern is in the destructive potential of technology, as *Apology for Heroism* was written in the shadow of the atomic bomb blasts that devastated Hiroshima and Nagasaki. *Untouchable* is clearly part of a much more exuberant defense of the liberating power of technology, but it isn't incompatible with the more careful position that Anand developed little more than a decade later: "Only, they have got to be new men, whole men, who have the critical spirit to see the machine age for what it is worth, to distinguish technology from the spurious ideas which have become associated with it, to sift the grain from the chaff. And they will have to be men who are sincere, disinterested and free, men who are willing to save the world so that they can live in and through it, men who are human, who represent humanity everywhere and seek a new way of life, in freedom" (Anand 1946, 145).

Other critics of Anand's have pointed out that Anand's own caste and class position make it impossible to avoid the appropriation of the untouchable's voice and that ventriloquizing for an untouchable is the same as claiming to represent him at the Round Table Conference:

> However, as readers, we must examine and remain aware of the difference between "a voice for" and "a voice of." We must take account of the fact that *Untouchable* represents the untouchables as they appear to the gaze of an upper class, upper caste Kshatriya Hindu, albeit a Marxist. This caste and class distance between the writer and the people he represents results in the erasure in the novel of the voice of the untouchable community as a dissonant discourse in the Indian social fabric. This absence is then substituted by the voices of the nationalist bourgeoisie speaking for the untouchables. (Mukherjee 1991, 36)

For Mukherjee, the problem of representation only compounds the problem of untouchable revolt, as untouchables here are seen as an irreducibly "dissonant discourse" and their speech as necessarily confrontational towards the status quo. It also easily blends back into a defense of authority, as Teresa Hubel argues: "The novel seems to demonstrate the necessity of elite leadership in the 1930s movement for untouchable uplift. It does not, moreover, endeavor to be conscious of the 'middle-classness' of its nationalism. This is particularly evident in the narrator's occasionally condescending omniscience" (1996, 170). This suite of elitist movements – appropriation, erasure and self-centeredness – is not the product of mistaken reading practices. Anand's text is indeed guilty of putting in place the rhetorical and emotional structures that enable nationalist appropriation of the untouchable's grievances as justifications for native rule. Untouchables do not speak for themselves in the novel, and as a result, the conclusion cannot be seen as the fulfillment of the untouchable demand for freedom. It appears, at every instant, to be the self-satisfied Congress member's view: that nationalism is sufficient to solve the problems of all, eventually.

But it should be obvious that the key reason that Anand's *Untouchable* is read in the postindependence world as an endorsement of the opportunist, rather than idealist, wing of Indian nationalism is because that idealist wing failed to produce the radical changes that it imagined were possible. There was no independent Indian sanitation regime with the concerns of untouchables at its heart, nor was there a consistent critique of the religious and social bases for caste hierarchies. Even minor reforms like temple entry, educational access and legal protections were a long time in coming. As a result, readings of the novel that highlight its misplaced confidence in the technological future of the Indian state are far from inaccurate. The only function of Sarshar's speech at the end of the novel is to satisfy middle-class audiences of their progressive credentials while making empty but emotionally powerful gestures towards untouchable freedom. The counterfactual may be unverifiable but is worth posing: had untouchables been able to mount as substantial an organizational and political force as, say, the Muslim League, the novel would have a completely different gloss. The kinds of futures that were being narrated in anticolonial novels in India are judged by the facts on the ground; more positive readings of the status quo, which I have ignored here, produce more positive readings of the novel. Any reading of an anticolonial novel, it seems, has to deal with reality: the particular outcome of the national liberation struggle, more than the content of the novel, determines the character of the postcolonial reading.

For that very reason, the novel opens up the possibility of alternative futures to nationalism and anticolonialism, ones that are not coextensive with the independent nation-state, futures that the novel can only imagine. This is not an exercise in utopian wish-fulfillment but an attempt to diagnose the different intellectual currents that simultaneously reveal themselves in acts of political solidarity. If the radical intelligentsia genuinely believes in the project of emancipation of the untouchable, is there any representation of that desire that can satisfy the postcolonial critic, armed as he or she is with the inevitability of the nation's failures, without resurfacing as an alibi for those very failures? In this respect in particular, Anand represents an important case study in understanding the rhetoric of solidarity and its bidirectionality. If appropriation can result in the papering over of genuine untouchable grievances by the state, there is also the possibility, as Anand argues, that the attempt to feel like the untouchable changes the radical intellectual in important ways, "changing [himself] before changing others." This inquiry has to be the undertaking of a much more sensitive, formal investigation of anticolonial novels that is willing to suspend the historical outcome of national projects to understand the intellectual history of anticolonial movements and the forces behind them. But such an inquiry could help to employ new strategies for understanding the risks and possibilities inherent in radical anticolonial narratives and could match those alongside the contingent histories of the nationalist movement. It could expose both the limitations and the potentials of the nationalist commitment to end chauvinism and traditional patterns of exploitation. It could also provide a necessary corrective to current accounts of anticolonial projects as necessarily reproducing Western models of statecraft. But most importantly, it could salvage an ethical relationship to the other that intellectuals could refine into a real political praxis of solidarity.

As a point of departure, there is a history of untouchable revolt (that neither Anand nor the Congress seems to have paid much attention to) that demonstrates a continuous arc of struggle against both British imperialism and Hindu orthodoxy. A wave of strikes led by untouchable sweepers had broken out across the subcontinent in the last part of the nineteenth century (1873, 1876, and 1889). These had been in response to the development of sanitation reform led by British municipal councils, which restricted the rights of untouchables and forced considerable wage reductions. The initial laws were framed to create a new, sanitized India that could avoid the cholera panics. But sanitation reform would also become labor reform, as public hygiene demanded the regulation of reliable untouchable labor. The United Provinces Municipalities Act of 1916 contained the following sanctions for untouchable work actions: "Should a sweeper who had a customary right to do the house scavenging of a house or building fail to perform such scavenging in a proper way, the occupier of the house or the building or the board may complain to magistrate. The magistrate receiving such complaint should hold an inquiry and should it appear to him that the customary sweeper has failed to perform the house scavenging of the house or building in a proper way or at reasonable intervals, he may impose upon such a sweeper a fine which may extend to 10 rupees" (Chahal 2002, 37). The Punjab Municipalities Act of 1911 contained similar provisions: "Should any sweeper (other than customary sweeper) who is under a contract to do house scavenging of a house or building, discontinue to do such house scavenging within 14 days' notice to his employer or without reasonable cause, he shall on conviction be punished with a fine which may extend to Rs. 10" (Chahal 2002, 38). The exorbitant fines placed on untouchables had the intended effect of deterring strikes, but also had the effect of generating a growing anti-British untouchable constituency. By the 1930s, untouchable revolts had been taking place all over India. A series of laws were passed by British legislators that created a monopoly on jobs, outlawed strikes and unions, and ensured that no strikes would occur in North India for almost twenty years. In 1931, the Communist Party of India had encouraged the formation of labor unions, the latter urging people to join "for the complete abolition of slavery, the caste system and inequality in all forms" (Ranadive 1982, 7). A 1926 strike of sweepers in Bulata crippled the town for weeks, and the success of the 1928 strike in Calcutta inspired the formation of sweepers' unions throughout India, one of which became famous for a skirmish in which "women threw pots of excreta at policemen, who tore off their uniforms as they ran away, vowing not to return without permission to shoot at the strikers" (Prashad 1995, 9). Little is known about the demands and the organizing that went into such labor actions, but they are at least a glimpse of the kinds of self-conscious activity that untouchables were engaged in. This political movement, had it grown, could have represented the future that Anand's Bakha looks out upon at the end of the novel.

A Novelistic Structure of Solidarity

Untouchable, then, can be mined for its formal strategies that enable the middle-class radical to see the project of untouchable liberation as his own project. There are two ways that Anand is able to accomplish this. First, the Joycean strategy of breaking down linear narrative in favor of the anarchy of daily experience allows Anand to ally Bakha's alienation with the alienation of the deracinated middle class (accomplished in the novel through a focalized itinerant character rather than linguistic experimentation). Because he cannot actually reproduce the experience of untouchability, Anand finds in middle-class alienation an acceptable corollary for encounters with chauvinism and then proceeds to demonstrate how the untouchable is, in fact, exactly like the middle-class intellectual seeking independence from the British. It is, then, unsurprising that for Anand the writing of the novel was in part framed and structured by his own encounter with chauvinist practices in British milieus: "Anand angrily retouched *Untouchable* after a P & O boat voyage from England to India in which the British treated him as a contemptible outcast" (Hemenway 1975, 15). This is precisely the essence of the pre-Gandhian version of the novel, which continues to animate the spirit of the truncated *Bildungsroman*. The Joycean flaneur is mapped onto the itinerant, laboring untouchable, and the profound disconnect between the subject and urban life provides some of the ideological texture of middle-class dissatisfaction with the visual offerings of modernity, except as consumable commodity. Bakha, armed now with Red Lamp cigarettes and a British soldier's jacket, encounters the inner city as a sensory overload that is so preoccupying that it allows him to forget, as he stares "absorbed and un-self-conscious," that he is, in fact, an untouchable in the city (Anand 1940, 46).[14] This experience of middle-class castelessness, then, produces the very encounter of accidental touching that is at the emotional center of the novel: "Bakha's mouth was open. But he couldn't utter a single word. He was about to apologise. He had already joined his hands instinctively. Now he bent his forehead over them, and he mumbled something. But the man didn't care what he said. Bakha was too confused in the tense atmosphere which surrounded him to repeat what he had said, or to speak coherently and audibly. The man was not satisfied with dumb humility" (47). In part, this scene draws its emotional power from the fact of its condensation of countless similar episodes that would likely have taken place across urban India. Indeed, it is the very reproducibility of the scene that allows Anand to get away with some rather clichéd and ideologically laden terms. It is also this reproducibility that allows Anand to step outside and watch the scene, despite its focalization, from the perspective of the sympathetic intellectual, still distant from the untouchable. It is precisely in his commitment to present Bakha as he is (which is, of course, an alibi for the upper-caste view of untouchables and contemporary history in which the untouchables do not, it is supposed, revolt) that Anand creates this poignant scene of caste chauvinism. This is fairly indisputable: Anand's attempt to capture the authentic untouchable ends up reproducing the ideological baggage of the upper-caste view of the lower castes. In fact, this is the only direction that purported authenticity, in this instance, could go. But despite this baggage, Anand's need to shore up the exterior of the untouchable with his internal, psychological vacillations ends up accomplishing what the external contact cannot: namely, the crossing of the moral barrier that separates untouchables from caste Hindus. Readers are, at least symbolically, entering quarters they would have otherwise avoided.

There is between Bakha and urban Bulashah an immense divide. At the moment of contact, Anand's narrator remarks, "But then he realized that he was surrounded by a barrier, not a physical barrier, because one push from his hefty shoulders would have been enough to unbalance the skeleton-like bodies of the Hindu merchants, but a moral one" (1940, 48). The distance is not only one of religious taboo but also of emotional and political significance: "But the barrier of space that the crowd had placed between themselves and him seemed to prevent his feeling from getting across" (49). And after being insulted and accused, when Bakha stands alone in the streets, the narrative overcomes what the social situation will not allow:

> But there was a smouldering rage in his soul. His feelings would rise like spurts of smoke from a half-smothered fire, in fitful, unbalanced jerks when the recollection of some abuse or rebuke he had suffered kindled a spark in the ashes of remorse inside him. And in the smoky atmosphere of his mind arose dim ghosts of forms peopling the scene he had been through. The picture of the touched man stood in the forefront, among several indistinct faces, his bloodshot eyes, his little body with the sunken cheeks, his dry, thin lips, his ridiculously agitated manner, his abuse; and there was the circle of the crowd, jeering, scoffing, abusing, while he himself stood with joined hands in the centre. (Anand 1940, 51)

Here the exterior perspective of the crowd has been replaced with a version that seems to approximate Bakha's interiority but is still short of the intimacy of free, indirect discourse. It relies on the kind of staccato phrasing of Anand's verbs ("jeering, scoffing, abusing") to mimic the emotional anxiety of Bakha's character, even though the language refers to the very people who are supposed to be incapable of sympathizing with the untouchable. At the same time, the extended metaphor describing Bakha ("his feelings would rise like smoke [...] kindled a spark in the ashes of remorse inside him") not only naturalizes untouchable rage (and perhaps allows the spontaneous rebel in through the backdoor) but also betrays the simultaneity of two worldviews. If Bakha's own feelings are a mystery to him and the caste Hindus who are abusing him are "dim ghosts" or faceless in the "circle of the crowd," then the slippage into critique of caste chauvinism in the passage ("his bloodshot eyes, his little body with the sunken cheeks, his dry, thin lips, his ridiculously agitated manner") points to both the retroactive condensation of the figure into a kind of satirical cartoon (similar to the depiction of Pundit Kali Nath, who fantasizes about Bakha's sister Sohini) and a stable anticaste ideologist capable of such satire. This version of rage and justice is still well within the worldview of the committed nationalist, but it has to work against the conventions for representational encounters with chauvinism. In fact, the smoky vistas of Bakha's emotion almost transform the event from actual caste-based violence to retroactive recollection, from immediate plot event to concrete set piece. The function of such a procedure is to provide an indirect avenue that will not "prevent his feeling from getting across." If the smoke and ashes of his rage move vertically and the feelings of the crowd move laterally, then the image that unites them ("the dim ghosts" and "the picture of the touched mind") is really only viewable by a postcaste readership.

But the perspective switches again, to a mix of free, indirect discourse and first-person speech, which is Anand's own version of stream-of-consciousness. The method here allows Anand to take the authentic untouchable consciousness and present it as a mirror of the middle class's reaction to the process of colonization:

> "Why was all this?" he asked himself in the soundless speech of cells receiving and transmitting emotions, which was his usual way of communicating with himself. "Why was all this fuss? Why was I so humble? I could have struck him! And to think I was so eager to come to the town this morning. Why didn't I shout to warn the people of my approach? That comes of not looking after one's work. I should have begun to sweep the thoroughfare. I should have seen the high-caste people in the street. That man! That he should have hit me! My poor jalebis! I should have eaten them. But why couldn't I say something? Couldn't I have joined my hands to him and then gone away? The slap on my face! The coward! How he ran away, like a dog with his tail between his legs. That child! The liar! Let me not come across him one day. He knew I was being abused. Not one of them spoke for me. The cruel crowd! All of them abused, abused, abused. Why are we always abused? The sentry inspector and the Sahib that day abused my father. They always abuse us. Because we are sweepers. Because we touch dung. They hate dung. I hate it too. That's why I came here. I was tired of working on the latrines every day. That's why they don't touch us, the high-castes. The tonga-wallah was kind. He made me weep telling me, in that way, to take my things and walk along. But he is a Muhammadan. They don't mind touching us, the Muhammadans and the sahibs. It is only the Hindus, and the outcastes who are not sweepers. For them I am a sweeper, sweeper – untouchable! Untouchable! Untouchable! That's the word! Untouchable! I am an Untouchable!" (Anand 1940, 51–2)

While the narrative wants to presume that this is a genuine epiphany, the idea that an eighteen-year-old untouchable encounters his own caste position for the first time in this way seems a little too staged for the accidental narrative of this day. It doesn't in fact work if it is only Bakha's emotional world, as the narrative would then collapse back onto the melancholic moods it began with. It is, rather, a combination of a readerly epiphany that is reflected in Bakha, a coming into realization of the contradictory emotional world of caste chauvinism through an already internalized and generalized sense of racial discrimination against Indians by the British, experienced as discrete events (the lying child, the Sahib, the crowd). But this has the effect not only of making Bakha's emotions legible, it makes that legibility contingent upon the similarity of that experience to the Indian intellectual's understanding of his own racialized body. And while Anand is drawing upon his own archive of racialized expatriate memory, it would have been easily understood by an indigenous readership. As Maria Misra has observed, the pattern of racist attitudes against Indians was pervasive in all forms of relations between the colonizer and the colonized, extending even into the kinds of commercial and entrepreneurial projects that the British would undertake in the subcontinent. Economic nationalism and British commercial suspicion worked in tandem to produce a fiercely combative relationship between Indian and British commercial and industrial interests, with the result that the British increasingly relied on a narrative of the failures in the Indian "character" as a way to resist the Indianization of their companies and of government. As a result, racism was no longer the exclusive experience of the nationalist expatriate; there were domestic corollaries that would have affected the middle class (and even sections of the nationalist bourgeoisie) as a specific indictment of its ability to harness the energies of industrial capitalism (Misra 1999, 123–42).[15]

These two processes – turning Bakha into the site of readerly emotional projection and mirroring middle-class alienation in Bakha's experience – are Anand's way of turning the narration of Bakha's sensitivity into a kind of *Bildungsroman* for the Indian middle-class reader. The procedure, though borrowed from Joyce, differs after Gandhi's intervention and his insistence on clarity and simplicity:

> Like a ray of light shooting through the darkness, the recognition of his position, the significance of his lot dawned upon him. It illuminated the inner chambers of his mind. Everything that happened to him traced its course up to this light and got the answer. The contempt of those who came to the latrines daily and complained that there weren't any latrines clean, the sneers of the people in the outcastes' colony, the abuse of the crowd which had gathered round him this morning. It was all explicable now. A shock of which this was the name had passed through his perceptions, previously numb and torpid, and had sent a quiver into his being, stirred his nerves of sight, hearing, smell, touch and taste, all into a quickening. "I am an Untouchable!" he said to himself, "an Untouchable!" He repeated the words in his mind, for it was still a bit hazy and he felt afraid it might be immersed in the darkness again. (Anand 1940, 52)

Anand lifts the "quickening" from the Joyce of *A Portrait of an Artist as a Young Man* (1916) and here extracts from it a strategy of realizing alienation. If, in the first epiphany, Anand's Bakha relies on the language of Indian encounters with British racism, then here the condition morphs into the vocabulary of existence and identity, so that the problem is not merely racist ideas in the crowd but the nature of his laboring body, now sensitive to the ideological forces that seek to discipline it and regulate it. Untouchability, like race, becomes an intolerable existential reality; the novelistic solution is engendered by a quest for the dissolution of both terms into the more expansive term, "human."

The second procedure is enabled by the introduction of Gandhi into the final pages of the novel. His presence here enables the possibility of a real merger between untouchables and the middle class, not only because of his political personality but because of Anand's association of Gandhi with the authentic masses of India. Anand's own feelings about Gandhi are interesting in this respect; despite their disagreements on politics, Anand felt that Gandhi was necessary if one was to have any serious engagement with India: "If I lost faith in the Mahatma, would I not be alienated from everyone at home – from the freedom movement itself? Gandhi was still my anchor. He had shown such a spirit of self-sacrifice, facing the Sarkar in campaign after campaign" (1984, 428). But Gandhi also represents something symbolic and important, and for that reason he can act as a focus of contemplation that unites disparate individuals in their simultaneous consideration of him:

> Bakha stopped short as he reached the pavilion end of the cricket ground. He leant by a tree. He wanted to be detached. It wasn't that he lost grip of the emotion that

had brought him swirling on the tide of the rushing stream of people. But he became aware of the fact of being a sweeper by the contrast which his dirty khaki uniform presented to the white garments of most of the crowd. There was an insuperable barrier between himself and the crowd, the barrier of caste. He was part of a consciousness which he could share and yet not understand. He had been lifted from the gutter, through the barriers of space, to partake of a life which was his, and yet not his. He was in the midst of a humanity which included him in its folds and yet debarred him from entering into a sentient, living, quivering contact with it. Gandhi alone united him with them, in the mind, because Gandhi was in everybody's mind, including Bakha's. Gandhi might unite them really. Bakha waited for Gandhi. (Anand 1940, 138)

This is the obverse of the nationalist problem; the middle-class nationalist looks upon throngs of supporters and sees "the tide of the rushing stream of people," indistinguishable, massive and incomprehensible. The middle-class nationalist's fear of the crowd – that it is insensitive, that it both claims and disavows him, that he stoops down to be one of them – is mirrored back in Bakha's fear of caste chauvinism. Where the middle class finds itself shuddering at its snobbery, the untouchable boy finds himself repulsed by prejudice. It helps that in other places in the novel, Bakha has already been cast as a nouveau bourgeois:

And though his job was dirty he remained comparatively clean. He didn't even soil his sleeves, handling the commodes, sweeping and scrubbing them. "A bit superior to his job," they always said, "not the kind of man who ought to be doing this." For he looked intelligent, even sensitive, with a sort of dignity that does not belong to the ordinary scavenger, who is as a rule uncouth and unclean. It was perhaps his absorption in his task that gave him the look of distinction, or his exotic dress however loose and ill-fitting, that removed him above his odorous world. (Anand 1940, 16)

By the time Bakha finds Gandhi, he can sit separated from the crowd and peer into it with the same vocabulary as the middle-class nationalist. The only solace that is provided is the linking discourse of Gandhism. In Bakha's fantasy, "Gandhi might unite them really." In the novel, the only other subject who is actually considering Gandhi at the same moment as Bakha is the reader.

The end of the novel reveals Anand's final exposition of the kind of sensitive humanism that he believes is necessary for a real solidarity to emerge between the nationalist and the untouchable. Amidst the heady afterglow of the Mahatma's speech in Gola Bagh, Bakha overhears a conversation between a poet, Iqbal Nath Sarshar, and a lawyer, R. N. Bashir, about the relevance of Gandhi's ideas for an independent India. The British-educated Bashir balks at Gandhi's retrograde ideas: "Gandhi is a humbug ... He is a fool. He is a hypocrite. In one breath he says he wants to abolish untouchability, in the other he asserts that he is an orthodox Hindu. He is running counter to the spirit of our age, which is democracy" (Anand 1940, 150). Sarshar responds in defense of Gandhi but then switches to a defense of the machine and the Indian spirit, even though Gandhi may not have advocated a technological path for India:

> "It is India's genius to accept all things," said the poet fiercely. "We have, through our long history, been realists believing in the stuff of this world, in the here and the now, in the flesh and the blood. Man is born, and reborn, according to the *Upanishads*, in this world, and even when he becomes an immortal saint there is no release for him, because he forms the stuff of the cosmos and is born again. We don't believe in the other world, as these Europeans would have you believe we do. There has been only one man in India who believed this world to be illusory – Shankaracharya." (152)

Here, Anand was borrowing from Ananda Coomaraswamy's critique of the British understanding of Indian philosophy in terms that anticipate Edward Said's *Orientalism*. The British interpretation of Indian society – unchanging, hidebound and metaphysical – was designed, Anand believed, to propagate a series of ideas in which Indians were ill-equipped for technical or technological innovation. But this belief in a constitutional antimodernity for all Indians mirrored the secular middle class's critique of Hindu orthodoxy; and its critique of Brahminical chauvinism relied on the idea that technological and scientific progress would break up the dominant ideologies that held the institutions of caste together. At the same time, in the rhetoric of the novel, caste enters into this defense of modernity only by analogy, as the suppressed term that will be smuggled in by the trajectory of the *Bildungsroman*. Technology, it seems, lifts all boats:

> The Victorians misinterpreted us. It was as if, in order to give a philosophical background to their exploitation of India, they ingeniously concocted a nice little fairy story: "You don't believe in this world; to you all this is *maya*. Let us look after your country for you and you can dedicate yourself to achieving *Nirvana* (release from the trammels of existence)." But that is all over now. Right in the tradition of those who accepted the world and produced the baroque exuberance of Indian architecture and sculpture, with its profound sense of form, its solidity and its mass, we will accept and work the machine. But we will do so consciously. We can see through the idiocy of these Europeans who deified money. They were barbarians and lost their heads in the worship of gold. We can steer clear of the pitfalls, because we have the advantage of a race-consciousness six thousand years old, a race-consciousness which accepted all the visible and invisible values. We know life. We know its secret flow. We have danced to its rhythms. We have loved it, not sentimentally through personal feelings, but pervasively, stretching ourselves from our hearts outwards so far, oh, so far, that life seemed to have no limits, that miracles seemed possible. We can feel new feelings. We can learn to be aware with a new awareness. We can envisage the possibility of creating new races from the latent heat in our dark brown bodies. Life is still an adventure for us. We are still eager to learn. We cannot go wrong. Our enslavers muddle through things. We can see things clearly. We will go the whole hog with regard to machines while they nervously fumble their way with the steam-engine. And we will keep our heads through it all. We will not become slaves to gold. We can be trusted to see life steadily and see it whole. (Anand 1940, 152–3)

This is a defense of a kind of sensitivity and emotional openness that the novel has been building towards. The ability to see without sentimentality and to understand the "secret flows" of life has been articulated in the representations of Bakha's own feelings and the development of a narrator capable of representing them "clearly." In fact, the kind of structure of solidarity that "stretches from our hearts outwards" depends entirely on the ability to see one's self in the untouchable, to see the common emancipation of both in the access to technological modernity and a Socialist ethic. And the payoff of such an ethics is a supercharged technological development without the pitfalls of capitalism and the servility of empire.

But there are pitfalls here. The operation – through which the untouchable, the machine, "race consciousness," and the radical middle class are all shown to be the products of six thousand years of development – is necessarily vague, even as this vagueness is masked by the breathlessness of the speech. The ambiguity in the terms necessarily hides a contradictory genealogy: race-consciousness can be marshaled to explain an Indian proclivity towards innovation, open-mindedness and change, but leaves the speaker vulnerable to prolonging the persistence of a naturalized caste-based chauvinism. This is particularly important as the novel has also put forward an alternative genealogy of Bakha's residual servility, "which he had inherited from his forefathers, the weakness of the down-trodden, the helplessness of the poor and the indigent" (Anand 1940, 17), and which had turned him into the "humble, oppressed under-dog that he was by birth" (58). At other times, Bakha also has inherited "the blood of his peasant ancestors, free to live their own life even though they may have been slaves" (64), while caste Hindus "did not relax the grin which symbolized six thousand years of racial and class superiority" (16). History is simultaneously the source of Bakha's immense, untapped potential and the explanation for his protracted enslavement. If Anand can only imagine the simultaneous development of middle-class and untouchable fortunes under the sign of race, it is because he transfers his experience with colonial racism onto the untouchable's encounters with caste prejudice using the only terms flexible enough to accommodate both oppressions. As long as anticolonial struggles continued to advance, it was possible to imagine that a Socialist humanism and an anticaste politics could share a common vocabulary, but once those struggles dissipated, this vague terminology could no longer guarantee coalition.

Because the solidarity between the middle class and the untouchable is fragile and contingent, it is all the more important that we take seriously the strategies that were put forward by those who were interested in its development, even as we are sensitive to the challenges that it eventually faced. The conclusion that Helga Ramsey-Kurtz arrives at bears repeating in this context: "[Anand] sees sameness where everyone else would see only insurmountable difference and endeavors to create sameness where others would interpret any assumption of likeness as sacrilege" (Ramsey-Kurtz 2007, 278). Cross-caste ventriloquism and genuine solidarity have identical rhetoric and grammar, even if they have completely different political ends and ambitions; humanist Socialism can sound like a politics of deferral as long as the broader pattern of social change is arrested. Disaggregating them from one another requires holding in suspension the idea that appropriative maneuvers are the default of all attempts at thinking about the problems of minorities in an anticolonial context.

Chapter 3

"THE MAHATMA MAY BE ALL WRONG ABOUT POLITICS, BUT ...": RAJA RAO'S *KANTHAPURA* AND THE RELIGIOUS IMAGINATION OF THE INDIAN, SECULAR, NATIONALIST MIDDLE CLASS

Religious and Gandhian Discourses in Karnataka

In July of 1921, Congress workers, as part of the national Noncooperation movement inspired by Mahatma Gandhi, picketed a liquor shop in Dharwar, a district in the southern part of the Bombay Presidency (now in modern Karnataka). Two young men had earlier fined an untouchable man for public drunkenness (as part of a local Congress temperance campaign) and were arrested by the police for looting and sentenced to six months' hard labor. The charge and the sentence were both commonly seen as unfair, and the Congress was working to organize opposition to the capricious punishment. Emotions were therefore raised and the pickets were larger than they had ever been in Dharwar. The police indiscriminately opened fire on the crowd that had gathered in Khilafat Maidan, and when the dust settled after the ensuing riot, three people were dead and several more injured (Narayan 1988, 112).

Gangadhar Rao Deshpande (later dubbed the "Lion of Karnataka" for his efforts in the movement for Indian independence and Karnataka unification) had rushed from Belgaum, where he had been organizing similar pickets at Gandhi's behest, to research the events on behalf of the All India Congress Committee and to preside over the funeral procession. He and 29 other Congress and Khilafat party members were arrested on trumped up charges of arson and looting in Dharwar; Deshpande and a few others were acquitted, since they had not actually been present, but most of the other activists were imprisoned, despite efforts by the party and its lawyers to mount a defense (Halappa and Krishna Rao 1964, 127).

On 14 July, Deshpande presided over the Dharwar District Political Conference in Navalgund where he presented his findings on the events at Dharwar and the callousness of the government response in firing upon a crowd of peaceful protesters. This concluded with a fiery speech in Kannada about the involvement of the district collector of Dharwar and the local police, in which he excoriated the actions of the British authorities. The meeting had been called to organize Congress activities in the area and so was monitored by British spies, one of whom reported Deshpande's speech to the police. The accuracy of the notes was suspect, but they included a section in which Deshpande supposedly described the British occupation as a "Satanic Government" and an instance of "*Ravana Rajya.*" The authorities were undoubtedly looking for any pretext to arrest Deshpande, and the police turned on these phrases as proof of Deshpande's sedition. In October, the government of Bombay issued a warrant for his arrest and charged him with sedition and inciting a riot for the content of his speech in Navalgund. Deshpande was arrested and stood trial.

The arrest of Congress agitators and propagandists was nothing new; the British authorities had been paying special attention to the Congress's activities and following the leadership very carefully. They had even extended their surveillance powers under the Rowlatt Act (1919), which gave authorities the power to arrest and detain agitators suspected of terrorism without trial (Ranadive 1986, 103). What was new in this instance was the criminalization, essentially, of political allegory, since calling the British Raj "Ravana Rajya," the courts argued, was tantamount to calling for religious insurrection against the empire. Religious language had been a part of political agitation against the empire for quite some time, but the courts had always treaded carefully around criminalizing religious speech. The political alliances the British had built required gingerly preserving religious traditions so as not to alienate the conservative forces on which the empire relied. The bulk of the charge against Deshpande had to do with his calls for an end to the British occupation and his use of certain key words in Kannada, Hindi and Urdu (*"swarajya," "nasht," "beleendshahi," "rajya padyathi"*) and whether they amounted to advocating sedition and violent revolution against British rule. Gandhi had made much work of references to the *Ramayana* (especially the dyad of Rama and Ravana) in his critique of British colonialism, but this had also produced substantial tension within the ranks of the movement for independence, even as it opened up a new political discourse on religion for the Congress to mobilize (Omvedt 1990, 726). Deshpande, a lawyer by profession, made a lengthy response to the charges against him (while claiming, "I don't wish to encumber the record of this case with any long statement") by allying himself with the Noncooperation movement and its aims, much of which relied on Gandhi's understanding of nonviolence, self-government and uplift. Deshpande had been unconvinced of the workability of nonviolent noncooperation at the Calcutta Congress in September 1920 and had joined the minority, who saw it as a symbolic half measure, in voting against it in Calcutta. But, "Between September and December I studied the speeches and writings of Mahatma Gandhi, the author of this movement, and also watched its wonderful effects on the masses" (Halappa and Krishna Rao 1964, 580). Deshpande, it turns out, was a deliberate convert to Gandhism.

The section of his response that the court was most interested in detailed Deshpande's recollection of the speech at Navalgund:

> I do maintain that the greatest injustice has been done in the Dharwar rioting case as well as other picketing cases. I think I used the word, "Yama rajya" in describing the injustice that was going on at Dharwar. But I am positive that I did not make use of the expression "Satanic Government or Ravana Rajya"; for I have long since decided that *to imitate parrot fashion Mr. Gandhi* in the use of the words "Satanic Government or Ravana rajya" *is unbecoming to followers of his like myself.* Of course the expression "Satanic" has been so

often repeated with impunity and referred to by high officials, from Viceroys downwards, Anglo-Indian journals like the Times of India and in Government publications, that it has by this time lost half of its charm and therefore most of its sedition, if there was any, but I know I have always enforced it upon myself purely as a point of discipline that *what is good for Mr. Gandhi is not necessarily good for me,* for I have not yet completed, as he has, the process of self-purification which justifies a critic to say anything that he honestly thinks proper to be said of this Government. (Halappa and Krishna Rao 1964, 586)

Much of Deshpande's argument rested on the fact that the government spy in the audience could not have possibly taken accurate notes, since he was "a fairly fast speaker" and the notes recorded only eleven hundred words for a speech that was two hours long. As the notes "contain some sentences which [he] never uttered and some which [he] could not have uttered," and as the spy had completely misrepresented the size and composition of the audience to which Deshpande was speaking (one thousand as opposed to three hundred primarily Brahmins, while all the witnesses against Deshpande were non-Brahmins). The bulk of his substantive argument, though, rested on the difference between the various allegorical terms for bad governance ("Satanic," "Ravana" and "Yama") as well as the distinction between applying these terms to the specific violence at Dharwar or to the essence of British rule (Halappa and Krishna Rao 1964, 582).

But Deshpande's argument is interesting beyond the challenge being made to the reliability of government moles and theological debates about the difference between sinners and their sins. The argument, for Deshpande, turns on what can only be described as a legalistic convenience that betrays the contradictory milieu in which the new, local middle-class leadership of the Congress must have found itself. Deshpande, after all, used his allegiances to Gandhi in the rest of his defense as proof of his nonseditious, nonviolent disposition and the complete legality of calling for swarajya and the peaceful transferral of power to Indians. Here, though, in order to show that the censor has clearly made a mistake, has heard "Ravana" when he should have heard "Yama," Deshpande has to establish his distance from Gandhi. Gandhi's rhetoric, Deshpande argues, is stale and perhaps superstitious; Deshpande's is not. Gandhi's use of "Satanic Government" and "Ravana Rajya" cannot be taken seriously as seditious, nor can it be used by "followers of his like myself," unbecoming as it is to parrot Gandhi as some kind of nationalist fashion. The very arguments he was using to defend himself from the charge of sedition were, unwittingly, undermining the political and religious authority of the Mahatma, whose uncritical use of religious allegory is rendered quaint. In making the legal defense of his political speech, Deshpande has to sacrifice any loyalty to Gandhi in order to proceed, even as he attempts to suture his fealty to the Mahatma back together. The proof that the censor has gotten it wrong, in this instance, is that there is a wide enough gap between Gandhi and the rest of the Congress that shorthand notes are no longer sufficient to decipher the political content of a speech; meanings must be carefully interpreted anew, perhaps even more radically than Deshpande had intended.

Or, more precisely, the reason that Deshpande can be certain which religious metaphor he used is because he is certain that "what is good for Mr. Gandhi is not necessarily good for me." Deshpande, an English-educated, progressive lawyer, already marked for his largely secular and political contributions to the Congress, confesses to his use of "*Yama Rajya*" in describing the British occupation of India, despite the fact that the differences between that term and the terms "Satanic Government" or "Ravana Rajya" would have been hard to parse while maintaining the rhetorical intelligibility of the original speech. Deshpande did attempt to explain his meaning: "Yama rajya: This epithet is the most innocent of the three. Yama is a deity in Hindu Mythology. It is believed that this deity is invested with the duties of dispensing justice according to the karma of the person concerned. [...] When I used this expression I had before my mind's eye the unjust and disproportionate punishments that were inflicted on two pickets" (Halappa and Krishna Rao 1964, 584). The distinction he draws between the reign of the God of Death and the reign of the Demon King of Lanka was perhaps self-serving and the mark of a clever legal strategist, especially since Ravana was mythologically no less dispassionately cruel than Yama and because taking Deshpande's exegesis seriously means that "Yama Rajya" is perfect justice ("according to karma of the person concerned") and therefore useless as a critique of British rule. So, in order to make the difference between "Yama Rajya" and "Ravana Rajya" clear, Deshpande attempts to police the semantic boundaries between the measured political speech of the lay Congress worker and the unfiltered, spiritual utterances of the Mahatma. Deshpande was, of course, concerned about the hypocrisy of the matter, especially if he was going to be singled out for using language that the largest newspaper in India and the head of the British Raj used regularly. But still, Deshpande's defense is marked by the need to show both that the intelligentsia saw the difference between drumming up religious sentiment by pandering to its audience ("to imitate parrot fashion Mr. Gandhi") and legitimate political analysis, and that between the Mahatma and the rest there had to be a carefully understood distinction when it came to language, politics and faith: namely, a distinction between rhetoric and religion. In fact, the differences in this rather similar religious terminology hinges not on theological differences between Christianity and Hinduism or the difference between Hindu deities and demons, but between the Mahatma and his followers. Religious language, in the hands of the intelligentsia, could be a precise analytical tool without leading to the perhaps illogical conclusion of religious injunction. The Mahatma made injunctions (famously, "Swaraj within a year"); the intelligentsia educated. The sessions court was wholly unimpressed with Deshpande's legal maneuvers:

> But by far the most important passage is the fifth which refers to the great injustice which had lately taken place in Dharwar. The accused denies that he has been correctly reported. He denies making use of the expressions "Satanic Government or Ravana raj," and pleads that the Inspector's notes showed that the epithets used by him referred to the injustice done by Government and not to Government itself. The epithets which are taken from the report are sworn to by the Inspector and several witnesses, and the accused has neither cross-examined them on the point nor called witnesses to contradict them. On the other hand on page 12 of his written statement he admits referring to the injustice going on in Dharwar, and as it appears in the charge, it seems to me that there is no real difference between calling Government Yama raj on account of its injustice

and describing as Yama raj the injustice of which Government has been guilty [...] Differing from both assessors I find the accused Gangadhar Rao Balkrishna Deshpande guilty of an offence under Section 124 AIPC, and sentence him to six months' simple imprisonment." (Halappa and Krishna Rao 1964, 597)

The case, though minor, amidst the tens of thousands of similar prosecutions of those arrested during the Noncooperation movement, was important for a number of reasons. Deshpande was a principal organizer in the region, and there were several large meetings in Karnataka in support of Deshpande, demanding his release. Moreover, E. H. Waterfield, the sessions judge, agreed that Deshpande's conviction was a test case, designed to measure whether the law could be used to criminalize speeches, and therefore marked one of the first times when certain kinds of religious allegory were sufficient proof of sedition, rather than outright calls for the overthrow of British occupation. Waterfield was also concerned that the proliferation of religious language to demonize the British government, while no defense against prosecution, could mean that the jails would soon be filled with seditious nationalists, and since religious language was used everywhere, it would be nearly impossible to know the difference between the truly spiritual and the deeply rebellious. Six months was the most that Deshpande could be reasonably sentenced to, despite the severity of the charge.

But even more interesting, perhaps, is that when representing religious ideas and mythological characters to the colonial court, authority no longer relied on scripture or scholarship (though Deshpande could count on his Brahmin background). There are no references to the *Vishnupurana* or the *Ramayana* or to the thought of a Shankaracharya to shore up the idea that Yama and Ravana are actually different and represent different kinds of approaches towards something as central as religious justice. Deshpande's entire posture toward the question of religious allegory signals how it had now become possible to ignore religious and scriptural authority and to produce new interpretive and exegetical outcomes. Deshpande certainly believes that he can represent religious thought and practice in a legal sense if not in a strictly theological one, but there isn't even the slightest hint of ambivalence that this might not be an acceptable procedure or that a religious argument might require a different kind of authority. It is telling that this democratic reading of religious myth is unconvincing to the courts, but more revealing is that such democratic interpretations are possible at all.

Deshpande, though, was no religious proselytizer; a practiced lawyer who had defended a number of important nationalist figures, despite his Brahmin background, he was representative of a layer of the new middle class: English-educated, privately religious while publicly secular, nationalist and progressive. He had also not been a Gandhian and had only recently become convinced of the need to organize as part of the Noncooperation movement. His political education and work prior to this point had been alongside the Marthi Hindu nationalist, Bal Gangadhar Tilak, whose influence over Congress Gandhi had been carefully undermining. His use of "Yama Rajya" to describe the British occupation, then, forces an investigation into differences between rhetorical and theoretical uses of religious allegories in making sense of and polemicizing against colonialism. Why after all did the secularists find themselves speaking religiously?

Or, to put it differently, how did the secularists expect their rhetorical deployment of religion to be understood? And by whom?

The Uneven Development of Literary Secularism

Deshpande's case was typical of a larger process of intellectual reorganization that was taking place amongst the nationalist intelligentsia, represented in the fiction of the period. By the end of the 1930s, the Indian middle class was beginning to see a way out of a certain intellectual impasse that had dominated its concerns, especially in its imaginative prose. The dominant literary trend up until the 1930s had been the progressivism of the writers who came to be organized under the Progressive Writers' Association. Progressive writing (also called *pragativadi* or *taraqqi pasandi*), in addition to its almost universal adoption of Soviet realism, had a number of thematic features in common, many of which circulated around a growing middle-class mistrust over Indian religious history, which was seen as responsible for the current enslavement to colonialism, the backwardness of the economy, the oppressive and chauvinistic character of the Indian home, and the antiscientific and irrational mood that hindered political mobilization.[1] At the heart of this view was an intellectual consensus that held that the peasantry was either incapable or unwilling to let go of a package of ideas loosely grouped as "religion" and that this stood in the way of attempts at broader social reform, which included but were not limited to nationalist agitation. Hinduism (and more precisely a particularly Brahminical variant of Hinduism, but also Islam) was so deeply embedded in the ideological and emotional architecture of the Indian peasant, the argument went, that its opposition to civil rights for the low caste, its superstitions, its ideas about female emancipation and particularly its sense that changes to the traditional pattern of village life represented the coming of the *kaliyug* (the "end of days" or "age of Kali"), all meant that liberalism and religion were seen to be mutual antagonists (Chauhan 1998). Perhaps the most famous example of this view of religion could be found in the famous Urdu short-story collection *Angare*, but it had its corollaries in the writings of Anand and later Premchand.

Much of this had to do with the class that produced imaginative writers in the 1930s and 1940s and the confrontation between the ideas that they encountered in their village homes and those in their urban schools. Despite Nehru's proclamations to the contrary, a substantial ideological and emotional rift had developed between the nationalist middle class and its peasant relatives. Their educations may very well have been financed through the explicit exploitation of rural labor through a network of both feudalism and capitalism, but once they left the villages for urban colleges they could not return to their homes as pastoral idylls any longer. It was not merely access to ideas in the cities that had transformed peasant students into cosmopolitan thinkers, it was also access to a rapid modernity (industry, science, development) that made the persistence of peasant life unimaginable except as escapist fantasy or as a source for emotional renewal to reinvigorate urban life. Students were not merely "Westernized" by ideas, they were modernized by life, more and more of which made the kinds of peasant worlds from which they had only recently emerged seem like a distant historical hangover, sometimes embarrassing, and nothing like a reasonable choice for the future: "The exotic [Western] education gave little scope for a correct understanding and appreciation of national problems by the students, and the English-educated youth became a class apart, with few things in common with the rural masses" (Halappa and Krishna Rao 1964, 24).

But this process of differentiation and distance between the urban intelligentsia and its rural relatives began to undergo a reversal as a consequence of nationalist agitation. Between January and March of 1921, the Congress Working Committee of the All India Congress Committee, began calling for students to boycott and leave government-controlled schools and colleges and for lawyers to give up their practices as a way to demonstrate opposition to the British occupation of India. Recent events in Amritsar and the passing of much more stringent restrictions on political expression and organization had pressed the nationalist middle class to respond, but they were also likely pulled into taking more aggressive political action by events that were happening in the countryside, where taxes to fund British wartime efforts, high prices and the monetization of rent had wrecked the rural economy, strained already tense landlord-tenant-moneylender relations, and had produced a substantial swell of peasant rebellions across the country (Rothermund 1993, 66–70). In response, the Congress had recently voted to implement an official all-India Noncooperation movement, and the student-lawyer boycotts were to be the first phase of its full strategy, which also included voluntary spinning of homespun yarn (*khadi*), distributing 2 million spinning wheels (*charkhas*), boycotting foreign cloth and liquor (*swadeshi*), flooding the prisons and jails with nonviolent protesters, boycotting elections and ultimately a no-tax and no-revenue campaign (Sarkar 1989, 204–5). Lawyers were not enthusiastic about giving up their practices, but students left colleges and universities in substantial numbers, with some estimates as high as twelve percent nationally (Bramford 1985, 103). While new nationalist colleges and universities were being established all over the country (like the Jamia Millia Islamiya in Aligarh or Gujarat Vidyapith in Ahmedabad), these were not nearly large or immediately attractive enough to absorb the students who had been radicalized by the call from the Congress. Small armies of nationalist students exited the classrooms and returned back to their villages and attempted to set up small nationalist groups and Congress branches. Returning to their villages in the 1920s and 1930s, they found they needed a new vocabulary with which to convey the urgency of their task while masking their own critique of peasant life.

As the decade drew to a close, some members of the progressive coterie were moving towards the idea that "religion" was no longer an impervious barrier between the urban intelligentsia and its peasant relatives. Many had refused to fall into the secularist camp from the beginning, but the question of religion was increasingly being reexamined by secularists who were attempting to find new explanations for the political and social changes taking place more broadly, and new methods for incorporating those changes into the texture of their literary output. Hinduism, in particular (though also Islam), possessed emotional and affective energies that could be used in the service of political and social change, and by the end of the 1930s, this group of writers set about experimenting with strategies to reflect these new ideas imaginatively. Part of this conclusion was due to the extraordinary and spectacular success of Gandhi's mobilizations during both the Civil Disobedience and Noncooperation campaigns and – perhaps most famously – during the Salt March, all of which used religious trappings to make political arguments for a shared nationalism. But there were other developments that also seemed to link religion to progressive mobilization, with real outcomes in peasant participation: the development of peasant organizations in Uttar Pradesh in the 1920s, the success of political theater in Maharashtra in the 1930s, and the spread of the Congress into the Indian hinterland in ways that had never before connected the urban and rural worlds in a seemingly static-free communication network (Wolpert 2001, 43).[2] In fact, there was something serendipitous in the timing of these changes, as the range and rapidity of religious reform meant that Hinduism was also subject to serious public debate and as a result available for creative reimagining. Gandhi was both a current within and a product of this pattern of religious reform. One of the consequences of such developments was the experimentation in imaginative writings on the ways that "religion" or "tradition" could be used in order to mobilize political sentiment (Mehta 1976). At the same time, Gandhi's entry into the scene of nationalist politics was demonstrating for many that religion was not an irredeemably conservative force, but that it carried with it an emotional content that could be used to induce people to act for change (Bilgrami 2011). More than a simple yoke on the necks of the peasantry and the poor, religious ideas could also be used to motivate social reform and social action; here, precisely, it was the ability of religion to provide an avenue for the activity of the oppressed that inspired modernizers.

But the progressives were interested in a specific kind of modernization. Even though the garb was saffron or *khadi*, the spirit underneath was still atheist; as a result, the goal was to use the conflicting emotional content of political religiosity in the service of abolition of religion altogether, akin to the way Deshpande was carefully deploying religious imagery to advocate for anticolonial politics. But the alliance with religious discourses was uneasy, especially since religion and orthodoxy were seen to be the very barriers to the desired political mobilization. In this provisional deployment, religion became something of a link language, connecting for the first time the political ideas of the urban nationalist with the worldview of the peasant through an idiom that he or she could understand. The gender of the peasant was also important, since one of the results of several decades of campaigning around the "women's question" was the consolidation of a belief that the most obnoxious feature of Brahminical Hinduism was the way that it not only abused women but seemed to succeed in reconciling them to their dismal fortunes. Religion in the pattern of Gandhi and Tilak, though, could be used to bring women out of their homes and peasants out of their sleepy apolitical hamlets and move them in the direction of secularism by slowly vitiating the key terms and underpinnings of Hindu thought. Unlike their nineteenth-century counterparts who sought to salvage religion by producing a variety of protestant reformations in Hinduism (e.g. the Arya Samaj, the Brahmo Samaj, etc.), when these students returned to the villages they were interested in finding ways to move the village into a nationalist, feminist, scientific and ultimately secular modernity. The theory of the evolution of the peasant had not, of course, been fully worked out, but the confidence in an evolutionary sociology and in a politics of radical social change compelled the nationalist middle class to take seriously the awakening of its peasant relatives.

This debate about religion and modernity filtered its way through the subcontinent, affecting the vernacular languages differently (Mugali 1975). Kannada was going through its renaissance in the 1920s and 1930s in a movement called *navodaya*, whose major figures included Srikanthaiah, Kuvempu, D. R. Bendre, Shivaram Karanth and Betgeri Krishnasharma (Amur 2001). Navodaya, like the other vernacular renaissance movements in British India, was led, for the most part, by Western-educated Indians who saw themselves rejuvenating the cultural tradition of South Asia by adapting European forms into vernacular languages and regional themes. Here, the models were British Romantic poetry (B. M. Srikanthaiah translated many of the British Romantic poets into Kannada), continental European fiction and Elizabethan drama. But no contradiction was seen between the nationalist sympathies of the leading figures (almost all were Congress members or sympathizers) and the adaptation of European traditions for the purposes of vernacular literary output. Furthermore, the social reform politics of this coterie were also quite forward-looking: anticaste chauvinist, antisexist (at least in some basic ways) and economically redistributive. It was characterized by a sort of paternalistic obligation toward the peasantry, not the least because so much of the movement was composed of Brahmin men with land and occupation, with the artist now playing the central role of patron and guardian saint. The point, though, is that a wing of the bilingual Indian intelligentsia made a conscious choice to write in the vernacular to pursue aims of social reform and popularize those aims within the subcontinent. Having been educated in the West, armed with ideas about social change and reform, and working towards independence, the generation of writers active in the 1930s and 1940s had to seek out new explanations for the contradiction between the reformist impulses that seemed to be growing in India and the conservative hold that religious ideas seemed to have. This frustration inched towards a confidence in the inevitability of change, even while it was hamstrung by a paternalistic belief in its own importance.

But Raja Rao's concerns were already broader and more complicated than the simple introduction of nationalism into the peasantry by the time he wrote *Kanthapura*. Even if that novel is read along a nationalist axis (as opposed to experimental, religious, modernizing, feminist, or psychological ones), his other writings demonstrate an attention to and an engagement with concerns that were clearly becoming distinguished from the range of issues that nationalism could easily encompass, and that the new, social novelists of the Progressive Writers' Movement were engaged with: representations of the worldviews of the peasantry, problems of modernity and modernization in village life, the durability of sexist ideas and their internalization by women, the irreconcilability of traditional familial expectations and urban social mobility, the viability of European languages in representing vernacular idioms and speech, the unwillingness of the low caste to challenge their oppression and the role of the intellectual in colonial India. Much of these concerns in Rao's writing, though, are occluded by the focus on his novels as opposed to his short fiction. Rao's 1934 short story, "Javni," for instance, details the rational divide that exists between an already secularized young man (Ramappa) and the conservatism of the women in his family, which binds them to a cycle of submission and brutality. Javni, a poor, low-caste servant (a midwife by birth, so likely from an untouchable caste), becomes the object of Ramu's attempt at social reform in his own family. She finds herself in the employ of Ramu's upper-caste family after the sudden death of her husband, the arrest of her brother-in-law and the internal rivalries in her husband's family make it impossible for her to live on her own. Her primary recourse in this circumstance is religious – "I wept and sobbed and wanted to go and fall into the river. But I knew Goddess Talakamma would be angry with me, and I stopped each time I wanted to kill myself" – though she does eventually run away to her brother's home before finding a job with a Brahmin family (Rao 1947, 17). Now working for the revenue inspector and his wife (Ramu's sister), Javni happily assumes the role of servant with all of the attendant submissiveness that grates against the sensibilities of the modern narrator: she eats "in the byre where her food was usually kept," she saves her absurdly low earnings to buy a lamb to slaughter for the goddess, and she accepts her condition despite Ramu's attempts at convincing her to protest (17).

But the constant string of tragedies in Javni's life also produces a deep attachment to the kind of calm that religion provides: "Should I live if that Goddess did not protect me? Would that child come to me if the Goddess did not help me? Would Mother be so good to me if the Goddess did not bless me? Why, Ramappa, everything is hers. O Great Goddess Talakamma, give everybody good health and long life and all the joys! Protect me, Mother!" (Rao 1947, 19). This humanist response to religion as a kind of salve butts up against the narrator's own rationalist critique of religion (especially of Javni's superstitious, animal-sacrifice version of Hinduism), which cannot tolerate the use of religion in propping up outmoded and outdated social customs and behaviors that should have long since fallen away. The two questions that the short story deals with – animal sacrifice and the injunction against intercaste dining – make for easy targets as objects of embarrassment for the newly educated. But it also produces quite a bit of social friction when objections are raised:

"And what, pray, is being irreligious?" I continued furious.

"Irreligious. Irreligious. Well, eating with a woman of a lower caste is irreligious. And Ramu," she cried desperately, "I have enough of quarreling all the time. In the name of our holy mother can't you leave me alone!" There, tears!

"You are inhuman, inhuman!" I spat, disgusted.

"Go and show your humanity!" she grumbled, and, hiding her face beneath blanket, she wept harder. (10)

There is no middle ground in the imaginative universe of the young modernizing narrator between himself and the women he wants to reform. The narrator's attempts to introduce more modern ways of thinking are immediately rebuffed, both by Javni, who finds his notions completely unworkable, but also by his sister who identifies them as being part of the new, urban ideology. The debate turns, though, inelegantly around the inevitable opposition between religion and humanism, between the democratic and dynamic impulses of the narrator and the rural conservatism whose emotional content he both understands and loathes. And it slowly becomes clear that Rao's narrator attempts, but inevitably fails, to get around the easy versions of village life upon which he reflects: on the one hand are men, modernity, secularism and progress; on the other, women, superstition, tradition and conservatism. As Ramu's sister reminds him: "Men, Ramu, can never understand us. [...] You are too practical and too irreligious. To us everything is mysterious. Our gods are not your gods, your gods not our gods. It is a simple affair." (Rao 1947, 6)

At the same time as the ideological divisions clearly harden for Ramu, he resists thinking of this state of affairs as permanent. In fact, his understanding of the neat oppositions between men and women, between modernity and tradition, is made possible only because Ramu's hopes for a democratic, humanist version of the world are frustrated by the reality of social relations in the countryside. As a result, even in the moments of epiphany, where the narrator's progressive politics could easily emerge, he collapses backwards into cliché and stereotype to describe Javni, only then to distrust his own impressions:

> I heard an owl hoot somewhere, and far, far away, somewhere too far and too distant for my rude ears to hear, the world wept its silent suffering plaints. Had not the Lord said: "Whenever there is misery and ignorance, I come"? Oh, when will that day come, and when will the Conch of Knowledge blow?
>
> I had nothing to say. My heart beat fast. And, closing my eyes, I sank into the primal flood, the moving fount of Being. Man, I love thee.
>
> Javni sat and ate. The mechanical mastication of the rice seemed to represent her life, her whole existence. (Rao 1947, 11–12)

Two things are worth underscoring in this passage. First, Ramu turns to millenarian language as a way to smuggle in the ideas of the Enlightenment. This rationalist reading of Hindu mythology was already extant in India, especially as Hindu reform movements sought to differentiate themselves from Islam and Christianity, but here the plea dissolves very quickly into secularist and Enlightenment terms. Rather than confront the question of fate as a debate within Hindu tradition, the narrator turns to a pathetic but stable humanism ("Man, I love thee"). Second, the experience of watching Javni eat in the dark, her food splashed with fresh cow dung, creates for the narrator a contradictory reaction. On the one hand, there is the easy return to clichéd characterizations of the content peasant, whose "whole existence" can be reduced to her act of eating bestially, while on the other, the narrator is absolutely unwilling to accept the solidity or the finality of that representation. In fact, the plea to a different kind of universalist divinity ("the moving fount of Being") is generated by a contradiction in an urban humanism whose empiricism cannot be reconciled with its idealism: the peasant seems at every point actually to be reducible to her stereotype when she shouldn't be. There is no progressive strategy of representation here: the peasant woman is simply a surface, easily troped as both animal and machine, incapable of producing an interior into which the narrative gaze can pierce or which the narrator can use as an exercise in demonstrating his own expressive humanism. Rather, Ramu confronts in many ways his worst nightmare: the indecipherable figure of the peasant woman unwilling and perhaps even incapable of being modernized. Perhaps more aptly, Ramu's reaction can be explained as a crisis in the paternalist view of Brahmin modernizers who were unable, immediately, to turn their caste-derived social authority into social change in the villages, especially when those reforms ran directly against extant versions of Hinduism in the villages. This is, of course, upper-caste elitism confronting its own chauvinism, but what is interesting is the persistent, negative pull of a reformist impulse that prevents the narrator from retreating ideologically back into stable ideas about social hierarchies.

But in many ways, it was this problem – of a reformist Brahminical impulse unable to produce the changes that it desired – which was the preoccupation of Rao's return to the village in literature. In "Akkaya" (which first appeared in French in *Cahiers du Sud*), Kittu (another educated, young Brahmin) cannot bear the site of the long, physical degeneration of his beloved great-aunt Akkaya. The problem once again is the contradictory way that Brahmin women imagine religion; Akkaya's religious beliefs on the one hand reconcile her to her degrading life as a Brahmin child-widow, while on the other produce in her an illogical and impulsive hatred of the Western medicine that can cure the typhoid that is destroying her. Her slowly decomposing body becomes a symbol for the suffocating hold that religion has on all attempts to introduce progressive change into the countryside. A similar problem emerges in "A Client," where a young student is tricked into an arranged marriage to "a charming girl of eleven or twelve" (Rao 1947, 141). In most places, the characterization of rural life in Rao's short stories bounces back and forth between an impulsive, paternalistic condemnation of superstitious practices and a sympathetic patience aimed at understanding the genuine hardships faced by the peasantry. There are, of course, formal similarities with landlord–peasant relationships that are not overcome, but the fact that the impatience has to do with the pace of progress, as opposed to the persistence of obedience, means that the effects of power are shifting. The slide into a benevolent paternalism was a necessary consequence of the middle class's underconfidence in its own charismatic authority.

Kanthapura and the Rearguard Action of Authenticity

To talk about the rhetorical and charismatic underconfidence of Raja Rao's *Kanthapura*, though, is more than slightly polemical, since the ambition of the novel is staggering. More so than any other anglophone Indian novel, *Kanthapura* succeeded at bringing into the orbit of English prose the fantasy of the perfect adequation of modern novels with the indigenous, rural forms of the vernacular languages. *Kanthapura* tells the story of a sleepy village in Uttar Kanara that awakens to political enthusiasm in the heady days of the Civil Disobedience movement but is ultimately destroyed by British troops when the peasants resist paying their taxes. What gives the novel its durability is that, as one of the few English-language fictional narratives about the reach of Gandhian nationalism into the villages, the novel attempts to resolve a longstanding anxiety that Congress nationalism was really an urban affair and that the urban intelligentsia really had nothing substantial to offer their rural relatives. If there was a general worry, shared by Gandhi, that writing in English was disconnected, insensitive, or simply incapable of representing India's cultural and psychological reality, then *Kanthapura* represented the most sustained attempt at overcoming the linguistic divide between the urban, cosmopolitan world of the anglophone writer and the vernacular world of the Indian, who in almost every case in late-colonial India was a peasant. It is telling, perhaps, that no novel before or since has attempted to reproduce what Rao's novel has done, which also demarcates the historical and literary moment of the novel's production as intimately bound up with the high point of an urban–rural nationalist compound. Other attempts at Indianizing English prose have, of course, been made, but none have attempted anything nearly as radical as what Rao attempted: the stylization of peasant oral tradition as the dominant form of a novel ostensibly about the inevitable Nehruvian urbanization of India. In fact, so successful is the form at occluding the content of the novel that few critics have given the novel credit for its ambition or its innovation, preferring instead to read the book as an idealization of peasant life rather than a call for its eventual disintegration.

The Indian nation needed novelistic forms that would suture together the disparate experiences and ideologies of its teeming population in fiction, in advance of what was possible in life (Gopal 2009, 74). Some of this, of course, was accomplished by translation of vernacular fiction into English, which allowed the urban reader to access the rest of the nation's literary output in whatever limited fashion. But translated novels carried with them a political warrant for the value of the vernacular, a political claim that threatened the possibility of Indian unification, at least linguistically. What *Kanthapura* was attempting was the elimination of the need for the translation altogether: if vernacular, folk and rural forms, rhythms and ideas could be captured in English, then one could fantasize about the homologization (if not homogenization) of literary tradition in India. Anglophone novels, then, would not need to feel threatened by their putatively more authentic vernacular counterparts, and a monolingual or bilingual English speaker would not need to feel anxious about the possibility of alternative nationalist processes. Raja Rao's novel accomplished this feat primarily through two formal devices that allowed his English prose to absorb something of the feel of rural storytelling. First, at the level of the sentence, Rao managed to defamiliarize standard English syntax enough through inverted word ordering and a heavy reliance on polysyndetons to give the novel an explicitly oral feel, or more precisely, give it the apparatus by which it could successfully masquerade as authentically rural. One example from the novel's conclusion gives a sense of the range of Rao's formal experiment:

> They say Rangamma is all for the Mahatma. We are all for the Mahatma. Pariah Rachanna's wife, Rachi, and Seethamma and Timmamma are all for the Mahatma. They say there are men in Bombay and men in Punjab, who are all for the Mahatma. They say the Mahatma will go to the Red-man's country and he will get us Swaraj. He will bring us Swaraj, the Mahatma. And we shall all be happy. And Rama will come back from exile, and Sita will be with him, for Ravana will be slain and Sita freed, and he will come back with Sita on his right in a chariot of the air, and brother Bharatha will go to meet them with the worshipped sandal of the Master on his head. And as they enter Ayodhya there will be a rain of flowers. (1963, 181)

The reliance on the polysyndeton to produce an effect of orality (we might also call it a chorus) in Rao's style relied on the (mistaken) urban belief that peasant speech and narrative was primarily composed of short, declarative sentences and commonly accessible allusions that produced the illusion of an authentic peasant consciousness. At the same time, though, that the form of the novel's orality moves to the foreground, what recedes is the political maneuver that happens in between the polysyndetons. If the first three sentences imagine a cross-caste political consensus of the village's women (from the Brahmin Rangamma to the Pariah Rachanna's wife), then the series of anaphoras that follow seamlessly extends the consensus from the village to states in the north (Bombay and Punjab) in a continuous prayer for the Mahatma. Throughout the novel, this formal attempt at reproducing a local, vernacular style was paradoxically connected to the creation of an all-India literary register that only an infinitesimal minority could read.

Part of Rao's stylistic procedure was derived from his amateur translations of the great Hindu epics into English and from his deep interest in folk narratives – *harikathas* and *sthalapuranas* – but the polysyndeton in English carried over something of its Biblical uses as well, linking the well-developed forms of Judeo-Christian religiosity with its Hindu counterpart. In the passage above, the polysyndeton bears a great deal of pressure to connect a number of distinct worldviews together: the Congress narrative of Gandhi's charismatic leadership merges into the return of *Ram Rajya*; the particular folk style of Kannadigan sthalapurana becomes a stand-in for a vernacularized all-India English; and the ideological and religious aspirations of rural women fold seamlessly into the secular, urban aspirations of Indian men (who speak completely different languages and live in completely different parts of the nation). That the folk, the epic, the modern, the Western, the religious, the prophetic, the political and the oral were all commingling in this stylistic experiment should at least be some index of the breathtaking ambition of the novel but also the inherent danger in such a politically explosive admixture; the form mirrored the fragile, motley and warring coalition that was being organized to challenge British rule under the banner of rural authenticity.

Second, Rao moved the novel explicitly into the domain of rural women, a psychology and logic heretofore almost entirely inaccessible to the novelistic narrator in general. This problem makes its appearance in a small vignette in *Kanthapura*, in which Moorthy, like so many other college-educated men, returns home and fails to convince sisters, mothers and sisters-in-law of the need to abandon superstition and orthodoxy. Even in Rao's Kannada short stories, his male, college-educated protagonists come up against the unwillingness of women to change their religious beliefs. Rao's novel inverts the procedure of these earlier narratives by organizing the tale retroactively so that the female narrator has already undergone the conversion from parochial to cosmopolitan consciousness, from orthodox to reformist versions of Hinduism, so that she can putatively explain how other women came to see the question of British imperialism as one of the most important questions of the day. By making the narrator a grandmother, the novel not only provides itself with an alibi against dissimulation, it also manages to politicize the very subject deemed resistant to politics. In fact, what the form of the novel manages to do is transform politics into grandmotherly morality, so that the only alternative to the coalition of chauvinism, orthodoxy and colonialism is cosmopolitanism, secularism and Socialism. The form of the novel and the choice of political content were not the necessary outcomes of the charisma of Gandhi and a commitment to Gandhian ideals, but the consequence of a momentary and fragile alliance that was possible when the Brahmins and the British were the faces of the same rural problems. That fragile alliance simultaneously held out the possibility for more radical changes in the village and the real historical outcomes of the failed rural economic programs implemented in the wake of India's independence.

But central to both procedures (the pseudo-translation style and the grandmotherly story) was the deliberate movement towards authenticity. For instance, a fairly recent retrospective on Indian writing of the 1930s that appeared in India's most widely read left-wing daily, *The Hindu*, argued for the authenticity of Rao's *Kanthapura*. *Kanthapura* succeeds, the article argues, exactly where history fails at making legible the history of the freedom struggle in the villages in South India:

> In more senses than one, this so-called record in *Kanthapura* happens to be a true history of the times. For, the forces of history bring in too many changes too speedily for the villagers to digest. One single sentence and the entire movement is brought to the historian to be fixed in proper place though he may not have a shred of diary or personal memoirs to recreate those days. For, this is how it exactly happened and Raja Rao's reference to jewels being hidden deep beneath the earth is how the poor villagers sought to safeguard their meagre riches. As an alternative, they placed the jewels in a niche in the wall and plastered it over leaving a private symbol or two to recognise the place. What follows also is pure history. The police charge upon men and women who refuse to budge. The police beat them up, pour gutter water and even pots of toddy on them. At last they manage to march them to the Santur Police Outpost. Only Rajah Rachanna and Lingayya and Potter Siddayya are detained. The others are taken in lorries and left in different places in the middle of the jungle. The Satyagrahis get back somehow and plant five twigs of toddy trees and a toddy pot as their Satyagraha trophies in the temple. Once again they go to the Skeffington Estate to stop the sale of toddy. The police get into action – a scene witnessed many a time during these days. (Nandkumar 2003)

We should, of course, be suspicious of the hyperbole ("One single sentence and the entire movement is brought to the historian to be fixed in proper place" and "what follows is pure history"), as it would require either some aggressive or naïve theory of representation in order to see the verisimilitude of fiction as a marker for reality, as such. But the account of the emotional effect and affect of the novel is still quite stunning. *Kanthapura* becomes authentic as a description of the process by which Gandhian nationalism inspires first one urbanized villager and then an entire village to engage in nearly unanimous protest against British colonialism.

The novel putatively does what diaries and records of the events cannot; it returns the gaze to the small, local details of the transformation of village life and by so doing manages to produce a seemingly irreproachable account of the nationalist fantasy of the past. This is something greater than the general production of truth-effects that we associate with realism or reportage, especially since the way this authenticity is recognized is by virtue of the presence of certain details that are supposed to be irretrievable to the historian ("jewels in a niche in the wall") and certain details that are too familiar ("witnessed many a time during those days"), mapped onto a historical event that seems to have no basis in the historical record: there are no recorded marches of villagers to coffee and tea plantations ("Skeffington Estate") to stop the workers from spending their money on toddy; there are no reports of villagers erecting barricades around their village to defend themselves against tax collection; and there are no reports of spontaneous support for Congress activists by indentured plantation workers. Some sixty-five years after it was written, the novel still is for much of the English-speaking middle class of India the standard narrative of the entry of Gandhian ideas and organization into idyllic settings, not because it happened this way but because this is the way it must have happened. *Kanthapura*, then, serves to fill the gap that seems to separate Indians from their national history; with its attention to hidden grain, local rituals, caste chauvinism, village geography, rural idioms and Gandhian politics, it is able to describe emotionally the contours of middle-class enthusiasm for peasant participation in nationalist mobilization. For postindependence readers, its authenticity is also a fantasy of a past that has become too remote to access regularly.

Rao was attempting to manufacture authenticity through a different, but parallel, relationship to the historical data that the novel marshals. The anxiety amongst many Indian writers who chose to write in English was that writing in English meant becoming unmoored from traditions, cultures and languages that were recognizably and meaningfully Indian, and that a novel about India in English could only ring false. In explaining how his novel attempts to render a sthalapurana (what Rao glosses over as "legendary history" but which is more accurately a "place story" or a temple or pilgrimage legend) in English, Rao drew attention to what he understood to be the axis between authenticity and representation (Prasad 2006, 25–32):

> The tempo of Indian life must be infused into our English expression, even as the tempo of American or Irish life has gone into the making of theirs. We, in India, think quickly, we talk quickly, and when we move we move quickly. There must be something in the sun of India that makes us rush and tumble on. And our paths are interminable. The *Mahabharata* has 214,778 verses and the *Ramayana* 48,000. The *Puranas* are endless and innumerable. We have neither punctuation nor the treacherous 'ats' and 'ons' to bother us – we tell one interminable tale. Episode follows episode, and when our thoughts stop our breath stops, and we move on to another thought. This was and still is the ordinary style of our storytelling. I have tried to follow it myself in this story. (Rao 1963, vii–viii)

This defense of the form of the novel is wedded to an ideology of culture, climate, geography and religion that is recognizably "Indian" but can get coded into English as infinite "tempo." Here, the hyperbolic ("we tell one interminable tale") is "ordinary" and speed and duration carry the burden of representing Indian-ness in English prose. As a defense of a particular kind of style – unpunctuated, breathless, naïve, ancient – this is a clever arrangement of social observation that aggregates easily into speed, but as an explanation for what counts as Indian-ness this is hardly compelling. It is all the more puzzling as a defense of Indian-ness in English as it is also supposed to be a specific kind of narrative for which the particular kind of tempo Rao is describing is, perhaps, ill-fitting: "It may have been told of an evening, when as the dusk falls, and through the sudden quiet, lights leap up in house after house, and stretching her bedding on the veranda, a grandmother might have told you, newcomer, the sad tale of her village." (1963, viii)

The soporific scene, the amateur history, the age of the speaker, the tragic note of the story and the ignorance of the audience all seem to rail against the kind of fast-paced narrative for which the novel wants to campaign; grandmothers can, of course, tell fast-paced stories, but this description, which locates the grandmother as the trope for the novel's authenticity, works against the authentic tempo that it wants to produce. There is a certain languorous and luxuriant way that Rao not only punctuates the sentence but relies on the intimacy of the gendered domestic space represented in the "stretching [of] her bedding on the veranda" that necessarily frustrates the demand for speed. In order to defend the form, Rao has to evacuate Indian-ness of any content; but in order to defend his grandmotherly trope, Rao has to abandon the logic of the form.

Authenticity, then, is both an overdetermined part of the composition and reception of the novel, as well as being contradictorily inscribed in it. Postindependence readers have sought to find in the novel heroic representations of the nationalist myths that they have received (inadequately) in textbooks, while Rao was searching for ways to shore up the indigeneity of his novel by connecting it to local forms. The problem with authenticity in making sense of *Kanthapura* is not that it undercuts the novel as a mirage, evading novelist and reader alike, but rather that authenticity means different things in different contexts, so that what is mislaid in any understanding of the novel are the stakes and the terms of the debate in which authenticity was rhetorically deployed. In postindependence India, authenticity is too heavily coded with the discourses of facile representational politics, conservative alibis for religion, and antimodernist romances of a lost past for it to be easily revived as a term for individuation, resistance, rarity and nonconformity, words that bear familial resemblances to authenticity and the authentic. In colonial India, authenticity was also the ground on which colonialism was resisted as an alien, invasive and disruptive historical phenomenon, even as religious reform and social change also used tropes of authenticity to give their projects rhetorical confidence. In fact, all claims to authenticity oscillate between these two registers of timeless universality and precious particularism; they need both simultaneously to serve as the reproducible halo that surrounds all artifacts and utterances by making them recognizable in their affective durability, in their historical fragility.

Another way of thinking about this problem of authenticity would be to think about is in relationship to Walter Benjamin's essay, "The Work of Art in the Era of Mechanical Reproduction" (1969), in which Benjamin argues, in part, that one of the consequences of technological development is that the ritualistic and cultic aspects of art deteriorate in favor of a more democratic and political engagement, which in Benjamin's formulation could aid either communism or fascism depending on the uses to which art was put. Benjamin argues that one of the functions of mass-produced art is its explicit politicization as it is removed from the domain of the sacred or the cultic and made popular and "progressive":

> An analysis of art in the age of mechanical reproduction must do justice to these relationships, for they lead us to an all-important insight: for the first time in world history, mechanical reproduction emancipates the work of art from its parasitical dependence on ritual. To an ever greater degree the work of art reproduced becomes the work of art

designed for reproducibility. From a photographic negative, for example, one can make any number of prints; to ask for the "authentic" print makes no sense. But the instant the criterion of authenticity ceases to be applicable to artistic production, the total function of art is reversed. Instead of being based on ritual, it begins to be based on another practice – politics. (224)

Following Benjamin we might consider that Rao's attempts at authenticating his own novel have less to do with the novel as an original artifact whose aura is threatened by the press than as an authentic reproduction of history and language as such, as necessarily an ideological maneuver. If Rao's novel was an attempt to shore up its own claims to authenticity, it was doing so under the pressures of both a regime of mass-produced novels in which authenticity no longer inhered in the artifact itself and under a historical regime whose meanings were hotly contested. It is valuable in this context to remember that Rao's technique for authenticity is derived primarily from *the fiction of the novel as a translation*, as a unique access point to an original that does not exist. Importantly for Benjamin, though, this was about the reproduction of the work of art itself, and not (perhaps) its translation from one media to another (live performance to novel) or from one language to another (Kannada to English).

Rao's novel offers up a particular kind of authenticity, which served the needs of anglophone writers before independence differently from readers of anglophone fiction after independence, even though the terms of authenticity would be remarkably similar. Authenticity as a formal problem is expressed in the novel in two important ways. First, since Rao was interested in making the case for Indian novels being written in English, authenticity had to appear as style, as coded into the form at the level of the sentence. Rao relies on formal innovations – inverted word order, translated idioms without gloss, the interminable chain of polysyndetons – in order to give the narrative the feel of being a product of both high, literary culture (of which the *Mahabharata*, the *Ramayana* and the *Puranas* are referents) and the traditions of local, folk storytelling (i.e. a narrative told by a grandmother in a village). The high Hindu epics provide a warrant for the novel's literariness, while the folk style brings the novel the feeling of indigenous knowledge. Secondly, the novel relies heavily on historical narrative, on the recent history of central, Western India in particular in order to shore up the quality of its content. The central pivot of this historicizing move is Gandhi's highly covered Salt March – when Gandhi led a hand-selected team of Congress members from Sabarmati to the coast at Dandi and manufactured salt in violation of the British monopoly – and the subsequent launching of the Civil Disobedience movement (Nanda 2002, 292–8). But smaller details also help make the novel's case. The harikatha and *kirtan* movements led by Bal Gangadhar "Lokamanya" Tilak, in which nationalist themes would be set to traditional stories and tunes and sung throughout the Bombay Presidency, finds a corollary in the novel as an explanation for the launch of the village's committee (Schultz 2002, 309–10).[3] The entry, too, of women into positions of political leadership in the Congress, especially Kamaladevi Chattopadhyay, becomes the inspiration for the village's *Sevika Sangh*, a local female volunteer unit (Chatterjee 2001). The presence of events, people and politics that "really happened," the novel's asymptotic relationship to lived history, all function to produce the aura of authenticity.

Finally, and perhaps most importantly, the problem of authenticity is also troped within the novel. At the end of the first chapter, Moorthy, an educated Brahmin who has returned from the city as a supporter of Gandhi, invites Jayaramachar into the village in order to perform a harikatha. But as soon as the harikatha is announced, the more orthodox in the village initially recognize the inauthentic character of the nationalist harikatha:

> "Today," he says, "it will be the story of Siva and Parvati." And Parvati in penance becomes the country and Siva becomes heaven knows what! "Siva is the three-eyed," he says, "and Swaraj too is three-eyed: Self-purification, Hindu-Moslem unity, Khaddar." And then he talks of Damayanthi and Sakunthala and Yasodha and everywhere there is something about our country and something about Swaraj. Never had we heard *Harikathas* like this. And he can sing too, can Jayaramachar. He can keep us in tears for hours together. But the *Harikatha* he did, which I can never forget is about the birth of Gandhiji. "What a title for a *Harikatha*!" cried out old Venkatalakshamma, the mother of the Postmaster. "It is neither about Rama nor Krishna." – "But," said her son, who too has been to the city, "but, Mother, the Mahatma is a saint, a holy man." – "Holy man or lover of a widow, what does it matter to me? When I go to the temple I want to hear about Rama and Krishna and Mahadeva and not all this city nonsense," said she. And being an obedient son, he was silent. But the old woman came along that evening. She could never stay away from a *Harikatha*. And sitting beside us, how she wept!" (Rao 1963, 10)

Venkatalakshamma, a Brahmin widow in Kanthapura, immediately recognizes that the content of the harikatha is not appropriate to the form; harikathas are for the divine and not for the mundane Gandhi. Connecting the divine to politics can be tolerated, up to a point, but the limit for Venkatalakshamma is the idea that a harikatha could be a secular allegory, mere "city nonsense." Religious allegories are one thing for Venkatalakshamma, since at least they preserve the content of the religious narrative, but secular allegories are merely self-referential. Still, Venkatalakshamma is won over for two reasons: "she could never stay away from a *Harikatha*" and the quality of the performance. Here, too, though, the quality of the form, the power of Jayaramachar's voice, demonstrates the dissociation of authenticity from content into style; as long as the harikatha is well done, the distance between the authentic and the inauthentic can be shortened substantially, but always at the expense of content.

Along the axis of the authentic and the inauthentic, a number of other terms suffer collateral damage; they are raised as equivalents of the authentic when the rhetorical function of authenticity is to evacuate those terms of their content. Consider the last example, in particular: the harikatha is literally profaned as it moves in the direction of the secular even though it is originally in the domain of the religious; the point of this performance is to smuggle in nationalist politics under the veneer of the authentic form. The transformation of tradition, religion and culture for new ends is now happening under the sign of the authentic, which means that if tradition, religion and culture are not substantially transformed by this innovation, they continue to serve the function that they served at the beginning of the paragraph: to separate the divine and the mundane, to keep nationalist politics out of the village. In fact part of the reason that tradition, religion and culture have to be used to make the case for authenticity is because they are the very terms that prevent innovation, change, and transformation from happening; they are the markers and borders that keep out the new, the foreign, the urban and the radical. But the hope in mobilizing those terms, in making the case for one's own authenticity, is that the borders will be loosened and that the categories can be made to dilate enough to accommodate the formerly inauthentic "city nonsense." If the inauthentic cannot move us (because we can see the con too clearly), then our response is a marker of the novel's authenticity, and here, the Mahatma's holiness serves as surrogate for the divine without reproducing it entirely. Once authenticity is transformed into style, the political content can be transformed at will, so that "city nonsense" can also make one weep. The move is necessarily risky because it risks confirming the categories it wishes to undo; in making the traditional, cultural and religious synonymous with the authentic, the novel risks ceding all of the ground to the conservative proposition inherent in all gestures of authenticity.

Another way to consider the problem of authenticity is from the perspective of the Venkatalakshamma's son, the postmaster "who too has been to the city," and so implicitly is also a Gandhian and a nationalist in the ideological dyad of the novel (urban-nationalist and rural-orthodox), but is also presumably closer in disposition to the middle-class, upper-caste author and reader for whom the terms of authenticity must be made pliable.

Venkatalakshamma's son is one of many young men in Kanthapura who are already excited about the possibilities for change in their village; early recruitment to the Congress in the novel is almost entirely based around young, upper-caste men: "He went to Dore and Sastri's son, Puttu, and Puttu went to Postmaster Suryanaryana's sons, Chandru and Ramu, and then came Pandit Venkateshia and Front-house Sami's son, Srinivas, and Kittu, and so Kittu and Srinivas and Puttu and Ramu and Chandru and Seenu, threw away their foreign clothes and became Gandhi's men" (Rao 1963, 12). Here he now stands in for an entire generation in Kanthapura, and by extension in India, that is attempting to move the peasantry into action, but which is frustrated by the reluctance of that peasantry, here coded by their allegiance to tradition, religion and culture. The son, who wants to win his mother over to secularism, nationalism and modernity, is rebuffed when he makes the case for the Mahatma's part in a harikatha in terms of authenticity; no harikatha that is inauthentic is desirable to his mother. So in order to move the debate, the son engages in a rearguard action ("but, Mother, the Mahatma is a saint, a holy man") in order to make the transition from religious orthodoxy to secular politics through the form of the harikatha. Authenticity is designed to connect the world of the urban, educated, nationalist son with his conservative, religious, rural mother.

This, of course, poses a problem. On the one hand, peasant life was abysmal and indefensible; on the other, the easiest way to deal with the politicization of rural life was to retain the ideal and charming pastoral view, placing such life under threat from colonial modernity. Both views, of course, found happy homes inside the Congress, since the debate between Nehru and Gandhi on the question of Socialism was never really allowed to come to a head. Still, the ideological and intellectual tension remained, and for a class now hoping to imagine its independent future, the stakes were quite high. If the point was to turn peasants into countrymen, then idealizing peasant life, rural ideals and pastoral aesthetics would necessarily be an emotional pull in the opposite direction. If the point was to preserve some sense of continuity with an unchanging rural idyll, then the hope that peasants could become urban would have to be abandoned. This was not merely a conflict over the pattern of social evolution that peasants would follow; it was also a debate over what kinds of emotional resources and ideological standards the middle class could mobilize to make its case to speak for and with the nation. The rural village could be, in Tabish Khair's formulation of Rao's project, "universalized and idealized" but this would mean simultaneously abandoning the didactic and reformist impulse that characterized petit bourgeois aspirations for peasant relatives.[4]

This is why there are both radical and conservative gestures happening at the same time in the novel. If the point of the harikatha is to get a peasant female relative to listen to a story about the Mahatma, the point of the story about the Mahatma is to induce a broad pattern of social change that leads from conservatism to secularism to feminism and finally to Socialism. Later in the novel, Rangamma, an educated Brahmin widow, reads aloud from newspapers that she gets from the city, producing, in miniature, a Socialist sthalapurana:

> [T]he country beyond Kabul and Bukhara and Lahore, the country of the hammer and sickle and electricity – it was onwards that she began to speak of this country, far, far away; a great country, ten times as big as, say, Mysore, and there in that country there were women who worked like men, night and day; men and women who worked night and day, and when they felt tired, they went and spent their holiday in a palace – no money for the railway, no money for the palace – and when the women were going to have a child, they had two months' and three months' holiday, and when the children were still young they were given milk by the Government, and when they grew older still they went to the universities free, too, and when they were still more grown-up, they got a job and they got a home to live in and they took a wife to live with and they had many children and the lived on happily ever after. And she told us many marvelous things about that country [...]. (Rao 1963, 29)

This is the inauthentic, the fantastical, the impossible that needs the cover of authenticity to sneak its way into the worldview of the peasant woman, especially since the fantasy that is on offer, even in the novel's formulation, is not the Socialism of the peasant, Brahmin woman but the Socialism of the urban, middle-class male. The ambition of the novel, and of its young, male characters is that nationalism will use the language of religion and open up the possibilities for a Socialist transformation of society.

Narrating from the Position of Underconfidence

But the explanation of politics seems to hit the wall of female understanding in the novel, even when it is done in vernacular style. Later in *Kanthapura*, when Moorthappa attempts to explain Dadabhai Naoroji's "drain thesis" to the villagers, no one understands (Naoroji 1901):

> "And the next harvest's agents will come and bring veritable motor lorries, such as they have in the Skeffington Coffee Estate, and they will take away all your rice and you will

have to go to Subba Chetty and buy perhaps the very rice that grew in your field, and at four seers a rupee too. The city people bring with them clothes and sugar and bangles. You will give away this money and that money and you will even go to Bhatta for a loan, for the peacock-blue sari they bring just suits Lakshmi, and Lakshmi is to be married soon. They bring soaps and perfumes and thus they buy your rice and sell their wares. You get poorer and poorer, and the Pariahs begin to starve, and one day all but Bhatta and Subba Chetty will have nothing else to eat but the pebbles of the Himavathy, and drink her waters saying, 'Rama-Krishna, Rama-Krishna!' Sister, that is how it is …"

"Oh, I am no learned person," explains Nanjamma. "You have been to the city and you should know more than me. But tell me, my son, does the Mahatma spin?" (Rao 1963, 18)

This, too, would have been reflective of the historical experience of the Congress in the villages, with intellectuals confronting their own inability to match their political and economic theories to the lived experience of the peasantry. After all, one thing a peasant should be able to understand better than an urban intellectual is the drain of wealth away from the countryside, towards the cities and ultimately to England; this is the crux of the peasant complaint. But here, the ideas of moneylender, landlord, tax agent, police officer and merchant are too complicated for the peasant woman to understand, despite the attempts at making the example personal ("the peacock-blue sari"), so she immediately turns back to the question of the Mahatma's personal example.

This narrative moment is a duplication of an earlier moment, in which the very process of the transfer of goods and commodities is ecstatically represented as an entrée into the geographical and cultural space of Kanthapura:

Our village – I don't think you have ever heard about it – Kanthapura is its name, and it is in the province of Kara. High on the Ghats is it, high up the steep mountains that face the cool Arabian seas, up the Malabar coast is it, up Mangalore and Puttur and many a centre of cardamom and coffee, rice and sugar cane. Roads, narrow, dusty, rut-covered roads, wind through the forest of teak and of jack, of sandal and of sal, and hanging over bellowing gorges and leaping over elephant-haunted valleys, the turn now to the left and now to the right and bring you through the Alambè and Champa and Mena and Kola passes into the great granaries of trade. There, on the blue waters, they say, our carted cardamoms and coffee get into the ships the Red-men bring, and, so they say, they go across the seven oceans into the countries where our rulers live. (Rao 1963, 1)

These are lines for which Rao is famous. The long polysyndetons, the enormous vistas, the poetical rhythms masquerading as translations of Kannada word order ("up the Malabar coast is it") and the ecstatic series of cultural referents ("elephant-haunted valleys") are all designed to set the stylistic tempo of the narrative as well as the folkloric mood of its narrator. Anshuman Mondal, for one, has commented on the accuracy of this representation of the economic nexus on which the Indian village rests: "The novel thus presents us with a matrix of space defined by a system of economic production (capitalism) at one end of which lies a terminus of production and the other end of which is a terminus of consumption (England). In between is a dislocated space filled by channels of mobility. The village of Kanthapura lies in this interstitial space, on one of these channels" (Mondal 1999, 104). At the same time, the circuit of commodities is described from a vantage point that betrays the peasant's own victimization; in Achakka's description, the exploitation is marginal and the movement is everything. (Incidentally, the caravan of goods, clearly the result of the colonial reorganization of the rural economy, has had almost no effect on the social relations in the countryside; Kanthapura is impervious to the modernity that might accompany capitalist penetration into the hinterland). In order to produce so detailed a political description, Rao is set up with a contradiction: a peasant woman can narrate the complex circuit of commodities that ends with British imperial consumption; but neither she nor her fellow peasants are able to see their own exploitation at the hands of such a process, when they are able to understand it all. The contradiction could, it seems, be resolved with recourse to the idea of the novel as a kind of narrative of development in which Achakka, the narrator, explains her own transformation, but that is not the novel's intention. In fact, the novel needs both images of the peasant woman (the naïve and the knowing) to be true simultaneously; it is symptomatic of its inability to imagine, even after the effects of the nationalist agitation, new, emergent patterns of consciousness and perception, which it claims have made their appearance on the scene. The transformation of the central character is almost imperceptible for two reasons. First, the narrative is told entirely after the fact, which means whatever epiphanic moment divides the informed narrator from the naïve one who still holds on to her religious explanations for the ways of the world is never reflected in the text, except obliquely. Second, because the novel needs a naïve narrator in order to make the emotional content of the religious form necessary, the novel has to transition seamlessly between the narrator who believes in Kenchamma and the one who has turned to Gandhi. This is not just a theoretical problem of representing the twists and turns of the colonial *Bildungsroman* in which the native character both learns and forgets. It also reflects Rao's own deep ambivalence about religious explanations for peasant consciousness.

There are, of course, consequences to this oscillation. One of them is that religiosity is both the explanation for the formal innovation and impossible to achieve within the novel itself. Religious forms and celebrations were being revived for political purposes not only because of the middle-class belief that the peasants could not understand politics, but because they were immensely successful. For instance, "The celebration of Basava Jayanti, started in 1913 on an extensive scale on the lines of the Ganesha and Shivaji festivals in Maharashtra, was a great force in rousing the people to work for social uplift and in bringing about cultural awakening" (Halappa and Krishna Rao 1964, 30). Not far from where *Kanthapura* is set, "Patriotic dramas such as *Bhavani Talwar, Simhagad, Bapu Gokhalyachi Pagadi* were staged in all the important towns. In Dharwar a dramatic troupe called 'Sri Sivaji Arya Samaj' was formed, which enacted nationalist dramas like *Rana Bheemadeva*. The Karnataka Vidyavardhaka Sangha had taken up literary activities and the Victoria High School was imparting education, both of them carrying on their work with a distinctly nationalistic bias and disseminating the new ideas of cultural revival and democratic government" (Halappa and Krishna Rao 1964, 83). Even the literati were successfully experimenting with the harikatha form, as Alur Venkata Rao's *Karnataka Gatha Vaibhava* (1912) became popular as an account of the glories of Karnataka's glorious past. But in *Kanthapura*, the experimentation does not produce the advertised ends. Even while the characters are moved by Jayaramachar's harikatha, the description of the harikatha itself falls completely flat, lacks any emotional or devotional character and borders on farce:

> And lo, when the Sage was still partaking of the pleasures Brahma offered him in hospitality, there was born in a family in Gujerat [sic] a son such as the world has never beheld! As soon as he came forth, the four wide walls began to shine like the kingdom of the sun, and hardly was he in the cradle than he began to lisp the language of wisdom. You remember how Krishna, when he was but a babe of four, had begun to fight against demons and had killed the serpent Kali. So to our Mohandas began to fight against the enemies of the country. And as he grew up, and after he was duly shaven for the hair ceremony, he began to go out into the villages and assemble people and talk to them, and his voice was so pure, his forehead so brilliant with wisdom, that men followed him, more and more men followed him as they did Krishna, the flute-player; and so he goes from village to village to slay the serpent of foreign rule. Fight, says he, but harm no soul. Love all, says he, Hindu, Mohammedan, Christian or Pariah, for all are equal before God. Don't be attached to riches, says he, for riches create passions, and passions create attachment, and attachment hides the face of truth. Truth must you tell, he says, for truth is God, and verily, it is the only God I know. (Rao 1963, 11–12)

If the function of the nationalist harikatha or sthalapurana is to translate political idiom into religious structures of feeling, then in the novel the translation takes place without the feelings to which it is aligned. Not only is Gandhi not given anything resembling the wonderfully mischievous childhood of Krishna, neither is he narrated in terms that might even explain his heroic deeds. Gandhi is supposed to be a mythological character; in Jayaramachar's harikatha he is merely a religious-political conjunction ("Fight, says he, but harm no soul"). In fact, so thoroughly secularized is the world of *Kanthapura*, that it is impossible even to reanimate the sthalapurana with nationalist figures. Quietly, perhaps, Rao even depopulates his harikatha with all of the stylistic innovations that make the rest of the novel interesting: the creative translations, the inverted word order and the emphasis on long, breathless sentences. It is not important, then, how the religious vocabularies are used to propel nationalist sympathies forward, merely that they are able to do so. In fact, the novel achieves its emotional result despite this momentary lapse because of the aesthetic benefit of the doubt that it is afforded as a putative translation; the emotional effect is presumed to be lost in a translation that has never been performed. Venkatalakshamma weeps, Achakka is moved and the rest of the town begins to organize a congress in Kanthapura as a result of the harikatha, but in the novelistic world, the religious idiom is a dud.

If the sthalapurana style of the novel has more successful moments, they are in the rendering of the internal space of the Brahmin nationalist, more easily readable as religious conversion narratives. In the fiction of the novel, Moorthy's conversion to Congress nationalism comes through his revelation of the Mahatma's political message:

> But Moorthy would have none of this. For, as everybody knew one day he had seen a vision, a vision of the Mahatma, mighty and God-beaming, and stealing between the Volunteers, Moorthy got onto the platform, and he stood by the Mahatma, and the very skin of the Mahatma seemed to send out a mellowed force of love, and he stood by one of the fanners and whispered, "Brother, the next is me." And the fanner fanned on and the Mahatma spoke on, and Moorthy looked from the audience to the Mahatma and from the Mahatma to the audience, and he said to himself, "There is in it something of the silent communion of the ancient books" [...] and beneath the fan came a voice deep and stirring that went out to the hearts of those men and women and came streaming back through the thrumming air, and went through the fan and the hair and the nails of Moorthy into the very limbs, and Moorthy shivered, and then there came flooding up in rings and ripples, "Gandhi Mahatma ki jai!" – "Jai Mahatma!" and as it broke against Moorthy, the fan went faster and faster over the head of the Mahatma, and perspiration flowed down the head of Moorthy. Then came a dulled silence of his blood [...]. (Rao, 1963, 32–3)

There are two things to be said at the outset about this moment. The first is that the line between the nationalist and the narrator is paper thin, not only because the revelation has been turned into legend ("as everyone knew") but also because the quickening is duplicated first in the immediate crowd and then again in the narration of the episode; the ecstasy is in part Achakka's. Second, the conversion completes the mythology of the cult of personality surrounding the Mahatma ("mighty and God-beaming"), since Moorthy's becoming a Gandhian is not only written as divine but is also emptied of any political content. The encounter with Gandhi then sets up the emotional relationship between the nationalist-as-supplicant and the peasant woman who tells the story, substituting the theory of political education of one for the other.

This political education, though, requires certain kinds of educators, and a fairly affected pedagogy. Moorthy, in Gandhian fashion, calls off the political campaign in the village after the riot that ensues when the peasants rush to defend him from the police. After returning from jail, Moorthy fasts in order to rid himself of the hatred that he feels is the source of the violence in Kanthapura:

> On the third day such exaltation came over him that he felt blanketed with the Pariah and the cur. He felt he could touch the stones and they would spring to his hands, he felt he could touch a snake and it would spread its sheltering hood above him. But as he rose he felt such a dizziness enter his head that he had to hold to the wall to move, and when he sat down after the morning prayers he felt his heart beating itself away. His eyes dimmed and the whole temple seemed to shake and sink, and the fields rose up with crops and canals and all stood in the air while the birds seemed to screech in desolation. And as he lay back on his mat, a languor filled his limbs and he felt the earth beneath him quaking and splitting. When he awoke he saw Rangamma and our Seenu and Ratna all in tears, and he moved his head and asked, "What's all this?" and Rangamma, so happy that he had at last awakened from his swoon, smiled back at him and said there was nothing the matter, and as he turned toward the courtyard he saw Pariah Rachanna

and Lingayya standing with joined palms. Something was the matter, thought Moorthy, and holding to the pillar he slowly sat up, and he saw the sunshine flooding through the valley, while the canal water ran muddy as ever, and up the Bebbur mound the empty footpath, quivering in the heat, ran up into the Skeffington Coffee Estate. Then suddenly he broke into a fit of sobs, and they stood round him and asked, "What's the matter? What?" and Moorthy would not answer. Or somewhere behind the dizzy blare was a shadow that seemed to wail like an ominous crow, and he broke into sobs despite himself. (Rao 1963, 65–6)

The power of the language is palpable. Moorthy begins with a kind of religious revelry after experiencing something akin to an encounter with divinity, though language is as close to high Romanticism as one can get. The fast-induced religious exaltation, though, ends abruptly, as Moorthy begins crying. In the logic of the narrator, there is no accounting for this emotional breakdown other than the conversion of Moorthy into a Gandhian figure. But the language of the passage bespeaks another, quiet crisis of confidence. The hope, even in the carefully exuberant prose, is that the fast will spread the democratic impulses of Moorthy out into the rest of the world, that the reorganization of the perceptual field will induce a social reorganization on the same pattern. It is not surprising, then, that the experience of divinity is coded as touching the untouchable ("blanketed with the pariah and the cur") and a complete mastery over the natural world. But even as the religious mood of the passage continues through the rest of the chapter, culminating as it does in one more set of Gandhi *bhajans* before Moorthy reconvenes the "Don't-Touch-the-Government campaign," it has to pause to notice the failure of religion to induce democracy on its own. What brings Moorthy to tears is the fact that the two untouchable men (Pariah Rachanna and Lingayya) remain standing outside the temple, and the scene outside remains entirely unaffected by the epiphanic structure of the political aspiration. The secular conscience of the author and the religious worldview of the narrator do not find themselves looking out upon the same world. If the use of the polysyndeton to approximate a spoken Kannada has in other places allowed Rao to press towards an authentic Indian-English, then here there is a quiet slippage between the telescopic polysyndeton of the pseudosociological Achakka (who describes in detail the traffic of commodities, the arrival of the coolies and the pomp of the religious festivals in near ethnographic detail) and the deeply internal, inaccessible, privately revelatory Moorthy. Moorthy is, undoubtedly, important in the novel, but this is the most intensely luminous examination of any memory or any feeling of a character; even the rape that takes place at the end of the novel is not afforded this kind of aesthetic attention. Achakka's narrative has to oscillate between the authentic naïveté of a Brahmin grandmother still wedded to religious belief and the slowly secularizing narrator that can communicate to her urban audience. Free indirect discourse is pressed into the service of religious ecstasy, but here the fantasy figuratively breaks down the socially organized religion in favor of a personalized, private one that can be made to stand in for an ideal secularism.

The other place where the sthalapurana style shines is at the climax of the novel, in the imagistic representation of the political combat between the peasants and the British. After months of refusing to pay taxes, the villagers are faced with the forcible seizure of their lands and begin to construct barricades and organize defense campaigns to protect their property from being attached.

> *And* there was a shuddered silence, like the silence of a jungle after a tiger has roared over the evening river, *and* then, like a jungle cry of crickets *and* frogs *and* hyenas *and* bison *and* jackals we all groaned *and* shrieked *and* sobbed, *and* we rushed this side to the canal-bund *and* that side to the coconut garden, *and* this side to the sugar cane field *and* that side to the bel field bund, *and* we fell *and* we rose, *and* we crouched *and* we rose, *and* we ducked beneath the rice harvests and we rose, *and* we fell over stones *and* we rose again, over field-bunds and canal-bunds *and* garden-bunds did we rush, *and* the children held to our saris *and* some held to our breasts and the night-blind held to our hands; *and* we could hear the splash of the canal water and the trundling of the gun-carts, *and* from behind a tree or stone or bund we could see before us, there, beneath the Bebbur mound, the white city boys grouped like a plantain grove, *and* women round them *and* behind them, *and* the flag still flying over them. *And* the soldiers shouted, "Disperse or we fire," but the boys answered, "Brothers, we are non-violent," *and* the soldiers said, "nonviolent or not, you cannot march this side of the fields," *and* the boys answered, "The fields are ours," *and* the soldiers said, "The fields are bought, you pigs." *And* a peasant voice from back says, "It's we who have put the plough to the earth and few her with water," *and* the soldiers say, "Hè, stop that you village kids," *and* the boys say, "Brother, the earth is ours, and you are ours too, brown like this earth is your skin and mine," *and* a soldier shouts out, "Oh no more of this panchayat – we ask you again, disperse, and do not force us to fire!" Then, it is Ratna's voice that says, "Forward, brothers, in the name of the Mahatma!" *and* everybody takes it up and shouts, "Mahatma Gandhi ki jai!" and marches forward. *And* a shower of shots suddenly burst into the air, *and* we close our eyes, *and* when we open them again there is not a cry nor a shout *and* the boys are still marching forward, *and* the soldiers are retreating, *and* we say, "So that was false firing." (Rao 1963, 168–9) [Emphasis added]

Here the novel has completed its task of transformation: the sthalapurana is reduced to the stylistic organization of polysyndetons and simple conjunctions, with the religious elements completely excised; the entirety of the drama of defending the land turns on the perceptions of the women who are both fleeing and leading the struggle; and the conclusion of the breathless, imagistic depiction is the entry of women into a combative consciousness and empowerment. Moreover, unlike other moments where the political epiphany has to be represented as religious allegory, here it is a perceptual epiphany alone. It has to be underscored that this is simultaneously the completion of the fantasy that the novel has set out for itself at the beginning and the very thing that the novel cannot provide an explanation for; women evolve in the novel despite themselves.

But this seems to be the unacknowledged contradiction at the heart of *Kanthapura*, because the effect of authenticity requires a suspension of the content of the novel: the slow secularization and democratization of village life. If the novel moves towards producing authentic representations of Indian forms and Indian life, then it needs a kind of imagined, static, stable identity on which it can rely. At the same time, if the novel persists in maintaining that the deterioration of Brahminical hegemony is necessary and inevitable, then this authenticity actually works to undermine its ideological aims. *Kanthapura* attempts to manage this contradiction by democratizing the form of the purana, and demonstrates its flexibility to deal with the present and the particular and not simply its origins, but this carries with it necessary risks: the forms of the democratic purana risk being indistinguishable from its conservative source material and make it easier for either an appropriation of the new content or a simple ideological backsliding of the form into the religious orthodoxy against which it wants to protest.

The novel attempts to democratize Hinduism in two ways. First, the content of the novel moves in the direction of performing a successful reform movement. The Bhatta is replaced by Moorthy, whose authority grows throughout the course of the book as an alternative kind of Brahminical leadership. Upon the death of Ramakrishnayya, religious education is then performed by women, where it had previously been the monopoly of men. And reading scripture and offering commentaries were not only the exclusive prerogative of the high caste, it was also confined to Brahmin men. Untouchables are integrated into the political life of Kanthapura: the symbolic authority of the *gram-devi* is undermined as the villagers leave their home. Religious processions are unproblematically used to advance political agendas. Second, the form of the novel furthers democratic impulses. Hindu religious forms are emptied out of their content and used to house nationalist ideas. Sthalapuranas can be told by women and can be about secular figures, like Gandhi, instead of gods and goddesses.

The puranic character of *Kanthapura* doesn't necessarily guarantee the novel's backsliding into a conservative Brahminical order, especially as the novel challenges the orthodoxy and chauvinism of that conservative Brahminism (in the figures of the Swami and Bhatta), and as the novel opens more democratic interpretations of texts and traditions. The novel can thus be read as part of the movement that is indigenizing, de-Sanskritizing, vernacularizing and perhaps problematically modernizing the puranic tradition. Here, the religious character of the form of the novel gives way to its secular content: no new gods or goddesses enter the village; at the end of the story the village burns down; the novel abandons the formal characteristics of the puranas (the *panch-laksanas*). These are as much interventions into the religious idiom as they are appropriations of it. The sthalapurana form gestures in the direction of producing an anti-sthalapurana: the story persists but the place and the gods who form the content of the narrative do not. And this is, essentially, the democratic move that the novel wants to open up.

The Congress in Karnataka

Another way that we might understand that underconfidence is as a product of the uneven and incomplete penetration of the Congress into Karnataka by the 1930s when *Kanthapura* was written. If in the 1920s the movement for Indian national independence was concentrated and far more explosive in the cities, by the 1930s the movement had shifted in important and substantial ways into the countryside, and the peasantry and its concerns were propelled to the forefront of the nationalist demands of the Congress. This process was, of course, uneven throughout South Asia (Punjab experienced little rural agitation during Noncooperation, while key cities in Maharashtra and Bengal saw even larger protests than before), but there was a renewed focus on the peasantry as both an untapped source of energy for the movement for independence and as an important political ally in the new democratic debates that political devolution and the census had opened up. Gandhi had already begun demonstrating the viability (and limited successes) of these tactics in visible ways earlier with his campaigns in Champaran in 1916, Kheda in 1917 and Bardoli in 1925, in which Congress-led movements were able to mobilize large chunks of the peasantry to fight around issues of wages, rents and taxes (Brown 1989, 110–12). These campaigns differed from the Congress's activities in places like Uttar Pradesh, where there had been a growing independent political leadership and peasant movement that was in existence before the Congress arrived on the scene, and where the Congress's involvement was designed to channel peasant protests in a safer direction against colonialism and taxation rather than the more radical demands of ending landlord–tenant property relations, abolishing rent and implementing more radical redistributions of land. In these more properly Gandhian *satyagrahas*, the Congress's infrastructure was a necessary component in the political mobilization of the peasantry, and it was this pattern that the Congress sought to reproduce in the Noncooperation movement of the 1930s.

As urban political fatigue set in and sapped the strengths of the city-based branches of the Congress, new political opportunities were exploited and opened in the countryside and fresh leadership was both cultivated and trained in some spectacular Civil Disobedience campaigns. Karnataka (then divided between the Bombay Presidency, the Madras Presidency and the Princely State of Mysore) had experienced very little political agitation in the 1920s and had become an important new front in the Congress's attempts to recruit new members, wage serious campaigns and win political victories. Uttar Kanara (in the Bombay Presidency) also fit the general pattern of the Bardoli campaign: increases in tax and revenue assessments followed by bad rains; heightened enforcement of laws governing local land use, which came into direct conflict with traditional patterns of cultivation and collection; development of peasant anger without political leadership or infrastructure; strong Congress influence amongst the landlord classes, especially the Brahmins; and an easy-to-organize defense campaign that would highlight the need for Congress-led political infrastructure. The Congress had, as a result, spent quite a bit of time and energy developing a political infrastructure in Karnataka (recruiting Kannada speakers, winning over the Tilakite leadership of local groups to Gandhian strategies and setting up new branches of the Congress throughout the countryside of Uttar Kanara, Dakshin Kanara and Mysore) and had begun salting the villages for more spectacular kinds of resistance to British colonialism. The proximity of Gandhi's 1930 Salt March along the Maharashtran coastline to the Kannada-speaking regions provided the Congress with the political theater that it required in order to inaugurate its no-revenue and no-tax campaigns.

But Karnataka was not entirely new to political struggle. In the decades prior to the establishment of large, organized Congress branches, there had been important local fights in which the peasantry, the new rural working classes (employed as migrant labor in large coffee and tea plantations in the foothills of the Ghats) and the middle classes in the smaller towns had demonstrated their willingness to take on authority and had even created regional networks through which they shared experiences and resources. Early political expressions were in the form of caste-based organizations, centered in the larger towns but providing resources and support to nearby villages, which were generally a part of the larger non-Brahmin movement that was spreading outwards from Tamil Nadu (in the Madras Presidency). In the early 1900s, the two most important non-Brahmin castes, the Lingayats and the Vokkaligas, organized the Veerasaiva Mahasabha and the Vokkaligara Sangha, respectively, and began work towards social reform in education, employment and social uplift. In 1903, the Bombay Karnataka Parishat inaugurated a series of protests throughout the Uttar Kanara district involving boycotting toddy and beedi shops, bonfires of foreign cloth, creation of swadeshi industries and large political meetings. In 1905–06, Bal Gangadhar Tilak toured Karnataka. But Sumit Sarkar's assessment that "of the four linguistic regions of south India, only Karnataka remained largely unaffected [by nationalist politics] – its political awakening would come in the 1930s" is fairly accurate (Sarkar 1989, 213).

By the 1920s, though, important economic and political changes were forcing the movement to shift away from largely symbolic actions towards more concrete challenges to authority and the legal apparatus. Uttar Kanara was a likely candidate for Congress agitation since its proximity to Mysore (where the Congress was still legal) provided organizers with political cover and because the peasants had legitimate grievances against the colonial state. There were two important economic questions for the peasantry of Uttar Kanara that the Congress attempted to mobilize around: access to wood and resources from nearby forests in places like Sirsi and Siddapur, and the increases in taxation that were affecting villages like Ankola. More serious enforcement of the Indian Forest Act (1878), which restricted the use of forestland and regulated the cutting of timber and the sale of wood, began to shave away at the resources that the local peasantry had access to and the income that they provided. In 1890, there were 240,399 acres under cultivation in the district. By 1915 that figure had dropped to 211,299 and by 1920 to 200,597 acres (Halappa and Krishna Rao 1964, 110). In 1914, there had been an upward revision in revenue assessments on land under the Revision Settlement, and this had only increased the financial burden on the peasantry. The combination of legal and financial pressures had also begun to force peasants to relocate or seek employment in other occupations, like the mines in Mysore or the plantations in Coorg (Gupta 1990, 27).

In 1924, at the Belgaum meeting of the Congress, the leadership of the provincial committee began the process of consolidating their infrastructure and penetrating politically into the Karnataka countryside. A number of organizations were established in order to spread Gandhi's constructive program throughout Karnataka, as were centers to train new volunteers and to coordinate a new upsurge in activity. In 1921, N. S. Hardikar, a Tilakite, established the Hindustani Seva Dal, a volunteer corps that worked in concert with the Congress; the relationship between the Seva Dal and the Congress was cemented when the Seva Dal helped to organize the grounds for the Belgaum meeting. The Karnataka Khilafat Parishat organized Hindu–Muslim cooperation on the demand for Khilafat, while the Bhagini Mandal Parishat set up training for women volunteers in the Congress. The All-India Khadi Board and the Khadi Association were both set up in Belgaum in 1925 and 1926 respectively, and worked to distribute spinning wheels to and collect homespun yarn from villages. Most significantly, though, the Karnataka Non-Brahmin Conference – which had previously abstained from participation in Congress activities, fearing them to be an upper-caste, Brahmin-led outfit – voted in 1930 to join the Congress. So, when the Congress decided to copy the model of the Bardoli Satyagraha in Uttar Kanara at the Dharwar Provincial Congress Committee in 1930, there were substantial organizations and leadership with sufficient training to help launch the project. The towns were more than willing to provide leadership in the rural areas and there was substantial spillover between British India and the prince states:

> By early 1931, preparations for a no-revenue movement had started in some Karnatak districts, while a Fortnightly Report dated December 1930 referred to attempts being made in parts of Maharashtra "to influence the Khots not to pay their revenue by inducing their tenants to withhold their rent." There were some signs also of a spill-over of popular agitation into neighboring princely states. Volunteers from Mysore participated in the Kanara movement, while a powerful no-tax campaign developed in the central Indian state of Chhatarpur in Bundelkhand between October and December, headed, interestingly enough, by a "notorious dacoit, Mangal Singh" who demanded reduction in land revenue and was "said to have visions of carving out a state for himself." On 30 December, a crowd of 20,000, including about a thousand armed with rifles, could be dispersed only by the timely arrival of a military contingent from British India; otherwise they would have "advanced on Chhatarpur and forced the Maharaja to accede to all their demands." (Sarkar 1989, 298–9)

But the experience of the 1930s in Karnataka ran counter to the model of organization, mobilization and cooptation that was the explicit strategy of the Congress in other places. Partly because the no-revenue movement was lead by larger landlords in the villages, and partly because the crackdown on the peasantry was substantial, the Congress had no problem in loosening the reins in Karnataka, actually allowing the protests to continue even after Gandhi had called off the Noncooperation movement nationally. So, when Gandhi ended the Civil Disobedience movement in 1931 (to negotiate with England) and then again in 1933, peasants in Uttar Kanara were not prevented from continuing their campaign against the forestry laws as well as their struggle to defend their properties from seizure by the British for nonpayment of taxes and revenues (one of the forms of civil disobedience called for by the Congress). Because landowners and tenants organized together against the colonial laws, there was no immediate rupture in the alliance between the landed and the landless, the high and the low castes. And the intransigence of the colonial state against the demands of both meant that the Congress was never in a position to face a serious political challenge from the Left. In fact, Karnataka may have been an exceptional instance of the party high command loosening the reins on a provincial committee with respect to following the national diktat.

Certainly, in other places, the Civil Disobedience movement of the 1930s was characterized by a strong, interventionist Congress, which attempted to control the movement of peasants, especially in those places where the renewed peasant militancy threatened to turn its ire on local landlords and moneylenders, many of whom were important backers of the Congress. This dynamic, of co-opting rural energies for nationalist campaigns, has led many to conclude rightly that the Congress attempted to channel rural forces into campaigns that would net them important electoral and bargaining victories, as well as to contain the peasant movements that were beginning to challenge the leadership of the landlords and Brahmins on which the Congress relied in most areas. Co-optation was most pronounced in Uttar Pradesh, where the Congress replaced existing *kisan sabhas,* which had produced their own political demands and leadership, and redirected the fights against local exploitative landlords and moneylenders towards the British. It was also the case that the new rural movements were not developing entirely because of the Congress's efforts, though in some places they played an important part. The effects of the First World War as well the global economic depression of the late 1920s had taken a heavy toll on the Indian peasantry. As the monetization of rural production had forced the peasantry to move away from subsistence production to production for the market and trade based on cash crops, a global economic slowdown threatened their livelihoods. The new, more militant peasantry turned its anger towards the unholy alliance between landlords, moneylenders and the state, whose demands of rents, interest payments and taxes were all becoming impossible to pay. In this context, the Congress's attempts at highlighting the British Raj (as opposed to local exploitation) played an important role in limiting just how far a number of these campaigns could go and how radical their demands could be.

In this sense, nationalism required a cynical and opportunist appropriation of peasant politics and concerns to gain advantages in negotiations with Whitehall. Connections to landlords and reliance on high-caste leadership meant that the Congress stopped short of more radical demands for redistribution of land, reduction, or even abolition of rent payments and an end to usury. This did not mean that the Congress could not net meaningful results for peasants, but it did mean that long-term solutions to peasant problems were held back for fear that they would threaten the march to independence. Gyanendra Pandey's description of the evolution of Congress is insightful:

> By the end of the decade, however, the provincial Congress had done much to bring popular nationalism under control. The party that emerged out of the experience of civil disobedience, widespread election campaigns and ministry formation was far more sophisticated but a great deal more progressive than before. For it developed a more self-conscious conservatism in the form of support for social stability and insistence on measured and "orderly" progress, even as it declaimed ever more radical slogans. One is tempted to say that the "poor man's party," as the new generation of Congress leaders described it in 1920, had become a rich peasants' party by 1940. (2002, 187)

There are two important problems with the generalization of the Uttar Pradesh experience to the rest of India (though it is important to point out that Congress opportunism and co-optation were not limited to the Uttar Pradesh experience). First, it flattens out the distinction between those places where the Congress had to be conservative in order to shore up its own landlord and high-caste base and those places where the Congress provided a meaningful infrastructure for protests and the development of campaigns. Secondly, it assumes that the peasantry had nothing to gain by being nationalist, or, more precisely, that peasant concerns and nationalist ones always moved in opposite directions. There would, of course, ultimately be no coevality of peasant and landlord interests, but it might have been possible for a while for the interests of the landlord (no-tax campaign) and the interests of the peasantry (no-rent campaign) to be expressed simultaneously, changing the character of both. So, while the criticisms of the Congress certainly hold, and there were in all places limits to how radical a project the Congress was willing to endure, it was certainly the case that in some instances Congress activity, even when modest in its scope, was quite radical in the eyes of the local population. Further, it is certainly true that the impoverished, low-caste peasant, faced with British revenue collectors and the police who enforced forestry laws, had genuine grievances against the state, even while his or her grievances against local elites and landlords were also meaningful. In Karnataka, too, where some of the Brahmin landowning classes were willing to sacrifice their own claims to land in support of the nationalist cause and the peasantry, there was the possibility of a solidarity that makes the critique of the Congress's opportunism less self-explanatory. Moreover, the middle-class intellectuals who returned to their villages as part of developing the Civil Disobedience campaign clearly did so in the hope of changing the social relations in their homes, not of entrenching old ones. The Congress's attempts at disciplining this class would have proved difficult indeed, not only because it would have been difficult to convince newly politicized students (the base of new membership in the Congress) that their job was to hold back peasant struggles, but also because many saw the politicizing of their families as a necessary part of modernizing them.

The no-tax and no-revenue campaigns that the Congress initiated were by no means confined to obscure taluks in Uttar Kanara. The movement for withholding taxes was both regionally contagious and had a distinct national coordination, but the driving force was not merely the economic demands of the peasantry. The Congress was responding to some new political realities as well. As Nehru would comment: "The cities and the middle classes were a bit tired of the hartals and processions," but "a fresh infusion of blood" could still come "from the peasantry," where "the reserve stocks were enormous." (1989) These two political realities – a looser control over the campaign from the top and new rural energies being released from below – produced a dynamic in which opportunities for a more elaborate and complicated network of grassroots organizing could be realized. If, in the end, the peasantry were needed to recharge the Congress's political battery, then the tendency would be toward more experimental forms of political expression.

One of the consequences of this political experimentation was a greater role for women in challenging the official decision-making process in the Congress. In 1930, Kamaladevi Chattopadhyay was part of the leadership of Gandhi's Salt Satyagraha. She not only organized a number of events along the route but was also responsible for organizing and leading the spectacular raid on the salt processing facilities in Dandi. Perhaps her most important contribution, though, was an argument with Gandhi over the inclusion of women in the march. The original composition of the march was 71 people, none of whom were women. A number of nationalist women protested Gandhi's decision:

Margaret Cousins, for one, excoriated against it in an article in *Stridharma*. While Gandhi had initially opposed the presence of women, arguing that, as the British would never hurt women, it would be cowardly for the movement to hide behind them, Kamaladevi argued that women had a right to participate in the nationalist struggle. Many credit her intervention into Gandhi's organizing efforts for creating a space for women to participate publicly in the satyagraha and for forcing the Mahatma to publish an official letter asking women to come out into the streets (Narasimhan 1999).[5] The letter was then used to convince the provincial committee, which had been even more recalcitrant than Gandhi on the question. She was in fact later arrested and jailed for her part in the organizing of the march (Thapar-Bjokert 1988). In 1932, as part of a Seva Dal camp in Borivli, Chattopadhyay was arrested when the police raided the camp. She was taken first to Arthur Road jail (which had newly been constructed to house overflow arrestees from Civil Disobedience actions) but was then transferred to Hindalga jail in Belgaum after she was suspected of inciting the inmates in Bombay to revolt against their jailers and protest the terrible conditions in the jail (Brijbhushan 1976, 70–97). Her long tenure at Hindalga brought her into contact with women, mostly from Sirsri-Siddhapur and Ankola in Uttar Kanara, who had begun to participate in Civil Disobedience in protest of the new tax increases and the more restrictive enforcement of forestry laws, which prevented peasants from taking timber and using it for their own purposes. Large-scale arrests had followed Civil Disobedience, some of which were coordinated with the local Congress leadership and had now filled the cells in Belgaum. As a result, Kamaladevi had occasion to meet "women from the remote corners of Karnataka […] the poorest women I had occasion to live in close contact with and get glimpses of their everyday life of want and hunger" (Chattopadhyay 1986, 174).

Her descriptions of the experience and her interviews are some of the only accounts that we have in English of the experience of the women of Uttar Kanara. As Kamaladevi recorded, "In 1932 this movement became a full scale No Tax Satyagraha and an integral part of the national political struggle drawing in participants from other sectors, especially the arecanut plantation workers, classed as among the most backward and poorest. It was reminiscent of Bardoli Satyagraha and though the Karnataka epic remains little known, nevertheless it was wide spread, involving thousands from all social and economic levels, the leadership however staying with agriculturists" (Chattopadhyay 1986, 176). Significantly, for Kamaladevi, the campaign in Karnataka had a mass character and a local leadership, distinguishing it from the Bardoli campaign. Kamaladevi also noticed that the Congress was in many ways the late-comer to the scene of peasant organizing in the region:

> Uttar Kannada [Kanara] district of Karnataka had a long history of Satyagraha, even before Gandhiji's arrival on the scene. Unlike my own district of Dakshina Kannada, it was a predominantly agricultural and forest area, with a large poor, landless population, many living mainly on forest produce, grazing the cattle they tried to breed. Their demands had been for cultivable land, improved breed of cattle, adequate grazing area, remission of grazing fees and the like. From 1904 sporadic agitations had been going on. Early in 1914 a Vana Dukha Navrana Sabha (forest relief committee) was set up for

better-organized action. The workers were politically moved by every freedom breeze. Thus when Gandhiji launched his Civil Disobedience, every programme he advocated found an echo here, each adding a new vigour to face the resulting tribulations. (Chattopadhyay 1986, 176)

Kamaladevi is, of course, retroactively writing the Karnataka epic seamlessly into the nationalist narrative ("moved by every freedom breeze" and "every programme he advocated found an echo here"). Her memoirs would be published well into the decline of the Nehruvian dream, perhaps as a kind of ideological buttress for a nationalism already facing significant critique. But the rest of her narrative is important in its taking stock of the range of peasant activity and organization that had occurred independently of the Congress. Guha and Gadgil confirm the narrative that Kamaladevi provides (Guha and Gadgil 1989).[6] Still, Kamaladevi's record, here, differs in many ways from the pattern that developed in the literature of the period, usually by upper-caste men, in which the only political impulse that a village feels has to be brought to it from without. In Kamaladevi's account, the organizing is initially spontaneous, indigenous and feminist.

Later in the same narrative, though, Kamaladevi backslides into the notion that political consciousness is not something that the women of Uttar Kanara possess, at least not without a Gandhian vocabulary into which their experiences have to be translated:

> How and why were these women here? I was overpowered by a million questions struggling to spill out of me. Quietly over the long evenings they told me stories. Since Gandhiji's call reached them, they had become aware of their own inadequacies, that they did not live as humans, in dignity, in self-respect. Their concept of what they wanted was not just mere food, better houses, proper clothes, etc. Yes, they needed these but it was more than that, they explained. They wanted freedom, not only for them, but all who were today in bondage like themselves. As the great leader had called upon every one of them to get free they must refuse to be in bondage. The heavy dues they were called upon to pay now seemed to them like the wages of slavery. They worked hard, they did not shirk from work but were not treated as humans. They repeated in a kind of anguish: "No one should be in bondage." Now they felt they were free for did they not prefer going to jail rather than be content to be slaves? "Had they seen the Mahatma?" I asked. No, but they brushed that aside – never mind – his call had reached them. It needed much more *punya* (merit) to have his Darshan. He too was in prison to bring freedom for all. He too suffered like them, did not only ask others to suffer. He was a true leader – "Were you not afraid of the consequences when you broke the law?" I asked. Came an emphatic reply: "No! We understand now that it is fear that makes us slaves. Our life circle was set that way from the moment of our birth. Our dharma, we were made to believe, was to drudge and live on the leavings. The Mahatma has made us free so we are not afraid. His care for us gives us respect. We are asked to serve, not slave." (Chattopadhyay 1986, 175)

The women of Uttar Kanara demanded not just bread but roses, too. Gandhi provided for them (in Kamaladevi's narrative) a vocabulary ("dignity," "self-respect," "freedom") through which to articulate their new political aspirations. There is, of course, a limit to how much Kamaladevi is willing to see, but despite herself, what emerges is a narrative not of Congress-led politics but of peasant women rewriting their own stories on top of other discourses. Never having met Gandhi, they feel free to interpret the Mahatma's political call for themselves; while still believing in religious restrictions, they now feel free to rewrite or reinterpret their own destinies. And even though the aphorism is most likely Kamaladevi's ("We are asked to serve, not slave"), the sentiment reflects in some ways the joint enthusiasm of the peasant woman and the middle-class intellectual for an emancipated class of peasant women.

On to this demand of emancipation, of course, Kamaladevi grafts her own set of notions for what genuine liberation would and should look like:

> My prison mates hailing from there were an eye opener to me. Their description of their life made my hair stand on end. A full meal was a rare luxury, they simply had to make do with what they could get. They covered their bodies with pieces of cloth. On a rare occasion like a marriage they got a full sari. Their horizon seemed non-existent. Did they ever dream of a different life? The question held no meaning. According to them for generations it had been so. There were no schools in their region, whereas I was used to at least one school in every village. Illiteracy was unknown to us. Their life was a far cry from what I had been familiar with. (Chattopadhyay 1986, 175)

The country woman is turned into a countrywoman by way of her embourgeoisement: educated, well-fed and clothed, the peasant woman now has the opportunity to "dream of a different life." There is some degree of arrogance to the notion that what the peasant secretly wants is to be like you, but this is because Kamaladevi only has a unidirectional notion of progress, even while there is no reason to suspect that she would not be open to others: "Such intimate communication was largely facilitated through my familiarity with their language, Kannada. But it had limitations. Their words and phrases sketched but the outline. The intensity of their passion and the depth of their sincerity which was the core and had stirred my inmost being seemed to elude my vocabulary to give appropriate shape to it in concrete phrases" (Chattopadhyay 1986, 175).

Kamaladevi cannot see anything but the reflexive economic and nationalist logic at work in the women's actions, as their political involvement in the campaign is not a signal of their conscious intervention but of their natures: "It was [impossible] in this context for the women not to jump into the fray, especially as each day a new repressive measure was unleashed. Household goods, movable property, apart from land, cattle were seized and sought to be auctioned in lieu of the tax that was withheld. Household goods were being ripped apart looking for hidden gold. In addition auctions had now to be picketed and frustrated. The women naturally became deeply involved. The slogan went: Each day brings a new hour of trial and every trial an ever new symbol of national force." At the same time, though, the heroism that the women manifest clearly strikes a chord with Kamaladevi: "At first they had a dreaded thought they would all be molested by the police. How could they survive such shame? A few knowledgeable women were not daunted. They stoutly scorned such fears which they affirmed arose from the age old superstition that women were weak." As her interview continues, Kamaladevi recounts the extensive and elaborate organizational network that the women developed: "In the forefront were Gauramma, Venkataramiah's wife, with a frail pale frame and Mahadevitai, even younger, hailing from a rich landed gentry. Eagerly a hundred women entered the arena. They did a million jobs as it were. They took long solitary journeys through the hoary forests, carrying messages, doing propaganda to rouse women in other villages, organized 'Prabhat Pheris,' pre-dawn singing processions, calling out women to action. The whole atmosphere became surcharged and all life in the region seemed to become enveloped in a conflagration." It is this self-activity, even when it is only rendered as nationalist campaigning, that draws out the enthusiasm of the middle-class nationalist, not because it stays within the ambit of the party high command ("enveloped in a conflagration") but because it turns the peasant woman into something that the urban intellectual can easily understand and empathize with (Chattopadhyay 1986, 177).

The standard critique of the nationalist mobilization of women is to emphasize its cynicism. As David Arnold argues, "Indeed rather than advancing the women's movement in the 1920s and 1930s, Gandhi seemed intent on imposing on women a new regime of moral obligations and social constraints. In particular he appealed to middle-class women to give up their finery, foreign cloth and jewellery and to spin and wear khadi instead. [...] Women's primary role was to manage the domestic environment, to be the 'queens of households,' and nurture swadeshi in the home. Except as servants of the nation they were not encouraged to venture much beyond the home" (Arnold 2001a, 190). As a critique of Gandhian politics and the view of the inner logic of the Congress, there is little here with which to find issue. What is astonishing, though, is how little resemblance such a controlled release of women into the public sphere has with Kamaladevi's own view of the women who are inspired by nationalist agitation; Kamaladevi's emphasis is not on the Gandhian dam but on the feminist current. It was not just a historical reality that women were entering into political activity in much more substantial numbers as part of the movement for Indian independence, it was also the case that it threw into relief a number of questions that the Indian middle class needed answered. On the one hand, the new belief in the confidence of women as important political agents meant confronting those women who were not in fact becoming more independent, freeing themselves of conservative ideas and the lot. In some ways the movement for Indian independence gave cover to changes already in the works in smaller, but important, ways in the villages and allowed women to challenge authority and come out into the streets under Gandhian banners. At the same time, the religious ideas under which women were becoming active might have been a problem for some of the more cosmopolitan middle class who needed to find more uniform strategies to characterize the development of their women. But the lack of progress of Indian women was not only a dominant theme in the case for continued British occupation, it was also becoming a persistent problem for the nationalist middle class, which needed to believe that it could offer up its own superior solutions to the problems in the villages.

Kanthapura and the Politics of Postindependence Communalism

The dangers inherent in the romanticization of religious language has preoccupied most critics of *Kanthapura*, where an affinity to Gandhian ideas is seen as an endorsement of religious partisanship in the postindependence communal antagonism between Hindus and Muslims. The main problem, critics argue, is that Rao's fiction is still seen as more or less aligned with Gandhian ideologies – especially Gandhi's views of utopian villages and a reformist, democratic Hinduism – with the result that his fiction is seen as the aesthetic arm of an ascendant bourgeois nationalism that would take the reins of the state after independence. Instead of looking for the places where the aesthetic project might run up against certain still raw, nationalist impulses, the trend in studies of Rao's fiction is to see it as a mirror of a religious nationalism of the Gandhian model. As one critic succinctly put it: "*Kanthapura* is a Gandhian novel. This is attested by its date of publication (1938), by the constant references to the Mahatma and by the very philosophy it sets out as an example" (Pousse 1989, 30). For those allied to nationalist historiography, such a relationship necessarily means seeing in *Kanthapura* the triumph of a pattern of values and politics operating under the sign of Gandhi and not a much more complicated set of interactions between ideologies that both despise and idealize the Indian peasant.

Rumina Sethi's *Myths of the Nation*, the only book-length study of Raja Rao's *Kanthapura*, takes this proposition as its central premise. Looking at the history of peasant struggles from the nineteenth and twentieth centuries, Sethi concludes: "Despite all the ambiguities and confusions, and the manoeuvres of the leadership, nationalist sentiment itself formed a very small part of peasant struggles, although it may be admitted that the national movement certainly provided an environment germane to the cause of the peasants" (1999, 115). In other places, her criticism is more scathing:

> But for those peasants, like Rao's, who had little to worry about, the need to join the national movement seems exaggerated. It is in cases such as these that we witness a contestation between fiction and history: the struggle to "get rid of the Redman" is motivated only by a pure appeal of nationalism dictated by religion, enabling the author to present an ageless and static, depoliticized Indian peasantry which nationalist intellectuals would find attractive – a peasantry that is not threatening in any way, that is not class conscious, but one that homogeneously embodies ancient ideals of duty, commitment, and sacrifice [...]. As a member of the nationalist intelligentsia, he is interested in depicting the peasants as having simple and romantic ideas of politics. Assisted further by using Gandhi as a deity, he marginalizes Gandhi's role in redressing peasant grievances, and confines it within the limits of divine grace, thereby keeping alive the iconography of a saintly agent whose presence and teaching would appear to be the only means of stirring the passivity of the population. (2003, 84)

The Congress, in this view, turned towards the peasantry cynically, molding their concerns to a more narrow, nationalist project, thereby running roughshod over the genuine, independent demands that might have arisen had the peasantry been allowed to lead its own struggles. Others, like Anshuman Mondal, find a variety of ideological positions available in *Kanthapura* (Socialist, Nehruvian, modernist, religious) but eventually see all of them subordinated to an "implicit and overdetermining Brahminical supremacism" (Mondal 2002, 932). And the consequences are to see the novel as complicit in leaving unchallenged the communalist attitudes again linked to Gandhi:

> Famously, in 1926, when his second son Manilal fell in love with a Muslim girl in South Africa, Gandhi refused to sanction any possibility of marriage. His argument is revealing, "Your marriage will have a powerful impact on the Hindu-Muslim question. Intercommunal marriages are no solution to this problem." We can note the adjacency of Gandhi's thought here to received notions of legitimate communal identities within the composite nation. It is unsurprising, therefore, to find this anxiety over intercommunal "contamination" reproduced in Rao's novel where the most graphic and horrifying act of violence centres on the rape of a Brahmin woman by a Muslim policeman. In the dark months of Partition, thousands of women would physically experience this paradigmatic act of communal violence. (Mondal 2002, 935–6)

The list of scholars who see *Kanthapura* as participating in reproducing the problems of Gandhian nationalism is in fact quite extensive.[7]

These patterns of reading Rao's fiction are descendants of the two main schools of historiography of Indian nationalism. Scholarship over the last twenty years has tended to see the nationalist deployment of traditional or religious idioms in one of two ways (though ultimately, these share certain key features). The first is to see in this move the triumphalism of Congress-led nationalism. Gandhi's genius, so this line of thought contends, was to find a way to use traditional patterns of religious belief in the service of making a certain bundle of nationalist ideas – opposition to British economic control over India, the idealization of village democracy as a model for national governance and mass political participation – available to the peasantry and the masses of Indians more generally. The second is to see in this idiom of nationalism a kind of naïve opportunism that more or less paved the way for more dangerous emotional energies that displayed their initial symptoms in the bloody rioting that erupted during and after the partition of the subcontinent, but which has since become a pattern of communal violence. As a result, attempts to think about the ways that nationalism and religion might have developed their respective ideologies in mutually constitutive and potentially progressive ways are normally short-circuited by the evidence of the late twentieth century: religion and nationalism produce a dangerous combination that leaves the nation incapable of dealing with communal extremism.

Common to both views, then, is the idea that religion was to be preserved through nationalism. The new mutually constitutive narratives of religious belief and nationalist mobilization worked in tandem to produce a set of ideas for an independent India, which produced either a pattern of secular democracy or of intolerant communalism, but was an irreversible process either way. But also common to both views is that Gandhian nationalism only moved in the direction of the nation-state, so that the intelligentsia's relationship to the peasantry could only be mischievous at best and predatory at worst. Ranajit Guha's critique of those who overlook peasant interpretations of their own political activity is important in this respect: "Unable to grasp religiosity as the central modality of peasant consciousness in colonial India, [Suprakash Ray] is shy to acknowledge its mediation of the peasant's idea of power and all the resultant contradictions. He is obliged therefore to rationalize the ambiguities of rebel politics by assigning a worldly consciousness to the leaders and an otherworldly one to their followers making of the latter innocent dupes of crafty men armed with all the tricks of a modern Indian politician out to solicit rural votes" (Guha 1988, 81). Subaltern studies has gone far in the direction of preserving the emotional and intellectual worldview of the peasant in this ideological transaction, whereby the peasant is able to carve out a space for political action and will that generates results that the nationalist could not have foreseen. The problem, though, is doubled when you have a class of intellectuals who were also attempting to move the peasantry into politics that were more radical than those imagined by official nationalism. In the readings that suggest either religiously orthodox or statist ends for nationalist politics, the affective energies that drew the middle-class nationalist to the peasant (the early twentieth-century homolog of the Subaltern Studies collective) are necessarily occluded.

The problem with such a view is not only its tendentiousness but also its inaccuracy. As late as April of 1948, Rao was still unconvinced of the intellectual and political direction of India. He and Iqbal Singh edited a collection of essays arguing that the trajectory of the nation was still as of yet undetermined and that the nation was in some danger of an anti-intellectualist mood with respect to the project of nation building. The introduction, while attempting not to sound alarmist, points to the pathology: "We are today passing through a phase of extreme intellectual confusion and disorder. Such confusion is inevitable after a prolonged period of political struggle; but while there is no need to take it too tragically, it would be the height of complacency to refuse to acknowledge that it exists. Symptoms of acute disorientation are discernible even at the highest level of leadership – and that at a time when the critical situation in the country demands the greatest lucidity of thought and purpose" (Singh and Rao 1984, vii). The problem is that the political mobilizations of the struggle for Indian independence had utilized a number of philosophical and theoretical terms in a derivative and sloppy way.[8] The theoretical apparatus of the nation relied overmuch on emotional output and not enough on finding an appropriate intellectual idiom to account for the specific features of the Indian condition, the consequence being a hollow Indian nation:

> As a people we have a reputation for being somewhat excessively preoccupied with theoretical and abstract problems; yet in the sphere of political we have tended to neglect all theoretical discussion and have failed to define general principles. This explains the distressingly ambiguous anatomy of most of our political movements and it leads in practice to some strange paradoxes. It is often difficult, for instance, to find a nationalist who can give a precise definition of his nationalism, a liberal who can explain his credo in terms which are not an insipid paraphrase of Mill and Bentham, a supporter of the Muslim League who can provide a coherent idea of the doctrinal implications of Pakistan, or even a revolutionary who can propound the dynamic logic of the *Communist Manifesto* except in borrowed phrases. Indian political movements appear for the most part to live on emotions rather than thought, heart rather than the head. The result is

a general intellectual mendicancy, an inanition of political thought. If this tendency continues unchecked there is some danger that, far from being a nation of philosophers, we may well become a nation of insufferable philistines. (Singh and Rao 1984, viii)

This is, interestingly enough, an underdeveloped counterexplanation for the derivativeness of nationalism, as it sees intellectual production in India as eventually being capable of overcoming its reliance on the West (and its bad paraphrases of Western idioms) and not being invariably trapped in the ceaseless repetition of European political thought. But what is also of interest here is that the genuine anxiety that there was much fuzziness to nationalist, liberal and revolutionary thinking, and that – far from being consolidated and confident ideologies – these were markers of political activity and expressions of political sentiment rather than articulations of developed political thought. Even if there were confident expressions of some aspects of political thought in India – and these are what the anthology attempts to group together – these were not understood except as caricatures by the cadre of political movements that fed the stream of nationalism.

For Rao and Singh, nationalism may have succeeded in producing a nation-state but it had not achieved a national program:

> There are points which seem to be common to Gandhism and Marxism: both, for example, are activist in their implications. Nevertheless, it would be a mistake to infer from this the possibility of their eventual reconciliation. They are two divergent world-views and as such do not admit of reconciliation. Ultimately, the choice for India in [the] field of political philosophy reduces itself to a choice between those two categorical alternatives. What would be her choice? It would be hazardous to enter the province of prophecy, but it may be pointed out that the assumption usually made by so many political writers in India, that the present dominance enjoyed by the Gandhian ideology is a constant of the Indian political situation, is not warranted by any rational considerations. Indeed, the lesson of history would be just the reverse. (Singh and Rao 1984, x)

For Rao and Singh, Gandhian political futures were not a foregone conclusion. At a minimum they were interested in investigating alternative political outcomes; at a maximum, they suggested that Gandhian politics were doomed, historically.

But beyond the larger trajectory of Rao's intellectual development remains the stubborn problem of accurately recording the intellectual inheritances of Rao's fiction. *Kanthapura* is a case in point. The suite of politics represented by the narrative arc of the novel are selected from a series of political thinkers and movements extant in India: Gandhian *sarvodaya* finds its representation in the swadeshi, untouchable reform and *panchayati raj* movements in the village; Kamaladevi Chattopadhyay's Socialist feminism characterizes Ratna's challenge to the sexist conventions of the village and Rangamma's Socialist sensibilities; the uses of yoga for political self-realization follow the same lines as those marked by Vivekananda; the view of the economic drain of Indian resources is taken from Dadabhai Naoroji; the hope for a secular future is troped as a turn toward Nehru and the Congress Socialists; the utopian promise of Socialism early on in the novel is Leninist and Russian. The figures that are explicitly and implicitly named in the novel mark both intellectuals who worked within and those who split from the Congress. The problem with reducing these to Gandhian nationalism depends on a reading of the Congress's activities in the 1930s and 1940s as characterized primarily by agreement rather than debate, and it falls to the critic to disentangle those ideological maneuvers in the novel that imagine themselves to be allied to Gandhi and those for which the alliance is clearly fanciful. At best, Gandhi is the screen onto which ideological fantasies about nationalism can be projected; at worst, the reference to Gandhi occludes a more substantial debate that is taking place within the novel's development and the unsettled enthusiasm with which the novel concludes.

Democracy and Authenticity

Kanthapura achieves its imagined national unity by reference to religious forms, but at the same time it corrupts and renders those forms more democratic. Or to put it differently, *Kanthapura* repeats the relationship of politics and religion that Gandhi had already inaugurated without reproducing Gandhian conclusions. Some, like Hemenway, have argued that, by leaving the characters "generally undifferentiated, undeveloped, rather uninteresting," and by highlighting how "it took thousands of anonymous Satyagrahis" in the movement for national independence, Rao "is consciously instilling a feeling of nationhood in essentially disparate peoples" (1975, 85). But this seems to dilute overmuch the local and rural details of the novel into an amorphous national whole; Rao's procedure is a little more nuanced and mediated. Gandhi had already made it possible to look at religious imagery in a much more mercenary way and to arrive at independent understandings of religious texts and traditions, thereby undermining Brahminical authority and prerogative as the guardians of religiosity. Rao seems to continue this pattern of interpretive and individual uses of religion and a newly intense engagement with exegetical practice by severing forms and terms from their traditions and yoking them to a secular, modern project. Rao also borrows from the techniques of European modernism a use of the past as myth and as form, which allows him to create an emotional buttress for completely different content. After all, if the harikathas and the religious discourses in the novel are designed to make its readers cry, the ending of the novel induces not tears but an intensified sense of the coming changes ("my heart, it beat like a drum"). It replaces this formal religious unity with unity in action.

By converting religion into a style or a marker of authenticity (as opposed to an ideological worldview endorsed by established institutions), the novel also opens up another contradiction: the very form that the novel needs to move the peasantry is undermined by the secularization of those forms. Peasants could be moved by harikathas, but once those harikathas were translated into novels, there was no way for them to be moving. There is an ideological sleight of hand at work here. The middle class can use secular or fabular village storytelling in a way that it has no need for the harikatha, which it used only tactically and, perhaps, cynically. It was part of creating what Mukul Kesavan has called a "portable culture" (Kesavan 2001).[9] By the time the nationalist movement is in its heyday, the Indian classical tradition was a composite invention, for there was no organic or natural connection between the cultural output of Indian antiquity, its purportedly Muslim middle ages and its new nationalist forms. But this was also contested, especially since the Muslim cultural contributions were deemed important by some and decadent by others. This has become something of a truism, but it is perhaps important to return to, especially as it helps readers of the development of this tradition understand the political, ideological, cultural and psychological investments that such inventions were both products and productive of. All the more so, if one wants to suggest, as this essay does, that the forms of imagining a shared cultural past did not necessarily mean an endorsement of majoritarian national narratives, an insensitivity towards the interests and histories of minorities, or the reproduction of subconsciously conservative worldviews. Tradition and cultural forms were being marshaled in the service of a number of different ideological positions – and in an India searching for the idiom of its own independence, the past became an exceptionally contentious battleground. Solidarity requires an idiom of unity, the terms of which are shaped by the received cultural heritage of the dominant groups, but the very imagination of that unity necessarily revises the original terms of the heritage, especially since the heritage does not produce spontaneous sympathy or political coalition. Each return to the past was, perhaps, out to establish a different view of the present and aspirations for the future, and was a response to differing perceptions of contemporary anxieties for which certain interpretations of the past were seen as potentially remedial and curative.

Rao's novel finds itself straddling two uneasy realities. On the one hand, it has inherited a belief in the inability and unwillingness of the peasantry to spontaneously modernize and the subsequent sociology of the peasant produced by the middle class: the peasantry is superstitious, conservative and parochial. This is clearly a problem for a middle class that wants to believe its nationalism is in the interest of the exploited peasantry and needs to see itself reflected in the enthusiastic support of its peasant ancestry. On the other hand, Rao has also inherited an uneasy relationship with tradition. If tradition and an idealized Indian past are necessary components for a nationalism that can voice its distinction from British modernity, then tradition also represents the very conservative and orthodox religious views against which nationalists are rebelling. So it turns towards formal solutions: religion and tradition are turned into styles and techniques rather than emotional architectures. In this way religion and tradition are preserved as markers of authenticity. This has the effect of democratizing the forms of religion and tradition and introducing secular, modern content into otherwise generically conservative structures.

But even his allies had a hard time swallowing Gandhi's views on religion. In the aftermath of the earthquake in Bihar, Tagore excoriated against Gandhi's view that the natural disaster was God's vengeance against Hindus for refusing to abolish untouchability (Bhattacharya 1997). Nehru found it utterly frustrating to contend with the Mahatma's personal view of religion, which relied on an "internal voice" that directed his political and personal decisions (Brown 2003). At the same time, the leading secular forces in the Congress treated Gandhi's view gingerly, as the Mahatma had clearly proven that deploying a religious idiom for political ends could net meaningful successes, even when the religious idiom merely translated political grievances into divinely sanctioned resistance (Sarkar 1989). The Congress, then, was an uneasy alliance between the forces of secular modernization and religious reform that engaged in a temporary coalition for national liberation. On the other hand, this fantasy also has at its core a much more radical project, namely the full secularization of peasant consciousness and the transformation of peasants into countrymen. This is not subconscious; it is actually a requirement of the first, elitist fantasy, that it embrace a more democratic outcome. It is the failure of the middle class to see its own spontaneously democratic impulses reflected in the peasantry that prompts it to accept an intellectual leadership whose authority it already suspects.

The original political impulse, though, sets the ideological contradiction – the fantasy is not national but individual and aggregate: that there can be a spontaneous, wide-scale, voluntary abrogation of Brahminical prerogatives. When this liberal, individualist self-projection meets with an immediate backlash as caste hierarchies are upheld, defended and reified by those religious forces in Rao's vision who are allied with empire, this allows the terrain to shift to reappropriation of the cultural past rather than a radical disengagement with it, since the audience for the change lies between an already secular, progressive worldview and the conservative apologists for empire, both of whom are vying for leadership of the peasantry. And this sets up the neat binary that was the intellectuals' version of nationalism: humanist, nationalist modernizers on one side; religious, conservative loyalists on the other.

The postcolonial reading of such a situation was to see in this, correctly, a false opposition; the modernist and the conservative could describe the same social outcomes, even if they claimed seemingly opposed worldviews. But such a reading fails to understand that the modernists were also a coalition of forces, from the Left and the Right, who could collaborate in their opposition to Brahminical authority (up to a point) and British imperialism, but who would dissipate upon independence. To lump the modernists together in this way makes it impossible to differentiate Nehru, Tata and Bhagat Singh, to create an artificially polemical example. It also allows postcolonial critiques to make a rather intellectually reductive move by which the consolidation of the repressive nation-state becomes the inevitable outcome of any anticolonial gesture rather than arriving at the contingency of that future. But more importantly, it gets the contradiction wrong, or more precisely mistakes the leadership for the coalition, and misses the participation of a small coterie of novelists in debates with the ruling ideologues in the Congress over the kind of future that would have been necessary for a successfully radical India. This is all the more complicated by the fact that the novelists were, for the most part, vague in their opposition and fuzzy in their proposals. The flexibility of the Congress's idioms and the intransigency of the British meant that the pressure was always focused on producing a critique of empire rather than on producing a critique of certain national liberation strategies, and so in many ways the emergent possibilities were often too nascent to be distinguishable.

But even still, the aesthetic and political project of *Kanthapura* bears little relationship to any variant of Gandhian nationalism. The village is destroyed, the peasants turn to violence, the women leave their homes and the central goddess is left without any worshippers. Rao's turn to Gandhi marks an important sense that something more was needed than intellectual discomfort with superstition, conservatism and obedience, which characterized the intellectual view of the villages (as opposed to the idealized village republics of the Gandhian variety) (Gandhi 1997). Gandhi, here, allowed the intellectuals to see the beginnings of a process of change that could reorganize the social patterns of Indian society, even as the terrain was not wholly compatible with the future they imagined. Importantly, Gandhi represented the first steps towards the evisceration of Brahminical hierarchy and challenges to empire simultaneously, even as Gandhi himself compromised repeatedly with both. And the terminus of this transformative impulse would be found, it was hoped, far beyond the reach of Gandhian prescriptions, perhaps even as anathema to them.

There is also a gendered component to the strategy, which sees the self-emancipation of women as part of the project, even when it is walled in by a kind of elitism that sees itself as benevolent in comparison to existing chauvinisms. On the one hand, this novel is part of the trend in South Asian fiction that saw intolerable sexism in the home and began to blame women for their lack of opposition to it; while on the other hand, it intersects with a competing intellectual trend that saw the role of fiction in educating women out of their inferiority. Both views shared an important elitist belief in the inability of women to create the conditions for their own emancipation, but the intersection of these ideas in the novel means that ideas of women's consciousness and their struggles are actually at odds and new forms are needed to find ways of describing the entry of women into the political sphere. That this comes on the heels of Gandhi's campaigns to encourage women to lead and participate in Civil Disobedience, as well as the conscious construction of women's organizations as formal parts of the Congress apparatus as a way to counterbalance the growing number of minorities represented by reservations in the central government that were allied against the Congress, means that even the entry of women into politics was not fraught with pressure from below and containment from above. As a result, the novel necessarily toggles between the docile stereotype of women (who incidentally needed the religious imprimatur before entering into the political fray) and the heroic stereotype of the nationalist woman (who would find themselves consciously reflected in the iconography of the goddesses in the Hindu pantheon). In fact, the patronizing attitude towards women in the novel is a result of the naïve theory of social change that lies at the heart of this nationalism, namely that Western-educated radicals were necessary to bring Gandhi's ideas back to their villages, because they were committed to the kind of social change that Gandhi could only preach about. While, on the other hand, alongside these patronizing ideas there exists another set of ideas about the self-conscious participation of women in acts of political heroism independently from men. Even at the symbolic level, ideas of women would have to change in order to accommodate the mobilizing needs of nationalism.

These patronizing and paternalistic attitudes receive more weight after independence precisely because the social transformation did not happen along the expected lines. Socialism remained a distant horizon, sexism persisted and religion remained conservative. But these were all contingent outcomes to the nationalist project, and part of the reason that *Kanthapura* settles for rearguard aesthetic decisions about authenticity is because Rao understands that very contingency: the confident expressions of a democratic future happen alongside the frustration of the democratic process. The alignment of the novel with the forces of statist reaction after independence is tied to the fact that the novel contains traces of both promise and impossibility in its text.

Chapter 4

THE MISSING MAHATMA: AHMED ALI AND THE AESTHETICS OF MUSLIM ANTICOLONIALISM

Nationalist Politics and Delhi

By 1940, when Ahmed Ali's *Twilight in Delhi* was published, it would have been increasingly difficult, though not impossible, to be a Muslim and a nationalist in the United Provinces. A few important figures had managed to navigate the problem of communal loyalties: Shibli Numani, Abul Kalam Azad and the Ali brothers had all publicly defended and made alliances with the Indian National Congress (Lelyveld 2004). In 1941, Jamaat-e-Ulema-e-Hind (later Jamaat-e-Islami), a relatively powerful collective of Muslim *ulama* from North India, would also come out in defense of an undivided India in opposition to Jinnah and the Muslim League and their "two nation theory" (Sarkar 1989). Furthermore, the Congress paid lip service to the idea of speaking for all of India by raising the slogan that Muslims were welcome under its large tent (Jalal 2001). Still, the contradiction between a Muslim identity and a nationalist one would have been palpable. Muslims appeared to give up longstanding internal debates and fall into rank behind the Muslim League by the 1942 elections, while the Muslims in the Congress were more and more seen as Muslims in name only, and were thoroughly critiqued for their heterodoxies. Leading Muslims in the Congress were devout, but the larger chunk of the Muslim membership would have been composed of secular, Western-educated, professional and left-leaning individuals. The Communist Party, when it entered into the Congress, brought with it thousands of young, secularized Muslims who were hostile to religiosity and saw only the trappings of orthodoxy in it. The cumulative effect of these processes was to make Congress nationalism appear to be anathema to an authentically Islamic identity (Pandey 2002).

This division posed certain problems for Muslims who were either guardedly optimistic about the promise of a secular modernity or who still had hopes for convincing the vast majority of Muslims that British rule was to be resisted and that making peace with colonialism was not an option, even if Congress nationalism was undesirable. There was no shortage of reform movements in South Asian Islam; in fact, the late nineteenth century and early twentieth century in colonial India saw a growth of movements for religious reformation and revitalization, which brought the question of Islam's relationship to colonial modernity to the fore of public debate. But few of these movements were moving in the direction of anticolonial politics, while more orthodox elements in Islam seemed to shun politics altogether in favor of political quietism. Part of the problem, of course, was the identification of anticolonial and nationalist politics with the Congress, especially since the Congress was making the project of winning Muslims over into its ranks difficult. First, the opportunistic use of Hinduism in order to win over large swathes of the peasantry and to generate alliances with Hindu reform organizations began to produce political effects that the leadership most likely did not endorse, though they did little to stop them. Communal rioting in the 1920s and 1930s, as well as the mobilization of Congress cadres on the basis of religious slogans and politics (like the defense of cows against slaughter), were beginning to convince Muslims that there would be no home for them in the Indian nation and that a country dominated by Hindus would necessarily trample all over the religious beliefs and pieties – not to mention political rights – of the Muslim minority. More to the point, the disastrous negotiations at both Round Table Conferences seemed to put the Congress squarely against representational protections for Muslims and give credence to Jinnah's argument that the Congress was a chauvinist, Hindu outfit. Despite the fact that Gandhi and other leading members of the Congress had campaigned against communal violence and sought to limit what they called "fratricidal politics," their commitment to unity at all costs prevented them from limiting mobilizations that sought to use religious themes to activate large masses of Hindus under the banner of nationalist unity (Arnold 2001a).

Even if the threat of covert Hindu politics was not enough to make Muslims weary, the alternative was a thoroughly secular set of politics that were hostile to Islam in a different way. The alternative to Gandhi and Madan Mohan Malaviya of the Hindu Mahasabha, of course, was Jawaharlal Nehru and his Congress Socialists, and for much of the secular Muslim intelligentsia – and the Progressive Writers' Association – it was this wing that was ideologically attractive. The secularists shared certain politics – a belief in uplift for women and minorities, a program of social distribution of wealth and land, a narrative of the syncretic past of India, a rejection of religion in favor secular modernity and a confidence in economic development to solve social inequalities – which made them an ideal fit for Muslim intellectuals who were already breaking away from religious ideas and embracing democracy and Socialism. It also had the benefit of offering intellectuals a strategy for social transformation since it connected them directly to the Congress's mass mobilizations and the party's ability to inspire large chunks of the population. The problem, though, was that the more one was excited by the Congress, the less likely one was able to draw out Muslims into the mass protests and the nationalist agitations. Troublingly for some Muslims, the very politics that attracted the ex-Muslim intellectuals were the very ones that they feared, since those politics often meant abandoning tradition entirely in favor of modernity, shunning anyone and anything that had even the slightest affinity for the past as a hopelessly backward relic of a decaying civilization. For Muslims who had come to see British colonialism primarily as a threat to their pattern of life and codes of behavior, the left wing of the Congress offered little in the ways of political solace or program to which it could be drawn.

The Muslim League, however, was hardly an option for those opposed to British colonialism in the United Provinces, if for no other reason than that the demand for a separate "Pakistan" would have dispossessed millions of Muslims in present-day India. Its collaboration with the British, opposition to nationalist agitation and its elite politics often brought them into conflict with those who saw the project of nationalism at a minimum as a package of social reforms oriented around independence from the British. Despite entering into compromise arrangements with the Congress on a few occasions and demonstrating a willingness to oppose British policies, the general arc of the league's development led it to the determination that the British were a more reliable ally than the Congress and that collaboration was a better means for winning concessions from the empire than protest. Furthermore, the league was seen by and large as a party of landlords, and that meant that the kinds of social reorganization that excited young Muslims about the Congress were removed from the league's table of demands. If the league could claim that there were tensions between Muslims and Hindus in India that deserved constitutional redress, its solution for a divided India meant a geographic nightmare for the majority of India's Muslims who lived in the heartland. Ultimately, the claim that there was a unitary Muslim identity that cut through differences of class, caste, language and sect was still being debated, and for many the idea of an Islamic state was not a move in a positive direction.

The decades between the Mutiny and independence had created, after all, substantial changes in the ways that Muslims understood their own lives and their relationship to British rule and modernity. Still, there was now a growing fear amongst a section of the intelligentsia that there might not be a single track leading from religious thought to nationalism, and that the variety of options available for expressing Muslim identity might lead into loyalism rather than rebellion, even as modernity was making it possible for internal debates within Islamic communities to receive new energies. The growth of movements for both reform and religious revival were at least one index of the complexity of the issues raised for Muslims attempting to make sense of their cultural inheritance amidst enormous political and social change. It is within this context that the specific aesthetic and political strategies of *Twilight in Delhi* become meaningful, especially since so many have considered the novel to be apolitical and antinational. Because of the complicated set of allegiances available for all minorities in late-colonial India, but especially Muslims with substantial class and sectarian differentiation, the automatic form of national allegiance that defined most patriotic writing in the 1930s and 1940s would have been hard to imagine. The earlier strategy of his friends in the *Angare* coterie – Sajjad Zaheer, Mahmud uz-Zafar and Rashid Jahan – had been almost entirely critical, leveling enormous charges against the aristocratic and orthodox sections of North Indian Muslims. But imagining how those same groups might imagine their own opposition to the British was not something that they had been interested in. So, by the time he had written *Twilight in Delhi* and parted ways with the Progressive Writers' Association, Ali was charting a different set of representational strategies to depict anticolonialism as it would have been felt by Muslims. Consider how Mir Nihal, the protagonist of *Twilight in Delhi*, remembers the Mutiny during the Coronation Durbar of 1911 as the royal procession passes in front of the Jama Masjid:

> It was this very mosque, Mir Nihal remembered with blood in his eyes, which the English had insisted on demolishing or turning into a church during 1857. As he thought of

this a most terrible and awe-inspiring picture flashed before his mind. It was on the fourteenth day of September, 1857, that most fateful day when Delhi fell into the hands of the English, that this mosque had seen a different sight. Mir Nihal was ten years of age then, and had seen everything with his own eyes. It was a Friday and thousands of Mussalmans had gathered in the mosque to say their prayers. The invaders had succeeded at last in breaking through the city wall after a battle lasting for four months and four days. Sir Thomas Metcalfe with his army had taken his stand by the hospital on the Esplanade Road, and was contemplating the destruction of the Jama Masjid. The Mussalmans came to know of this fact, and they talked of making an attack on Metcalfe; but they had no guns with them, only swords. One man got up and standing on the pulpit shamed the people, saying that they would all die one day, but it was better to die like men, fighting for their country and Islam. His words still rang in Mir Nihal's ears. (Ali 1994, 106)

In the context of two simultaneous historical recollections (Ali looking back in 1940 to the Coronation Durbar in 1911 and Mir Nihal looking back in 1911 to the events of 1857), we have the basic terms that establish the mood of what Ali imagines to be Muslim anticolonialism. For Mir Nihal, colonialism is understood as a battle between religions and governments over space and identity: in fact, it is a contest between Islam and the British Army for control over the Jama Masjid that most clearly produces the emotional response that the novel seeks ("His words still rang in Mir Nihal's ears"). It is the territorial conquest of Delhi that inaugurates the cultural decline of the city and ultimately the political enervation of its martial resistance. In 1857, Mir Nihal remembers, men had been willing to die "for their country and Islam," while in the present moment, the same Jama Masjid has been "vulgarly decorated with a garland of golden writing containing slavish greetings from the Indian Mussalmans to the English King" (Ali 1994, 106). Religious thought used to lead organically to anticolonial resistance in Mir Nihal's memory; now it preaches loyalism of the worst kind.

But by 1918, and the close of the novel, Mir Nihal's position has become even more depressed about the possibilities for meaningful anticolonial resistance:

Memories of days and hours came swarming like flies upon him, and he thought of his life from childhood to the present day. Delhi had fallen, he reflected; India had been despoiled; all that he had stood for had been destroyed. Only a year ago a new wave of freedom had surged across the breast of Hindustan. People had become conscious and wished to come back into their own. The Home Rule Movement was started, and there were prophetic rumblings of distant thunder as the movement went sweeping over India. But, somehow, all this did not affect Mir Nihal. It was not for him, the martyrdom and glory in the cause of the Mother Land. His days had gone, and a new era of hopes and aspiration, which he neither understood nor sympathized with, was beginning to dawn. His world had fallen. Let others build their own. He was one of those who had believed in fighting with naked swords in their hands. The young only agitated. Let them agitate. He was unconcerned. (Ali 1994, 175)

If the problem in 1911 for Mir Nihal was the betrayal by the religious establishment of political principles and the absence of anticolonial resistance of any kind, then in 1918, the problem is that the resistance is too Gandhian and the demands of the movement are too modern. The implication for Mir Nihal, then, is that an anticolonialism that does not value the cultural past is worthless and vacuous. In the drama of the narrative, this posture of political resignation mirrors the paralyzing stroke that Mir Nihal has just suffered, forcing him to remain in bed without any visitors who remember the past. But the passage is cleft with contradictions. The use of free indirect discourse alongside the third-person omniscient narrative makes the emotional isolation of Mir Nihal palpable even as it undercuts his conclusions. As Mir Nihal falls deeper into passivity, the narrator reminds us that the anticolonial movement is on the move in rather heroic terms ("a new wave of freedom had surged across the breast of Hindustan"), only then to be undermined by Mir Nihal's return to martial and masculine strategies of authentic anticolonialism ("fighting with naked swords in their hands"). The ability of the narrator to preserve the romance of swadeshi agitation comes up against the sheer patronizing (though pathetic) arrogance of Mir Nihal's dismissal of it, but neither seems to cancel the other out. In another context, Mir Nihal's inability to become a nationalist would mark him off for critical derision; here, the narrator's nationalist sympathy supplements Mir Nihal's political demoralization, sneaking sympathy for Gandhi in through the back door while preserving Muslim critiques of contemporary nationalism.

Earlier, Ali had adopted the posture of many of the writers involved with the Progressive Writers' Association, where distance from Gandhian agitation was a mark of aristocratic decadence and sympathy for the British. For instance, in "Tasveer ke do Rukh" (The picture has two faces), published in *Shole* (Flames) (1934), Ali describes the world of Mir Sahib, a *sharif* man from Delhi, whose son, not unlike Mir Nihal's son Asghar, is about to marry a woman not to his liking and therefore is disowned. Mir Sahib, his wife tells us, is obsessed with the hobbies ("these are not hobbies, they are ruination itself") of the sharif man, in particular training pigeons (a favorite of Mir Nihal's as well). Mir Sahib's day is marred by the mention of his disobedient son and by the insult he receives from the lower orders on the street, who refuse to apologize for bumping into him. He is rescued by his friend, Nawab Sahib, only to then be trapped in the phaeton during a stand-off between people protesting the Rowlatt Act on one side and the Delhi police and British Army on the other. The resulting curfew and street blockade leave the two stranded:

> The noise of the commotion dimmed. It appeared as if people were confronting the police. Suddenly, another cry was powerfully raised:
> "Repeat: Long live Mahatma Gandhi!"
> And people chanted even more loudly:
> "Long live the revolution! Long live the revolution!"
> Nawab Sahib lived in Farashkhana. It seemed to him that it would be impossible for the phaeton to get there from here and so he thought it best to take another route down Nayi Sadak through Chandni Chawk. (Ali 1985b, 20)[1]

In "Tasveer," Ali's indictment of the *ashraf* elite (who are unwilling to accept change in patterns of social behavior – from filial obedience, to marriage, to dress, to ideas about politics) is evidenced by their unwillingness to participate in Gandhian Civil Disobedience (already merging into more radical kinds of politics in this scene) and their own hypocrisy. Willing to say that injured protesters get what they deserve, since they have the audacity to spit in the face of the benevolent British administration, Nawab Sahib ends his harrowing day with a visit to a courtesan while demonstrators are shot indiscriminately by British security forces, as two beggars slink away into the darkness. Here, the aristocracy is entirely irredeemable and its cultural fixations are markers not of its colonial victimization but of its arrogance, idiocy and obliviousness. Moreover, between *Twilight in Delhi* and "Tasveer," the charismatic power of Gandhi to stand in perfect metonymy with anticolonial politics has been vitiated.

In Gandhi's place, the novel offers the emotional attachment of Delhi's residents to the city, its architecture and its culture as the foundation for an anticolonial politics and aesthetics. Despite its reputation as a "moody" novel, *Twilight in Delhi* quite lovingly documents the Delhi-ness of Delhi through a kind of cinematic celebration of its continuing culture, by reversing the previous pattern of social critique and turning away from the aesthetic priorities that had defined the *Angare* project. In fact, almost everything that was previously critiqued in *Angare* and *Shole* finds itself reinjected with aesthetic and emotional content in *Twilight in Delhi*. Pigeons are not domestic menaces but triggers of ecstatic contemplation ("the sky was full of wings, ever so many") (Ali 1994, 17). Beggars do not mark economic ruination but reinforce a religiously sanctioned social safety net ("they went away praying for the souls of those within") (14). Marriages to social lessers are not protracted familial battles but beautiful occasions ("the wedding was rounded off with happy fun and merriment") (131). Religion is not repressive orthodoxy but a channel for hopeful conviction in the future ("his heart was filled with the glory of God and the fervor of Islam") (58). Courtesans are not objects of male sexual depravity but genuine companions who offer relief from the world ("a quiet corner for himself where he could always retire and forget his sorrows") (79). The anthropological documentation of Delhi's culture is perhaps the most salient aspect of *Twilight in Delhi*, with its lengthy depictions of kite battles, Eid feasts, weddings and household arguments. In addition to describing the urban space of Old Delhi and the variety of men (usually distinguished by the shapes, sizes and colors of their beards and headgear) who populate its narrow streets and crowded spaces, Ali painstakingly translates over sixty poems and songs that would have made up a part of the standard repertoire of a connoisseur, almost all of them overheard by a character quite accidentally but always serendipitously.

> A hopeless weariness was in the atmosphere; and the dust blew more often than before. The glory had gone, and only dreariness remained. The richness of life had been looted and despoiled by the foreigners, and vulgarity and cheapness had taken its place. That relation which existed between the society and its poets and members was destroyed. Perhaps the environment had changed. Society had moved forward, and the people had been left behind in the race of Life. New modes had forced themselves upon India. Perhaps that is why that unity of experience and form, which existed in Mir Nihal's

youth, had vanished. Whatever it was, a new world had come into being and, he felt, he was not a part of it. (Ali 1994, 176)

However, this problem of the desires of women, and specifically how they measure up to the fantasies of modern Muslim men, becomes the axis on which the sensibilities of Ali's politics turns, and which – more clearly than anything else – exposes the contradictory resolution he arrives at to the competition between nationalism and Islam. For if Ali is interested in women's desires as a litmus test for the sexist attitudes prevalent in ashraf homes, then this desire is always reduced to the conservative and petty image of women as ideologically bound to domesticity, arranged marriages, traditional patterns of family and service to husbands. In fact, the criticism launched in the novel at the modernizers is that they are unable to recognize in their own women the foundations of social and sexual conservatism, as they leapfrog over the necessary developments in the female mindset that must take place before they are ready to accept existence outside the home.

In some complicated ways, too, Ali's novel begins with some implicit assumptions about the necessity of a modernist, feminist impulse. Ascribing very little agency to the women in his novel (they are always lounging, fighting, non-reproductive, mad, etc.), Ali finds their condition to be less than admirable. The idiom is already steeped in the clichés of the embarrassed modernizer who discovers that the women of the home are exemplars of the decay, decadence and backwardness of society at large:

> In the zenana [women's quarters] things went on with the monotonous sameness of Indian life. No one went out anywhere. Only now and then some cousin or aunt or some other relation came to see them. But that was once a month or so during the festivals. Mostly life stayed like water in a pond with nothing to break the monotony of its static life. Walls stood surrounding them on all sides, shutting the women in from the prying eyes of men, guarding their beauty and virtue with the millions of their bricks. The world lived and died, things happened, events took place, but all this did not disturb the equanimity of the zenana, which had its world too where the pale and fragile beauties of the hothouse lived secluded from all outside harm, the storms that blow in the world of men. The day dawned, the evening came, and life passed them by. (Ali 1994, 29)

More problematically, the women in Ali's novel don't seem to want to their own liberation. This should come as no surprise to those who would see in Ali the kinds of patronizing ideologies common to male, liberal modernizers who saw women's improvement as the burden that only they could bear. Still, Ali does seem to be groping towards a position in which women's improvement is necessary for radical changes in Delhi/Muslim society at large. In fact, sexism sets the upper limit for personal and aesthetic satisfaction in the novel. The romance narrative is truncated because of it; the political narrative has its horizons shortened because of it; and as a consequence of it, the narrative refuses to find another idiom in which to imagine internal dynamism in Muslim society.

For Ali, the privileged place for working out a strategy of social development and conflict is the domestic space; yet the home is also an idealization and as such it allows us to bring into sharp relief the narrative and ideological differences between an ashraf,

Urdu literary idiom and a modernist, sociological approach to the effects of colonialism. For the home is both an overdetermined ideological space and a specific site for the transaction of real, family business: it is both an outmoded, conservative relic and the site where contradictions in the ideologies of home, family and religion (and later, poetry, culture and politics) abide. Outside the space of political street fighting and a microcosm of it at the same time, the sharif home becomes the place where the rarefied world of social conservatism is shown to be simultaneously teeming with radical politics just barely beneath the surface, where conservative sexual mores are experienced as both limits and possibilities, where culture and religion are both isolating forces and means for political transformation. So the home becomes the place where Ali can savagely critique both colonial social relations and persistent feudal ones, simultaneously finding comfort in the ideological moorings of the Muslim, landed aristocracy – especially its proprietary view of the city and its command of poetry – and being horrified by them. Asghar's contemplations of Delhi and its transformation, his passive observations that are transformed into novelistic symbols, have this dual quality built in to it:

> As he came into the by-lane a strong gust of hot wind blew dust into his eyes. A small cyclone formed itself, and particles of dust, stray bits of paper and feathers rose in the air circling and wheeling, rising up above the house-tops in a spiral, and as the force of the cyclone died down they descended limply, fluttering and tumbling back to the earth. Somewhere nearby two women were quarrelling inside a dilapidated house:
> "O God, give me death. I am tired of this life ..." (Ali 1994, 21)

It is not merely that the home is the last refuge against the ecological and social devastation created by the uneven modernity of colonialism, but also that the sexist strictures of the home bleed out into the world as anticolonial critique. It is the woman's complaint about her life that reproduces and vocalizes the city's complaint about its colonial masters and the subsequent decay and deterioration that it brings about. The *zenana* becomes the unwitting site of social critique, precisely because it is the rarefied symbol of an ashraf elite that has to confront colonial modernity head-on and fails to do so, a hallmark of the sexist and secluded world that it manufactures for its women, and a locus of anticolonial politics.

In Ali's novel, the perfect adequacy of the domestic squabble for Asghar's moods cuts in both directions. Perhaps the complaint is launched at the world outside, in which case the emotional world of the home provides some respite from the decay of colonialism. Here, it seems, the complaint is also internal to the sharif home, and as such seems to work in the direction of undermining the claims of the sharif household on progressive politics. In fact, the image turns on itself, since it is precisely into this world of domestic complaints that Asghar (whose foreclosure occasions his moody travel through Delhi) is seeking entry. But Ali wants to have it both ways: the progressive reform of the sharif household alongside the preservation of ashraf literary culture. It was precisely this notion of a complete rupture with the cultural past that Ali resisted most in his debates with Sajjad Zaheer in particular. But it was not simply a return to a putative past that Ali wanted – in fact, the novel retains all of its distaste for the social patterns that persist in the home. What it wants is social reform in the home alongside the best of Urdu poetry. And it is that preoccupation – the preservation of a cultural past – that becomes the dominant theme for Ali's anticolonialism and provides Ali with the intellectual and emotional vocabulary from which to connect the isolated world of the sharif home with the heady days of nationalist politics. This was, after all, something that the nationalists could do – preserve the buildings and the music and the emotional space of sharif culture, something that the British were decidedly uninterested in doing.

One index of the failure of the nationalist movement to actually meet the needs of Ali's novel is the 1966 introduction to *Twilight in Delhi*. In 1966, he revised his introduction to reflect the changed historical realities since the novel had been printed. "The raison d'être of *Twilight in Delhi* [was to show that] the damage done by colonial powers to the heritage of conquered peoples is irreversible" (Ali 1994, xi). The lengthy introduction begins by detailing the consequences of imperialism on the colonized, from the Aztecs to Africa, and goes on to explain how the British slowly destroyed the best aspects of Muslim and Mughal culture in India in general and Delhi specifically. But the final paragraph of the introduction changes direction:

> Seldom is one allowed to see a pageant of History whirl past, and partake in it too. Since its publication, the Delhi of the novel has changed beyond nostalgia and recognition. *For its culture was born and nourished within city walls that lie demolished today; and the distinction between its well-preserved, jealously guarded language and the surrounding world has disappeared in the rattle of many tongues, even as the homogeneity of its culture has been engulfed in the tide of unrestricted promiscuity.* The British had only built a new capital outside the city walls. *The present rulers have removed the last vestige on which the old culture could have taken its stand and are moving it farther away towards Indraprastha, affirming the prophecy of the book*: Seven Delhis have fallen, and the eight has gone the way of its predecessors, yet to be demolished and built again. Life, like the phoenix, must collect the spices for its next and set fire to it, and arise resurrected out of the flames. (Ali 1994, xi–xx) [Emphasis added]

Here, the independent and partitioned Indian nation joins the long legacy of Delhi's conquerors, as one more imperialist that has devastated the country. Ali's problems with the construction of this Indian nation are already easily identifiable as a postcolonial dissatisfaction with the promises of independence and the horror of partition; India's new Hindu identity ("moving it farther away towards Indraprastha") has irreparably damaged the possibility of another renaissance of Urdu letters. Instead of producing a national renaissance with Delhi as its capital, the Indian nation merely reproduced and accelerated the pattern of previous conquerors ("removed the last vestige on which the old culture could have taken its stand").

What makes this cultural loss even more poignant is the distance that paragraph marks from the impossible-to-find introduction to the 1940 edition of the novel, which at least contained some hope that independence might allow the cultural past to persist in the present. This is the same paragraph:

> Seldom is one allowed to see a pageant of history whirl past, and partake in it too. Ever since becoming capital in the early thirteenth century, imbibing knowledge and

ideas and imparting cultures, becoming *homogeneous and cosmopolitan* in spite of the origin and ethnicity of its rulers and inhabitants, it had remained *the embodiment of a whole country, free of the creedal ghosts and apparitions* that haunt some of modern India's critics and bibliographers chased by the dead souls of biased historians of yesterday. Enmeshed in the prejudices and rules and rulers, they gainsay by the very nature of their studied silence, his rightful place to the author among his contemporaries; *and in their self-seeking separateness deny the city of the novel its Indianness and wider cultural view and representational character, as against the verdict of history*. (Hasan 2005, 241)

The concerns for Ali are to find in Delhi the embryo of a national identity that can stand in for the whole country. Delhi was ideal because of its history and because of its composite character as the hub through which different ethnic and religious groups could pass and intermingle. But Delhi was also important because allegorizing it secured in the Indian nation a place for a Mughal and Muslim past. *Twilight in Delhi*, then, was part of the project of overcoming the divide-and-rule politics of the British ("enmeshed in the prejudices and rules and rulers") and reanimating a humanist principle that could have found in Delhi the foundations of a Hindu–Muslim collaboration and amity, and could have used that humanism to revivify a more confident anticolonial politics predicated on the syncretic character of Delhi. There is, of course, a sleight of hand at work here, since this anticommunal Delhi is more or less a fantasy, but it does mark Ali's novel as a different kind of national allegory. After all, colonialism happened to the Muslims as well as the Hindus, Ali might have reminded us; and a new nation-state would have to embrace both of its cultural heritages, not only to fight against colonialism but in order to secure itself. There is also an attempt to remap India and Delhi, turning India not into the land that the Muslims invaded but the land that Muslims helped to develop, contributed to and even cared for. *Twilight in Delhi* makes Delhi both stand in for the rest of India and prove the longevity of Muslim cultural contributions to the subcontinent.

Muslim Literature, Identity and Weddings

By the early twentieth century, the Muslim literary world of North India had been engaged in a long discussion about how both to represent weddings in fiction and also what kinds of marriages would be produced by more or less successful weddings. This was part of a larger pattern of reconsidering how one ought to feel about such large concepts as gender, sexuality, religion, culture and politics, in which individual choices reflected certain kinds of political dispensations and allegiances that were publicly visible and legible, now that the British had handily defeated the erstwhile Mughal kings and ushered in a new pattern of governance and colonial modernity. What bothered late nineteenth-century reformers (like Syed Ahmed Khan and Maulana Ashraf Ali Thanawi) about Muhammad Hadi Ruswa's *Umrao Jan Ada* (1869) was in part the novel's opulent presentation of weddings and the decadent lifestyles of the aristocrats it depicted. In response, they put forward another view of Muslim weddings that were to be more correctly in accordance with *sharia* and less costly, more in line with the leaner times that the now-disenfranchised Muslim middle class faced under new colonial patrons, and more able to revive their religious convictions, which had suffered from heterodoxy and cultural contamination. Their vision for marriage ceremonies – chaste, small and thrifty – had not fully taken hold even by the 1920s or 1930s, but the books that advocated this kind of wedding were reproduced widely, and Maulana Thanawi's *Behishti Zewar* (Celestial ornaments) and Nazir Ahmad's *Mirat ul-Urus* (The bride's mirror), for instance, sold massively (Thanawi 1990).

At the same time, liberal reformers and traditionalists were not the only ones bothered by big weddings. Left-wing writers and intellectuals also came to agree with a number of the conclusions advanced by the reformers at Aligarh Muslim University and the traditionalists at Deoband. When the cause célèbre of the Progressive Writer's Association, *Angare,* was written in 1932, its authors also attempted to rethink what marriage meant in colonized Muslim homes, where sexism meant that companionate marriages were almost impossible and radical thought would have no truck with orthodox or aristocratic weddings. In doing so, they were extending the critique raised by the reformers into questions of sexism and sexual repression: if the reformers were worried about waste and corruption, the progressives worried that no matter how reformed the wedding, the marriages that resulted would inevitably produce sexist relationships. So, by the time Ali broke from the *Angare* group and penned *Twilight in Delhi*, he had also been participating in the long arc of feeling about weddings in colonial Muslim homes. The difference between most other representations of marriage that had preceded *Twilight in Delhi* and Ali's novel was that the marriage normally succeeded or failed in direct relation to the success or failure of the wedding. Reformers who wanted and got chaste weddings wrote about how those produced successful marriages; progressives who wrote about mismatched and boring weddings would go on to describe the failures of the marriage. But in Ali's novel, the wedding itself is so lovingly depicted, its lavish customs and petty familial debates described in such detail, that the failure of the marriage that results is almost jarring. Even more astonishing: why in a novel about the decline of Delhi under British colonialism did Ali seemingly turn back to representations of excessive customary practices whose social worth had already been found wanting?

For instance, as Part III of *Twilight in Delhi* opens, soon after the Delhi Durbar of 1911, the Nihal family is busily making preparations for Asghar's (the youngest son) wedding, at which we are told, more than a thousand guests will be in attendance:

> The women laughed and talked at the same time, the children wept and cried, and a loud din filled the house where no one really listened to another and people shouted all in vain. Women worked away, embroidering, tacking laces and borders, serving food and talking. Those sets of clothes which were ready were tucked with thread and kept in huge wooden trunks. They were the clothes which are sent to the bride from the bridegroom's side.
>
> "You know at my marriage …" someone would recall the past. "And at mine …" another would wax reminiscent.
>
> They talked of clothes and clothes, admired someone's dress, criticized another's taste. They talked of what they had worn at a particular wedding, or what they should wear now.

They had so many things to do, and their own clothes to set in order. The children would not let them work, but in spite of their shouts and demonstrations of self-will the work continued and progressed. (Ali 1994, 113)

This passage derives part of its intensity and its energy from the implicit ideological procedure that it is enacting, coming as it does at the end of a lengthy tradition of discounting lavish weddings as sources of both aristocratic excess and moral turpitude, and therefore inverting the conclusions of that tradition by valorizing the very thing that had fallen out of favor. It is the auditory and visual density of the wedding that the narrator seems most taken with, which seems connected to the function that the wedding plays, both in the drama of the novel and the knotty symbolic structure of its ideological claims. First, weddings are places of female activity and vibrancy in Ali's novel, in a way that the mundane world of the zenana is not; women are not only supremely industrious but at the center of the action that will dominate the nuptials. If only temporarily, women's activities and energies are unleashed. Second, it is implied that all weddings are temporally doubled, in the sense that every wedding must be set in comparison to some previous wedding or another (usually of one of the attendees), in order to measure social victories and economic failures within a large family or broader community; as such they serve as both sites of nostalgia and occasions for collective memory. Third, the novel uses scenes from Muslim weddings in North India but has to provide a certain anthropological explanation of the activities for English-reading audiences: that the bride's clothes are made at the groom's house is not news to any native reader but would provide interesting texture for an English-reading public. Finally, and perhaps most importantly, in an otherwise gloomy and despondent novel, the marriage scene stands out as the one place where the majority of characters are actually happy. What marks this passage (and the following ten pages) out from the rest of the novel are the specific kinds of emotional and affective pleasures that are derived from novel's rich descriptions of the wedding ceremony: comforting, domestic, noisy, intimate, beautiful, inertial and permanent.

The Urdu Literary Antecedents to *Twilight in Delhi*

To understand this nostalgic romance with cultural and customary practices, it is important to understand just how serious the debates about gender, religion, and custom actually were in the world of Urdu letters. When Ahmed Ali participated in the production of the now infamous collection of short stories, *Angare*, the project that had united him with his collaborators – Sajjad Zaheer, Mahmud uz-Zafar, and Rashid Jahan – had both been relatively clear and politically unified. The collective goal had been to illuminate the repressive atmosphere that existed under the weight of Muslim orthodoxy and to attempt to open up new spaces for critiques of sexism and class stratification (Ali 1974).[2] Mahmud uz-Zafar's "In Defence of Angare, Shall We Submit to Gagging?" – penned in response to the scathing attacks the collection received from Muslim circles as well as the proscription of the book by the United Provinces government – explains in part how the coterie imagined their literary intervention into Muslim life:

> The stories of my friend S. Sajjad Zaheer are concerned chiefly with the criticism and a satire of the current Moslem conceptions, life and practices. His attack is directed primarily upon the average Moslem in this country – a burden that leads to a contortion and a cramping of the inquisitive or speculative mind and the vital vigours of body of both man and woman. Ahmed Ali essays into the realms of poverty, material, spiritual and physical, especially the poverty of the Moslem woman, and imagination and admirable boldness breaks through the veils of convention to expose the stark reality. Rashid Jahan, who is also a Doctor of Medicine drawing on her practical experience, also portrays the ghastly plight of the woman behind the purdah. My own single contribution, is an attack on the vanity of man which seeks to find an outlet at the expense of the weak and defenceless womanhood. Nobody can deny the truthfulness of these portraits [...]. (Mahmud 1996, 451)

The two main preoccupations of the collection are the basis of the authors' defense: a ruthless attack on sexism and sexual repression on the one hand, and a need to expose the hypocrisy of social conventions on the other, in favor of a "stark reality" that everyone experiences but no one discusses.

There were two assumptions here that would later drive a wedge between Ali and the other figures involved in *Angare*. The first was an implicit sociological theory about the relationship between art and life that was most likely borrowed from Soviet theories of Socialist realism. The idea, in part, seems to have been that exposure of hypocrisy would lead to an awakening of consciousness and produce an automatic social transformation – so that transformed internal states of mind would induce external social change. Here, an aesthetic vocabulary of modernism was yoked to social criticisms of repression; because internal feeling and external realities did not match, they had to be brought together through epiphanic moments where events in the narrative memory were retroactively reorganized in favor of social critique. Almost all of the stories in *Angare* work in this way, beginning with the assumption that the reader knows (or suspects) that the world is not quite right, jarring them into a recognition of the extent of the depredation through, in most instances, racy exposé, with the intended effect of "social awakening." If we consider the dramatic strategies of the *Angare* collection broadly, they turn on the didactic energies that are supposed to be produced with the exposure of hypocrisy: husbands force their invalid wives to have children to prove their virility; liberal-minded and European-educated men seduce the family slave only then to have an arranged marriage to a respectable woman; God visits prostitutes in heaven; middle-class clerks who hate their superiors for cheating them turn and cheat their own servants; religion is trumpeted as a real solution in a world of poverty. The best example is Sajjad Zaheer's "Jannat ki basharat" (A vision of heaven), the most controversial piece in the collection, which depicts a pious *maulvi* who refuses to have sex with his young wife during Ramadan but has a pornographic fantasy with fairies in paradise. The transformation of a set of radical, secular humanist politics into literature relies on the protracted revelation that external appearances and internal realities do not match, that the public world and private life ought to be brought into closer connection. Part of the reason for the repetition of this drama is that it relies so heavily on a naïve sociology in which the revelation of contradiction is supposed induce a revelatory experience in the reader and move forward the process of social radicalization: once the clerisy has been exposed as corrupt and depraved it is supposed to be impossible to believe in the institutions that prop up religion, for instance. Ali came to be unconvinced that this didactic moment ever arrived.

Second, and perhaps most importantly, was the relationship between "custom" (*rasm*) – individual practices – and "culture" (*tehzeeb*) – entire systems of belief and tradition – and the determination of which of the two was more responsible for the state of Muslim society. Sexual repression and intellectual stagnation, the argument went, came from somewhere, and rooting it out required understanding its precise origins and determining how much of the past had to be thrown out in order to make way for the future. In drawing its own conclusions about the roots of the problem, the collective left few sections of society out; the responsible parties included modern, liberal men who hated their uneducated, backward wives; aristocrats who controlled their sons' sexuality only to cavort with courtesans; and, of course, the religiously orthodox, whose external piety was a veneer for their internal corruption. In part, this debate was inherited from the debates about Urdu poetry and Muslim society that had been ongoing since the 1857 Mutiny as an attempt to explain why the once-great rulers of India had fallen so easily to the British. The *Angare* group in some ways shared the criticisms of aristocratic Muslim culture that the intellectuals connected to the reformist Aligarh Muslim University had also developed (specifically Altaf Husain Hali and Muhammad Husain Azad), finding literary culture in particular to be the source of the political degeneration of a class and a race of people as a whole. In *Muqaddama-e-shair-o-shairi* (The introduction to poetry and poetics), Hali blames erotic poetry for aggravating the corruptions of Muslim life: "In the beginning the corrupt taste of society ruins poetry, but once poetry is spoiled, its poisonous atmosphere inflicts extremely severe harm on society" (Pritchett 1994, 177). For Hali, the problem centered on the explicit discussions of sexual and erotic themes in Urdu poetry, and specifically the *ghazal*, which became synonymous with decadence, excess and prurience. But there were important differences between the reformers and the radicals, since in the main, the *Angare* coterie were atheists and wanted to throw the entire cultural past out entirely, while Hali and Azad were looking to preserve a chaste Urdu poetic idiom, and would have settled for a return to more accurate customary practices from which to produce better believers. Still, in their search for the source of the problem, the Muslim reformers and the *Angare* progressives shared at least this in common: the health of Muslim society could be understood best by evaluating the sexual ideologies that its cultural past had aided in producing. For the *Angare* collective, Ali included, the liberation of the nation required the liberation of its women.

Sajjad Zaheer was later more clearly on the side of eliminating everything from the cultural past, but his contributions in *Angare* were closer to Ali's later position – that culture, especially literary tradition, had to be saved even as custom was being eliminated. In "Neend nahin aati" (I can't sleep), Zaheer's antihero, a poet named Akbar, balks at being asked to write new, nationalist poetry: "*Mister Akbar, you are, knock on wood, a marvelous poet. Why don't you give us a patriotic poem* [qaumi nazm]. *How long will you write fables about nightingales and gardens?* To hell with the nation. What has the nation ever done for me that I should give up my nightingales and wag my tail and wiggle my hips for the nation?" (unpublished manuscript). Zaheer, at least initially, seemed to be in favor of a more selective understanding of poetic tradition that was now being edged out by the tastes of new nationalist and communalist patrons. Nationalism and communal solidarity may have been important, but they certainly could not immediately produce good cultural outputs, nor did they possess the solutions to the most enduring problems facing Muslims. So as the narrative proceeds, this aesthetic debate about poetry becomes subordinated to another more important debate about marriages. Akbar has, more or less, been pressured into a costly wedding by his mother's guilt and his relatives' greed, and under the weight of the economic hardships he and his wife and infant son are now forced to endure, the marriage crumbles into violence and eventually murder. The emphasis, though, is on the economic wastage and ruin produced by certain customary practices associated with weddings:

> When we had found a bride, when we had picked a wedding date, and when the day of the wedding neared, those same people who badmouthed the wedding were suddenly ready to be in the party. All of mother's scraped together savings were spent on the wedding and the guests. Oil lamps, silken vests, rice, music, fancy cushions, joking around, crowds. There wasn't enough food. Turned out, the cook cheated us. Someone stole Badshah Ali Sahib's shoes. Not a stone was left unturned, but still *You idiot, why couldn't you take better care of the shoes?* But sir, it's not my fault – then began the arguments about the dowry. Would the dowry be the kind paid immediately after the wedding or the kind paid only after the divorce? About the custom of showing faces. The custom of salutations. Joking, flowers, insults, and the wedding was over. Mother finally got her wish. (Zaheer, unpublished manuscript)

Weddings are not social or sexual relations between individuals or communities but mere economic transactions between family members, opportunities to leech resources out of and extend authority over the couple's families. In fact, the serial representation of the trappings of a Muslim wedding ("Oil lamps, silken vests, rice, music, fancy cushions, joking around, crowds") already has the feeling of insufficiency and inadequacy built into it, as everything is absorbed into that composite crowd, which manages to turn family industry into undifferentiated consumption. But already, Zaheer's aesthetic sensibilities and his sensibilities about customs are heading in opposite directions. If poetry can afford to be decadent and even frivolous in times of nationalist agitation ("how long will you write fables about nightingales and gardens?"), weddings can have no such luxury, as every economic excess is directly related to a burden that the new couple will face. Poetic tradition ought to be preserved in the face of nationalist prudishness, but marital customs are not only silly but wasteful: no meaningful emotional or economic resource is to be found in them.

Here, perhaps, Zaheer is developing on and critiquing ideas from Nazir Ahmad's *Mirat ul-Urus*, a widely popular novel written in 1869, which depicts the lives of two sisters

(Akbari and Asghari – the names will be repeated throughout the literary discussions of weddings) in order to demonstrate the "value" of correct Muslim living. Where Akbari is senseless and profligate, Asghari displays all of the virtues of a sensible Muslim daughter and wife, and that sensibility allows her to survive economic hardships where Akbari fails. The challenge for *Mirat ul-Urus*, though, was to intervene in long-standing customary practices and reorganize social preferences by adjusting aesthetic judgments: customs that were attractive had to be made to appear unattractive and shown to be unreasonable so that Muslims would abandon them. Asghari's reorganization of the aesthetics of marriage is a necessary intervention before Zaheer's Akbar can complain easily; initially, the argument has to be made patiently and deliberately:

> As far as mere clothes and mere ornaments go, they are useful enough. But those heavily-embroidered costumes: I ask your honor, of what use are they? Why, my own are lying there simply rotting. I hate putting them on, worse luck! inside the house. Now and again I have worn them at weddings; or perhaps on the Eed they have been taken out for an hour or two. Except for that, there they are tied up in my bundle the whole year round. Putting them in the sun, when I have to do it, gives me a headache for the day which might well be avoided. And if you should want to sell them, you don't get the value of the material. People won't offer you the price even of the trimmings. And it is just the same with the made-up jewellery. (Ahmad 2001, 178–9)

Asghari's complaint is about the wastage produced by marriage and its trappings; every last bit of capital leaks out from the household economy: clothes lie fallow and jewelry depreciates while domestic labor must be spent trying to slow the economic ruin (as opposed to producing wealth). The implicit rhetorical procedure in the paragraph is to recalibrate aesthetic value against economic virtues: wastage is not luxury but ugliness and pain. Ahmad's intervention into the colonial home and the lives of women is taking place under the backdrop of the reorganization of North India after the declaration of the British Raj in 1857. Middle-class professional Muslims were now unmoored from their previous Mughal patrons, dispossessed of their property in many instances, and without any real occupational choices as long as they held on to anti-British and pro-Mughal politics. Ahmad's polemical agenda in *Mirat ul-Urus* is to try to find ways for Muslim homes to survive and flourish under these new conditions by shoring up the walls of the house and making sure that wives are equipped to stop the ever-present leaks. But the ethic of frugal living coincides with another critique of customary practices that have seeped into Muslim homes, largely, Ahmad concludes, from Hindu practices. From both directions, then, the Muslim home is threatened with enervating waste and contamination.

The other place in *Angare* where weddings are perhaps most thoroughly critiqued is Rashid Jahan's one-act play, *Parde ke picche* (In the women's quarters). In the play, two women, Mahmudi Begum and Aftab Begum, detail the long list of complaints that they have against the men in their family: sons who marry Christian daughters and abandon their mothers, husbands who force their wives to have operations so that they are still sexually viable partners after nearly a dozen pregnancies, husbands who threaten second marriages in order to get sex regularly. Weddings lead to nothing but disaster, as Aftab Begum exclaims, "Wherever I look, it seems as though it's the same trouble. The men get what they want every time. It's unbearable!" (unpublished). At one point in the drama, though, the two women are interrupted by a fight between two of Mahmudi's children. Her son accuses his sister of reading erotic fiction, who defensively claims that she is instead reading Thanawi's *Behishti Zewar*, a religious text detailing ways for Muslim women to live more pious lives. The difference between the marriages that Aftab and Mahmudi Begum describe and the ones that Thanawi advocates could not be more dramatic, perhaps driving home the worthlessness of the religious intervention into sexual relations. After delineating 103 sins related to contemporary marriage customs (involving waste, improper ritual, etc.), Thanawi argues for a more chaste ceremony with few attendees: "The groom wore clothes from his own house. [...] After the Friday prayer, there was a brief sermon describing the errors of customs. [...] After the sermon, the marriage was solemnized, and dates were distributed both inside and outside the house. They were also sent to the houses of those who could not come. Everything was completed before the late afternoon prayer. [...] After the night prayer, the same kind of sermon was delivered for the women. It had a great impact on them, too" (1990, 143). The bright optimism of Thanawi's reformism has no place in the real lives of Muslim women in Jahan's play, where religion is just another tool in the arsenal of men to get women to do whatever they want. Here, too, bad weddings produced bad marriages.

Ahmed Ali and the Fallout from *Angare*

By 1938, Ahmed Ali had broken with the Communist Party-led Progressive Writers' Association, then only a few years old. Throughout 1937–38, the *Angare* coterie had intense discussions in London to try to settle the question of what counted as "progressive writing." The bitterness of the break is clear in the afterword to his short story collection, *The Prison House* (1942), in which Ali criticizes Sajjad Zaheer for maligning his record and erasing him from the history of the Progressive Writers' Association, but the crux of the debate was simple: Zaheer held to a Stalinist Socialist realism as the model for progressive writing; Ali felt that class struggle was irrelevant to the production of progressive writing (Ali 1986). But when the break happened, Ali was the one left standing alone, as everyone else seemed to close ranks inside of the Progressive Writers' Association. Whatever the personal hurt felt at this moment, it necessarily meant that there was a change in the way that Ali produced literature and thought about aesthetics. Part of this was characterized by his slow shift from Urdu to English (and his later canonization as an anglophone rather than vernacular writer), in which he could engage audiences and find patrons (like E. M. Forster) less familiar or concerned with the debates that had been conducted in Urdu, and perhaps where he found literary production less restricted. The other part of it was also a conscious attempt to think about form and content anew, as well as to reconsider the relationship between politics and art established by the Socialist realists.

Some of the hurt is documented in his fiction, even as his essays adopt a more measured posture of respect to the various parties of the debate. The first indication that something was happening that required a rethinking of *Angare* appears in *Shole*.

Aesthetically, Ali shifts from the stream-of-consciousness writing that had characterized both of his short stories in the *Angare* collection – "Baadal nahin aate" (The clouds aren't coming) and "Muhavaton ki ek raat" (A night of winter rains) – in favor of a more straightforward realism and more psychologically wrought drama, grounded in a third-person omniscient narrator. Gone, too, is the female-centered narrative voice of both pieces, which had used female desire to critique both orthodox restrictions on female sexuality and the ways that poverty was experienced doubly by women. Ali had always maintained that women were capable of sexual longing that wasn't merely masculine projection onto empty female objects (more or less the same critique of male sexuality that emerges in the pieces by his fellow writers).

In "Shaadi" (Wedding), for instance, the narrative begins with a marriage between Akbar (once again) and Hameeda, a marriage that Akbar accedes to but does not want, and which has "no pomp or circumstance, very plain, a modern-day [*jamana-e-jadeed*] wedding" (Ali 1985b, 183).[3] Akbar, an England-educated man, returns home after having read D. H. Lawrence and Havelock Ellis, only to discover that his modern ideas about sex and romance are frustrated by the backward ideas about marriage and women that persist there. Female seclusion turns everything into "a barren and desolate, womanless [*baghair aurat*] wasteland" and he is unable to find a real companion (184). At the same time, these romantic notions of companionate marriage are mixed with seedier images of Akbar's past: "All he could think about were those nights in hotels and the lips of young women and nothing else" (185). He eventually consents to marriage because years of sexual frustration have worn him down, but Akbar stubbornly retains his opposition to backward marriage customs that subordinate women, refusing even to help his wife out of the palanquin or to see her on their wedding night, since this would be like "visiting a courtesan." The narrator, however, pans to the bride's chambers, where the "poor girl" sits in utter isolation on her wedding night, imagining that she has been "married to this room," all the while waiting for husband, confused about why he doesn't arrive. Despite being told by the narrator that Akbar "had no idea whether his wife had consented to the marriage or not or what her desires were," the implication is that, as she falls asleep at three o'clock in the morning, she is waiting for her husband and bemoaning her sexless fate (184).

Meanwhile, after his friends offer him homilies of the fates of men who do not visit their wives on their wedding nights – "and you can see what happens – divorce!" – and drag him back to his house, he tries to sleep but can't because he's fantasizing about the very wife he refuses to see (Ali 1985b, 185). In order to distract himself Akbar recalls (incorrectly) passages from *Angare*:

> Our society is so full of repression and stupidity. Customs have turned everything upside down so that everyone now is worthless and good-for-nothing, like that *guy who was always staring at Akbar's cap and his achkan. Sing me a song about roses and nightingales, do me the honor of accepting this cigarette, and puffs himself up. Hey Mister Akbar ... My name is Akbar, too! How strange that I didn't realize it sooner. Shall I sing a thumri or a dadra? Wonderful, Munni Jan, wonderful. Coy and spicy.* Has anyone put it better? Coy (cottony cheeks bouncing up and down) and spicy. *Like cloves and black pepper. Darkness, darkness in whiteness. Ink pots, inkpots of*

dirt, that poem about reeds, and the carpet. Carpets and carpets, now come the maulvi's strumpets. The maulvi sahib and his dream of fairies, fair skinned, long legged, fearless, and delicate, and beautiful, beautiful ... and then that beautiful figure and that shuddering waist. (194)[4]

These last words repeat the fantasy that he has already had about his wife and lead him to imagine that she longs for him, and decides to go to her. But at the moment he decides to go to his wife, he has a change of heart: "Akbar got up quickly, and entering the courtyard, he made his towards his wife's room. Just as he stepped off the platform, he suddenly had a thought: 'Perhaps people criticize *Angare* to keep up appearances. After all, many people read the book in secret, like thieves, in the same way as I am sneaking up to my wife like a thief. Actually, most people read *Angare* in secret.' A smile spread across his face as he thought that last thought. 'Lies, all lies. People live out their lives in lies'" (Ali 1985b, 196). He turns away from the bedroom at exactly three o'clock, convinced that he has deluded himself that his wife is waiting for him.

There are at least three issues in this narrative that raise interpretive problems for thinking about Ali's relationship to both aesthetics and politics as well as his representation of sex and sexuality. First of all, "Shaadi" is decidedly intertextual and critical; the reference to *Angare* and its full condemnation of customs (*rasoom*) and society as repressed and ignorant here produces the ironic result of first unleashing and then frustrating actual sexual possibility. *Angare*, Akbar thinks, gets it right; no one in colonial India is capable of real and meaningful sexual desire (even as real sexual desire is happening, albeit under conditions of deplorable sexism). The lines are obviously lifted from Sajjad Zaheer's "Jannat ki basharat" and "Neend nahin aati" in order to reinforce the similarities between the arrogance of Akbar and the hubris of the *Angare* group. Incidentally, Ali groups his own story in with the rest; the reference to the "poem about reeds" is lifted from his story, "Baadal nahin aate." The rejection of the *Angare* project, it seems, is total, even as he indexes his dependence on the short story collection for his present intervention. Second, the jabs at *Angare* are not only political but also at the level of structure: in both "Neend nahin aati" and Mahmud uz-Zafar's "Javanmardi" (Virility), romance and sexual desire are distant horizons that cannot be found in the present, and so the male protagonists (themselves also educated and liberal) are forced almost literally to murder the women in their lives out of frustration at sexual and social pressures. "Shaadi" takes the same narrative – a modern man married to an uneducated woman – and makes the reading of sexual repression and the lack of sexual options a mistake: Akbar's wife literally is his fantasy. For Ali, it is liberal arrogance that imagines uncoerced sexual desire as merely a product of modernity; if Akbar had bothered to ask, good sex and potentially a good marriage awaited him. Moreover, *Angare* does nothing to change the social order, since the only way it gets read, for Akbar, is as pornography. To drive the point home, the narrator reminds us, "He read the novels of D. H. Lawrence [...] but Lawrence only poured oil on the fire (*aag*) that was raging inside Akbar" (Ali 1985b, 177). And finally, Ali's "Shaadi" makes a point of making fun of "modern weddings," where a commitment to antisexist principles actually turns into humorless moralizing and boring parties. *Angare* was, in the end, a bad wedding and produced a bad marriage.

If this allegorical reading of "Shaadi" is compelling as a long retrospective on the political and aesthetic antipathy between Ali and the Progressive Writers' Association, it is because the critical reception of Ali has always been dominated by those who see his fiction as an important corrective to Sajjad Zaheer's condemnation of him as "retrograde." The problem of making sense of Ali's aesthetics and politics is long standing, since all determinations and judgments of Ali's work almost always center on either his debates with Zaheer and the Communist wing of the Progressive Writers' Association or his anglophone fiction, and even then almost exclusively relying on *Twilight in Delhi*, the function of which is to make Ali out as an identitarian writer. The relationship between the two and the complicated ways the shift from Urdu to English participated in larger political debates is almost always occluded. Gobinda Sarma, in a move of consciously communalist literary criticism has written that *Twilight in Delhi* is not a political novel because "the nationalist spirit breathed by the novel does not belong to any recognized phase of our freedom struggle" (Sarma 1990, 23). Harish Trivedi rightly criticizes Sarma but turns communal critique into virtue: "The new hopes and aspirations [of the Home Rule Movement] are not for Mir Nihal not only because the emotional thrust of the whole novel is backward rather than forward but also because the quiddity of Mir Nihal as well as of his little world is essentially and intensely Muslim in a way that the countrywide nationalist movement could not be" (Trived 1986, 64–5). The wonderfully evocative phrase "intensely Muslim" is all the more problematic given that what it meant to be Muslim in late-colonial India was the subject of intense debate and discussion, and the notion that it was "backward not forward" seems to smuggle Sarma's communalism in through the back door. Even Priya Joshi's wonderful account of the way that Ali indigenizes the novel by adapting the *shehrashob* to European forms turns the "historicide" of Delhi's past into a tragedy, since it means that "a hodgepodge, hybrid culture with no center and no place would become pervasive and perhaps the norm," already anticipating a postcolonial rather than anticolonial reading (Joshi 2002, 226). This is at least part of the legacy of the fallout with the Progressive Writers' Association: that Ali is seen as apolitical, Muslim, nostalgic and formally (rather than socially) transgressive.

The Marriage in *Twilight in Delhi*

Ahmed Ali has fit uneasily into the canon of nationalist writing from the Indian subcontinent, largely because his critique of the politics of Indian nationalism (in both its Congress and Communist variants) does not fit with the established strategies for making sense of late-colonial India and its attendant aesthetics. *Twilight in Delhi*, Ali's most important work from this period, does not end as nationalist novels are supposed to end: the main character, Mir Nihal, is slowly dying after having had a stroke, while the nationalist agitation to which he is unsympathetic rages outside, and as a Muslim he cannot bring his hatred of the British to turn into sympathy with Gandhi. The democratic and secular character of Indian nationalism has always needed to believe that it was making a space for its Muslim citizens, even more aggressively so in the aftermath of partition, and so the novelistic turn away from the possibility of Hindu–Muslim unity seems to betray the very idea on which Indian nationalism has staked its flag. For Muslims to talk openly about this issue would have seemed impolitic in the heady days of nationalist agitation, as the critical tradition would have it. Moreover, the public debate with Sajjad Zaheer over the character of *taraqqi pasandi* (progressive) writing – in which Ali accused the Progressive Writers' Association of being a dogmatic mouthpiece for the Communist Party – has meant that he is seen either as a decadent artist (by his Communist detractors) or as an apolitical formalist (by his anti-Communist supporters); that he put his lot in with the Muslims who migrated to Pakistan seems to have sealed the deal with mainstream nationalists (Ali 1986, 162–3). Much of this has to do with how literary debates are still politicized in the subcontinent and how deeply felt is the commitment to preserving the nationalist credentials of literary work from the period.

But explaining this history and the history of representations of weddings in Urdu literature is designed as a corrective to these instrumentalist and symptomatic readings of Ali's prose. Anticolonial politics are deeply connected, as I have suggested, to both representations of gender and the aesthetics of weddings; in fact, even if he was able to abandon certain ideals of the *Angare* collective, Ali continued to be a progressive (in admittedly idiosyncratic ways) and was deeply committed to opposing sexism and empire, even if his politics were more imaginative and utopian than practically possible. The problem for Ali was less that empire ought not be opposed or that sexism ought to be tolerated, but how to do that while retaining the best parts of Urdu literary tradition, especially since it seemed to be coming under attack from the very people who were critiquing empire. Unlike the Progressive Writers' Association, Ali's political desires map onto a complicated process in which custom (individual practice) is preserved and culture (larger patterns of society) is abandoned; but the contradictory nature of this salvaging operation, where memory is mined for its most precious artifacts and then abandoned, does not fall easily onto critical expectations for either progressive (i.e. antisexist) literature or anglophone (i.e. secular nationalist) literature of the late-colonial period. It was one thing to talk about how the British had sacked Delhi, but to argue for a return to Mughal styles of architecture, poetry and religious worship as emotional resources against the onslaught of colonial modernity was, the progressives might argue, to abandon any commitment to antisexist principles. Anglophone critics found it easier to reconcile Ali's nostalgic aesthetics with his anticolonial politics but had no sense of the kind of intervention that the novel was making into Urdu literary traditions and debates (Askari 1994).

Interestingly enough, Ali would produce his image of a good wedding in the middle section of *Twilight in Delhi*, the part of the novel that most critics almost always ignore. The marriage between Asghar (having abandoned the Akbar-named models) and Bilqeece is fraught from the start. Asghar's father, Mir Nihal, objects to the wedding because "you don't want to bring a low-born into the family" (Ali 1994, 48); Bilqeece's family are descended from Mughals, while Asghar is a Saiyyed, a direct descendent of the Prophet. The ultimate acceptance of the marriage by the father is supposed to be a mark of two simultaneous processes in the novel: the liberalization of orthodox thought (by agreeing to a mixed marriage) and, contradictorily, the contamination of Delhi's purity by external forces. A mere two weeks before the wedding, George V has forced the citizens of Delhi to observe his lavish Coronation Durbar – "All this show and prosperity is temporary" (99) – while Mir Nihal seethes inside, recalling the carnage that Delhi underwent in 1857. If there is any comparison to be drawn between the two lavish ceremonies that happen right next to one another, they are consciously suppressed by the narrator. Instead, Ali's narrator takes some anthropological delight in his rich description of the wedding itself: "The day of the wedding arrived at last. In the morning the bridegroom's clothes from the bride's house, a sherwani of gold brocade, a silk shirt, a turban, silk handkerchiefs, a white paijama with a screaming red paijama-string, shoes with flowers embroidered on them in gold; and other things like buttons, attar, collyrium, etc. These clothes were strewn over with parched fluffy rice. There were also the sehra and baddhi in a separate tray" (120). The wedding is an exercise in conspicuous consumption and display, each item of clothing lovingly detailed for the reader as it would have been for the attendees, so that the status and position of the families could be reasserted publicly and the moment of communal solidarity could be experienced broadly. At the same time, the indulgent imagery of this moment means that the connection that had been asserted earlier about internal and external realities has also been broken: weddings are not emblematic of the moral and ethical condition of the people getting married. Weddings are now simply weddings, a fusion between the people involved and the things that they will wear and own. In fact, the more lavish the wedding, the greater an imaginary emotional resource it could be for a community facing the slow vitiation of its public cultural power. Surely the red paijama-string "screams" for Ali's narrator because those in the present no longer do; the wedding itself becomes an occasion not only to celebrate but also to memorialize a past about to vanish.

The wedding also inaugurates other processes that Ali has not abandoned as preoccupations from earlier works. First, Asghar, unlike the Akbar of "Shaadi," actually goes to his wife: "It was not until one o'clock in the morning that he could go to his wife who had been put in the bridal room. The house was quiet now as everyone was tired after the whole day's strain and had gone to sleep. The sky was heavy with millions of twinkling stars; a cold wind was blowing. And with a fast beating heart Asghar went to his bride" (Ali 1994, 129). If *Angare* foreclosed the possibility of good sex under colonialism, Ali was not willing to make that polemical intervention again in this novel. Still too prudish, perhaps, to depict the sex act itself, the narrator simply pans out to the atmosphere in suggestion of the romantic moment – a naïve, expressionist move repeated throughout the novel to both suggest the possibility of connecting internal and external states as well as their ephemerality. But marriages are still unhappy in the novel and the critique of sexism remains. In fact, once married, women face unbearably suffocating conditions in the zenana, where "things went on with the monotonous sameness of Indian life" (29). Men might have sexual urges but women lack emotional and sexual maturity; they are stifled by "inhibitions which grow in the repressed lives of Indian women like cobwebs and mushrooms" (30). And ultimately, Asghar turns out to be just as bad a husband as the husbands from *Angare*, literally killing his wife by neglecting her and then as widower turning his desires onto her younger sister.

What Ali attempts to do in *Twilight in Delhi*, then, is to reorganize the connections between the emotional resources that culture provides and the customary ways those cultural practices are understood and lived. Marriages were indefensible but weddings were good. Muslim homes were sexist but Muslim architecture was worth preserving from the ravages of colonialism. Religion was oppressive but religious worship was beautiful. The aristocrats were decadent but the poetry they produced was beyond compare. This decidedly antihistorical and antimaterialist reading of Dehlvi culture also helps to explain the anthropological procedure at work in Ali's fiction: in addition to describing the urban space of Old Delhi and the variety of men (usually distinguished by the shapes, sizes and colors of their beards and headgear) who populate its narrow streets and crowded spaces, Ali painstakingly translates over sixty poems and songs that would have made up a part of the standard repertoire of a connoisseur – almost all of them overheard by a character quite accidentally but always serendipitously – as well as multiple festivals, varieties of pigeons, kite flying battles and even the different kinds of street beggars. The function of aestheticizing weddings served the same function as aestheticizing Delhi's past: one had to have a basis from which to critique the ugliness of colonialism. At the same time, though, nostalgia, in Ali's fiction, is not merely recollection but aesthetic revaluation: the past had been written off as irrelevant; in order to be recuperated, the past had to be carefully reimagined as not only important but also as beautiful.

But for now, the preservation of Delhi's culture was linked to the critique of the British stewardship of Delhi. The streets and structures are in disrepair; the wall that surrounds the city is being torn down; the very feeling of the city, the feeling responsible for the characteristic Dehlvi ghazal, is being ruined by British rule. This trope in the novel works in two ways. First, it is a realist rendering of the decay of the domestic and commercial spaces in Old Delhi. Hosagrahar's groundbreaking architectural history of Delhi documents the depth of deterioration in the urban landscape: "By the turn of the twentieth century, however, the city was far more fragmented. [...] Tantalizing remains of skilled craftsmanship jarred with the workshops and shacks that crowded once elaborate courtyards, while mansions had become decrepit tenement houses or warehouses. With the establishment of New Delhi in 1911, historic Delhi became an embarrassment to the shining new capital of the British empire in India" (2001, 26). The urban space was undergoing a vast transformation, a combination of dispossession by the British of ashraf property and the influx of capital drawn to Delhi by the shift of colonial power from Calcutta to Delhi:

> Between 1858 and 1862, a land transaction of bewildering complexity was carried through. The confiscation of the houses of all Muslims who could not prove themselves innocent [of involvement in the Mutiny], the demolition of a large number of houses in order to build the Cantonment and the railway line, and the necessity to compensate the owners of these houses, were all linked up into a single operation. It led to one of the most remarkable revolutions in the ownership of urban property. Broadly speaking, it gave much of the property which had belonged to suspect Muslims into the hands of comparatively few individuals who had liquid cash, and involved the government, because of its own amateurishness, in an unnecessary loss. (Gupta 1981, 29)

The situation had repercussions for the organization of the sharif home as well: "The loss of income made it impossible for the *haveli* owners to sustain either the patronage or the earlier opulence. The impoverished *rais* (aristocrats) were caught between their old elite ways and the reduced incomes. Having never worked, the gentry of yesteryear did not consider employment an option. Their sons were unskilled and quite often entirely uneducated. Incapable of selling their services, the new generation of impoverished highborn became increasingly destitute" (Hosagrahar 2001, 32). This is more or less the dynamic at work in the drama of *Twilight in Delhi*, the slow deterioration of a feudal economy and its replacement by a colonial capitalist one produces profound changes in the private and public worlds of the ashraf. In *Twilight in Delhi*, the question more or less becomes who will run the Nihal household and how: the eldest son has died; the youngest has abandoned tradition and moved out; the patriarch lies paralyzed. The effects of colonialism on the Nihal household, then, are a kind of national allegory in miniature on the claustrophobic world inhabited by Muslims after the 1857 Mutiny. The unique intervention of the novel is to map this urban and domestic decline alongside a cultural stagnation.

In order to do so, though, the novel mobilizes a conceit that strains at the realism of its recording of Delhi's decline. In Ali's novel, every poem maps perfectly onto the mood of its listener; in fact, a ghazal or a *qawwali* or even the stray bawdy song cannot be heard without an immediate and precise mood being struck in the closest character. As Asghar describes his romantic troubles to his sister, a Sufi *qawwali* about unrequited love begins next door; as he climbs the steps of the brothel for an unexciting encounter with a courtesan, "from nowhere, as it seemed, a man appeared singing a verse from Dard" (Ali 1994, 52); when the narrator complains of the claustrophobic domestic world that suffocates the women who are trapped there, a beggar's song reproduces the narrative emotion; and when Asghar feels guilty about having emotionally abandoned his wife, a tonga-driver begins to "sing in a hoarse voice the latest sad and melancholy tune" (174). This is an almost cinematic soundtracking. Part of this, of course, is derived from the mystique of Delhi, with its reputation for being steeped in its poetic traditions. But that reputation is used, here, in the service of an extended trope that connects the internal world of the residents of Delhi to the perfect adequacy of the poetic atmosphere in which they experience their moods.

That poetic adequacy then bleeds into a network of expressionist symbols through which it is not only the poetry but the whole of the immediate external world that reflects and gives shape to the psychic one. Asghar's unsuccessful visit to Bilqeece's home is mirrored in a pigeon that "misbehaved in its flight and the dropping fell near Asghar's foot" (Ali 1994, 20); the "repressed lives of Indian women" (30) is similarly reflected: "the wind blew the leaves to and fro, dust floated in the air, at night the cats quarreled over bones under the wooden couches or miaowed and caterwauled on the roofs" (31); and occasionally the poetic and the material compound the effect of both on the characters in the novel: "Only now and then a dog barked somewhere, or an engine shrieked far away touched by the beauty of the voluptuous song" (39). In another way, this why Ali's expressionist procedure is so poignant. The city literally becomes the perfect representation of the complex internal moods of its residents, whose unhappy moments find the perfect *qawwali* being sung just next door or whose philosophical moments find their perfect referents in the wildlife. There is in Ali's Delhi an immediate and unmediated compatibility between the inner consciousness of his characters and the world that they are able to experience. The destruction of this world, as a consequence, becomes all the more problematic since it threatens to ruin the architecture, physical and psychic, that buttresses the poetic and literary compositions of the city itself.

But even in the descriptions of the city, there is a remarkable tension. On the one hand, any description of old Delhi's landscapes results in a picture of Eliotic urban decay: "Heat exudes from the walls and the earth; and the gutters give out a damp stink which comes in greater gusts when they meet a sewer to eject their dirty water into an underground canal. But men sleep with their beds over the gutters, and the cats and dogs quarrel over heaps of refuse which lie along the alleys and cross-roads" (Ali 1994, 3). On the other hand, the city has a spiritual interior that is both impervious to colonization and resistant to decay: "Yet the city still stands intact, as do many more forts and tombs and monuments, remnants and reminders of old Delhis, holding on to life with a tenacity and purpose which is beyond comprehension and belief" (3). And then again, the very structures that resist decay are themselves falling apart: "Yet ruin has descended upon its monuments and buildings, upon its boulevards and by-lanes" (5). In some ways, this tension between a city that is both survivor and victim, timeless and time-bound, is both a product of and reason for the political and philosophical contradictions that the novel has its heart.

However, this decision to memorialize by aestheticizing sets up a contradiction in Ali's anticolonial aesthetics that begins in the opening pages and winds itself through the entirety of the novel. The narrator remarks on the first page:

> But the city of Delhi, built hundreds of years ago, fought for, died for, coveted and desired, built, destroyed and rebuilt, for five and six and seven times, mourned and sung, raped and conquered, yet whole and alive, lies indifferent in the arms of sleep. It was the city of kings and monarchs, of poets and story tellers, courtiers and nobles. But no king lives there today, and the poets are feeling the lack of patronage; and the old inhabitants, though still alive, have lost their pride and grandeur under a foreign yoke. Yet the city still stands intact, as many more forts and tombs and monuments, remnants and reminders of old Delhis, holding on to life with a tenacity and a purpose which is beyond comprehension and belief.
>
> It was built after the great battle of Mahabharat by Raja Yudhishtra in 1453[sic] BC, and has been the cause of many a great and historic battle. Destruction is in its foundations and blood is in its soil. It has seen the fall of many a glorious kingdom, and listened to the groans of birth. It is the symbol of Life and Death, and revenge is in its nature. (Ali 1994, 3–4)

The function of these lines at the beginning of the novel (set sometime in 1910) is to establish clearly the longevity of Delhi against the sieges of its many conquerors, beginning with the Hindu epics that detail its beginnings and continuing on through to the present British Raj – a four hundred-year legacy of multiple conquests and outright devastation. In the logic of the narration, the chief characteristic of Delhi is the impossible durability of the city against the impermanence of its inhabitants: the city and its residents have been decoupled in order to preserve the identity of the urban space, no longer defined by its denizens ("no king lives there today"). Delhi, in this passage, is the thing that conquest cannot kill; the residents do not share the city's invincibility. It is perhaps to make this point that the last thing the narrator introduces in this section is the Nihal family itself, made marginal to the drama taking place on and about the urban landscape.

A page later, the narrator continues:

> But gone are the poets too, and gone is its culture. Only the coils of the rope, when the rope itself has been burnt, remain, to remind us of past splendor. Yet ruin has descended upon its monuments and buildings, upon its boulevards and by-lanes. Under the tired and dim stars the city looks deathly and dark. The kerosene lamps do light the streets and lanes; but they are not enough, as are not enough the markets and the gardens, to revive the light that floated on the waters of the Jamuna or dwelt in the heart of the city. Like a beaten dog it has curled its tail between its legs, and lies lifeless in the night as an acknowledgement of defeat. (Ali 1994, 5)

The Delhi from the first passage is temporally and spatially identical with the Delhi in the second passage, but the triumphalism of the earlier passage is here replaced with the mood that will become the more pronounced one in the course of the narrative: this time, the ineffable Delhi-ness of the urban space has been despoiled beyond recognition, impervious to the attempts of colonial municipal administration to make the city vibrant and lively, and unable to hold on to the architecture that defined it, architecture that is surprisingly still standing in the first passage. If in the first passage the city was impervious to colonial conquest ("lies indifferent in the arms of sleep"), now urban ruination stands in for the kinds of misadministration conducted by the colonizers and depersonalization of Delhi into a mere colonial capital ("gone is its culture"). The emphasis here is on colonial misrule and the specific manner in which the British urban planning and administrative changes that came with the transfer of the capital to Delhi from Calcutta have emptied the city of its content and its character. The only thing that links these two Delhis together is a putative timelessness, which may or may not survive.

But which Delhi, then, are we encountering in Ali's novel: the one about to be irretrievably lost ("Only the coils of the rope, when the rope itself has been burnt") or the one that cannot be destroyed ("It is the symbol of Life and Death")? Or perhaps, more importantly, why does Ali's narrator draw powerful emotional resources from both ideas of Delhi, and why does his idiosyncratic variant of anticolonial aesthetics seem to undo itself at the moment it should be the easiest to decide whether to celebrate the inevitable end of British Rule or to lament the ruin that has ravaged Delhi? One clue is provided in two sentences that link the two passages together, which come right after a quatrain from a translated poem:

> I'm the light of no one's eye,
> The rest of no one's heart am I.
> That which can be of use to none
> – Just a handful of dust am I.

> And, as if to echo the poet king's [Bahadur Shah "Zafar"] thoughts, a silence and apathy of death descended upon the city, and dust began to blow in its streets, and ruin came upon its culture and its purity. Until the last century it had held its head high, and tried to preserve its chastity and form. (Ali 1994, 4)

It would be far too easy to resolve the debate in favor of a ruined Delhi, resolving the contradictory descriptions into points on a temporal line, even if one could ignore that terribly annoying word in the first passage, "today"; instead, the novel needs at least two other things to suture together both of the ideas that it needs in order to induce the intended emotional effect. First of all, it must make reference to Urdu poetry, especially Urdu poetry of the Dehlvi school for which Delhi was renowned. That the poet in question was also the last king of Delhi helps to make Ali's point more forcefully: the removal of the king and the end of poetry are simultaneously linked to the decline of Delhi (Petievich 1992). But there is a subtle twist at the end that betrays another contradiction in Ali's conception of Delhi: the chiasmus of phrases ("its culture and its purity" and "its chastity and form") link and affix the language of urban cultural notoriety and literary formalism with a sexualized (and sexist) vocabulary of female fidelity and a racialized prohibition against intermarriage. The fantasy of a chaste and pure Dehlvi culture is at odds with its long history of multiple ravages; Delhi's genealogy – and the genealogy of its poetry – is hopelessly mixed. The wedding, which is supposed to preserve the aesthetic past, is also the occasion of its thematic undoing in the novel.

This contradiction (between two simultaneously extant versions of the past) sets up other problems that the novel is at pains to acknowledge, because it needs the aesthetics more than it needs the local resolution of political ethics to be on terms favorable to its ideology. First, one way to resolve the initial contradiction would be to insist that every other sacking of the town left the culture intact, that it preserved the "Indian-ness of Delhi" so that what is at stake this time is purely nationalist; the character of Delhi is threatened not by the sacking itself but by the transformation of its culture under foreign rule. This is something that Ali tries a number of times in the novel, as when his narrator remarks, "Many activities were going on in Delhi, for the English king was going to hold his Coronation Durbar in the ancient seat of the mighty kings of Hindustan" (Ali 1994, 97) or when Mir Nihal waxes nostalgic, "Here it was, in this very Delhi, he thought, that kings once rode past, Indian kings, his kings, kings who have left a great and glorious name behind" (105). Here, metonymy does the work of telescoping all of India into Delhi, making it not only the capital of the conquered nation but emblematic of a common political and cultural subjection. But this comes up against its limits almost immediately, since Delhi's cultural primacy is predicated on regional rivalry, not on national unity:

> Besides, a new Delhi would mean new people, new ways, and a new world altogether. That may be nothing strange for the newcomers: for the old residents it would mean an intrusion. As it is, strange people had started coming into the city, people from other provinces of India, especially the Punjab. They brought with them new customs and new ways. The old culture, which had been preserved within the walls of the ancient town, was in danger of annihilation. Her language, on which Delhi had prided herself, would

become adulterated and impure, and would lose its beauty and uniqueness of idiom. She would become the city of the dead. (144)

That the threat to Delhi comes internally – as a result of British redistricting that placed Delhi in Punjab rather than the Northwest Provinces as a part of the strategy to weaken local elites in the wake of the 1857 Mutiny – means that the metonymy that connects Delhi to India only works in one direction. Even before Lutyens has demolished large chunks of the old city and begins the process of building a modern, New Delhi to the east, Delhi faces cultural threat from other Indians. Delhi's Indian-ness can only be purchased by excluding Indians from it, by marking it off as a city and not as India itself.

If one wants to preserve Dehlvi culture, in fact preserve its linguistic and literary repertoire, then doing so in an anglophone novel already is one mark of defeat. So, even as he is, in Priya Joshi's wonderful phrase, "indigenizing the novel" (by yoking Urdu genres to European novelistic conventions), he is also anglicizing and deracinating Urdu. The genesis of this contradiction, the simultaneous feeling that Delhi will survive and will not, is a particular aesthetic crisis that may have been unique to Ali but which also reveals something about the nature of Muslim politics and aesthetics at the end of the British Raj. Having already marked himself off a secularist and having broken with Sajjad Zaheer and the Communist-led Progressive Writers' Association, the number of aesthetic and political strategies available to Ahmed Ali to represent his particular brand of anticolonialism must have been limited. The Congress, the party of Gandhi and Nehru, had a few Muslim members, but these were unable to mobilize sizeable constituencies; the Muslim League appeared to have the ear of most of North India's Muslim population, but few maps of Pakistan included Delhi; and the Communist Party's dogmatism was already troubling Ali, who had broken off his ties with Zaheer by 1938.

Incidentally, there is another way to read the invasion of Delhi by Punjabis in the 1920s. As Delhi became the capital of the United Provinces and more people moved in, they brought with them religious revivalist movements that had spread throughout the Punjab. The Hindu Mahasabha and the Arya Samaj, two communal organizations, moved into Delhi and began staging *shuddhi* (reconversion) and *sangathan* (consolidation) projects on a large scale, in part to reassert Hinduism as a unifying force of Indian nationalism. Swami Shraddhanand, a leader of the Hindu Mahasabha, became president of the Bharatiya Hindu Shuddhi Sabha in 1923 and set about to try and reconvert Muslims in the United Provinces to Hinduism. The harassment this produced of Muslims in Delhi eventually led to Sharaddhanand's murder by Abdul Rashid, an incident noted in Ali's "Hamari galli" (Our lane), usually cited as source material for *Twilight in Delhi*: "Just then Abdul Rashid was condemned to death for the murder of Swami Shraddhanand, leader of the Hindu Revivalist Party. The Mussalmans of the city were angry and excited. On the day of execution thousands of men collected outside the jail to receive Abdul Rashid's corpse. When the Police refused to hand it over, the fury of the mob became uncontrollable. They wanted to tear down the jail and bury that martyr in a manner befitting a saint" (Ali 1985c, 17). The communalism of Delhi in the 1920s and 1930s must have been one more reason why the project of cultural revival was worth trying for Ali, over the objections of his erstwhile collaborators.

By the 1940s, the idea that critique did not end in nihilism or that reconstruction was not a pipe dream was increasingly difficult for Ali to sustain. Redemption becomes not simply a distant horizon but an impossible one, as none of the characters in *Twilight in Delhi* are capable of anything other than fragile and momentary acts of contrition, easily dissipated by the more generalized sense of moral turpitude. Because whatever culture was, for Ahmed Ali it was paradoxically reprehensible and praiseworthy, and blunt critique could no longer do the work of preserving a more refined aesthetic sensibility. It is unclear whether the fight with Zaheer produced a turn towards more classical Urdu poetics or vice versa, but suffice it to say, falling out with the social realism of the Progressive Writers' Association was for Ali synonymous with a turn to a more properly Urdu idiom. But this was also a problem, since what made the *Angare* project coherent (if inchoate) was that it had no problem abandoning both tradition and culture as relics of some outmoded, feudal and orthodox past. Even when it relied on that tradition (referring to Nazir Ahmad's fiction, for instance) it erased records of it; a mere three Urdu couplets are quoted in the entire collection and most of it attempts to reproduce an honest colloquial idiom, shorn of the phraseology of classical Urdu poetry. This was not an option for Ali, who could not rejoin the ranks of the Progressive Writers' Association nor find his lot with either the communalists or with the Congress. Instead, he settles for the riskier strategy of trying to preserve a sanitized version of the past in the hopes of a future political struggle, in terms more favorable to culture.

In this reorganization of the past, weddings and the kinds of emotional resources they (and other bits of personal and collective memory) provided became important features of Ali's novelistic imagination. What the anglophone novel occludes, however, and what most anglophone literary critics miss, is how the particular valences of Ali's nostalgia (or rather his conscious aesthetic revaluations of memory) have to perform two contradictory functions at once, because, even though the novel is written in English, it clearly has Urdu interlocutors, relies on Urdu literary debates and traditions, and resurrects a Dehlvi cultural past that could only be accessed in English with some difficulty. One of the casualties of the conflict with Zaheer has been to relegate Ali's novel to an almost exclusively anglophone critical terrain on which the cultural past can only be accessed as nostalgia, and not as a residue exerting demands on the present. What emerges, once Ali's novel is situated against the Urdu tradition of which it is clearly a part, is less a desire for a return to Mughal patterns of governance and life, and more an understanding of the complicated processes by which Muslim identity navigated the choices that were thrust upon it by the literary and political debates of the time. The reorganizing of the aesthetic and ethical codes that accompanied weddings cut in two directions at once: against the progressives who abandoned culture and against the British who did not understand it. In order to accomplish both, the political content of the wedding had to be consciously connected to a larger project of reinvigorating the aesthetic codes through which the past was understood. Anglicizing the Urdu Dehlvi past was not only an act of triumphantly preserving Delhi against colonialism, even preserving it in colonial time, but also an admission of defeat that Delhi had already died, and the nation that was going to be built shared only traces of the cultural past that it sought to preserve. Nostalgia for Ali simultaneously marked the distance from the greatness of Delhi's past and the future of nationalist promise, an idiosyncratic resolution to the contradiction produced by the conflation of culture and nation on which the novel relies.

The Politics of Ali's Delhi

The second ambition of *Twilight in Delhi* is to explain the simultaneous ubiquity of Muslim hostility to British rule (expressed either as anticolonialism or as opposition to colonial modernity) and its concomitant absence from the world of nationalist politics, and – by explaining the contradictory emotion – find a way to overcome it. This has, of course, the benefit of also solving the first set of problems about preserving culture; if the ashraf classes have an incipient anticolonial ethic, though muted and complacent, then the culture that shapes their internal worlds has a politics that can be legitimately workable for nationalist purposes. As a result, Ali looks for politics in the elite, while the progressives and reformists would look for political change to come from below. But the ashraf, though angry, were politically quiet. In the closing pages of the novel, the decline of a culture and the decline of the city turn into the pathetic, political death of Mir Nihal:

> Memories of days and hours came swarming like flies upon him, and he thought of his life from childhood to the present day. Delhi had fallen, he reflected; India had been despoiled; all that he had stood for had been destroyed. Only a year ago a new wave of freedom had surged across the breast of Hindustan. People had become conscious and wished to come back into their own. The Home Rule Movement was started, and there were prophetic rumblings of distant thunder as the movement went sweeping over India. But, somehow, all this did not affect Mir Nihal. It was not for him, the martyrdom and glory in cause of the Mother Land. His days had gone, and a new era of hopes and aspiration, which he neither understood nor sympathized with, was beginning to dawn. His world had fallen. Let others build their own. He was one of those who had believed in fighting with naked swords in their hands. The young only agitated. Let them agitate. He was unconcerned. (Ali 1994, 175)

This is the tortured political landscape of the novel, one in which all but a handful of characters see the British as something to be resisted if not hated, and where simultaneously the sharif home is impervious to the political agitations that are taking place on the streets of Delhi. There are multiple explanations for the political complacency that persists in the novel, and here it is the feeling of a loss of glory of a civilization, while in other places passivity is the product of a fatalism that is linked to Islam and the domestic space. Politics takes place on and in the streets, while quiet resignation dominates the home. For *Twilight in Delhi*, this mood of Muslim anger at the occupation of Delhi by British troops and the garish Durbar of George V is the necessary corollary to the mood of fatalism and defeat that seems to govern the emotional retreat into domesticity. The constant oscillation between the domestic and the urban spaces, between resignation and protest, sets the emotional landscape for a novel interested in charting the sociology and psychology of the purportedly apolitical Muslim.

It seems to have been clear to Ali that charting a course towards nationalism from Islam would require different logics than modernity and progress, terms that seemed to gravitate in favor of British rule, even though he seemed to be attracted to the political and moral impulses that those terms implied. Their opposites – tradition and stasis – had the advantage of evoking anticolonial politics, as they tended to produce ethics and aesthetics that were resistant to British colonial modernity and rule, but the social order that they defended was itself hardly worth the effort. This was not a unique problem for the Indian intelligentsia, as reformist, revivalist and loyalist movements publicly debated the variety of ways that tradition and modernity might be used to best create a set of values that the present could draw from. But in Ali's novel, the debate is carried out in a formal register: the novel deliberates on the variety of ways to salvage an Urdu culture through a novel written in English. There is, of course, no need for such a strategy to be contradictory. Many have in fact noted that it was through English that the vernacular languages and literatures became revitalized (Chaudhuri 2004, xvii–xxii). But in the novel, the tension between British modernity and Urdu tradition is consciously felt in the decision to write in English. The translation of a classical idiom into a modern one, across languages, had the function of producing a relatively unique aesthetic ideology, one in which the terms of the tradition/modernity debate were freely mixed and selectively deployed. As a result, Ali's novel shifts between the worlds of the classical and the reformist literati (the Old and the New Light, or *Nayi Roshni*), between the modernizers and the antimodernizers, hoping to save sharif Delhi from the hands of the British and in spite of the Muslim elite who were presiding over its decline. The only preservation that was possible, it seemed, was a nostalgic recollection, or rather a present already prepared to be nostalgically recollected.

The translation, though, necessarily papered over the debates that persisted within ashraf circles, where modernity was legible as a pattern of behavior and a set of beliefs about the world, and could not be hidden by poetic repertoire. This meant, in part, that the kind of culture that Ali was preserving also needed to fit his needs: a cultural tradition worth preserving rather than shedding as decadent holdover; a poetic past that was commonly seen as threatened by British rule; and an aesthetic worldview that was inclusive of India but resistant to colonization. As a result, it was to Urdu poetry rather than Islam that Ali turned for a cultural vocabulary that extended through the ashraf classes and beyond. For one thing, Urdu literary culture had the benefit of inheriting the syncretic tendencies of North Indian Mughal rule:

> Here [North India] many Muslims lived in towns, and the higher orders, the ashraf, were a much larger proportion of the Muslim population than in other parts of India. In upper India, much of the old order had survived the vicissitudes of British rule, and not only Muslims continue to have a large share of government posts but many of the big landowners in the region were Muslims. Despite their successful propaganda to the contrary, Muslims enjoyed a solid educational base both in the old learning and in the new secular instruction. But these notables of north India belonged to an elite which by tradition was not exclusively Muslim. In the heartland of the Muslim dynasties, the Faithful lived among a sea of unbelievers, who were not to be converted by persuasion or

by the sword. Accordingly, their system of rule had to be tempered to fit the necessities of peoples beyond the range of Muslim doctrine, whether at the summit of society or at its base. The ruling groups around the courts of northern India embraced a striking medley of peoples, Muslim as well as Hindu, for the most part more committed to their own fortunes than to the integrity of their creeds. [...] From these accommodations, there emerged an Urdu-speaking elite with its famous syncretic culture, neither wholly Muslim nor Hindu, but a creative combination of influences from both, recruited from several communities, floating upon society like an oilslick upon the water, but destined to be broken in modern times by the waves of populism from below. (Jalal and Seal 1981, 419)

Additionally, Urdu poetry had the benefit of being substantially flexible to incorporate the variety of feelings that modernity itself was producing.

Ali had no complete theory for how the Urdu poem might accomplish this feat, but his feeling that it might be useful certainly explains the ever-present translated poem in *Twilight in Delhi* as well as his attempt to preserve pre-1857 poetry in his anthology of Urdu poetry, *The Golden Tradition* (1973). Retrospectively, we can even see the viability of Ali's nascent feeling:

The Urdu *ghazal* and the constellation that surrounds it – metrical structures, histories of composition and reception, Persianate vocabulary and thematic conventions, and the image associated with it of an imperial culture in decline – retain a distinct place in the postcolonial Indian cultural imaginary, from popular 'Hindi' cinema to such a work of Indo-English fiction as Anita Desai's *In Custody*, despite the massive effort in recent decades to denaturalize and alienate Urdu to contemporary Indian culture and society. Perhaps like no other poetic form in northern India, the history of this lyric genre is inextricably tied up with the emergence and development of national culture, and in no other form, not even the Hindi *git*, or 'song' that is sometimes said to be the national-popular poetic genre par excellence, are the contradictions of the social so deeply inscribed. (Mufti 2004)

Consider the fact that *Twilight in Delhi* laments more than anything else the decline of Urdu poetry in Delhi, already designed both as miniature representations of the culture and geography of the whole of India. The list of Urdu poets that Ali translates – Bahadur Shah Zafar, Shauq, Dagh, Dard, Mir – all come from the Mughal court in Delhi and all are made to stand in for the culture of an India (even when Delhi competes with Lucknow in the novel) now under threat from British rule.

Only some monuments remain to tell [Delhi's] sad story and to remind us of the glory and splendor – a Qutab Minar or a Humayun's Tomb, the Old Fort or the Jama Mosque, and a few sad verses to mourn their loss and sing the tale of mutability:

I'm the light of no one's eye,
The rest of no one's heart am I.
That which can be of use to none
– Just a handful of dust am I.

And as if to echo the poet king's [Bahadur Shah] thoughts, a silence and apathy of death descended upon the city, and dust began to blow in the streets, and ruin came upon its culture and its purity. Until the last century it has held its head high, and tried to preserve its chastity and form. Though the poet who sang its last dirges while travelling in a bullock cart to Luknow, city of the rival culture, managed to keep silent and, to preserve the chastity of his tongue, did not indulge in conversation with his companion [...]. But gone are the poets too, and gone is its culture. (Ali 1994, 4–5)

In the poetic history that Ali creates for Delhi, derived as much of it is from Azad's *Ab-e-hayat* (Water of life), Delhi was intimately linked to its poetry, so much so that a mere recollection of Bahadur Shah's poetry produces a spontaneously fabricated response ("a silence and apathy of death descended upon the city"). The virginal city, protective of its "chastity" and "purity," now ravaged by British rule, has produced a corollary bastardization – if not out-and-out devastation – of the cultural products of British-controlled Delhi. It is important to mark here that the idea that Delhi was simultaneously syncretic (Hindu and Muslim) and "pure" is, of course, a contradiction that the novel cannot resolve without some effort. Here, the resolution is papered over through an Indian identity: Islam, Buddhism and Hinduism are Indian, British colonialism is not. In fact, there are daily reminders of the composite character of Delhi that Mir Nihal sees on his walks:

Right in front of him was the Red Fort built long ago by Shah Jahan, the greatest of artists in mortar and stone, but which was now being trampled by the ruthless feet of an alien race. On his right, beyond the city wall, was the Khooni Darwaza, the Bloody Gate; and beyond that still was the Old Fort built by Feroz Shah Tughlaq many more centuries ago. Still beyond stretched the remnants of the past Delhis and of the ravished splendor of once mighty Hindustan – a Humayun's tomb or a Qutab Minar. There it was that the Hindu kings had built the early Delhis, Hastinapur or Dilli; and still in Mahroli stands the Iron Pillar as a memory of Asoka; and other ruins of the days of India's golden age, and dynasties greater than history has ever known. Today it was this very Delhi which was being despoiled by a Western race who had no sympathy with India or her sons, thought Mir Nihal. Already they had put the iron chains of slavery around their necks. (Ali 1994, 106)

That the monuments Ali lists are literally commemorations of the sacking of Delhi by one or another invading force is here presented in an unironic fashion. It is something of Ali's style to place these contradictory ideas next to one another unselfconsciously, though it might be helpful to hold on to the possibility that this was both inevitable and innovative as an attempt to resolve the problems produced by nationalism. Most nationalist histories have to rewrite the past in order to tell the story of lost grandeur, but here that lost grandeur is literally a list of ruins and relics destroyed by successive empires, at the very moment that the novel wants to criticize the British for doing the same.

Such a lack of irony is only possible in late-colonial India, after the publication of books like Nehru's *The Discovery of India*, with its goals of explaining to the British and to Indians themselves that India was, in fact, a single country. This is not to argue that theories of composite nationality did not exist before Nehru, but rather that the idea that "sympathy with India or her sons" ought to be the touchstone for good imperial rule is marshaled against the British only after some patient reorganization of the historical past for a nationalist end. That "sympathy" means something like democracy or political devolution; here, by metonymy, it also comes to mean poetry and architecture in the double sense of stewardship over the aesthetic past and something akin to the reproduction of an indigenous structure of feeling, Hindu and Muslim, impervious and superior to British urban planning.

But this sense of stewardship is also in part proprietary and aristocratic. At the very moment that the coronation procession moves past the Jama Masjid, Mir Nihal recalls the last uprising of Delhi's Muslims against the British in 1857, when defense of religion and defense of city merged into defense of a building:

> It was this very mosque, Mir Nihal remembered with blood in his eyes, which the English had insisted on demolishing or turning into a church during 1857. As he thought of this a most terrible and awe-inspiring picture flashed before his mind. It was on the fourteenth day of September, 1857, that most fateful day when Delhi fell into the hands of the English, that this mosque had seen a different sight. Mir Nihal was ten years of age then, and had seen everything with his own eyes. It was a Friday and thousands of Mussalmans had gathered in the mosque to say their prayers. The invaders had succeeded at last in breaking through the city wall after a battle lasting for four months and four days. Sir Thomas Metcalfe with his army had taken his stand by the hospital on the Esplanade Road, and was contemplating the destruction of the Jama Masjid. The Mussalmans came to know of this fact, and they talked of making an attack on Metcalfe; but they had no guns with them, only swords. One man got up and standing on the pulpit shamed the people, saying that they would all die one day, but it was better to die like men, fighting for their country and Islam. His words still rang in Mir Nihal's ears. (Ali 1994, 106)

It is important that the structure is a mosque; it's not likely that five thousand Muslims would have defended, for instance, the Red Fort, should Metcalfe have wanted to turn that into a church. But in the slippery aesthetic and emotional categories set up in the novel, the Jama Masjid is already almost secular, and here what Mir Nihal recalls is not the religiosity of the rebellion but its bravery. The crowds around him now cannot see that the Delhi Durbar in the way that Mir Nihal sees it, as an extension of the urban devastation and cultural humiliation of 1857, because they have lost a fighting spirit ("blood in his eyes").

If colonialism was something that happened to the Muslims rather than to the Hindus, if colonialism was primarily about replacing one set of rulers (Mughal) with another (British), and replacing one set of values with another, then the primary victims of colonial occupation would have been Muslims. *Twilight in Delhi*, though, reflects a profound anxiety about this understanding of colonialism (which empiricism and cultural nationalism prevents it from critiquing). Not only have Muslims failed to revolt against colonialism in any serious way, they are in fact moving towards the worst aspects of colonialism, allying themselves to it, abrogating their own cultural and moral traditions. Asghar's modernist ethic clearly triumphs over the traditional views of marriage, family and life (represented by his father, both emotionally and actually, in the first half of the book), only to give way to a much more corrupt, selfish and decadent kind of modern romance in the last half, when Asghar turns his affections to his recently dead wife's sister. Mir Nihal's traditional worldview is increasingly claustrophobic and foreshortened, and therefore his robustly anti-English views cannot be the foundation for a vague nationalist polemic, which Ali clearly sympathizes with. The fact that there is no good basis for a clean nationalist, Islamic ethic from which to narrate the decline of the city means that Ali has to piece together the worldview from a series of inadequate perspectives. Furthermore, having already been burnt by the reception of his polemics in *Angare*, Ali's restrained criticisms of Muslim orthodoxy restrict the ways in which Ali can arrive at a robust picture of the importance of an Islamic past to a syncretic nationalism.

This is also the reason that Ali has to return to an almost pre-political Delhi to stage his family drama. The historical bookends of Delhi's interregnum, between the end of the 1857 Mutiny and the transfer of the imperial capital to Delhi, mark perhaps the last days of Delhi's independence from Britain and the last time that Delhi would be confined to its traditional borders. Afterwards, Delhi would expand north and south and the walled city would be transformed and modernized – a suburb for a new, Indian Versailles. But if the relationship between the poetry and the city is supposed to be the mark of a lost grandeur, then the compatibility between the current urban setting and the denizens of Delhi poses some difficulties. After all, unity between the public and private worlds cannot both be lost and preserved simultaneously; or put differently, the decline of Delhi cannot both kill art and produce a fine novel. This, however, is the very murky atmosphere that the novel hopes to preserve, since its loyalties are so evenly divided. On the one hand, the novel wants to retain the cultural vocabulary of the past as a reminder of the Indian-ness of Delhi's Muslims. On the other hand, Ali finds the world of the sharif home dangerously moribund. Not only is the home the space of uniformly sexist attitudes towards women, it is also bound up with religious orthodoxy, superstition and political passivity, and is suspicious of science. The problem for Ali throughout *Twilight in Delhi* is that the nostalgic voice of cultural preservation and religious masculinity is coupled to the critical vocabulary of social modernization, secularism and feminism that he has not abandoned from the *Angare* project. So while Ali laments the slow vitiation of the urban space that gave rise to the ghazal and the aesthetic unity of Delhi, the novel is also at pains to defend the walls of the sharif home as anything other than the bastions of superstition, sexism and stagnation. This produces an odd tension in the novel between the inner spaces of the Nihal household and the larger vistas of the urban world of Delhi. If the former is seen as the feminized and petty space of domestic conservatism, that conservatism is necessary both as a place from which to launch a radical critique of the effects of colonialism on the city at large and as the source of the emotional vocabulary of the ghazal that the novel is also trying to preserve.

This combination of modernist sensibilities grows out of a literary idiom of "traditional" Muslim culture in the north that gives rise to what many critics have identified as the uneasy mood of *Twilight of Delhi*. It is a political novel that eschews any lengthy discussion of politics; it is a social novel that centers on a more or less cloistered family; it has a poetic content grafted onto a novelistic form; it is an Indian sensibility depicted uneasily in English. These oscillations are simultaneously necessary for the emotional impact of the novel (which relies on a coeval disgust and sympathy with the domestic and political situation) and produce the central contradiction of the novel: cultural decay only uneasily produces a political rallying cry. English has already replaced Urdu, the Muslim elite have already been removed, the religious sensibilities have already been transformed – the past can only be imagined back into existence as a motive for political struggle at great imaginative costs, many of which undermine the very foundation on which they are built.

But this tension between the insides and the outsides of the homes refracts a larger contradiction that the novel is at pains to articulate openly. The vocabulary from which a confident, Muslim, anticolonial nationalism could emerge has all but vanished by the late-colonial period, after the Muslim League had (more or less) captured the mantle of Muslim politics in North India, while dissolution into the purportedly Hindu mainstream nationalist movement would have satisfied some of the political desires but left none of the cultural and emotional registers intact. This, then, becomes Ali's preoccupation in *Twilight in Delhi*: how does one critically preserve a sharif culture in Delhi while not becoming a loyalist? Or more importantly, what does one do with the fact that anticolonial Muslim identity seems to have built into it a preservation of some of the most reactionary political and social ideas? Most of the ashraf had, after all, moved steadily closer and closer to the Muslim League's politics and farther and farther away from the kind of confrontational anticolonialism that Mir Nihal fantasizes about in his recollections of the "men of 1857" (Ali 1994, 107). And the novel's setting between the 1857 Mutiny and the years immediately after the Delhi Darbar (1911–14), leading up to the first wave of the Gandhian Civil Disobedience movement (1919–22), mark perhaps the last time when Muslim identity and nationalist belief might not have run at odds with one another. And it is only for the brief period of time between the coronation and the Second World War (or between Khilafat and the rise of the Muslim League) that such a political and aesthetic rapprochement is possible. The strategy for such a reconciliation is a pan-Indian nationalism, which finds its representatives in people like the Ali brothers and Maulana Abul Kalam Azad. The matrix of ideas that these people represented were not only contradictory but also marginal: the secular nationalism of the Congress; modernizing in education; private religiosity; the anti-imperialism of the middle class.

In many ways, the debate in the late-colonial period was an extension of the debate that had begun in the aftermath of the 1857 War of Independence, with the formal declaration of British rule over India. Then, the debate was between those who retreated into private religiosity (and retained their hostility to the British) and those who entered into public life, attempting to reform Muslim identity in search of new British patrons. In his social history of the Urdu ghazal, Ralph Russell explains the divisions that emerged after the suppression of the mutineers:

> Those in the first camp maintained their strong (if now mainly silent) hostility to the British, withdrawing from the political arena and clinging firmly to their traditional

religion and culture in the hope that conditions might one day emerge in which they could regain their former dominance. The other camp took a very different stand, calculating that the old Muslim elite could never fully regain its old ascendancy, but could hope to persuade the English to take them on as junior partners provided that they made a complete break with the past, and identified their interests completely with those of the British. To do this they needed to acquire a modern education and adopt, wholesale, British cultural norms. It should be stressed that it was not merely to win British approval, fundamentally important to them though this was, that they took this view. They were convinced that it was the mastery of modern science and the adoption of modern ways of life that had been the basis of British pre-eminence, and that they own Muslim community would never prosper or win a place of honour in the modern world unless it did likewise. (Russell 1995, 180)

But this picture of North Indian Muslim politics presents a problem for anyone interested in reading *Twilight in Delhi*, a novel ostensibly produced in this intellectual crucible, in the last possible moments of meaningful intervention into the debates about Muslim nationalism. Ali's novel lacks all of the moralizing quality of the New Light fiction, represented perhaps best by Nizar Ahmed's *Ibn ul-Vaqt* and *Mirat ul-Urus*, with its need to lay out the arguments in favor of modernity with all of the zeal of new converts. At the same time, this is a novel that bemoans the domestic decay of the households of the orthodox, with their repressed women and their psychological stagnation.

This may not have been entirely wishful thinking, as Ayesha Jalal explains; the cracks were beginning to emerge in the politics of Muslim loyalism well before the Durbar of 1911:

Already by the late 1880s Britain's imperial policies in India and new colonial conquests in the Islamic world were leading more Muslims to shun Sayyid Ahmad's policy of non-participation in the Congress and stolid loyalty to the raj. Muslims from the North Western Provinces had taken to attending the annual sessions of the Congress in increasing numbers. [...] Since 1895 Shibli Numani had been publicly opposing his old patron's policy of Muslim non-participation in the Congress. Differences with his colleagues at Aligarh led Shibli to help found the Nadwat-al Ulema in 1898, an institution which he believed would give fillip to his personal aspirations of greater status as an intellectual leader of India's Muslims. (Jalal 2001, 93–5)

Still, there are problems with Jalal's formulation, since it relies on explicit membership in the Congress (the numbers disprove rather than prove this trend) and leaves out the larger trend of Muslim identity-formation in the complicated world of communal awards and rioting in North India. The number of people who followed Numani into the Congress were few and far between. But the point is still important: it was possible to imagine a politics of opposition to the British beginning from one's identity as a Muslim, and as long as this was possible, then collaboration with the Congress and Gandhi were not entirely out of the question. The Muslim League is, though, absent in this novel, as are Gandhi's attempts at collaborating with the Ali brothers in the campaign to preserve the

Islamic caliphate in Turkey. The absence of those sections of the political establishment that have become important in understanding the postindependence narrative of the movement for independence makes reading the expressionist oversensitivity of *Twilight in Delhi* all the more difficult, precisely because it does not seem to conform to the pattern of Muslim politics in any recognizable way. The ideological field had not been closed, and Ali moved into the debates about Urdu poetry in order to find a common resolution.

In his study of early twentieth-century literary histories of Urdu, Shamsur Rahman Faruqi reveals the variety of ways that Urdu greatness was perceived as lost and how the attempts to reclaim it were articulated. Faruqi argues that there were "three dominant models": the first saw the literature of the past as superior in its "naturalness" and marked Urdu literary history as one of perpetual decline and in desperate need of revitalization; the second saw revitalization of the past greatness of Urdu literature through an admixture of British pragmatism and voluntarism; the third imagined that Urdu's literary greatness was impossible to reproduce and all that could be done was to "selectively cultivate the best of the past." As Faruqi contends:

> These positions are not always clearly stated, but are like major premises, though inarticulate at times, running though the writings of three greatest modernizing Urdu critics who wrote between 1875 and 1914. The first model bears the stamp of Altaf Husain Hali (1837–1914), the second bears the stamp of Muhammad Husain Azad (1830–1910), and the last one is derived from the writings of Shibli Numani (1857–1914). The most interesting thing about these authors is that while they might not have always agreed on quite what constituted the past, they were agreed on the point that literature, at least Urdu and Persian literature, seemed to have an inveterate tendency to decline with the passage of time. (1999, 15–16)

The first two positions, interestingly, correspond to the views that were circulating around Aligarh Muslim University. Hali's *Muqaddama-e-shair-o-shairi* was written in consultation with Syed Ahmed Khan, while Azad's *Ab-e-hayat* continues to be standard reading for Aligarh students today.

The end of the Urdu renaissance in Delhi coincided with the rise of the Muslim League in North India, though neither occupied exactly the same cultural or political space as the other. If the former was concerned with interventions into education, culture and religion, the latter saw itself primarily as a counterweight to the Congress in matters of political devolution in negotiations with the British Raj. While most nationalist histories have tended to view the former as the progenitor of the latter, some critics, like Mushirul Hasan, contend that the cluster of figures around Hali, Syed Ahmed Khan, Zaka Ullah and others held a range of views that could not be condensed into the two-nations theory in any reasonable way and betrayed a nascent anticolonial ethic (Hasan 2005).

Urdu letters at the turn of the century were turning towards Aligarh. Its two most important figures, Hali and Nazir Ahmad, were already aligned with Aligarh and working towards more serious reorientation of the whole of Urdu letters. The most serious polemic was waged against conventions in Urdu poetry, which were held to be responsible for the decline in the morality of the ashraf classes and for the decadence that had found its way into Islam. Ahmad, in *Fasana-i-mubtala* (A story of one infatuated), famously declared, "What else is there in our poetry other than lovemaking and vulgarity?" (2003, 48). Hali's *Musaddas* went farther and found that Urdu poetry had left the backdoor open not just for immorality but for heresy, as the prime figures in the ghazal moved in the direction of idolatry and adultery.

This reform movement was the cultural expression of the loyalist middle classes, who despite having been affected by the repression following the 1857 Mutiny found themselves finding opportunities with British rule that had not been open to them before: employment, patronage, education and religious freedoms. This was done with the aim of both producing a loyalist faction of Muslims as well as bringing about social uplift:

> The notion that Muslims as a "class" were "backwards" received support, then, from well-publicized statistics, and elicited a good deal of official British solicitude. Muslims of the *kacahri* milieu were probably the first people in India to benefit from such a designation, but at the cost of altering their own estimate of themselves. Muslims now were laggards, all sulking in their tents, dreaming of lost empires and reciting decadent poetry. Some Englishmen who interpreted the 1857 Revolt as an effort to restore Muslim rule felt some urgency in winning over Muslims, drawing them into the system of British rule and British values. An 1859 Educational Dispatch from the Secretary of State in London had urged special attention to problems of Muslim access to education. Hunter's polemic in 1871 on the Indian Musalmans, his reiteration of these concerns as chairman of the Educational Commission in 1902, and a petition from a Calcutta-based Muslim political association in the same year all prompted full-scale governmental enquiries and a large literature of diagnosis and prescription for the problem of Muslim education. Muslims required special attention and, some argued, special treatment. (Lelyveld 2004, 86)

The class thus produced found it necessary to advance a different cultural idiom: chaste in its taste, didactic in its literature, loyalist in its politics and Islamic in its faith. While they were split on the question of language, Zaka Ullah advancing Urdu and Syed Ahmed Khan in favor of English, they were united in the belief that Islam had declined and needed to be revitalized, and that revitalization would happen through cooperation with the British and adding Western rationalism to a Unitarian version of Islam. And their opponents were found in both the orthodox *masjids* of Delhi as well as the newly nationalizing groups of Delhi. They excoriated against the feudal remnants in Delhi who were not only unable to adapt to the challenges faced by colonialism but were also unwilling to take advantage of opportunism to insert a dynamic force into the religious and cultural idioms of Muslims.

Mir Nihal represents a kind of visceral anti-English ethic, rooted in his being "an aristocrat in his habits, a typical feudal gentleman" (Ali 1994, 28), opposed to Aligarh. He detests Asghar's modern habits (wearing English clothes and shoes) and has convinced Asghar that had he "stayed in Delhi he wouldn't have even allowed [him] to learn to English" (36). Instead, Mir Nihal prefers traditional pastimes: pigeons, courtesans, alchemy and religion. There is even a fairly clear generational divide between Mir Nihal and his children, who are unable to express their own emotional worlds without recourse to an almost clichéd poetic idiom (which would have been the vernacular of a certain kind of ashraf upbringing); Mir Nihal on the other hand remains decisively prosaic. Habibuddin, Mir Nihal's son, on the other hand, is the model for the growing Khilafatist sentiment in the city. His son recites "*Sarfaroshi ki tamanna*" (The feeling of sacrifice) to much praise from his friends. Habibuddin ("friend of the faith"), a government official (who has yet to abandon his post as part of the Khilafatist boycott), is self-consciously nationalistic: "The English frankly say that they fear no one but Muslims in India and that if they crush the Mussalmans they shall rule with a care-free heart" (183).

Saeed Hasan becomes the model for the Deobandis, who consciously absent themselves from politics (in favor of a quiet personal religiosity and political critique):

> Saeed Hasan did not much believe in patriotism. He had completely failed to sympathize with the movement and was disinterested. He was one of those who accept an order of things and come to believe in it. For they did not wish to take any trouble to think for themselves. So long as a thing did not disturb the placidity of their lives they never said anything against it. The game of Politics was too difficult for Saeed Hasan to understand. Besides, British rule did not meddle with his life, although a foreign modernity and ways did go against the grain because they directly affected him. That is why, whereas he raved against English ways of living and thought, he never said anything against the foreign rule. Life went on peacefully for aught he cared; and that was all he was interested in, like most Indian fatalists. (Ali 1994, 185)

Here, the idea of political passivity is found to be a pervasive cultural problem, and Saeed Hasan is immediately molded into a national type: objecting to the style but not the political content of empire, Indian fatalism made it possible to reconcile life under Britannia. But there is also the seemingly strange idea that British imperialism is characterized as a kind of banality – "so long as a thing did not disturb the placidity of their lives" – or at least a kind of low-grade and slow-moving violence whose most obvious features were cultural rather than economic, juridical, or geopolitical. In such a context, Ali's intervention serves not only to show the decay of the city (the destruction of the architecture of Delhi, a long-standing convention of the shehrashob) and the growth of a substantial underclass (the omnipresent beggars), but also to move the debate into why questions of culture and ways of life also warranted more political confrontation on the part of Muslims in Delhi.

The debate between the characters, though, is never fully resolved, because it cannot be. At best, the various positions elicit momentary sympathies and then dissipate, frustrated. But in each instance, the frame of Ali's novel is to turn the political debates into debates about poetry and debates about the city. This was both a formal innovation and an inheritance of specific emotional and aesthetic theories circulating in Delhi at the time (as well as, perhaps, theories from British modernist texts that Ali was reading at the time). At the same time, though, Ali's cosmopolitan and nonmoralizing idiom sets him apart from the rest of the Delhi elite that was looking for other solutions to the political and intellectual crisis created by British rule. While most of Delhi was looking either outwards to Aligarh or inwards to Jama Masjid, Ali's gaze constantly moves through the decaying remnants of a Delhi that stood in opposition to the British pattern of life. And as a result, his preservation of the ghazal in translation meant taking a side in the cultural skirmishes that were taking place in Delhi at the time. But at the same time, *Twilight in Delhi* seems to share some of the conclusions that have been reached about Urdu poetry by the reformers, since the novel is characterized by a sense of an arrested cultural and political development. Between 1857 and 1911, nothing really seems to change for Muslims living in Delhi. It takes a few years for Muslims to return to the city after having been thrown out in the aftermath of the Mutiny, but little changes in the Muslim worldview. It is telling, too, in this vein that Ali's intertextual practice relies very heavily on eighteenth- and early nineteenth-century Urdu poets from Delhi in order to maintain the fiction that there has been little or no interesting cultural output in Delhi in the 80 years between the Mutiny and the publication of the novel. Clearly this is part of the polemic against colonialism and the effects of colonialism on not only the imagination but also the urban landscape that gave rise to the complicated and unique linguistic innovations of the Dehlvi ghazal. But there is also a kind of political polemic against the cultural output of Muslims in the intervening years. These cultural failures had failed to produce the desired political and aesthetic outcomes, and *Twilight in Delhi* would be an attempt to solve them.

Ali's Novelistic Politics

Urdu poetry contains a specific genre for the occasion of the decline of a city and its empire. The shehrashob, also extant in Turkish and Persian, becomes important in Urdu poetry around the eighteenth century when Urdu began to replace Persian as the court language and came into its own as a literary language. Other poetic forms also follow the Mughal court into South Asia (the *ghazal, masnavi, musaddas, nazm, qasida, soz*), but in some ways Delhi was uniquely suited for the shehrashob since it had been the capital of several empires in the subcontinent and overtaken, the novel reminds us, at least seven times. Shehrashobs are poems occasioned by the sacking of a city; they tend to be formally varied (the *musaddas* – the six-line stanza – and the *ghazal* – the two-line stanza – being the two most common metrical and rhyme schemes) but common in their content. Shehrashobs describe the decline of a city, either before or after conquest depending on the political orientation, through a cataloging of the features of the city: its marketplaces, its artisans, its structures and most of all, its poetry. Either because of the depravity of the conquerors or the corruption of the residents, cities that were once grand have now come upon ruin, and so the elegiac structure and tone of the shehrashob simultaneously reproduces past greatness even as it contends that that greatness is completely irretrievable.

The Urdu shehrashob differs from its Persian and Turkish cousins in many ways, but the one that contemporary Urdu critics are keen on reminding readers of is that the Urdu shehrashob eschews the homoeroticism of the Persian and Turkish forms. One of the conventions of the shehrashob, in this respect, is to describe the denizens of the city, from the perspective of an itinerant, *bazaari*, public spectators, their occupations, but also the beauty of their young men (*"ladkon ki khubsurati ka hazliya andaaz"*) (Ahmed 1967, 9). The sacking of a city, after all, brought with it not only the destruction of the architecture and the monuments that had made a city unique, but also created a situation where the streets were now filled with new bodies, which the poems necessarily depict as unattractive in order to expose the depth of the decline between the former paradise and the current hell. As a result, the critics remind us, the shehrashob in Persian and Turkish often lingers on the bodies of young men in the streets and how their beauty makes a particular city the envy of all men. The point here is not to debate the virtue of homoerotic urban poetry but to demonstrate that the shehrashob itself was a flexible poetic form, shaping itself to the moral and political conventions of its generation. The modern Urdu shehrashob, after all, develops in the conflict with colonial modernity and is in many ways a product of the debates taking place in Urdu about the decadence of the ghazal (itself a homoerotic genre) in order to preserve a sanitized version of the cultural past.

The other important debate that affected the shehrashob in the modern period was the debate about the benefits of material and worldly poetry. Unlike other genres of Urdu poetry that lent themselves to the metaphysical and the introspective, the shehrashob was seen as decidedly and decisively material and worldly (Ahmed 1967, 9). There has been, in recent years, an extensive debate about the materiality of the ghazal (some believe that the ghazal is the product of historical circumstances, while others argue for the inviolability of its lyric frame), but the shehrashob's credentials in this respect are more or less acknowledged by most critics. Naeem Ahmed, who has written one of the two key texts on the history of the shehrashob, argues: "Shehrashobs are both a description of life and an investigation of it. These poems are not a consequence of thoughts of pain (*khayaal-e-arayi*) but a product (*takhliq*) of the conditions of their times. For this reason this genre is a reflection of its environment (*mahaul ki akaas*)" (Ahmed 1979, 272). In Ahmed's history, the shehrashob's unique qualities (*ahmiyat aur azmat*) are characterized by its reliance on realism (*vaqayat aur haqiqat* – literally "comprehension and reality") through plainness, seriousness and comprehensiveness (*sadaqat, girayi, geharayi aur sadagi*) (Ahmed 1979, 272). Ahmed is, it should be clarified, continuing the Aligarh distaste for the ghazal by resurrecting the shehrashob as a chaste and grave poetic tradition, but his explanation of the stylistic features of the shehrashob is still persuasive.

The shehrashob describes not only the events of the sacking but the political, social, cultural, economic and financial (*siyasi, samaji, tehzibi, maashi, aur maasharti*) transformation of a city under new rule (Ahmed 1967, 10). Beginning with Mir Jafir Zetli and Mahmud Shakir Naji, the shehrashob became an important index of the allegiance of poets and writers to particular heads of state and their unwillingness to accept fealty to new leaders. This particular type of shehrashob Naeem Ahmed and others call the "*tabahi o barbadi*" shehrashob. The other variety of the poem (not given a precise term by the major critics) is about the internal decline of a city already in ruin, mismanagement and decay, ready for new leadership and deserving of conquest. The shehrashob was, in this respect, flexible enough a genre to accommodate the poetry of protest and the poetry of loyalism, looking forward and backward historically, depending, of course, on the particular poet and his patron. It also relied on a specific theory or interpretation of history, one in which the sacking of a city was decisive politically, even if poetically productive.

And for a novelist like Ali, who was looking for a form capable of linking a Muslim emotional frame with a nationalist politics, experiments with the shehrashob could, in fact, be productive. In a different context, Priya Joshi has argued that Ali's method was to take indigenous narrative conventions and selectively graft them onto the novel, thereby creating a unique formal and ideological structure that the novel could deploy selectively:

> His was a form of literary indigenization that had severed all ties with the Victorian literary world and in which empire is represented largely as a distorting and corrosive power rather than a productive cultural influence. [...] *Twilight* was a singular attempt at vernacularizing the novel with almost exclusively local preoccupations. [...] Ali's formal and cultural influences in *Twilight* tend to be from the Urdu and Persian poetry that flourished in Mughal India. The transaction he engages within *Twilight* is an oddly paradoxical one, freely utilizing an imported language and form but vigorously eschewing other cultural influences from them altogether. Few Indian novels before or since *Twilight* have been as sternly selective. (Joshi 2002, 212–3)

Consider, in this vein, the difference between Altaf Husain Hali's famous shehrashob, "*Jite ji maut ke tum munh mein, na jana hargiz*," and the temporality and idea of history in *Twilight in Delhi*.

> Hearken to me, do not go into the ruins of Delhi.
> At every step, priceless peals lie buried beneath the dust,
> No place in the world is so rich with hidden treasure.
> Even the traces of what reminded us of the city's destruction are gone,
> Dear Heaven, can there be greater oblivion than that?
> Those are gone have forgotten us. We too have ceased to think of them.
> Times have changed as they can never change again.
> Can you point to any family that which does not bear scars?
> Dear Heaven, that made us weep, cease, I beseech you,
> But do not let strangers mock us.
> If they were to know our plight, not only friends
> But the whole world would pity us.
> O cup-bearer, who passes the last round of wine.
> Do not fill it to the brim, and let no thirst be fully quenched.
> For now their long spell of good fortune lies asleep.
> Do not awaken them, O wheel of time, they are in deep slumber.
> O mirth and joy, hasten hence, Delhi is no place for you any more,
> Yes, once Delhi was the center of art and science
> But the art of poetry is dead, never to be born again.
> Do not grieve for the glories of the past.
> "Ghalib," "Shefta," "Nayyar," "Azurda" and "Zauq" will never come again.
> After "Momin," "Alavi" and "Sehba," who is left to speak of that art of poetry. (Gupta 1981, xviii)

Not only does the emotional logic of Hali's shehrashob require a complete rupture between the present and the past, it also binds its listeners into a shared community of loss, one that experiences the trauma of losing a city in the same ways. The death of poetry (*"shairi mar chuki"*), the destruction of the distinctive architecture (*"mit gaye tere mitane ke nishaane bhi"*) and the loss of intellectual capital (*"ilm-o-hunur"*), make it impossible to return to the past. There is, of course, always a tension in poems of lament, which reproduce the very thing they claim is irretrievable, but this tension does not undo the symbolic axis of the poem, which turns on the impossibility of recuperating a loss (*"chipe chipe peh hain yan, gauhar ekta teh khak"*). What the shehrashob requires, of course, is the utter victimization and devastation of an urban space and a way of life in order to both explain the political change as trauma and produce a version of that trauma as a unique episode, not just in collective memory but also in history (*"aisaa badla hain na badlega zamanaa hargiz"*).

Certainly there are elements of the shehrashob in Ali's novel. The detailed description of the landscape and particularly the buildings and monuments, the cataloging of more than sixty different pieces of poetry (both high and low brow) and the repeated refrain of the loss of Delhi's grandeur and its patrons are all formal features of the shehrashob. Though Ali borrows not merely the content but also the form. Consider this passage from earlier in the novel:

> But gone are the poets too, and gone its culture. *Only the coils of the rope, when the rope itself has been burnt*, remain, to remind us of past splendor. Yet ruin has descended upon its monuments and buildings, upon its boulevards and by-lanes. Under the tired and dim stars the city looks deathly and dark. *The kerosene lamps do light the streets and lanes, but they are not enough, as are not enough the markets and the gardens, to revive the light that floated on the waters of the Jamuna or dwelt in the heart of the city.* Like a beaten dog it has curled its tail between its legs, and lies lifeless in the night as an acknowledgement of defeat. (Ali 1994, 5)

The intense symbolism – "coils of rope," "the kerosene lamps," "the light that floated on the waters" – is a staple of the shehrashob (in Hali these are the "priceless pearls" and the "cup-bearers"). There is also the repetition of "they are not enough, as are not enough," simultaneously rhyming and setting the stage for the light to literally be extinguished from Delhi. There are other places where the novel appears to lift entire passages from Hali's shehrashob and use them as its own:

> What happened to the great poets of Hindustan? Where were Mir and Ghalib and Insha? Where were Dard and Sauda or even Zauq? Gone they were, and gone with them was the wealth of poetry. Only a poverty of thought had come to stay, reflected Mir Nihal, and in place of emotion and sentiments a vulgar sentimentality. Time had reversed the order of things, and life had been replaced by a death-in-life. No beauty seemed to remain anywhere and ugliness had blackened the face of Hindustan. (Ali 1994, 176)

It is no longer, though, a shehrashob being turned into a novel – here as in many places in the novel a quiet substitution is being made. Hindustan slips in for Delhi. It is not the case that the shehrashob wasn't capable of myths of national glory, but it presumed that the nation was telescoped in the city. Or rather, there was no need to talk about the whole of the nation since its capital and its culture was destroyed. Here, that culture is nationalized: Dard, Sauda and Zauq are no longer Dehlvi poets but national ones. The destruction of Delhi and its poets no longer affects simply the city but the entirety of the nation.

But Ali takes the conventions of the shehrashob – a genre of male, public spaces – and moves them into the domestic, private world. The domestic space is then subject to the same kind of telescoping procedure. The home is not merely the home but a reflection of homes throughout India. Ali's narrator tells us, in a rather typical moment of feminist sympathy: "In the zenana, things went on with the monotonous sameness of Indian life." Women are not merely women in the household but representations of the patterns of sexism writ large in the subcontinent, as when Mehro's fantasies about her engagement are described as "the inhibitions which grow in the repressed lives of Indian women like cobwebs and mushrooms." There is also a pattern of throwaway phrases like "women hold a subordinate position in Indian life." The sky in Delhi doesn't just darken, it darkens "with a beauty peculiar to India, bringing associations of joy and love and spring."

And there is, of course, Mir Nihal's eventual retreat into his home after his stroke, which occasions another transformation of the emotional space of the world into the political space of colonial India:

> New ways and ideas had come into being. A hybrid culture which had nothing in it of the past was forcing itself upon Hindustan, a hodge-podge of Indian and Western ways which he failed to understand. The English had been beaten by the Turks at Gallipoli. Even this had not affected his heart. He had become feelingless and *was not interested whether the Caravan stayed or moved on*. The old had gone, and the new was feeble and effete. At least it had nothing in common with his ideals or his scheme of things. (Ali 1994, 1975–6)

There is something in that line – "not interested whether the Caravan stayed or moved on" – that is indicative of Ali's procedure. Conventional lines of Urdu poetry are smuggled back into the English prose of the novel as accounts of the feeling of the characters. At the very moment when Mir Nihal is contemplating his unfitness for the changes being wrought on Delhi, the narrator, in a rhetorical flourish, makes the idiom of the poem Mir Nihal's own. And so the experiences of the city, its poets, its monuments and its residents all become linked in a network of filiations held together by a shared, though translated, idiom of Urdu. The shehrashob structure of the novel moves it in the direction of generalizing the experiences of a family, of a city, to stand in for the whole of the nation. And here is perhaps the most interesting of Ali's arguments in *Twilight in Delhi* – colonialism was first and foremost felt by the Muslim population of India. These visions of urban decay – of a past splendor rendered permanently irretrievable, of ruins that serve only to remind of the gulf that separates the past from the present – these are consistent with the structures of the shehrashob. In many ways, this would be the emotional architecture that not only made up the world of Mir Nihal's generation but also provided some connection to the world of anticolonial politics as well. There is also the possibility that this novel imagines that it is not a part of the tradition of novels written with the didactic purpose of educating the passive into becoming political agents, but sees the need for reconsidering the casual, organic methods that we have for narrating the process of radicalization and all of its troubling and disarming suburbanizations. Politics here is not only domestic but domesticated, transferred as it is to the zenana where the sexist attitudes of the narrator mix with a purported empiricism about the lack of desire of women in the Muslim home to uplift themselves.

As a result, for Ahmed Ali, the novelization of the shehrashob is not simply the translation of a shared feeling from one genre to another (and one language to another), it is also an attempt to take a lost worldview – militant opposition to the British through an idiom of Muslim masculinity – and transform it into a politics and poetics that can be salvaged for the present. At issue here are both the intellectual's sense of his separation from his cultural past and also the sense that it should be possible to manufacture a Muslim anticolonial radicalism. As he watches the Durbar procession pass the Jama Masjid, and recalls the last Muslim uprising in Delhi against the British, Mir Nihal is overwhelmed with a feeling that the past is irretrievable:

> There were those men of 1857, and here were the men of 1911, chicken-hearted and happy in their disgrace. This thought filled him with pain, and he sat there, as it were, on the rack, weeping dry tears of blood, seeing the death of his world and of his birthplace. The past, which was his, had gone, and the future was not for him. He was filled with shame and grief, until the tears of helplessness came into his eyes and he wiped them from his cheeks. People were busy looking at the show, and the children were curious and shouted. They did not know yet what it all meant. It all seems a fair to them, thought Mir Nihal; but soon, when they have grown up Time will show them a new and quite a different sight, a peep into the mysteries of life, and give them a full glimpse of the sorrows of subjection. *But happy are they who feel not, for they do not know, and miserable are they who see and suffer and can do nothing. A fire burns within their breasts; but the flames do not shoot up. Only the soul is consumed by the internal heat* and they feel dead, so dead, alas…. (Ali 1994, 107)

Mir Nihal, of course, has it wrong: the people do feel, the novel reminds us, since they will only a few pages later challenge the British rule in Delhi quite spectacularly. But the question for Ali is how to overcome Mir Nihal's isolation from politics, itself a projection of the novelist's isolation from a cultural past. But in this instance, the moment of translated poetic idiom (and here it is almost cliché) – "A fire burns within their breasts; but the flames do not shoot up" – is oddly a simultaneous figure for political quietude and expansive sympathy. The fire burns doubly, for both the apolitical and the frustrated, joining in them in a shared affective, albeit imaginary, structure. This is also why the figure of disenchantment has to be repeated twice in the passage: first, when Mir Nihal recognizes the impossibility of recovering the spirit of 1857, and second, when he exposes the Durbar (presumably for the men of 1911) as a hollow, political spectacle. This last maneuver, though, is outside the scope of the shehrashob, which presumes a shared history and interpretation of the past, and in fact relies on that shared collective memory to move into figures of exaggeration and hyperbole. Disenchantment is novelistic, and novelistic precisely in the ways that the progressives from the 1930s hoped to use literature as a didactic form.

The difference between the shehrashob and Ali's novel is precisely the transformation of the intermediary classes between the late nineteenth and the early twentieth centuries. It may have been possible to believe that there was a collective expression of loss in Delhi after the Mutiny. In fact, the publication of *Fugan-e-Dilli* (1931) and the massive *Mushaira* (1845), which collected together some of the greatest poets of Delhi in order to mourn the loss of the city, were testimony to the ways in which certain patterns of literary and political community still existed in the immediate aftermath of the British crackdown on Muslims in Delhi. After the British had consolidated power, though, and after the waves of Muslim reform and modernization movements, it was no longer really possible to believe that there was a shared experience of the trauma of colonization. In Mir Nihal's terms, this is the split between the "men of 1857" and "the chicken-hearted." In fact, Ali has to look in the most unexpected of places, the well-to-do and orthodox sharif home in order to find instances of anticolonial revolt and a recollection of the trauma of the Mutiny. It is from this space that anticolonialism can extend its political reach, since Mir Nihal becomes increasingly political not because of his access to the larger political world but as he retreats farther and farther into his own domestic and private life. Ali's novel has to borrow some of the conventions of the shehrashob, not only because so much of the experience of colonization and the complaint of Muslims in Delhi was linked to the destruction of an entire pattern of life, but also because it becomes the one way to retrieve that moment of anger that will unite Muslims as Muslims against the British. This was also metonymy – Delhi was India writ large and Delhi was Muslim. As a result, India could be the land of the Muslims as well. This was a problematic gesture, but nonetheless interesting in how it completely ignores the hegemony of nationalist parties, forging instead an alternative explanation for political solidarity and for the engagement of minorities with the nationalist mainstream, making a nationalism all of their own.

But the shehrashob, by itself, would have been inadequate, because its temporalities are far more abrupt, which brings it markedly close to the didactic literature from the 1930s. Cities once sacked are permanently transformed in the logic of the shehrashob. The trauma is immediate and the urban space is irretrievable, except imaginatively. There is nothing in the present that recalls the grandeur and the splendor of the past. The shehrashob relies on a complete rupture in history; new rulers are so different from past ones that the poetry reels on superlative axes in order to demonstrate how different the vistas and the sensibilities are between past and present. *Twilight in Delhi*, on the other hand, relies on two different temporalities: one that extends the process of decay over decades (rather than a single traumatic episode) and another that recycles previous narrative and ideological frames to make sense of the present. Moreover, the shehrashob was ultimately a public poem, not only because of its importance as a political utterance designed to demonstrate loyalty to patrons and an unwillingness to sell one's pen to the most recently empowered, but also because its eyes were intensely fixated on the bazaar and the street. The city as a whole faced ruin: its artisans, its merchants, its professionals and its poets. In *Twilight in Delhi*, not only do the *bazaari* classes benefit from the transfer of the capital from Calcutta to Delhi, but the ashraf classes fare well, too, as both Asghar and Habibuddin have lucrative careers working for the British government. More to the point, the novel's complex moods and its need to demonstrate the local patterns of life in Delhi and their charms and significances mean that the novel cannot have unambiguous views about the processes of change that the city is undergoing. Resentment of the British exists alongside of resentment of the past, even as those positions fight over the symbols to produce their necessary meanings.

It is in this vein that the novel also produces two kinds of explanations for its twin versions of historical decline: on the one hand, decay is the product of a hidebound Indian civilization that has left Indians unable to progress; on the other hand, decay is the unique product of British colonialism. There is the linear time of colonial modernity that produces the steady deterioration of the sharif household and the cyclical temporality of a long, purportedly Muslim view of history that has already absorbed the decline of the British Raj as an inevitability of moving the colonial capital to Delhi. Delhi, after all, has seen the rise and fall of seven empires, and this reality makes it possible to insert an anticolonial worldview without a concomitant revolutionary sensibility. Islamic opposition to misrule does not require a thoroughgoing reorganization of the social order. In many ways, though, this reflects a conservatism in Ali's thinking, burnt by the reaction of the Sunni orthodox elite in North India for participating in the *Angare* project, but still hoping to find a way to reconcile a respect and a love for the cultural products of a conservative world. There is a genuine, nonironic nobility in Ali's representations of Mir Nihal, even at the moments of his pathetic decline. This same respect for conservative culture appears in both the semi-ethnographical account of Asghar's wedding, clearly written for outsiders, as well as in the detailed and unavoidable encounter with the ghazali moods of young, sharif men.

This oscillation between the novel as critique and the novel as pedagogy is also part of the ideological tension of the nationalist who is also a modernist and a Muslim, whose cultural identity is at odds with his own political beliefs and who finds only unsatisfying outlets for his political concerns. For instance, even if Gandhi is the only solution for more radical kinds of challenges to British rule in Delhi and South Asia more generally, Gandhi has no solution to the crisis of patronage that the changing rule in Delhi has inaugurated. In fact, in order to get to Gandhi both literarily and politically, one has to have already abandoned the prospect of returning to a literary Urdu ashraf culture, and that is the compromise that remains absolutely untenable throughout the course of the novel. The pains of colonialism are felt in the Nihal household precisely because the family are the scions of the feudal privilege of Mughal Delhi; but that cultural idiom holds no real emotional intensity from which to raise a challenge to colonialism, both because it had been defeated in 1857 and because that idiom finds the audience that it can attract increasingly diminished by the changes in power. Moreover, the permanently transformed landscape of Delhi in the aftermath of 1857 has not only made the defeat of Bahadur Shah a permanent memory, but it has also defeated and demoralized a leadership that challenged empire and might have risen to challenge it again. The decline of feudal power has the ability to turn India's Muslims into nationalists, but this emotional trajectory is fraught with certain pitfalls: the sexism of this worldview leads it towards self-destructive and decadent ends (Asghar); the inability to assert the remnants of its prestige towards political ends tends towards passivity (Mir Nihal); and the religious trappings of its politics leads it to rationalize an abandonment of politics even when this is its natural proclivity. And it is this double bind that Ali finds himself attempting to solve, seeing as he does the necessity of anti-imperialist politics but being dissatisfied with nationalism, seeing the problems with Islamic practice but also its necessity in constructing viable communities of resistance. Into this mix must also be added the complicated tone of the novel – a mix of nostalgia and disgust and desperation – which seems to cut against the possibility of a utopian future, normally the standard fare of nationalist literature. The concluding sentence of the novel, for instance, abandons any possibility of human intervention in the political future: "And night came striding fast, bringing silence in its train, and covered up the empires of the world in its blanket of darkness and gloom [...]" (200). This is a narrative pose that is both victim of and unaffected by the powers of empire, which can imagine both the passing of empire as a natural phenomenon and can find no character throughout its survey of Delhi capable of leading such a revolt. Moreover, the only effect that the novel maintains is possible is a kind of moodiness about empire, a mood that must be aestheticized before and while it is being politicized.

Part of this was the consequence of being unmoored from the movements for change from which they were alienated, but part of it was also the desire to be able to voice the strategies and ambitions of individuals for their own emotional, psychic and social improvements. And in *Twilight in Delhi*, these desires are contradictory: romance produces problematic family arrangements; careers produce alienation; and literary ambitions are separated from patronage and languish in obscurity. As a result, the escape from feudal hierarchies and rigidities opens up a world of both dizzying freedom and radical alienation. These formal contradictions are not the function of bad writing, but the symptoms of an intellectual class that has become unmoored from tradition and yet still depends on it, that is deeply critical of the past but still derives pleasure from it. And in many ways, this is precisely the problem of the progressive nationalist with genuine classical training: a new kind of form is needed in which the coming into being of a new world retains in important ways the defining characteristics of the old one.

And here is where the intellectual problem becomes an aesthetic one for Ali. However one tries to reorganize the terrain, the British imprint will be felt as part of the heritage of Delhi and there is no way to undo the fact of its conquest and its reorganization of the urban space. In the novel, this is the problem with Asghar's wedding being set right next to the Coronation Durbar. If in the one instance religious orthodoxy has to give way to modern ideas about love and romance that threaten the purity of the bloodline, then in the other the new regime brings about the obsequy and decay of the old order through its interpenetration of the otherwise pure. There is, in fact, no place from which one can be principled: hybridity is not preferred over purity, but neither is the obverse; the old is preferred to the new, except when it comes to attitudes about women, religion and politics; the upper classes are not preferred to the lower, except when they demonstrate the ability to oppose the British.

The only way that the past can be smuggled into the present is through art and architecture, the only redeemable aspects of tradition that can be preserved. In Ali's

Delhi, it is not the city as such that survives (since even Indraprastha bears only a faint geographical and urban similarity to the Delhi of the novel's present) but the artistic tradition of the past. And this is what makes Gandhi important, or more precisely, why a vague nationalism, that could have been everything to everyone but was understood precisely every time it was deployed, was so productive of the kinds of narrative ambivalence that Ali needs. Shehrashob simply will not do, since we have no allegiances to any of the rulers of Delhi, even if the British are the most despised of the bunch. The novel's attempts to preserve the literary heritage and jettison the rest is only possible in the ranks of a movement that has already come to question an unadulterated modernity and an orthodox tradition, a movement that happily and uncritically borrows from both in order to construct its idioms of the future.

For Ali, then, there was a serious problem with the kinds of political options that were available to Muslims as nationalists in late colonial India, and in some ways, the novel oscillates between a view of an aestheticized apolitical Dehlvi past and a political horizon, bounded by Gandhi, that it is struggling to approach. Gandhian politics and ideas are only obliquely a part of the novel, perhaps as collaboration with Gandhi was foreclosed more generally in Muslim politics in India with the collapse of the alliance between Gandhi and the Ali brothers. The failure of Ali to produce a compelling narrative for the unity of Islam and nationalism is in part his failure, ideologically, to see the kinds of barriers that really did stand in the way of an unambiguous Muslim nationalism. They were, however, also failures of the Congress to articulate politics that could connect with the ashraf in Delhi and bring them into the nationalist fold. That may have already been an impossibility given the ways that the British were able to insert themselves into the class conflict that existed in the United Provinces and make that conflict manifest as communal rather than economic. But that is hardly the problem for Ali. The novel itself bears testimony to a creative intellectual engagement with the terms of nationalism to make them meaningful for a minority community, and with a number of formal experiments in order to overcome intellectual contradictions, in the terms of that community.

Chapter 5

THE GRAMMAR OF THE GANDHIANS: JAYAPRAKASH NARAYAN AND THE FIGURE OF GANDHI

The Gandhian sobriquet is widely deployed in the twentieth century by a variety of political and social actors with a range of interests. To give just three examples: Anna Hazare's movement against corruption in India in recent days has been termed a "Gandhian movement" and has earned Hazare the moniker of the "modern Gandhi," even though many have found him to be an opportunist rather than a principled *ahimsavadi*; in the fight against the Indira Gandhi–led Emergency in 1975–77, Jayaprakash Narayan's movement for an end to authoritarian rule earned him the title of "Gandhian Socialist" (though he had been using "Gandhian Socialism" as an analytical term for some time) and his call for *sampurna kranti* ("total revolution") was supposed to induce a moral regeneration in India; and as we have seen in this study, in the 1930s, Indian writers writing in English for largely European audiences came to be canonized as "Gandhian writers" because they depicted scenes from the movement for Indian independence in their novels and because Gandhi routinely appeared – as a character, as a trope, as a symbol, as a topic of discussion in their pages. There are, of course, others who have both self-identified as descendants of Gandhi (Vinoba Bhave, Martin Luther King Jr., etc.) and others who have been dubbed Gandhians by virtue of their heroic activism against greater powers (e.g. the Chipko movement in India). In fact, Gandhi is widely regarded as having intellectual and political offspring all around the globe; Gandhi and Gandhians are reproduced everywhere, with varying degrees of family resemblance.

But in all of these instances, the deployment of the term "Gandhian" does at least as much work of assigning moral probity to the cause in question as it does in providing an index of the political proximity to Gandhian ideas (however we understand them). Gandhi has come to mean many things to many people, as Claude Markovits reminds us, but the term "Gandhian" has come to guarantee the moral righteousness of the person it describes: Gandhian politicians are incorruptible; Gandhian movements are persuasive and compelling; Gandhian ways of life are sustainable and laudable. At the same time, "Gandhian" is never reducible to the historical person of Gandhi; Gandhi serves as something of an inspiration and something of a justification simultaneously for a range of political and philosophical propositions that were uncharted in his idiosyncratic and provisional ethics. Usually, the term "Gandhian" marks an additive and subtractive procedure, a selective appropriation of ideas that are more or less recognizably associated with Gandhi. Take for instance Anthony Parel's concluding thoughts on the relationship between Gandhi and Nehru: "Nehru shows how one may disagree with Gandhi on specific policies without disagreeing with his public philosophy. Today, most Indians – barring right-wing Hindus, Marxists and Maoists – find themselves more or less in Nehru's situation. They believe that they can have both industrialization and Gandhi's public philosophy. He survives in India in and through their 'abiding sense of hope'" (Parel 2011, 236). Parel's attempt at yoking what he sees as more or less unqualified goods for contemporary India (industrialism and morality) also includes his sense of what is bad (communalism and armed struggle), which is regulated and defined by invoking "Gandhi," even when the historical Gandhi's public philosophy would have had a hard time squaring industrialism with his own idiosyncratic economic strategies. "Gandhian" has come to mean specific things in specific historical moments that have more to do with contemporary preoccupations than they have to do with the ways that Gandhism might be a kind of aggregate term for all of the political, ethical and performative aspects of Gandhi's life: more than being a mark of principled nonviolence, "Gandhi" actually comes to mark the ground between activists and the state, as each seeks to regulate the behavior of the other with respect to political futures.

If "Gandhian" can be an omnibus term for all kinds of nonviolent strategies deployed in the service of social change and used in the rhetoric of policing otherwise unruly activists, in India it also comes to mean a set of political ideas and ethical practices that are unquestionably Indian and beyond reproach, that are replicable as recognized pieces of political theater, that represent in many ways the arrested development of the dialectic of nationalism within the postcolonial nation-state: at no point has the nation that Gandhi imagined actually arrived, so whatever is understood to be Gandhi's message must be made relevant again. It is deployed by both state and nonstate actors, nationalists and separatists, communalists and anticommunalists, and industrialists and environmentalists, as each seeks out a recognizable idiom for its political theories and practices. In fact, by tracing the understanding of the term Gandhian over the long duration of its deployment and the intellectual engagement with Gandhian ideas, what emerges is less a picture of convergence with Gandhian thought and more a picture of historically differentiated views of the Mahatma that were important for particular polemics. What, then, does "Gandhian" mean and how does one come to be seen as a Gandhian, in as much as Gandhism is both a political philosophy and a style of politics? What rhetorical power does the Gandhian appellation provide and what political differences and disagreements with the Mahatma does it necessarily obscure? And how was it that some of Gandhi's fiercest critics also came to see in Gandhi something to be replicated, admired and followed?

The answers to these questions differ from the conclusions most scholars have arrived at when it comes to Gandhi's legacy. Claude Markovits finds that "the Gandhi we hear of has little to do with the flesh-and-blood man" (2004, 165), while David Hardiman concludes that, in a number of important contemporary activists, "Gandhi – their model – still lives" (2003, 301). Gandhi is either completely evacuated or entirely resuscitated in what are still the two dominant schools of scholarship: "Gandhian" is either is seen as a marker of the misappropriation of genuinely and authentically Gandhian ideas or the creative reimagining of an authentic Gandhian spirit. The problem with both of these formulations is twofold. First, in the deployment of "Gandhi" by antagonistic forces in a given historical struggle – as in the Emergency in 1975, when Narayan and Vinoba Bhave, two "Gandhians," confronted each other from opposite sides of the question of support for the Indira Gandhi government (even though most scholars tend to find Narayan the more "Gandhian" at that moment) – such analytical frames are rendered unhelpful and even contradictory. Second, since the frame of reference for these studies tends to be a kind of family tree beginning with Gandhi and radiating outwards, other genealogies for contemporary "Gandhians" are often occluded in the service of reproducing (or smashing) the myth of the Mahatma; is Narayan, for instance, best understood as a relative of the Mahatma or of Marx? In order to develop a more nuanced account of the deployment of Gandhi (as a figure in both the historical and rhetorical sense), this essay looks at the long career of one "Gandhian" in order to understand the variety of gestures that were performed to become Gandhian. A different picture is revealed, too, when one examines the rhetorical procedures through which the Mahatma is invoked into the present. All deployments of "Gandhi" are necessarily figurative and so bear an uneasy relationship to the historical figure; by tracking these figures, though, we can also understand something about the longevity of "Gandhi" as well as the specific political uses to which the figure is being put.

In the final decades before independence, the Indian Left widely debated its political orientation towards anticolonial nationalism and Gandhi. Revolution, they believed, was the order of the day with the massive increase in political activity, and the Indian Left was enthusiastically organizing inside of India for a more radical transformation of Indian society. Two questions were inevitably raised: first, was it possible to attain Socialism in a predominantly agrarian society like India; and second, were the people at the head of the Indian National Congress, and in particular Gandhi, radicals or reactionaries in the coming struggle against capitalism? What is revealed by tracing the legacy of some of the debates had in the Left about the figure of Gandhi are the complicated ways that the figure of the Mahatma was seen as part of a large, symbolic political chain. Sometimes the chain of signification showed Gandhi's reactionary credentials (Gandhi – nationalist bourgeoisie – capitalism), while at other times it pointed to an unmistakably progressive character of Gandhian politics (Gandhi – mobilized masses – Socialism). In the course of the last two decades of the Indian movement for independence, both of these images of Gandhi existed side by side as the various Left parties tried to rationalize the contradictory positions that they found themselves in. These also produced a variety of strategies with respect to collaboration and critique: a Gandhi with mass appeal could be admired; a Gandhi whose influence was waning could be isolated; a Gandhi engaged in mass struggle could be pushed; a Gandhi too close to the bourgeoisie could be abandoned. The reactionary and the progressive credentials of Gandhi were variously brought into play depending on the various strengths and weaknesses of the Socialist and Communist Left.

Two important conclusions emerge from this picture of leftist engagement with Gandhi and Indian nationalism. First, even until the moment of independence, scathing criticism of Gandhi went alongside enthusiastic endorsement of the mass mobilizations that Gandhi was credited with producing. While the Communist Party of India never altered its argument that Gandhi was deeply conservative (one Communist called him "the acutest and most desperate manifestation of the forces of reaction"), even its leading members were forced to concede at different moments that he had a unique ability to draw out large crowds of people in opposition to British imperialism (Bharati 1987, 39). As early as 1924, M. N. Roy, the head of the Communist Party, was convinced of the utterly conservative role of Gandhian ideas on the movement for national liberation; he could only write in uncontrolled invective: "To you or those like you, 'Non-violent Non-cooperation' may be a case of political wisdom or expediency, but to the stalwarts of pure Gandhism it is a fetish, and positively counter-revolutionary at that. [...] Yes, once more the Empire is saved, once more the blessed Indian society is rescued from the threat of a Revolution! Victory to the name of the Mahatma and to his cult of Non-Violence! Alleluja, Amen!" (1924, 9). As such, Roy was convinced that collaboration with the projects of the Congress could only give cover to the conciliatory strategies of the bourgeoisie and advocated instead the organization of independent revolutionary parties. Roy's position, though, was part of a larger debate taking place within the Communist International (Comintern) about strategies for advancing the revolutionary struggle in India, which came to a head in 1925 at the meeting of the Colonial Bureau in Amsterdam. Roy's chief antagonist at the meeting was R. Palme Dutt, who argued instead in favor of working within nationalist organizations in order to clarify the political differences between the Congress and the Communists; Dutt was to later swing around to Roy's position in 1927, only then to shift again to advocating for collaboration with the Congress in the famous Dutt–Bradley thesis of 1935, which argued that the Congress and Gandhi should be brought into a united fight against imperialism.[1] This was merely the beginning of a long series of twists and turns in the Communist Party's orientation on the question of bourgeois nationalism, the united front and Gandhi, which only ended when the Communist Party swung back again in 1942 to supporting British imperialism against Hitler and ending all ties with the Congress during the Comintern's Popular Front period. The Congress Socialist Party, on the other hand, fully entered the Congress soon after its constitution in 1934 and followed a course of increasing appreciation for the contributions of Gandhi to the movement for national liberation. The study of these political characterizations of Gandhi and the concomitant shifts in strategy that the Left in India pursued is already the subject of a vast corpus of literature.

Second, and more importantly, "Gandhi" was seen as a link in a process that did not terminate with the words or actions of the Mahatma, but, in the discourse of the Left, could only be diagnosed by considering the relevant players who were attached to him. Multiple attempts were made at diagnosing his political philosophy from his writings, but even these were inconclusive. Gandhi was variously "holding back" the movement for independence and "pushing it forward"; his satyagrahas were both "mass struggles" and religious "hocus-pocus." Variously, Gandhi represented not only himself but also the "bourgeois" and "right wing" elements within the Congress as well as the "Socialist" factions that were vying for influence as well. At different points, Gandhi came to stand in for "the nation," "the masses," "the peasants," "the Congress," and "the bourgeoisie" – the various aggregations for which he was seen as the representative. This is at least part of the reason that there were almost as many pamphlets talking about the "Bolshevik

Gandhi" as there were talking about him as the "mascot of capitalism." Gandhi's Socialist and capitalist credentials were shored up by reference to the very people and groups that he was immediately positioned next to, making him something of a metonym for them. The tension in these images of Gandhi in the leftist literature of late-colonial India was a product of the uneasy relationship between the Left and its understanding of the prospects for radical social change. For instance, Nehru's characterization of Gandhi underscores this tension between leftist confidence and inadequacy with respect to organizing radical politics at the all-India level: "All this [the various estimations of Gandhi's politics] shows that we were by no means clear or certain in our minds. Always we had the feeling that while we might be more logical, Gandhiji knew India far better than we did, and a man who could command such tremendous devotion and loyalty must have something in him that corresponded to the needs and aspirations of the masses. If we could convince him, we felt that we could also convert these masses" (Nehru 1958, 255). Here, too, Nehru shows the circuit that connects Socialists – through Gandhi – to the peasantry, a circuit that Nehru felt he had to rely on because of his inadequate understanding of India but whose future he also felt confident he understood better than did Gandhi. In the worldview of the Left, the process went something like this: Gandhi would deliver the masses into activity that the radicals could not; the radicals would use the activity to move the masses beyond Gandhi by raising demands that the people wanted but Gandhi could not fulfill.

This sense of confidence and inadequacy, of theoretical certainty and practical incapacity, characterized the relationship between a large section of Indian Socialists who, like Nehru, both criticized Gandhi and knew that without him they had few chances to find mass audiences on their own. "Gandhi" came to mean something more than the historical personality; he came to represent both the obstacles and occasions for the growth of revolutionary Socialist possibilities in the subcontinent. It is precisely this duality in Gandhi, his conservatism coupled with his ability to ignite mass protest, that seemed to give Socialists in India the most difficulty. In the process of attempting to understand the class character and political trajectory of the Congress, for instance, Socialists like Narayan were unsure about how to add up the sum total of the forces working inside of the Congress; here is how Narayan saw others inside of the Socialist Party thinking about the nationalist movement:

> However, to return to the question whether the Congress could become an instrument of socialism. There are many contradictory trends and forces in the Congress. Some of these tend to pull the Congress in the direction of socialism. There are the socialists, for instance, and a small number of other leftists. There are also many, whom one may describe as constructive Gandhians, who are in sympathy with democratic socialism. There are towering men in the Congress such as Pandit Nehru and Maulana Azad, whose sympathies are the same. And above all, there is Mahatmaji who, as a servant of *daridranarayan*, is a socialist in his own original way. It was perhaps not wrong to believe that these forces could together succeed in taking the Congress and the country towards socialism. And, therefore, there were many among us who did desire, and some still do, to give this course a chance. (1980b, 135)

This was partly the result of an elastic definition of Socialist, which in this passage stretched to include voluntarist social work ("constructive Gandhians"), nationalist modernizers (Nehru and Azad) and idiosyncratic concern for the poor (Gandhi), as well as self-identified Socialists campaigning for a revolutionary transformation of the social order. But the picture that develops from this presentation of Congress's political future is first a vertical integration of Socialist thought within all ranks of the Congress and second a horizontal movement of the entirety of the Congress from the outside. At a minimum, this was an attempt to see Socialist prospects in every act of nationalist resistance; at a maximum, it was a serious misreading of the political situation that the Socialists confronted.

Narayan is important in this story because he is most widely understood as one of the most capricious Indian political thinkers, vacillating from Bolshevism to democratic Socialism to liberalism, philanthropy, and finally to Gandhism at the end of his life. For J. P. (as he came to be known in the 1970s in his fight against the Emergency) had by that moment in time a varied political career: he had joined Congress in 1930, started the entrist Congress Socialist Party, walked out of Congress in 1948, joined Vinoba Bhave's Bhoodan campaign in 1954, formed the Gandhian Praja Socialist Party in 1957, led the Bihar student movement in 1974, organized the People's Union for Civil Liberties in 1976 and helped to form the multiparty Janata Party in 1977. Some have characterized Narayan's political flexibility as a mark of his deep commitment to on-the-ground realities over doctrinaire applications of Marxism, though much of this scholarship seems to use Narayan to wage Cold War polemics against Socialism in general (Handa 1985). In fact, it is the extraordinary flexibility that Narayan seems to have with political formations and organizations that makes him an important part of the story of how the figure of Gandhi has been deployed over the last century.

Narayan, though, saw things differently on the eve of independence than did his comrades in the Congress Socialist Party. Unconvinced that the Congress was dispositionally bourgeois, Narayan felt that the concentration of "individual self-interests" within the leadership of the Congress would prevent it from ever becoming Socialist: "The question then is, can the Congress change structurally? [...] Here, I think, the answer is uncertain. It does not appear to me to be possible. All the individual self-interests will join together, as they are doing today, to obstruct a change and thwart Mahatma Gandhi as well as to check socialism" (1980b, 138). If in the first picture Gandhi was part of a vertically integrated Socialist strain within the Congress, here the image is one of an isolated Gandhi standing alone defending the party and enabling a move towards Socialism. What seemed to happen during the last years of the movement for independence was the reduction of all national aspirations (in all of their variety) to the figure of Gandhi. At every point, Gandhi stood not for himself but, through the masses that he was able to mobilize, for a variety of different possible futures of the postindependence nation. The ease with which Narayan slides rhetorically between the effects of the "do-nothing" politics of the Congress elite to Gandhi and then to Socialism reveals what Narayan is at pains to point out. The Congress Socialists were unable to see any path to Socialism that did not first pass through Gandhi. Gandhi, here, functions both as a historical and rhetorical figure, as metonym for populist politics, as metalepsis for Socialism, which is to say that Gandhi comes to stand in for a political process that is disconnected from his actual political philosophy: the Congress Socialist Party routinely described Gandhi as a political figure they would bypass and as a necessary link in the symbolic nexus between mass agitation, populist politics, and Socialist futures. This figurative operation happened alongside a longer compromise with Gandhi and bourgeois nationalism in which the Socialists helped to preserve unity in the Congress and withheld certain criticisms of its politics; at its heart it was a political theory of revolution in stages, which imagined that radical social change would be the necessary result of mass mobilization for independence.

This is how Narayan understood the transformation of the movement for independence into a more general movement against feudalism and international capitalism:

> After the removal of British power, the abolition of Princes and of the zamindari and capitalist systems should be a comparatively simpler problem. If the Indian people proved strong enough to destroy the British Raj in India, nothing could stop them from destroying feudalism and capitalism if they desired to do so. The only limiting factor would be the stage of development for the political consciousness of the masses. In other words, if the socialist movement were to become strong enough to move the masses in the right direction, all these changes could be made without much difficulty or opposition. (1980a, 121)

The movement for Socialism, then, was only the necessary next step once the masses were sufficiently strong enough to throw off the yoke of imperialism. Narayan's understanding of the weakness of the Indian bourgeoisie relative to the strength of empire meant that for him, the bourgeoisie would have been unable to achieve independence without bringing the masses of Indians into open conflict with the British Empire. At the same time, though, the more the masses were activated, the more they also threatened the power and position of the indigenous rulers (the princes and the capitalists). This meant that while independence was necessary, in the minds of the Socialists it was not sufficient for radical change, and Socialism would mean an open conflict with the people who were at the helm of the Congress. Gandhi was helpful in bringing out the masses but unhelpful in advancing "the stage of development for the political consciousness of the masses." So critiques of Gandhi, while always present, were mapped alongside compromises with Gandhi and the Congress, so that every time Gandhi was represented, he was represented anxiously. Unable to turn him into either an unqualified good or unproblematic bad, intellectuals of the period found themselves using increasingly figurative language in their depictions of Gandhi in order to produce a picture of the Mahatma that suited their ends. What emerges, ultimately, is a pattern of symbolization, or more precisely certain tropes of "the Mahatma," which were necessary corollaries to this posture of critique-and-collaboration: the aggregation of these figures of the Mahatma produce a Gandhian grammar.

The phrase "Gandhian grammar" has been chosen for two reasons. First, it signals the way that political debates with Gandhi were had through the extensive network of newspapers, magazines, journals and published speeches that were produced in the 1930s and 1940s. Gandhi was a diligent correspondent, and the sheer volume of political letters and articles in which Gandhi develops a specific idiom and a set of phrases then picked up by his interlocutors begins to resemble its own linguistic archive of allusive references that are historically remote and idiosyncratic uses of English specific to the class in question. Second, it is designed to signal how Gandhi became "Gandhi," a rhetorical figure that could be deployed for argumentative, emotional, persuasive, or political ends. In fact, much of the political debate about tactics that the Congress would conduct had to make explicit reference to whether or not "Gandhi" would approve of the specific kinds of terms that were used. When Narayan wanted to move a resolution for a national general strike, Gandhi immediately responds by calling this "violence"; in his response, Narayan begins to more clearly define the character of his strike:

> In his article Gandhiji, quoting my words that we had emphasized labor and peasant organization as the basis of a revolutionary mass movement, adds that he dreads the language used. To a revolutionary like Gandhiji, who had played with fire and stirred up millions to action, the words need not cause any fear. I do not mean by them bloodshed and chaos. Revolution need not always be red in tooth and claw. We had explained to Gandhiji at Delhi and I had again explained it to him at Abbottabad that our aim was to lay the basis for a country-wide non-payment of rents, revenue and taxes and general strike by workers in industry and transport. We mean by these peaceful and regulated but might mass conflicts that would paralyze and end British rule. (2001a, 26–7)

First, Gandhi the interlocutor, the one who disagrees with the language of "strikes," is now counterposed to "a revolutionary like Gandhiji," a fictional creation of Narayan's mind, and rhetorically designed to move class-based struggle ("non-payment of rents" and "general strike") into the lexicon of Gandhi-led satyagraha. The negotiations and arguments by which political debates were conducted in and around the Congress necessarily led to the production of a Gandhian grammar, that Gandhi both defined and that eventually defined "Gandhi."

In the 1930s, though, before he had become disillusioned with both Nehru and Soviet Communism, Narayan, recently returned from the US, was crucially involved in the mass contact campaigns that the Congress was undertaking in the 1930s. The aim of his newly formed Congress Socialist Party was – as he described in "Why Socialism?" – "to elucidate certain problems arising out of the present stage of the national movement and the problem of its future direction. The growth of the Congress Socialist Party has created a thought-ferment within the ranks of the Congress and has brought issues of fundamental importance to the fore. A conflict of ideologies, a juxtaposition of programmes, demands clear-cut decisions" (2001d, 1). Narayan's hope with the pamphlet had been to open up a discussion with Congress workers to answer some of the more basic objections to Socialism but also to convince the Congress to adopt a more radical program that would make it possible to transform the Congress from a limited organization to a mass organization. Narayan lays out six specific minimum demands that the Congress ought to take up in its agitational work:

1. Complete independence, in the sense of separation from British Imperialism.
2. All political and economic power to the producing masses (including brain workers).

3. Nationalization of all key and large industries, banks, mines, plantations, etc.
4. Abolition of landlordism in all its forms.
5. Land to the tiller of the soil.
6. Liquidation of all debts owed by peasants and workers. (86)

Narayan knew this program would immediately put him into conflict with the leadership of the Congress, much of which was closely allied to large landlords in India and some of which relied on patronage from prominent capitalists in order to fund their operations. But his hope had been that Nehru's presidency in the Congress would open up space for more radical debates, so that any movement in the direction of a more radical program would immediately shift the Congress towards a mass-based party. In this project, Narayan relied on a theoretical understanding of the relationship between the Congress and the Congress Socialist Party, in which entering into the Congress allowed the Socialists to get closer to the real anti-imperialist forces in the country. As Narayan put it: "The argument advanced is that by remaining within the Congress, [the Congress Socialist Party] is strengthening the bourgeois hold over the anti-imperialist elements within the Congress. Nothing can be further removed from reality, however. The very purpose of the Party remaining in the Congress is to weaken, by inside propaganda and opposition, that hold; and ripen the anti-imperialist elements for a final break with it" (2001d, 87). Narayan imagined that by pushing the Congress towards developing a mass, populist base he would be forcing a rupture within it: the bigger the movement grew, the harder it would be for Gandhian ideas to hold on to the reins of the movement.

At the same time, though, Narayan wanted to make sure that Congress workers were armed with a good understanding of the differences between the Congress and the Congress Socialists so that the "final break," when it happened, would at least happen along the lines that he had envisioned. This was the crux of the debate with Gandhi that Narayan takes up in the pamphlet: Narayan was interested in "permanently destroying the basis of exploitation and inequality," while Gandhi said, "I shall be no party to dispossessing the propertied classes of their private property without just cause. My objective is to reach your hearts and convert you so that you may hold all your private property in trust for your tenants and use it primarily for their welfare" (2001d, 46–7). This is fairly straightforward and part of the more general criticism that had emerged from both the Communists and the Socialists of Gandhi and the Congress by the 1930s: that it was a party of the national bourgeoisie, that Gandhi's strategies for *sarvodaya* were conservative with respect to upending the social order of the countryside, that moral appeals for social change would fail because they left the underlying social structure intact.

What is less obvious, though, about the terms of his debate with Gandhi is that Narayan has to make the case that he is both more Indian and more Socialist than Gandhi, who was already seen as representative of both. In fact, Gandhi's ideas of village republics were to many observers akin with notions of primitive Communism, and because this idea was rooted in Indian tradition it had a better chance of working in India. Narayan summarized the argument thus: "[Gandhi] speaks of 'indigenous socialism'; the 'essential genius' of India; the 'fundamental conception of Hinduism.' Western Socialism is based, according to him, on conceptions that are fundamentally opposed to those of Hinduism.

He implies, naturally, that his 'indigenous' Socialism, is much better suited to India than our foreign variety" (2001d, 49). And against the charge that Socialism is Western but Gandhism is Indian, Narayan responds, "Gandhiji's views are essentially what in socialist history is known as reformism. Its language is Indian but its substance is international. The chief interest of reformism lies in maintaining the established order of society. Only it sees the forces of disruption, and, sensing danger, wishes to neutralize and quieten them. It therefore advocates the administration of palliatives. All that Gandhiji tells the landlord and the capitalist, is that they should improve their relations with their tenants and laborers" (2001d, 50). Here, the problem that Narayan underlines is the universalist nature of a politics of accommodation with the ruling order, which, while Indian in style, is at least European in content and theory. In Narayan's view, then, Gandhi's Socialism is briefly, temporarily and polemically not indigenous enough. Narayan goes on to delineate the many problems with Gandhi's putative Socialist future: Gandhi's notion of trusteeship tacitly endorses exploitation of peasants and workers; Gandhi's belief that moral suasion can change the minds of capitalists misunderstands why capitalists are greedy in the first place; Gandhi eschews machinery without considering its real potential for human development; and finally, "Gandhism may be a well-intentioned doctrine. I personally think it is. But even with the best of intentions, it is, I must admit – it gives me no pleasure to do so – a dangerous doctrine. It is dangerous because it hushes up the real issues and sets out to remove the evils of society by pious wishes" (62). The difference between Gandhi and Socialism could not have been clearer for Narayan – what was needed was a sharp distinction between Socialist ideas and Gandhian ones if the movement for independence was going to move from anti-imperialism towards a more Socialist pattern of governance quickly.

Less than a year later, though, Narayan's position had become more complicated, both with respect to Gandhi and with respect to the Congress. First, as a consequence of the Dutt–Bradley thesis, the Communist Party sought to enter into a united front with the Congress; because they were banned, they did this first by entering into the Congress Socialist Party. The project of both the Communist and Socialist Left became to help move the Congress leftwards by engaging the party in as much mass mobilization work as possible. Critiques of the leadership were acceptable, in this period, but the Congress came to be seen as synonymous with the expression of the will of the entire nation. Second, only a few months after the publication of "Why Socialism?" Narayan was already convinced that the Congress resolutions passed at the Lucknow session in 1936 were proof that the party was actually shifting leftwards. In his report to the Congress Socialist Party, Narayan now advocated for a different approach to Socialist politics:

> It may appear strange that those who profess Socialism should say that they do not want to raise the issue of Socialism in the Congress. This may look like a ruse, a camouflage. It is neither. Our policy is dictated by the simple consideration that an organization the task of which is to unite all genuinely anti-imperialist classes on one front against imperialism needs not a Socialist but a broad anti-imperialist programme. We have no anxiety regarding Socialism. We know that the march towards it is inevitable and that complete freedom from imperialism is the first step towards Socialism. (1936, 3)

Here we ought to consider two things: first, the trope of dissemblance and ingenuity; and second, the logic of inevitability. For Narayan, Gandhian garb (his terms are "a ruse, a camouflage") and Congress activity is not a veneer for genuinely Socialist propaganda but merely the shell of an inevitable kernel that will eventually be sundered. The logical connection for Narayan is that "Socialism" need not be the policy of the Congress since "anti-imperialism" (which comes close to meaning the kinds of Popular Front tactics that characterized some of the Comintern's approaches to anticolonialism) was the order of the day. At the same time, though, the implicit response to the charge of a putative disingenuity is Narayan's belief that anti-imperialism inevitably leads to Socialism. The logic of inevitability, though, was really a deferral, since what it implied was that Socialism was not a demand to be raised in the immediate. Both of these will be important when we think about the nature of the term "Gandhian" and how many different expectant processes lurk beneath its mobilization.

Now, instead of openly campaigning against the more conservative elements inside of the Congress, he encouraged the Congress Socialist Party to vote wholeheartedly for Congress candidates in the 1937 ministerial elections. Despite months of previous argument that elections to the ministries would change nothing because the constitution hamstrung all elected officials, this is how Narayan responds to the Congress victory:

> The response and enthusiasm of the people have been a revelation to us. And such touching faith in the Congress! Simple peasants, they enter the booth as if it were a place of worship, drop their cards in "Gandhiji's" box and joining their hands devoutly make their salutation. Thousands come trekking from distant homes without inducements, defying threat and coercion, and shouting *Swantantra bharat ki jai* to vote for the Congress. The Congress is their hope – it will relieve them of their distress. This march of the hungry peasant to the polling booth is a prelude to the march to the battlefield. (2001b, 153)

Narayan is not known for his more colorful prose, writing as he does mostly polemical articles in the service of political skirmishes with contemporary adversaries. But in this instance, his genuine excitement at the prospects for activating the peasantry overwhelms his usually contained prose. Here, the symbolic chain of associations runs from the Congress through Gandhi (via religious associations) to the peasants and to revolution, and is supposed to mirror the growing political consciousness of the peasantry (though, in fact, it is more a measure of Narayan's optimistic reading of the outcome of the Bihar elections). Narayan's paternalism ("simple peasants") is as palpable in this passage as is his genuine solidarity with the peasants ("defying threats and coercion").

At the end of the same article, Narayan can barely contain his own sense that something radical is taking place within the consciousness of the peasantry:

> The other night as I was returning from an election meeting perched on a rustic *ekka* I happened to pass by a smithy. Suddenly I heard the cry *Swantantra Bharat ki-jai* followed by the age-old cry *Raja Ramachandra ki-jai*. Apparently a group of workers was listening to a recitation of Ramayana which is periodically punctuated by the most popular of cries, "Raja Ramachandra etc." *But the thought that a national cry had gained such respectability*

as to be coupled with this religious and deeply devout cry gripped my mind. It signified nothing short of a great mental revolution among the people. The Revolution has almost matured, I thought. (2001b, 156) [Emphasis original]

This set of associations is difficult to read with the same sanguine optimism after the rise of the Hindu Right as a political force in independent India. But for Narayan there are a series of equations that aggregate into his enthusiasm: secular nationalism has the same form as religious ecstasy; respectability is the same thing as popularity; and perhaps most radically, a "great mental revolution" is the harbinger of "The Revolution." There are clear vectors of possibility for Narayan that lead from this postelection scene directly into a final contest with international capital. But what ought also to be clear is that even journalistic reporting in the days of the movement for Indian independence could not be bothered by the flatness of the fact; everything became automatically a symbol to be diagnosed and reinterpreted for political purposes. "Gandhi" was no different.

Between the angry polemic of 1936 and the enthusiasm of 1937 is not some radical transformation in the content of Narayan's politics, which are still confidently Socialist. What has changed is the sense that critiquing Gandhi can and should be held in abeyance because the mass character of the movement is creating new opportunities for political awakening and radicalization. By 1939, Narayan went so far as to side with Gandhi in his maneuvering against Subhas Chandra Bose for the leadership of the Congress, because it was clear to him that siding against Gandhi would have wrecked the unity of his anti-imperialist front.

> But, at the same time, I am very clear in my mind that it would do the greatest possible injury to the cause of freedom in this country if we were to leave the Congress and form a parallel mass organization. There is no doubt that there is going to be a growing divergence between our line of work and that of the present Congress leadership. [...] But at the same time, if we carry on our work among the people with energy and devotion, we shall undoubtedly be in a position to rally the Congress masses around us and resurrect the Congress from its parliamentary debris. (1980c, 103)

Splitting from the Congress meant wrecking it, though it is not at all clear how many members would have walked out with Narayan. Narayan here imagines salvaging the Congress from within by energizing a new anti-imperialist current within it and leveraging that for a more activist (rather than election-oriented) Congress. Here, though, there is a double motion: in order to protect the cause of freedom, a split must be avoided so that at a future moment Narayan can take advantage of a split. In the first formulation, the Congress is indistinguishable from the masses; in the second, the masses have already abandoned their erstwhile leaders. At other times, though, Narayan was more straightforward; it would be important to "wreck" the Congress:

> We should work with the object of bringing the anti-imperialist elements under our ideological influence, through propaganda and work among the masses, so that finally they come to accept a proper anti-imperialist programme. I am not saying that by working

in this manner we shall win the right-wing to our programme, and thus "convert" the Congress. The Congress, as it is construed at present, cannot hold together very long. The more successful we are in pushing our programme, the nearer the day when a split will occur in it. (1946, 131)

These two positions were the result of Narayan's awkward position inside of Congress, both structurally dependent on the organization and at once working for its eventual dissolution into something more radical.

In January of 1947, Narayan penned his article "The Transition to Socialism" in the hope of laying out the course by which a soon-to-be independent India would move from a bourgeois nation-state into Socialism. A mere six months before India would be independent, Narayan already saw the possibilities of moving the country in more radical directions and he attempted to lay out three scenarios in which that transition from new nation-state to Socialism could come about. First, assuming that "a full democratic state has been established in India" after the British had left, Socialism could be brought about, Narayan argued, through "the democratic method," by which he meant "a victory at the polls" of the "future Socialist Party of India" (1964b, 50–52). Narayan had spent quite a bit of time over the past decade trying to convince the various smaller Socialist groupings to unite under a common platform, and democratic opportunities after independence offered up one important moment to inaugurate such a venture (2001c, 214–7). Second, assuming that compromises made between the British, the Princely States and the forces of communalism produced an undemocratic outcome in which colonial legacies persisted and gave birth to "such a sickly and diseased India that life for her would hardly be worth living," then the only path to Socialism would be "to renew the demand of 'Quit India' and to mobilize the people into a final challenge with the foreign power," in order to move the nation to full democracy and "a considerable way on the road to socialism" (1964b, 53). Both of these fit within the political framework developed by the official Left in India under British rule; part of the argument that runs through the article is a polemic with members of the Communist Party, especially M. N. Roy, who had critiqued Narayan and the Congress Socialist Party for remaining too closely tied to the bourgeois Congress (Sarkar 2006). Had either of the first two situations come to pass, both the Congress Socialists and Communists would have seen the transformation of India along similar lines. The third scenario was perhaps the one for which Narayan was theoretically prepared but for which, it turned out, he was not tactically equipped, and the one that actually came to pass.

Narayan was worried that a "violent revolution" might be necessary if "it is found that the Congress had forsaken the revolutionary path and was determined, whatever compromises it might have to make, to remain in the offices of Government" (1964b, 55). In the months leading up to independence, Narayan was convinced that the Congress was an unstable political formation in which the more conservative representatives of the bourgeoisie and the more populist elements of the "the peasants, the workers in the factories, the students, the city poor and the middle classes" were vying for control over the decisions and policies that the Congress would adopt (1964b, 54). The most recent Congress meeting at Meerut in November of 1946 had left Narayan cautiously optimistic that it was the Left that was ascendant, though he worried that the capitalists still firmly held on to the reins of the political apparatus:

> The Congress, which has been and remains the spearhead of the national revolution, has been slowly taking note of the economic urges of the people. The resolution on social objectives adopted by the Meerut session of the Congress goes a very long way towards socialism. The difficulty, however, seems to be that to the dominant section of the Congress, which seems at the bottom to be guided by capitalistic ideas but which *exploits the name of Mahatma Gandhi*, these declarations of social policy are merely tactical moves to placate the masses in order not to lose their support. (1964b, 54) [Emphasis added]

The tension in this description of the political forces within the Congress is not merely an analytical error on Narayan's part (though it is that, too, since it is hard to imagine simultaneously going "a very long way towards socialism" in an organization "guided by capitalist ideas"); Narayan was unable to decide whether the resolution he was able to move at Meerut meant that the Congress was amenable to being pushed in the direction of greater economic redistribution or whether this was a cynical ploy to provide a populist cover for otherwise overt power grabbing. He was prepared to move in the direction of a "dictatorship of the toiling masses" if the Congress were revealed to be a reactionary organ, but the hope running throughout the article was that the growth of the Congress Socialist Party's size and influence and the growing confidence of peasants and workers within the Congress would produce a pincer action that would shift the Congress along a more democratic path. Violent revolution was the threat designed to ensure a peaceful and principled transition to genuine democracy, to discipline the Congress into keeping its democratic promises and to stave off sectarian critique from the Communists.

The instability inside of the Congress for Narayan was simultaneously an index of possibility, in which the Congress Socialist Party could seize its advantage, and an index of an impending betrayal, in which the bourgeoisie's interests found hollow populist rhetoric to secure support and consolidate its own power under the aegis of the new nation-state. There are historical and political reasons for Narayan's inability to read the political situation clearly, not the least of which is his unwillingness – except rhetorically – to stomach a break from the Congress and his misplaced faith that Nehru genuinely believed in a Socialist future for India. What is of interest, though, is that in Narayan's essay, it is the "name of the Mahatma" that is poised between a genuinely democratic Congress and an opportunistic one, between a Congress that wants to solve the problems of the economically downtrodden and one that wants to secure the advantages of independence exclusively for the elite. At the same time, for Narayan, "the name of the Mahatma" is a perfectly flat phrase, one whose meaning should be clear and unobjectionable, aligned as it seems to be with "the masses," but which also threatens to be the sleight of hand under which the bourgeoisie can "placate" the democratic aspirations of the people. There are at least three simultaneous processes at work in the phrase "the name of the Mahatma" that are worth paying close attention to in order to unpack the complicated way in which nationalism, Socialism and democracy came to be seen as isomorphic and indistinguishable in their relationship to statism, capitalism and corruption.

First, in the sense that Narayan means the phrase, "the name of the Mahatma" is supposed to be a stand-in for nationalist unity, opposition to communalism and political noncooperation with the British, all of which lead automatically to anticolonial activism. In this sense, Gandhi is equivalent to a set of political ideas and practices that bring India closest to conditions for Socialism without actually getting to Socialism proper. Second, in the sense that Narayan fears Gandhi is being "exploited," "the name of the Mahatma" sutures over the difference between opportunistic deployment of rhetoric and meaningful action to secure democratic reforms: "If we review the work of Congress Governments in the provinces and at the centre, we shall find, apart from words and resolutions, no concrete roof that the social policy laid down in Congress manifestoes and resolutions has any binding or compelling force behind it" (1964b, 102). In both of these senses, "the name of the Mahatma" functions as metonymy for a set of politics that the historical Gandhi could be easily affiliated to.

The third sense of the phrase, though, is one that neither Narayan nor the bourgeois in Congress see, but is revealed by examining the rhetorical figure of "the name of the Mahatma" itself. In fact, if "the name of the Mahatma" means what the bourgeoisie wants it to mean, than it can hardly be "exploited," since it is merely performing the function it was designed to perform; alternatively, if "the name of the Mahatma" refers clearly to some set of populist politics that resonate with and activate the masses, then it also cannot be exploited. The exploitation of the phrase is only possible if the "name of the Mahatma" means neither and both. "The name of the Mahatma" is actually an impenetrably dense phrase produced by two metonyms joined together, a metalepsis, or as Harold Bloom has described it: "a word is substituted metonymically for a word in a previous trope, so that a metalepsis can be called, maddeningly but accurately, a metonymy of a metonymy" (1975, 103).[2] In fact, "the name of the Mahatma" is first a metonym for the historical figure "Mohandas Gandhi" (the autonomasic function of metonymy) and not merely the sound of the name, and then later reveals itself to be a reference to something that the historical Gandhi represents (the synecdochic function of metonymy); "the name of the Mahatma" passes first through the historical personality of Gandhi and then moves to something for which Gandhi is a surrogate, something more suggestively figured as "the name of the Mahatma" because it is not named specifically. The range of things that "Gandhi" could mean are legion: the politics that Gandhi represents, the charisma that Gandhi radiates, the national unity that he symbolizes, the resistance for which he is famous, the nonviolence he popularizes, the masses he represents. In another context, Madhavi Menon has described how metalepsis works rhetorically: "Metalepsis is the rhetorical term designated to bridge the gap between two worlds even as it is the trope that undermines any absolute opposition between the two. Indeed, metalepsis insists that every claim to absolute identity […] is differentially constituted in relation to the other. Metalepsis might be described as the trope that inhibits the formation of lasting bonds; as such, it often needs to be hidden away from the light of day" (2004, 68–9). The terms that Menon uses to describe metalepsis – "bridge," "gap," "absolute identity," "differentially constituted," "hidden away" – all help to unpack the way that "Gandhi" seems to function as more than the historical person in the debates about anticolonialism and Socialism. In fact, it is only because it is a metalepsis that "the name of the Mahatma" can have both a strong sense and an exploitable quality, and be simultaneously coherent and vulnerable; in this instance it is supposed to both smuggle democratic Socialism into the nationalist movement and erase the traces of capitalist opportunism.

Metalepsis becomes the dominant rhetorical device for most radical anticolonial politics because it is at once confident that a Socialist transformation is both necessary and the order of the day, and feels palpably that the dominant discourse and political tendency within nationalism is actually resistant to Socialism. This double motion – consisting of overconfidence and underconfidence – produces a particular grammar of radical nationalism in which the terms of bourgeois nationalism are deployed in the hope that their populist ability to move large numbers of people will overwhelm the specific, controlled way that conservative elements inside of nationalist circles use them, the tropological function of the terms overwhelming the realpolitik in which they are deployed. As a result, utilizing popular and populist imagery, Gandhi in particular, also meant disarticulating the "Mahatma" and repackaging him in ways that could be useful. For Narayan, and for others, what the movement for national liberation was bringing to the fore was the possibility of exposing economic and social grievances and providing an idiom in which those grievances could be expressed and large numbers of people could be mobilized; that Gandhi might have actually opposed Socialist revolution did not seem to preclude Narayan's attempt to reformulate the Mahatma's functions for his own ends: "In other words, I clearly see a major revolution intervening on our road to Socialism. I see further that the success of that revolution depends as much on its political as its social ends. In fact, I do not see that revolution succeeding if only 'Quit India' were inscribed on its banners. Other objectives too its banners must proclaim: 'land to him who tills it'; 'wealth to him who produces it'; 'Praja Raj (People's Government) in the States' and others" (1964b, 101–2). In order to suture over the differences between "revolution" and "Congress," Gandhi was being invoked in vague language to smuggle in the Socialist aspirations of the people who worked around him.

As it turned out, violent revolution never materialized. In 1948, despite his problems with the Congress ("the Congress is so identified with the Government that it has lost the power to protect the rights of the people"), Narayan found himself unwilling to advocate for a politics in which the Indian government would have to be "overthrown by violence" (Narayan 2002). Part of the reason was his disillusionment with actually existing Socialist governments, especially Stalinist Russia, which he understood as "amoral" and "totalitarian," and whose origins in violence left him uninterested in repeating its mistakes. In distinction, Narayan preferred the moral calculus of Gandhi: "But the greatest thing he taught us was that means are ends, that evil means can never lead to good ends and that fair ends require fair means" (2002, 111). This was not an abandonment of his Socialist ideals, Narayan argued, but a unique fusion of political philosophies: "according to Gandhi and Karl Marx, the highest stage of democracy is that in which the State has withered away" (113). For Narayan, the central question now was the creation of a separate Socialist Party and the beginning of a process of activating the masses through constructive work to begin to transform India's future. This was no longer a project of pushing forward with "Quit India," but one in which "building up a Socialist society" was the result of an accumulated series of projects: "constructive work in creating a sound trade union movement; in mobilizing the youth and children as voluntary servants of the nation; in creating cultural influences that go down to the most backward sections of the people; if we succeed in eradicating caste, superstition and bigotry; if we succeed in enlisting the co-operation of hundreds of thousands of selfless workers to whom the seats of power hold no attraction" (114).

It would take another ten years before Narayan moved decidedly into what he imagined to be the "Gandhian" fold; in 1951, Narayan began the process of reconsidering Gandhian ideas and trying to find some way of mixing them with his erstwhile Socialist preoccupations. In his 1951 article, "Socialism and Sarvodaya," for instance, Narayan argues that "Socialism will neglect Gandhi at its peril" (1964a, 95). And by 1953, Narayan had penned the pathetic "A Plea for Gandhianism," in which Narayan felt compelled to say that Socialism and Communism had been shown to be inadequate because of their failures in Europe and Russia and that Gandhian ideas hadn't received the credit they were due for winning independence in India by the Socialists. While many historical events led up to Narayan's conversion, his return to Gandhism and the figure of Gandhi are perhaps the most important in making sense of the various ways that anticolonial nationalism confronted those who clearly seemed to have a hegemony over large sections of India. Even at his most critical of Gandhi, Narayan is unwilling to break from the Mahatma's embrace, as he sees the Congress as a legitimate and important part of the development of the anti-imperialist struggle. The decision, later, to embrace the Congress's electoral strategy and withhold criticism of the Congress in favor of a joint slate of candidates (all Congress candidates) led directly to the conclusion that more was to be gained from calling oneself a Gandhian than from not. In fact, "Gandhian" as a term has always been additive, supplementary and translational. If in 1936 Narayan was not afraid that Socialist ideas would get a larger hearing than Gandhian ideas would, at least by 1937 he begins to find that he needs "Gandhi" as a signifier to reach out to broader swaths of people than he can convert by the logic of his own Socialist rhetoric. By 1951, after independence and the Mahatma's martyrdom, it becomes nearly impossible to advocate for justice without recourse to the Mahatma.

Gandhi himself makes the task of pinning down "Gandhism" all the more difficult since his provisional system of ethics, what David Hardiman describes as "dialogic – one in which knowledge is seen to arise from discussion, rather than from a unified philosophical system," has served as grist for the mill of a minor industry of hagiographic texts that have all attempted to define the elusive term "Gandhian" (Hardiman 2003, 7). Gandhi was also fond of drawing attention to his own iconoclastic posture towards the already developing cult of the Mahatma:

> As a matter of fact, you must give up the very name of Gandhism. If not, you will be falling into a blind well. Gandhism is sure to be wiped out. I love to hear the words: "Down with Gandhism." An "ism" deserves to be destroyed. It is a useless thing. The real thing is non-violence. It is immortal. It is enough for me if it remains alive. I am eager to see Gandhism wiped out at an early date. You should not give yourselves over to sectarianism. I did not belong to any sect. I have never dream of establishing any sect.

> If any sect is established in my name after my death, my soul would cry out in anguish. What we have carried on for all these years is not a sect. We do not have to subject ourselves to any "ism." Rather, we have to serve in silence in keeping with our principles. (Gandhi 1969, 377)

And still, something lingers of "Gandhism" and "Gandhian" in the present that includes but is not reducible to nonviolence, despite Gandhi's insistence on defining his own legacy. "Gandhi" is not quite a blank screen onto which anything can be projected – colonialism, for instance, would have a hard time claiming Gandhi – but there are clearly many versions of the Mahatma that can be strategically invoked.

What is one doing when one calls oneself a Gandhian? Or, perhaps more precisely, what is the figurative operation being performed in the act of taking the name of the Mahatma as a descriptor for a person, a set of politics, or an action? And how closely does the adjectival "Gandhi" resemble the historical "Gandhi"? Is the operation aggregational (measuring degrees of similarity or quantities of Gandhian acts) or performative (claiming a mantle for oneself)? The transformation of the historical personality into an adjective is necessarily a figurative operation, but is it rhetorical or analytical (if those two terms can signify opposing poles on the spectrum of proximity), casual or formal? Does "Gandhian" in this instance function as a metaphor, repackaging the chaotic mess of the present with the clean, well-trodden lines of the past, or does "Gandhian" function as metonymy, in which case, might we see the relationship between Gandhi and the "Gandhian" thing as contingent, arbitrary and temporary? Does the deployment of "Gandhian" signify the spectral return of a past that has not yet found completion in the present or does it anoint the present with a meaning and justification unique to it? And, of course, to ask the question as polemically as possible, is not one of the reasons that the "Gandhian" appellation continues to be deployed that we want to rescue some vision of the future from the horrors of the present; to salvage, too, an instrumentalized Gandhism from the historical Gandhi?

Critiques of and compromises with Gandhi occurred at the same time because the priority of the day was the inclusion of the masses, the peasants, the laborers, which the radicals had only limited access to and hoped that their proximity to Gandhi would open up new vistas and opportunities for engagement with more radical thought. As the myth of the Mahatma dilated, the opportunities for radicalization proportionally shrank. But from the beginning, even with the critique of Gandhi, the theory of additive or stagist interpretations of Gandhi has been a part of all Gandhian rhetoric, that Gandhi represents some minimum, common understanding of a democratic future upon which all other futures can safely build themselves.

> In these circumstances India alone actively represents the aspirations and promptings of the disinherited and dispossessed of the earth, India's fight for freedom is at once anti-imperialist (and therefore also anti-fascist, for imperialism is the parent of fascism) and a drive to end the war through the intervention of the common man. Neither allied nor axis victory is our aim, nor do we pin our hope on either. We work for the defeat of both imperialism and fascism by the common people of the world and by our struggle

we show the way to the ending of wars and the liberation of the black, white, and yellow. (Narayan 1980c, 93)

Narayan's vision for India's future far outstripped Gandhi's, though he never found it useful to make clear those distinctions and differences through a fundamental break with Gandhi. The aspiration in Narayan's India is internationalist (as opposed to territorial) and cosmopolitan (as opposed to parochial), but it still purports to be Gandhian. Even by 1977, when Narayan was a self-proclaimed Gandhian, he was advocating for a strategy of industrialization and nationalization that would have undoubtedly made the Mahatma cringe. The idea that "Gandhian" is a baggy term is perhaps not a novel intervention to be made, but the disaggregation of the various streams operating under the sign of the "Mahatma," the "Congress," and "nationalism" gives us some sense that nationalism is not a singular concept, and that even when unity was prioritized to diversity, the function of that unity was always being negotiated anew. It also explains how the terms "Gandhian" and "nonviolence" have served as polemical adjectives rather than categories of historical analyses in most instances; and if we begin with the argument that Gandhi and success are not synonymous, then we can begin to ask what kind of work the Gandhian sobriquet is actually being asked to perform. Both the Left and the Right sought to occupy the space on which Gandhi cast his long shadow, precisely because of the success of the myth of the Mahatma. Attempting to understand this as a performative rather than a philosophical or categorical maneuver allows us to return to the project of understanding the content operating under the sign of "Gandhi."

Chapter 6

THE MAHATMA MISUNDERSTOOD: THE ARRESTED DEVELOPMENT OF THE NATIONALIST DIALECTIC

In much of the thinking of the Socialist and Communist Left in the 1920s and 1930s, anticolonial liberation was connected to the development of the struggle for international Socialism. If the Russian Revolution inaugurated an international belief in the possibility of "non-Western" and underdeveloped nations to successfully conclude revolutionary processes, then anticolonial activists across the world sought to find ways of replicating this in their own countries, of engaging the fight against imperialism and strengthening the movement for Socialism at the same time. This was not only aspirational but theoretical, as the international Communist movement organized under the Comintern regularly debated whether it was possible to overthrow imperialism in the colonies without also unleashing the collective power of the proletariat and the peasantry. This became the source of inspiration for much of the radical thinking in India, in particular, where a number of Socialists and Communists attempted to understand how the processes that would liberate the nation from colonialism might also inaugurate a whole series of dynamics, resulting in a more egalitarian society. In so doing, Indian leftists were sometimes inheriting and sometimes inventing new theoretical tools in order to understand the process by which the radical reorganization of production by the direct producers might be possible. They did so under great strain – with the repressive apparatus of the British colonial government highly sensitive to any signs of Bolshevik activity – but were ultimately unable to develop the organizations or the social forces that might have led to different conclusions than the compromised solution that was the negotiated independence signed between the leaders of the Indian National Congress, the Muslim League and the British government.

One of the most important contributions to understanding this failure of the movement for independence to produce more radical change has been Partha Chatterjee's text, *Nationalist Thought and the Colonial World*, in which Chatterjee powerfully shows how the particular kind of nationalist discourse that the Indian movement for independence relied on upon locked it into a contradictory strategy in which "even as it challenged the colonial claim to political domination, it [nationalism] also accepted the very intellectual premises of 'modernity' on which colonial domination was based" (1986, 30). Chatterjee's book is now a classic in postcolonial studies, not only because his engagement with the discourse of nationalism continues to be one of the most original examinations of Indian decolonization, but also because it helps to crystallize the main arguments about the relationship between the nationalist intelligentsia – which comes for Chatterjee to mean anticapitalist and antimodernist radicals – and the official leadership of the nationalist parties that were committed to bourgeois statecraft. Chatterjee uses the formulations of the Italian Communist Antonio Gramsci to explain why the Congress was never going to deliver on radical social change, since its strategy depended on an ambivalent attitude towards the masses of people that it would have to mobilize in order to challenge colonial structures of administration and power. In Chatterjee's argument, all nationalism produces a "passive revolution," a formulation he borrows from Gramsci's reading of the Italian *Risorgimento*, and which he takes to mean the attempt of the nascent bourgeoisie to turn "the old dominant classes into partners in a new historic bloc and only a partial appropriation of the popular masses, in order first to create a state as the necessary precondition for the establishment of capitalism as the dominant mode of production" (30). For Chatterjee, the struggle of the Indian bourgeoisie against colonialism was shackled into a commitment to reproduce the very thing that it was supposedly struggling against – colonial modernity.

The reason, Chatterjee argues, that a more radical transformation of society does not emerge, why the movement for independence leaves intact most of the very systems of colonialism it putatively rejects, is because ultimately those sections of the radical intelligentsia within Indian nationalism (the figure that Chatterjee relies on is Gandhi, for reasons that will become clear) were unable to foresee the intentions of the more conservative elements inside of the nationalist movement; therefore, "the forces of 'moderation' succeeded in appropriating the results of popular initiative for the purposes of a partially reorganized and reformist state order" (1986, 46). Unable to reconcile peasant modes of thought with nationalism, the nationalists faced two choices: "either peasant consciousness would have to be transformed, or else it would have to be appropriated" (81). The first "could hardly seem a viable political possibility. The other possibility then was an appropriation of peasant support for the historic cause of creating a nation-state in which the peasant masses would be represented, but of which they would not be a constituent part. In other words, a 'passive' revolution" (81). Radical anticolonial figures like Gandhi were responsible for articulating a vision of a future India that was anticapitalist and that rejected the social arrangements that colonial modernity had inaugurated, only then to activate the peasantry and deliver them into the hands of people like Nehru who were only interested in using their energies to win a modernist nation-state.

To do so, Chatterjee explains that in India a "war of maneuver" (insurrection) against the British was impossible, so the bourgeoisie relied on a "war of position" (hegemony/ideology), allowing it a certain kind of rhetorical flexibility in its populism, which he traces from Bankim to Gandhi to Nehru, and which enabled it ultimately to establish capitalism under its control rather than attempting a wholesale transformation of the relations of production or the juridical apparatus of the state. Borrowing from Gramsci, again, Chatterjee explains, "there are two contrary tendencies [in the formation of nation-states] – one of gradualism, moderation, molecular changes controlled 'from the top,' the other of popular initiative, radical challenge, war of movement. The equilibrium that would result from the struggle between these two tendencies was in no way predetermined: it depended on the particular 'moments' of the relation of forces, especially on the relative quality of the 'subjective forces' which provided political-ideological leadership to each tendency" (1986, 46). Chatterjee argues that the moment of popular initiative is best understood through the figure of Gandhi. Gandhi, Chatterjee explains, allows the bourgeoisie to take advantage of the popular initiative that he can generate in order to bridge the gap between the bourgeoisie, which desires colonial modernity, and the masses, which are dispositionally antimodern and anticapitalist, and harness its energy to force the hand of the colonial state to negotiate rather than to dismantle it.

Chatterjee's argument has been powerfully critiqued by a number of scholars including David Hardiman and Sumathy Ramaswamy, who have argued that the totalizing framework that he produces more or less consigns all national liberation struggles to failure and makes the project of resisting colonial domination nearly impossible. If nationalism as a discourse always plays into the hands of the statist progeny of colonial modernity, then the struggle against imperialism is locked into a pattern of reproducing the very social arrangement it critiques. A few scholars have noticed that this particular pessimism about the project of national liberation is in fact a kind of "presentism," which resulted from a more general understanding of the anticolonial liberation struggles as creating a whole series of "failed states" that were in many ways responsible for the problems of ethnic cleansing and antiminoritarian politics that characterized much of the 1980s and 1990s. Rather than reflecting the particular problems of nationalist discourse or the various theoretical articulations of the strategies of nationalism, Chatterjee's understanding of the Indian context reflects a more general disillusionment with the project of nationalism altogether. Indeed, between 1980 and 2000, there were few theoretical contributions to the debate on nationalism that saw the nation-state as little more than a necessary evil at best, or responsible for some of the most horrifying excesses of modernity at worst (Jusdanis 2001).

More recently, though, new scholarship on Gramsci has argued that many of the thinkers in an around the Subaltern schools, including Chatterjee, have relied on a reading of Gramsci that they have inherited from Eurocommunist interpretations that selectively reproduced Gramsci in order to derive "a non-revolutionary approach to socialism."[1] Critics of Chatterjee have already noticed that this reliance on discourse means that he abandons the material questions of India's development, overemphasizes elite thinkers (Sarkar), homogenizes Enlightenment thought (Cheah), homogenizes and flattens nationalism (Choudhary) and produces a fatalistic portrait of anticolonial movements in general (Chrisman).[2] This scrutiny has prompted important reconsiderations of the value of anticolonial nationalism and has brought attention back to the contingent nature of anticolonial outcomes. And though Sarkar invites a reintroduction of class struggle as one of the important categories of historical investigation, the precise relationship between intellectuals and the Subaltern groups (in a Gramscian sense) still remains undertheorized, and the specific application of the Risorgimento analogy to late-colonial India has not been tested. More provocatively, very few scholars have challenged Chatterjee's specific application of Gramsci's understanding of the Risorgimento to the Indian nationalist struggle, which at a minimum warns of a "Danger of historical defeatism, i.e. of indifferentism, since the whole way of posing the question may induce a belief in some kind of fatalism, etc. Yet the conception ["passive revolution"] remains a dialectical one – in other words, presupposes, indeed postulates as necessary, a vigorous antithesis that can present intransigently all its potentialities for development" (Gramsci 1971, 114). Gramsci would have found the inevitability of the particular kind of Italian state anathema to his own thinking about the Risorgimento, especially since he argues repeatedly that had revolutionary forces been more "Jacobin," more steadfast in their opposition to the Piedmontists, "the Italian State would have been constituted on a less retrograde and more modern basis" (108). The remodeling of Gramsci's revolutionary optimism into postcolonial pessimism is strange, indeed, even though it follows a long legacy of postmodernist thinkers who have sought to turn Gramsci into a feature of their anti-Marxism, as Timothy Brennan has powerfully shown (2001).[3]

This re-evaluation of Gramsci has important implications for Chatterjee's critique of nationalism and in particular his assessment of the contributions of Gandhi and Marxists in the late-colonial period. First, the problem of fatalism, which Chatterjee turns into a problem of "discourse" in his essay, has to be re-examined as a problem of politics and contingency; nationalism contained within it both a capitalist and an anticapitalist wing and the victory of one over the other was not a foregone conclusion, especially as Socialists and Communists were attempting to find ways of pushing the movement forward by deepening their roots into labor and peasant-based organizations. Gramsci, after all, used "passive revolution" to describe both the Risorgimento and the development of fascism in the twentieth century, hardly something that he would have accepted passively, given that Gramsci was one of the most important theoretical contributors to the fight against Mussolini before his death. If the problems of nationalism are not discursive, then it becomes important to evaluate anew why the circuit between nationalism and international Socialism was broken and whether it could be forged again. Second, if part of the reason that Chatterjee relies on a Eurocommunist reading of Gramsci is so that he can sustain a critique of Marxism as Western and Eurocentric, he can only do so by obscuring his deep dependence on Marxist debates that were conducted during the 1920s and 1930s on the question of nationalist politics. What Gramsci calls "passive revolution," Indian Socialists and Communists called "a compromise with imperialism" (what Lenin, in a different context, referred to as "the Prussian way") and it was a central component of their attempts to engage theoretically with the possibility that nationalism might already be a lost cause that the influence of the bourgeoisie and the relative weakness of the proletariat might already mean the deck was stacked against them. Here, too, the contributions of Indian Marxists to understanding the relationship between Gandhi and the bourgeois state become important indices of detecting just how a process of critique-and-collaboration structured their relationship to bourgeois nationalism, especially since it is to these thinkers that the historical Gramsci was hoping to speak. And finally, if the key figure of radical possibility in Chatterjee's reading of Indian nationalism is indeed Gandhi, then it matters that we understand just how far Gandhi might have been able to push the struggle for Indian independence by mobilizing the peasant masses and whether this was the intention of Gandhian mobilizations at all; at least some on the Communist and Socialist Left believed that he was not only no longer interested in mass protest but that the peasants and the workers were tiring of being called out to protest only to be forced to retreat with little to show for it.

The reason for a return to Chatterjee at this particular moment, some twenty-five years after the publication of his book, is not merely to add to the corpus of critical material that has engaged with his essay. Part of the reason is to revitalize an understanding of the period of anticolonial struggle in precisely the way that Chatterjee gestures but has also foreclosed, namely a historical-materialist approach that seeks to explain how it was that the nationalist bourgeoisie managed to contain mass protest activity in the subcontinent. After all, if Chatterjee wants simultaneously to abandon Marxism for its teleological impulses and to smuggle back Marxism for its critique of capitalism, then one is left with a contradictory approach to the problems faced by national independence struggles throughout the world. Even if "modernity" is turned into a synonym for "capitalism" in Chatterjee's account, there is no strategy to escape the problems produced by the theme of nationalism. After all, there was no subaltern force that challenged Gandhi and Nehru successfully. One important danger of his reading of nationalism is still extant in academic circles today, namely that extant national liberation struggles (Kashmir, Afghanistan, Tamil Eelam and Balochistan) are only seeking their own place at the table of modernity and are therefore projects to dismantle rather than to push in more radical directions. The processes that might have more fundamentally challenged the framework of capitalism were the ones being interrogated by the official Left in the colonial context. One of the other implications of a historical-materialist account is to put the Indian Left back into the story of the development of nationalism in order to understand the reasons that they were ultimately unable to play a more decisive role in the story of national liberation.

Mazzini Misunderstood

In his "Notes on Italian History," Antonio Gramsci attempts to understand how the Italian bourgeoisie was able to unify the various Princely States under the banner of a unified Italy without also going through a period of radical change along the lines of the French Revolution. In so doing, he follows a line of historical debate first begun by Marx and Engels and developed more thoroughly by Lenin about the revolutionary potential of the bourgeoisie after the failed revolutions of 1848 in Europe. Gramsci is primarily interested in developing a theory of the intellectual leadership of the revolutionary classes, which he groups into two factions. The "Moderates" were a relatively homogenous group representing those members of the nobility who also participated in capitalist economic enterprises and composed of men like Cavour, D'Azeglio and Balbo. The "Action Party" was a more diverse group composed of the radical petit bourgeoisie (artisans, journalists, professionals) and the urban proletariat, and is represented in Gramsci's writings by Mazzini, Garibaldi and Pisacane. In Gramsci's mind, the reason that Risorgimento was a movement "without terror, a 'revolution' without a 'revolution,'" was a result of the fact that the Moderates managed to exert hegemony over the more radical Action Party and absorb them into more conservative program (1971, 78). That process could have been avoided had the Action Party more closely resembled the French Jacobins, "who opposed every 'intermediate' halt in the revolutionary process, and sent to the guillotine not only the elements of the old society which was hard a-dying, but also the revolutionaries of yesterday – today become reactionaries. [...] They were convinced of the absolute truth of their slogans about equality, fraternity and liberty, and, what is more important, the great popular masses whom the Jacobins stirred up and drew into the struggle were also convinced of their truth" (78). Unfortunately, because it was unable to develop into a Jacobin Party, "the Action Party was in fact 'indirectly' led by Cavour and the King" (57).

In attempting to understand why the Action Party did not become a Jacobin Party, Gramsci offers two contradictory explanations. The first, the counterfactual thesis, is the one that Chatterjee references in his book:

> Talking about the relationship between Cavour, a classic exponent of the war of position, and Mazzini who represented to a much greater extent the element of popular initiative or war of movement, Gramsci asks: "are not both of them indispensable precisely to the same extent?" The answer is: yes, but there was a fundamental asymmetry in the relation between the two tendencies. Cavour was aware of his own role; he was also aware of the role being played by Mazzini. That is to say, Cavour was not only conscious that the change he was seeking to bring about was a partial, circumscribed and strictly calibrated change, he was also conscious of how far the other tendency, that of a more direct challenge to the established order by means of popular initiative, could go. Mazzini on the other hand, was a "visionary apostle," unaware both of his own role and that of Cavour. As a result, the Mazzinian tendency was in a sense itself appropriated within the overall strategy of the war of position. (Chatterjee 1986, 45)

In this explanation, Gramsci is describing "what the Risorgimento did not do rather than what it did," a central part of most revisionist historiography in Italy (Cammett 1967, 215). Cavour, Gramsci argues, was never really interested in much more than establishing the hegemony of Piedmont over the entirety of a unified Italy, but he required someone like Mazzini to help popularize the notion of Italian unification. Mazzini, unable to understand his role in this dynamic, was subordinate because only Cavour had access to all of the resources of the Piedmontese state and army. Mazzini was unable to understand the difference between his attempts at unification and Cavour's and was necessarily appropriated by what Chatterjee calls "the overall strategy of the war of position." Since Mazzini was never able to develop a Jacobin Party, the necessary counterfactual about his ability to push the movement for unification in a more radical direction, while important, remains speculative in Gramsci's larger critique of the Risorgimento.

Chatterjee points this out in part by explaining the difference between Mazzini and Cavour: Mazzini never knew his relationship to Cavour was antagonistic and therefore could never come to realize that he must behave like a "Jacobin" towards him, i.e. understand that only one of them could dominate the movement for national unification. Cavour never had to come to that realization since he represented the dominant interests and had as a consequence a natural pull on the intellectual class and hegemony over the subordinate groups in Italy. But where Gramsci differs from Chatterjee is that he believes that, even in a backward country with a weak bourgeoisie that is willing to compromise with the monarchist elements, it would have been possible to move from a war of position to a war of maneuver – the missing element was the self-consciousness of even a "skeleton organization" that would have allowed the nationalist middle class to press for a more democratic end to the Risorgimento.

The second explanation as to why the Action Party did not become more radical is the organizational thesis, which Chatterjee ignores. Gramsci argues that one of the other ways that the Action Party could have become more radical was "if support was won from two directions: from the peasant masses, by accepting their elementary demands and making these an integral part of the new programme of government; and from the intellectuals of the lower and middle strata, by concentrating them and stressing the themes most capable of interesting them" (1971, 74). This, Gramsci argues, was a dialectical process, since spontaneous actions on the part of the peasantry would have excited the radical intelligentsia to reach out to them, while radical pro-peasant politics from the intelligentsia could have helped to crystallize peasant struggle around them: "if the peasants move through spontaneous impulses, the intellectuals start to waver; and reciprocally, if a group of intellectuals situates itself on a new basis of concrete pro-peasant policies, it ends up by drawing with it ever more important elements of the masses" (75). But because of the "dispersal and the isolation of the rural population," it was more important to understand the history of the intellectual groups that would have played a central role in shifting the terrain of peasant struggle in a more decisive direction (75). In order to do so, the Action Party would have had to been vying for hegemony amongst the peasantry for years and would have had to seed revolutionary ideas into the peasantry and win their confidence over the long struggle. The absence of agrarian struggle in Italy, though, limited any development of any radical tendencies within the Action Party. As John Cammett reminds us, Gramsci is also a historian who explains "why such a movement was not historically possible" (Cammett 1967, 220).

The contradiction between the counterfactual thesis and the organizational thesis is important for an understanding of the Indian context. If the first implies that the problem was merely dispositional (i.e. Mazzini did not understand the historical role that Cavour was going to play), then the second implies that the reason for that disposition has to do with the historical circumstances that conditioned it (i.e. there was no radical movement of the peasantry to inspire Mazzini). What differentiates India from Italy in this instance is precisely what Chatterjee gives Gandhi credit for: mass mobilizations of the peasantry. The historical record on the Noncooperation movement, the Civil Disobedience movement and the Quit India movement are clear enough, but Chatterjee himself concedes the point: "it was the Gandhian intervention in elite-nationalist politics in India which established for the first time that an authentic national movement could be built upon the organized support of the whole of the peasantry" (1986, 124). Unlike Gramsci, though, who argues that there would have been a dialectical relationship between the mass movement of the peasantry and the radical intelligentsia in which the intelligentsia breaks from the bourgeois leadership and attempts to draw the peasantry towards it, Chatterjee concludes that "the working out of the politics of non-violence made it abundantly clear that the object of the political mobilization of the peasantry was not at all what Gandhi claimed on its behalf, 'to train the masses in self-consciousness and attainment of power'" (124). Despite the fact that there is a range of historical evidence – even from the Subaltern Studies school – indicating that peasants were moving in a more radical direction and chafing at the reins placed on them by the politics of the Congress, the picture that emerges here is one of a limit placed on the movement by the politics of Gandhi. The dialectic that Gramsci says is central to understand is the development of Jacobin political formations, namely revolutionary parties.

A more flexible and determined middle-class radical formation would have been able to push towards revolution, against the odds: "the popular intervention which was not possible in the concentrated and instantaneous form of an insurrection did not take place even in the diffused and capillary form of indirect pressure [...]. The concentrated or instantaneous form was rendered impossible by the military technique of the time, but only partially so; in other words, the impossibility existed insofar as that concentrated and instantaneous form was not preceded by long ideological and political preparation, organically devised in advance to reawaken popular passions and enable them to be concentrated and brought simultaneously to detonation point" (Gramsci 1971, 110). At all points in Gramsci, after the French Revolution, revolution is a political rather than economic question, since the objective conditions have already developed far enough to pose the possibility of revolution. Unlike Chatterjee, who has more or less accepted the notion that decolonization can only culminate in an uneasy compromise between the elites and colonial remnants with a limited reform agenda, Gramsci holds out for the possibility of an alternative outcome.

That Chatterjee relies on a conscious misreading of Gramsci is not the central problem here, even though this is important since Gramsci is not interested in demonstrating the inevitability of bourgeois consolidation of power but in explaining why the bourgeoisie never can represent the interests of the entire nation and why independent parties must be organized to combat their ideological hegemony in the field of nationalist politics. The central problem is that the shift from a historical-materialist to a discursive account of the problem of nationalist politics leads to an analytical problem (namely, the reintroduction of the very problem that Chatterjee believes that he is avoiding: Marxism). At every stage in his reading of the Risorgimento, Gramsci attempts to show how an alternative trajectory might have been possible if Mazzini had only been able to shake his dependence on the Moderates and offer meaningful reform to the peasants, something that Mazzini is willing to consider but not fight to the death over. The bourgeoisie in colonized countries, argues Chatterjee, had to rely on a war of position rather than a war of maneuver, since the state was too strong and organized for Indians to coordinate effective, immediate military confrontation with the state. The difficulty with this argument is that it takes one reading of the movement for Indian independence (one in which events like the mutinies in the Royal Indian Navy and the Royal Indian Air Force or the construction of the Indian National Army or even the large peasant uprisings that took place in the south play a remote role) and makes them stand in for all movements for independence, even those in which the military confrontation with the state was the primary form of the movement (Algeria and Vietnam, for instance). And it ignores Gramsci's more central point that the limitation of the war of maneuver was the ideological preparation of the independent popular forces for such a war in the first place. The questions that Gramsci raises about the development of productive forces, the role of culture, the strength of the clerics, the confidence of the radicals, all become subsumed under the problem of colonial/statist modernity.

Part of the reason that Chatterjee is uninterested in this development is because he sees the problem as inherent in nationalism, as such, and not in the balance of forces that exist in any given national context. But the primary reason is that Chatterjee's attempt to situate his critique of nationalism within a postmodernist critique of the Enlightenment means that he needs to abandon the revolutionary parts of revolutionist Marxist theory. In drawing the now-common connection between Marxist and Enlightenment understandings of universal theory, Chatterjee argues, "more often than not, [Marxists] have adopted exactly the same method as those of the liberals – either a resort to sociologism, i.e. fitting nationalism to certain universal and inescapable sociological constraints of the modern age, or alternatively, reducing the two contending trends within nationalism, one tradition and conservative and the other rational and progressive, to their sociological determinants, or invoking functionalism, i.e. taking up an appropriate attitude towards a specific nationalism by reference to its consequences for universal history" (1986, 22). And in favor of the Marx of Reason and the Enlightenment, Chatterjee prefers the romantic Marx who "was convinced that capital in its global form had reached a stage where it was definitely 'against science and enlightened reason' and he saw even in the 'archaic' resistance of the popular masses in countries still not enslaved by capital the possibility of a new beginning" (170). Other critics have responded to the charge that there was a late, romantic turn in Marx's writings; here, the antinomies in Chatterjee's thought are what are important.

Chatterjee's version of Gandhi best fits this picture. In his reading of Gandhi, especially *Hind Swaraj* (1909), Chatterjee finds that, rather than being a critic of modern civilization, Gandhi is interested in "a fundamental critique of the idea of civil society" (1986, 85). Unlike other nationalists who are trapped in the thematics of nationalism, Gandhi believes that "it is not because Indian society lacked the necessary cultural attributes that it was unable to face up to the power of the English," an understanding that characterizes almost all of the nineteenth-century reform movements in India (86). The problem with colonialism is that it produces too much modernity, too much consumption, and therefore raises the specter of widespread exploitation and ruin. It is in this context that Gandhi argues both for village republics as the model of governance and for anti-individuality as the basis for morality and ethics; this is also what leads him, in Chatterjee's view, to embrace an antirational universal religiosity. The net result of Gandhi's views was to produce a series of contradictions: "a nationalist which stood upon a critique of the very idea of civil society, a movement supported by the bourgeoisie which rejected the idea of progress, the ideology of a political organization fighting for the creation of a modern national state which accepted at the same time the ideal of an 'enlightened anarchy'" (101). Moreover, in the deployment of nonviolence, Gandhi managed to yoke together a private morality with a disciplined, political force, such that political leadership had less to do with a program that appealed to the broadest number of people, but the willingness to die, which allowed Gandhi to make concessions on his demands without sacrificing his moral perfection. This is, for Chatterjee, the fundamental problem of Gandhism: "While it insisted on the need to stay firm in its adherence to its ideal, it was no longer able to specify concretely the modalities of implementing this as a viable political practice. Now that there were powerful and organized interests within the nation which clearly did not share the belief in the Gandhian ideal, there was no way in which the Gandhian ideology could identify a social force which would carry forward the struggle and overcome this opposition in the arena of politics" (117). As a result, Gandhi mobilizes the peasantry in the service of nationalism but never creates the conditions for their self-emancipation.

Leaving aside the main problem with this characterization, namely that it never asks whether it was indeed Gandhi who mobilized the masses, what is important about Chatterjee's understanding of the Gandhian moment of maneuver is that it is identical to the critique of Gandhi developed by the Communists in India. In 1935, M. N. Roy wrote *The Manifesto for the Revolutionary Party of the Indian Working Class*, and laid out an argument about the ability of Gandhi to play the role of mobilizing – but not activating – the peasantry in India:

> Thus the National Congress outgrew the old [nineteenth-century] reformist leadership not to follow [a] revolutionary course, although it placed itself at the head of an objectively revolutionary mass movement. The spectacular rise of Gandhism appears to be an enigma. How could a revolutionary movement come so completely under the domination of an essentially counter-revolutionary ideology which, by its very nature, was bound to be its undoing? [...] For the time being, in the earlier days of the anti-imperialist mass movement Gandhism, particularly the personality of its prophet, performed a useful function. It quickened the political consciousness of the masses by interpreting policies in terms of religion. [...] Even though caught in the ferment of the revolutionary agitation, destined to change the conditions of earthly life, the Indian masses lacked the confidence that they could bring about any such changes without the intervention of some superhuman force. To make up the lack of self-confidence, the movement created the MAHATMA, who could perform miracles, do the impossible. What the masses could not think of doing themselves would be realizable under the leadership of the Mahatma. [...] This objective function of Gandhism, for the time being, was overshadowed essentially its subjective significance which is counter-revolutionary. It served as the might lever for the development of the forces of revolution, destined to disrupt the social condition that constitutes its material background. (1997, 196–7)

This, Roy argued, locked Gandhi into a strategy of holding the movement back every time it attempted to use the mantle of the Mahatma to advance its own interests:

> Consequently, the National Congress, dominated by Gandhism, performed the meritorious task of involving larger and larger masses in the anti-imperialist agitation, but checked the development of militant activity. The result of this policy of going one step forward only to retrace two or more, was defeat whenever there was any encounter with the enemy. And in the atmosphere of mass discontent such encounters could not

always be avoided. Every defeat meant [a] check upon the further development of the movement. (1997, 197–8)

And as the Congress had only just recently announced its decision to enter into the provincial governments, Roy was convinced that the nationalists were only interested in statist conclusions: "From non-cooperation to His Imperial Majesty's constitutional (if not loyal) opposition – that is the road the Congress leaders have already travelled. The completion of the next stage will see them proudly functioning as administrators of fraudulent self-government granted graciously by the Imperialist masters of India" (1997, 219–20). Gandhi would then be leading the masses straight into the Congress's orchestrated "passive revolution."

While Chatterjee's reading of Gandhi avoids the "progressive/reactionary dyad" that he associates with Indian Marxists, both Chatterjee and Roy agree on the fundamentals: Gandhi's style speaks to the masses, his social program is countermodern and religious, and the fundamental impulse in his method is to demobilize mass action once he has called it out into the streets. In fact, the main thrust of Chatterjee's argument about Gandhi initiating the moment of maneuver in the passive revolution of capital is in fact the central argument being made by the Communists throughout much of the 1930s and 1940s. If Roy and Chatterjee disagree about anything it is about the potential of the movement to outstrip Gandhi's control. Roy, of course, is writing from the heady days of the movement for national liberation in which the prospects for a wider confrontation with landlords and capitalists must have seemed to be around the corner, while Chatterjee writes from a vantage point substantially higher and later.

What is important in this instance is how both of them seem to misunderstand the central role that Gramsci ascribes to the possibility of an independent Left actually being able to break free of the grip of Gandhian mobilization. The essay will conclude with a more complete evaluation of the Gramscian argument, but it is important to point out that even during the composition of "Notes on Italian History," Gramsci noticed that Gandhi was not Mazzini: "Gandhism and Tolstoyism are naïve theorizations of the 'passive revolution' with religious overtones. [...] In the struggle Cavour–Mazzini, in which Cavour is the exponent of the passive revolution/war of position and Mazzini of popular initiative/war of maneuver, are not both of them indispensable to precisely the same extent?" (1971, 107–8). Gramsci's other notes on the Indian situation also mention Gandhi but use Gandhi as a metonym for India, while still differentiating nonviolent struggle from a war of maneuver: "Thus India's political struggle against the English [...] knows three forms of war: war of movement, war of position, and underground warfare. Gandhi's passive resistance is a war of position, which at certain moments becomes a war of movement, and at others underground warfare. Boycotts are a form of war of position, strikes of war of movement, the secret preparation of weapons and combat troops belongs to underground warfare" (229–30). Gramsci only made passing reference to India; there are in fact only a handful of places where he talks specifically about the Indian context in *The Prison Notebooks*. But what is definitely clear is that he thinks that it was possible for the movement in India to advance beyond the war of position (propaganda). Ultimately, neither Roy nor Chatterjee maintain that belief.

The Communists in India

M. N. Roy is idiosyncratic in the history of the Communist movement in India. Originally a part of the Communist Party of Mexico before becoming an official in the Comintern, Roy would go on to found the Communist Party of India and be one of the Comintern's liaisons in China during the Chinese Revolution (1927–31). Roy was later expelled from the Comintern because of his disagreement with Stalin over the question of the role of the Communist Party of India and its relationship to the Congress. As a result, his career becomes an important part of evaluating the debate about the relationship both between nationalism and international Socialism but also between intellectuals and the dominant forces of the bourgeoisie in a nationalist struggle. More so than any other member of the Left, Roy was perhaps one of the fiercest critics of Gandhi's role in the movement for Indian independence, a position he did not relinquish until 1940 when he abandoned the nationalist movement in favor of supporting Britain's role in the Second World War, coming to the conclusion that the campaign against fascism was more important than the immediate fight for independence in India. But perhaps most decisively in Roy's case was the five year prison sentence he served for the Kanpur conspiracy, which further isolated him from the political struggles in which he had been involved. Completely cut off from any of the independent formations that could have challenged the Congress from the Left, Roy's transformation from a Jacobin to a nationalist would be complete by the end of his life.

This biography is important to make sense of the periodization at issue here, roughly between 1920 and 1937 when the central terms of the Left's alliance with the Congress were to be settled. In 1920, two simultaneous processes came together: namely, the launching of all-India agitation led by the Congress and the development of a specific orientation by the international Communist movement on the question of accelerating the prospects for revolution in India. By 1937, three things had happened that ended the possibility of the Left playing an important role in moving nationalist agitation in the broader populist struggle. First, the Communist Party of India had been thoroughly discredited for following the Comintern's ultra-Left "Third Period" line, in which it denounced all nationalists as reactionary; this both limited their ability to grow and cut off access to any kind of collaboration with the nationalists. The repression of the leadership of the Communist Party by the British government added to these political difficulties. Second, the Congress Socialist Party entered into an alliance with the Communist Party in an attempt to push the Congress leftwards, but they were thoroughly routed by Gandhi at the Congress session in Tripuri in 1938, ending all possibility. Third, the assumption of the Congress presidency by Nehru, believed to be an ally of the Left, meant that all criticisms of the Congress were now deferred in favor of complete entry into the Congress by most on the Left.[4]

In their attempt to formulate the perspectives of the movement against colonialism internationally, the various Communist parties of the world grouped under the Comintern came together in 1920 to try and theorize the relationship between the movement for nationalism and the movement for Communism. There were two important questions that were debated in the Comintern with respect to the "nations of the East": would the anticolonial revolts also be Socialist revolts, and if not, would the nationalist bourgeoisie be a partner in the fight for freedom. For Lenin, the central issue in the colonized countries was initially the question of independence and anti-imperialism; at the Second Congress of the Comintern, an alternate position was put forward by Roy, who argued that Communists had to distinguish between bourgeois democratic movements and mass revolutionary movements – only the latter deserved support. Lenin's initial formulation in the "Draft Theses on the National and Colonial Questions" argued that

> the Communist International should support bourgeois-democratic national movements in colonial and backward countries only on condition that, in these countries, the elements of future proletarian parties, which will be communist not only in name, are brought together and trained to understand their special tasks, i.e., those of the struggle against the bourgeois-democratic movements within their own nations. The Communist International must enter into a temporary alliance with bourgeois democracy in the colonial and backward countries, but should not merge with it, and should under all circumstances uphold the independence of the proletarian movement even if it is in its most embryonic form. (1965, 160)

In the debate that followed the submission of the "Draft Theses," Roy, the delegate from Mexico and future leader of the Communist Party of India, argued that the struggle in the colonies had already outstripped the bourgeois-democratic stage, as colonial modernity had already begun the process of creating a combative and sizeable proletariat capable of leading the struggle against imperialism:

> In recent years there has been a new movement among the exploited masses in India that has spread very quickly and expressed itself in mighty strike waves. This mass movement does not stand under the control of the revolutionary nationalists. It develops independently, although the nationalists try to use this movement for their own purposes. One can say of this mass movement that it is at all events revolutionary, although no-one would say that the workers and peasants who form this movement are also clearly class-conscious. (1920)

As a result, one could now distinguish between nationalist movements that were bourgeois in character and mass revolutionary movements in the colonies that were peasant and proletarian in composition (Gupta 2006). This assessment led him to disagree with Lenin's formulation that the Communists should support "bourgeois-democratic national movements," and he continued to argue for much of his life for a decisive break with nationalist politics in India. Lenin was not fully convinced of Roy's argument that the nationalist bourgeoisie was counter-revolutionary. Partly in response to this debate, Lenin reformulated the original draft and replaced "bourgeois-democratic" with "national revolutionary"; but for Lenin this only clarified the original position: "The significance of this change is, that we, as communists should and will support bourgeois liberation movements in the colonies only when they are genuinely revolutionary, and when their exponents do not hinder our work of educating and organizing in a revolutionary spirit the peasantry and the masses of the exploited. If these conditions do exist, the communists in these countries must combat the reformist bourgeoisie" (Maitra 1991, 43). The implication of these successive revisions was to make sense of whether or not there were sections of the bourgeoisie in the colonial countries that were committed to the prospect of anticolonial revolution or not.

Over the course of the next several years, the Comintern and the Communist Party of India attempted to apply this formula to an understanding of the nationalist movement in India. Three issues were at the heart of the debate. First, as we have seen, was whether the nationalist bourgeoisie was "genuinely revolutionary" or not. Roy remained unconvinced that the bourgeoisie in India would fight to the end against British imperialism and attempted to explain why the only really revolutionary classes in India were the peasants and the workers. He based this primarily on two pieces of evidence: the reactionary nature of Gandhi's religious symbolism and politics, and the calling off of the Noncooperation movement after the peasant rising in Chauri Chaura (Haithcox 1971, 32–4). Lenin and the majority of the Comintern continued to believe that as long as the Congress continued to oppose British imperialism, they were revolutionaries (Maitra 1991, 74). Second, Roy and others in the Comintern debated over whether or not the working class was of sufficient size and organization to be able to lead a revolutionary struggle in India. This question flowed from the first, since, as Roy argued, the stronger the proletariat the more the bourgeoisie would need to rely on it to dispel imperialism, while at the same time the stronger the proletariat the more the capitalists would fear it. In his study of the Indian working class, *India in Transition* (1922), Roy consistently overestimated the size and development of working class organization in India, a position he later altered after the Communist Party of India began its labor organizing in earnest a few years later.

Third and most important for this discussion, central to the dialogue and discussion between Roy and Lenin had been a debate about the role of Gandhi in the movement for Indian independence. Roy had been a consistent critic of the role that Gandhi had played in the movement for Indian independence, returning repeatedly to the role that Gandhi's religious ideas had on derailing the movement for more radical ends. In explaining why the Indian proletariat would need to lead the revolutionary process in India, Roy was ruthless in his condemnation of the Indian bourgeoisie and its chief representative, Gandhi: "The Indian bourgeoisie is even innocent of the radicalism which prevailed among the intellectual wing of the Russian bourgeoisie, in the latter decades of the nineteenth century. All the reactionary cults, which find expression in Gandhism, are more hostile to revolutionary ideas than was the Pan-Slavism of the Russian intellectuals. The Indian bourgeoisie are closely bound up with landlordism, and, the majority of the intellectuals are generally conservative in their social outlook" (1923, 85). Throughout the 1920s and 1930s, Roy rarely wavered from this view of Gandhi. Lenin, on the other hand, never published his opinions about the situation in India, but Roy recalls in his *Memoirs* that Lenin argued with him privately that Gandhi was a "genuine revolutionary" (1964, 379). The difference between Lenin and Roy continued to center around the question of how to draw in the largest number of peasants and workers to the nationalist struggle while retaining political independence; if Roy thought that this was a nonstarter, for Lenin, it was the only way that the Communist Party would win hegemony amongst the masses of people who were clearly inspired by Gandhi's message. In the parlance of the Comintern, this was the united front.

Despite their disagreements over the specifics of the class relations in India, Roy was convinced of Lenin's method, of political independence while supporting the bourgeoisie in its revolutionary aspirations. Rather, Roy's idiosyncratic reading of the Indian situation meant that his organizational theory converged with Lenin's even though he disagreed about the basics. If, after all, the only way to win independence was through mass working class and peasant organizations, then building these to fight for independence would provide some measure of strength against bourgeois cooptation at the end of the day. But, if the Congress was setting the agenda on the pace of the nationalist struggle, then bringing the masses out under independent banners would also have the effect of supporting the nationalist fight. Throughout the 1920s, he attempted first to organize the Communist Party of India and then give it an orientation on the working class. When he was expelled from the Comintern in 1928, he immediately set out first to convince the Communist Party not to follow Stalin's Third Period line (which encouraged abstention from and ruthless criticism of the Congress): "the Communist party cannot advocate that India will immediately be a Soviet Republic. That will be running after a Utopia. [...] In India, the way to Communism lies through the national revolution. [...] To this end it [the CPI] must work through the national mass organizations – the National Congress, Youth League, student organizations and volunteer corps" (Haithcox 1971, 170). When that failed, he set about organizing the Revolutionary Party of the Indian Working Class through his supporters scattered throughout the country. The process, though, was interrupted by his arrest and imprisonment for his involvement in the Kanpur conspiracy case. When he emerged from prison, his party was small and isolated.

The way that the question of collaboration with the Congress was resolved determined in many ways how the Left saw the prospects for independently calling out the masses on a more radical footing. Acharya Narendra Deva, leading member of the Congress Socialist Party, took a very measured approach with respect to the prospects for transforming the nationalist struggle into a struggle for Socialism; as a result he concludes that collaboration with the Congress is the order of the day: "But whether or not socialism will be established in our country simultaneously with the winning of freedom cannot be categorically answered. Capitalist democracy is any day preferable to serfdom and subjection to alien rule. And he will be a short-sighted and a very narrow socialist who will refuse to take part in a national struggle simply on the ground that the struggle is being principally conducted by petit bourgeois elements of society although he will make ceaseless efforts to give it a socialist direction" (1987, 5). This comes very close to an abandonment of the fight for Socialism altogether in favor of a more diffuse participation in the nationalist project without any real emphasis on radicalizing the movement. Even Deva had to admit that this in many ways was the result of the fact that, even by 1940, the Left had been unable to win influence amongst the wider layers of Indians: "It is a hard fact that today no struggle will have a nation-wide character and attract the attention of the world unless Gandhiji associates himself with it. This may provide a sad commentary on the state of our political advancement, nevertheless we cannot afford to ignore it.

Today we want a powerful mass movement and unless Gandhiji gives the call, the masses and the classes will not be drawn into it in large numbers" (133). As a consequence, Deva argued, it was impossible either to ignore the Congress or engage with any systematic critique of Gandhi. The Congress Socialist Party ended by liquidating itself entirely into the Congress, doing exactly the work that Chatterjee accuses Gandhi of doing: putting its supporters behind a bourgeois program.

Shapurji Saklatvala, on the other hand, had been sent by the Communist Party of Great Britain to India to help propagandize about the Comintern's Third Period line. Saklatvala, the first Indian elected to British Parliament, made the case that Gandhi made bourgeois politics appear to be radical by choosing boycotts that were beneficial to the bourgeoisie: "Since then he has been shouting for a compromise, and by dramatic vestures he is striving to force a speedy compromise between the British and would-be Indian bourgeois leaders to stem the growth of proletarian revolution. He selected the Salt Law in March as the point of his attack because he knew that for twelve months the Indian salt manufacturers had been begging the Viceroy for protective measures against the foreign European salt trust – measures which they were very likely to obtain as a price of peace between Indian bourgeoisie and British imperialists" (1930, 23). Saklatvala's implicit claim was also that imperialism was not threatened by the political theater of the Salt March, since it would have been easy enough for the British to concede the demand. But perhaps more importantly for the hardliners in the Communist Party was the fact that Gandhi produced revolutionary situations only to cripple the revolutionary process: "He neglects the revolutionary side of the salt proposition. He does not call upon millions of Indian villagers to expel the special Salt Police from their villages and he does not call upon his own friends, the big Indian salt manufacturers, to refuse to pay the taxes and to go to prison. He does not call upon his propertied and mill-owning friends to refuse to pay income tax and have their property confiscated. He does not support the railway strikers and textile strikers who were shot down" (1930, 26). The list of Gandhi's crimes could be legion.

Saklatvala and the rest of the Communist Party, though, went in the exact opposite direction of the Congress Socialist Party following Roy's expulsion. In place of liquidation, the Communist Party abstained from all nationalist struggles, accusing the Congress of being reactionary agents. This had disastrous consequences for the future of the Communist Party, as it hemorrhaged members throughout the early part of the 1930s. Added to this was the almost wholesale arrest of the Communist Party's leadership in 1928 by the colonial government. The cumulative effect of the political sectarianism and state repression was to make the Communists a relatively weak force in nationalist politics. Ultimately, neither the Communist Party nor Roy was able to produce a consistent strategy by which they could compete for hegemony against Gandhi and mobilize revolutionary classes at the same time.

Gramsci on Transformism

The consequences of that failure have had lasting effects on how anticolonial history in India is still studied and how the Left is understood and how it understands itself.

The failure of the anticolonial struggle to produce a more democratic, let alone Socialist, outcome has meant that historians and activists alike have more or less abandoned the project of nationalist anticolonialism as too complicit in the development of bourgeois nation-states. There is no longer a search for the circuit that might ultimately connect, through a Jacobin party, the nationalist struggle to international Socialism. In India, this is represented by the dominance of Stalinism amongst the official Left and liberalism amongst the activist Left – both of which have abandoned any serious commitment to the overthrow of capitalism or revolution more generally. In fact, the role of Stalinism on the national liberation struggles throughout the newly decolonized world has been a seminal part of the reason that the dialectic between nationalism and international Socialism has been arrested. In academic circles, this process finds its parallel in poststructuralist theory, which, after the failure of the French rising in 1968, joined the postcolonial disillusionment of the nation-state with the Western disillusionment with Marxism to produce a variety of theories no longer interested in the processes of radical social transformation.

Here, again, Gramsci is instructive to explain why. The failure of the Italian Risorgimento to produce a more radical democracy meant that the populist intellectuals were absorbed into the hegemonic position that the Moderates now acquired at the head of the Italian state. Gramsci argues that the success of the Moderate Party over the Risorgimento depended on its ability to accomplish two things at the same time: first it was able to "dominate antagonistic groups, which it tends to liquidate"; and second, it provided "intellectual and moral leadership" over "kindred and allied groups" (1971, 57–8). This was the predicate for holding power: "A social group can, and indeed must, already exercise 'leadership' before winning governmental power (this indeed is one of the principal conditions for the winning of such power); it subsequently becomes dominant when it exercises power, but even if it holds it firmly in its grasp, it must continue to 'lead' as well" (57–8). As a consequence, it was able to exert influence over groups and classes that had wavered in their opposition to it. This process, Gramsci called "transformism":

> The Moderates continued to lead the Action Party even after 1870 and 1876, and so-called "transformism" was only the parliamentary expression of this action of the intellectual, moral, and political hegemony. Indeed one might say that the entire State life of Italy from 1848 onwards has been characterized by transformism – in other words by the formation of an ever more extensive ruling class [...]. The formation of this class involved the gradual but continuous absorption, achieved by methods which varied in their effectiveness, of the active elements produced by allied groups – and even of those which came from antagonistic groups and seemed irreconcilably hostile. In this sense political leadership became merely an aspect of the function of domination – in as much as the absorption of the enemies' elites means their decapitation, and annihilation often for a very long time. [...] It was precisely the brilliant solution of these problems which made the Risorgimento possible, in the form in which it was achieved (and with its limitations) – as "revolution" without a "revolution," or as a "passive revolution" to use an expression of Cuoco's in a slightly different sense from that which Cuoco intended. (58–9)

In this sense, the success of the "passive revolution" in India was not simply to demonstrate the hegemony of the Indian state over the peasantry who had followed its leadership in the fight for independence. "Passive revolution" also meant the conversion of the intellectual class of the newly independent state, not simply to blind adherence to all of the state's policy, but to at least abandon those antagonistic strategies that might put it into permanent conflict with the state.

This has had the effect in much of the scholarship about the movement for Indian independence of discounting the prospects for revolutionary transformation, even from those who were erstwhile revolutionaries. There are multiple reasons for this hegemonic position of the dominant state form, even over people, like Chatterjee, who are antistatist dispositionally. Historically, the period of decolonization (roughly 1950 to 1980) coincided with the largest boom in global capitalism. That had the effect not only of shoring up the ability of nation-states to win over supporters but also had the benefit of strengthening the coercive arm of the state globally. Secondly, the decline of the nations in the so-called "Second World" (nations allied to the Soviet Union) at the end of the 1980s meant that even when there was opposition to capitalism in the economic shocks of the 1970s and 1990s, it was usually accompanied by the politics of TINA ("there is no alternative") and the growing influence of neoliberalism and pragmatism over state actors and activists respectively. Finally, in the Indian context, the continuing political vacillations of the official Communist parties has meant that most activist intellectuals come to radical politics in opposition to Marxism rather than through it. The cumulative effect of these developments was the production of a historical consensus about the non-reciprocity of nationalism with international Socialism.

Gandhi became an important part of the story of how this happened in the Indian context. As a figure he was perhaps most responsible for winning over the radical Left to the Congress in the 1930s and 1940s, and then became the primary figure through whose legacy the state exerted hegemony over the activist Left in the years after independence. In the context of the academic Left, the abandoning of class as a category means that the discourse of nationalism (even postindependence) looks like derivativeness even when it is the marker for techniques of innovation. Here's Gramsci again: "the class relations created by industrial development, with the limits of bourgeois hegemony reached and the position of the progressive classes reversed, have induced the bourgeoisie not to struggle with all its strength against the old regime, but to allow a part of the latter's façade to subsist, behind which it can disguise its own real domination" (1971, 83). The reasons that nationalism did not turn into Socialism had everything to do with class and the development of significant and confident enough sections of the Left to combat empire and capital. The failure of that process to come to fruition has left a legacy recognizable in all of the intellectual output from the subcontinent ever since.

Conclusion
DANGEROUS SOLIDARITIES

Most readers of nationalist and anticolonial literature are drawn towards this material because of the radical worldview and affect that it contains. The list of writers who deployed nationalism and anticolonial themes is long and has now become the standard syllabus in most courses on postcolonial literature in universities. In the first half of the twentieth century, literature became an important tool in the hands of anticolonial nationalists who sought not only to understand the processes by which entire swaths of humanity had been enslaved and dominated by primarily European powers, but also to imagine into existence the conditions under which that enslavement and domination could come to an end. This was not a process unique to literary inquiries and experiments: the entirety of the colonized intelligentsia was engaged with trying to imagine what the consequences of colonialism were on a subject population and what alternative political and social arrangements might do for the welfare of the people in general. If we take Gregory Jusdanis's definition, that "[Nationalism] is a revolutionary, progressive, and utopian doctrine, seeking the transformation of the inherited, and quite often, unjust and oppressive order," it becomes easier to understand why this literary corollary to the independence movement was, in fact, inspiring (2001, 10). The fact that writers from the Indian subcontinent could also rely on an anticolonial figure with as global a reputation as Gandhi plays no small part in the creation of this attractive, politicized canon.

The literature of the period shared in the development of speculative nation formation; the nations that were being imagined were simultaneously reorganizations of the past and utopian projections into the future, most of which bore strong family resemblances to Socialism in no small part because of the Comintern's interest in promoting anticolonial struggles. Part of the reason that radical writers were interested in nationalism was because they felt that the changes that were going to accompany the end of imperialism and the advent of modernity were going to usher in a process that would completely transform society. At its core, this literature has become a part of the nationalist canon because it provides a left-wing populist narrative of what the nation-state was imagined to be, a narrative of its potential and promise: solidarity with the marginalized, equitable redistribution of wealth, democratic control over the institutions of power, an end to religious orthodoxy and hope for an improved future. It bears underlining that the texts in question could not have played this role if they were simply the radical alibis of a more conservative worldview, the utopian veneer of a dystopian project.

But if in the first half of the twentieth century it was still possible to be inspired by a version of nationalism that bled into some variant of Socialism, by the second half of the twentieth century it seemed both impossible to believe in such a conjunction and naïve to have believed it in the first place. In place of egalitarian and just nation-states, the midcentury movements for decolonization brought into the world a number of states that were illiberal, chauvinist, violent, unjust, or otherwise undesirable. The number of examples was legion and the lesson was nearly universal: anticolonial struggle produced premature states with little protection for their minorities. In the parlance of the Right, this was the era of "failed states," and the experiment of the Non-Aligned Movement was merely a collection of states with immense social conflicts that they had no ability to resolve. For the Left, this was part of a more general demoralization that set in with the collapse of the Soviet Union and the now global opinion that Socialism meant statist authoritarianism of one variety or another; there was still some hope through the anti-imperialist resistance in Vietnam, but once that war ended, the Left collapsed thoroughly, as did any confident belief in the promise of nationalism. And once the sun had set on the various European powers in their colonial possessions and decolonization was a more or less completed process, it became possible to speak of a postnational world, a world that moved from the prison of the nation-state into new, liberated organizations without the restrictions and repressions that all nation-states seemed to embody. The general consensus seemed to have been that decolonization changed precious little and in many instances may have even made the problem worse.

One of the casualties of this revaluation of nationalism and the movements for decolonization has been the critical reception of the literature of the period. If postindependence nation-states extolled the virtues of its nationalist poets and writers, then postcolonial criticism tended to see in the same writing early formulations of the problems with nationalism. Nationalist writers may have been important parts of the process of animating anticolonial struggle, but their texts revealed, this consensus argued, an important complicity with the majoritarian, chauvinist, faux-populist and bureaucratic statist ideologies with which nationalism came to be identified. In imagining that the end of colonialism was also the end of all forms of domination, nationalism showed its own limits as a politics of genuine liberation. Radical political aspirations now became populist veneers for the inevitable betrayal by both indigenous bourgeois leaders and conservative social forces that putatively turned the newly independent states towards a course of ethnic violence (since every state necessarily contained multiple nations and majorities attempted to secure their advantage at the expense of minorities). It was the elites of every state who benefited, who then used the language of nationalism – which relied on tropes of a revived ethnic past, exclusive to only certain parts of the nation-state – against its social competitors in order to accrue the gains of capitalist development for itself. Novelists who admired the mass campaigns of indigenous peasants and workers against their erstwhile masters had not laid enough of a foundation to inoculate those same peasants and workers against their new masters and had, perhaps inadvertently, handed to the state the very terms and ideologies with which the elite could organize against those who had not yet felt the changes trickle down to their lifeworlds.

Alongside this revision of the promise of nationalist resistance to imperialism came a re-evaluation of the figures who had attempted to connect anti-imperialism with Socialism; instead of being radical theorists of future social organizations, the same intellectuals were now seen as complicit in the creation of states with venal administrations and massive inequalities, especially since in many places it was the Socialists who took control over newly independent nations. Moreover, those states that relied on a discourse of state Socialism in Latin America, Africa and Asia were also engaged in spectacular amounts of accumulation and concurrent exploitation, creating a bureaucratic clique that benefited from its connections to the state and mass immiseration everywhere else. This was partly an extension of Cold War rhetoric in which the Non-Aligned Movement was seen as a gateway into the formal Socialist orbit, but it was also the disenchantment with Socialism that set in after the defeats of the revolutionary movements of the 1960s and 1970s. In many ways, the commonsense notion that Socialism was a failed project grew up alongside the notion that nationalism was anything other than a byword for ethnic cleansing, militarism and chauvinism, and neither term has found much support amongst either political pundits or academic critics. Both of these legacies were partly the result of the specific strategies of post–Cold War capitalists in order to break into the states that were aligned under the aegis of the Second and Third World groupings by way of international financial institutions and "shock therapy."

There were multiple reasons for this shift. First, and perhaps most importantly, was the fact the nationalist movements of the immediate postwar era had resulted in states that had failed to deliver on the promises of radical social justice on which they were founded. Nationalism came for left-wing critics to mean an alibi for the politics of the comprador bourgeoisie and ethnic and elite male chauvinism; for the right wing it came to mean failed states and the seemingly endemic problems of ethnic conflict that seemed to plague all newly decolonized states and gave lie to the notion that postindependence nationalism could suture together a multiethnic polity in colonially created territories. In short, majority populations everywhere trammeled over the rights of minorities. Second, new criticisms of historiography had come to see decolonization as more of the same rather than a decisive break in the direction and shape of history. Part of this was an extension of a radical critique of the failures of nationalism from the perspective of the subaltern, who saw few, if any, gains from the postindependence state, but it was also an extension of postmodernist views of history into colonial historiography. Third, and perhaps most dangerously, the critical consensus had been that with the end of the Cold War, imperialism and colonialism in their classical form were more or less over. Aggressive territorial ambition was no longer the order of the day; the objectives of international finance capital could be accomplished with the help of international aid and lending institutions and the pliable leaders of the developing world. Finally, there was a growing sense that the nation-state was dead and being replaced by international or transnational networks of power that offered better possibilities for radical humanism. As a result, nationalism came to be seen as either a completely outdated and inaccurate ideological framework or an impossibly dangerous set of allegiances that could only unleash primordial passions.

The consequence of all of these processes was to move the debate about anticolonial nationalism into a debate about discourse, rather than a debate about the balance of forces in the colonial encounter. As Laura Chrisman puts it:

> Such political shifts fed the tendency of postcolonial studies to regard nationalism as inherently dominatory, absolutist, essentialist, and destructive. [...] The cultural turn of

social and literary theory, post-structuralist critiques of Enlightenment rationality and modernity — these encouraged postcolonial studies to view nationalism as a primarily cultural and epistemological, rather than socio-political, formation. This accompanied the view that nationalism was, as Gayatri Chakravorty Spivak suggested, "a reverse or displaced legitimation of colonialism," doomed to repeat the "epistemic violence" of the colonialism it rejected. (2004, 183)

This frame of reference has been the dominant strain of postcolonial studies in literature departments. And one of the consequences of this development is a tendency towards reading for complicity — by which nationalist writers are seen as necessarily and inevitably complicit in setting out the intellectual and ideological frame through which the postcolonial betrayal could happen. Now this was an incredibly important procedure when it came to showing how the class of Indians who putatively made the nation in the image of the people was betraying those very people after the fact, but it has also brought with it a series of ancillary problems for the contemporary political situation.

The developments of the first decade of the twenty-first century, though, have forced a widespread re-evaluation of both of these academic and political notions. The revival of the national question and classical forms of imperialism (rather than corporate globalization, which had characterized the style of control over the global economy by the large capitalist powers after the Vietnam War) at the beginning of the twenty-first century means that critics have to contend with the national question and national liberation anew. The primary issue under which this monograph was written was the unresolved question of Palestine and the resurgence of the second intifada in 1999; but to this can be added the American occupations of Afghanistan and Iraq; the imposition of American military bases throughout Central Asia; the revival of the movement for Kashmiri independence through the nonviolent struggle of the Jammu Kashmir Liberation Front; the Israeli invasion of Lebanon and its subsequent repulsion by Hizbollah in 2006; the renewed demand for an independent Tamil Eelam in Sri Lanka and the genocidal campaign against Tamils by the Sri Lankan government; and the military campaigns against Balochi and Pashtun separatists by the Pakistani army. This, of course, conflates three kinds of imperial and national questions that need to be disentangled: the resurgence of American imperial control over Southwest Asia by military means and the establishment of satrapies in Afghanistan and Iraq in particular; the long-standing colonization and occupation of land by newly independent states with interests opposed to the indigenous populations, especially in Kashmir and Palestine; and the civil rights struggles of minorities in newly independent states that were taking on the shape of demands for separation, as in the case of Sri Lankan Tamils and the Gurkhas in Assam. The problem still seemed to be that the national question, rather than having been resolved, was asserting itself anew in interesting and complex ways, since in many instances these demands for separation were being made against states that had been established as the result of successful anticolonial liberation movements themselves. The justice of the demand for secession and self-rule seemed to be at odds with the pervasive view in academic circles that nationalism was ultimately a doomed project and that its partisans were necessarily chauvinist and elite and its outcomes failures. But the durability of these late twentieth- and early twenty-first century movements for national self-determination, as well as the global revolt against the International Monetary Fund and the World Bank, have led a number of theorists to begin to re-evaluate the nation-state and nationalism as potentially useful in the struggle against global capitalism and empire.

But the problem now is different. Insofar as nationalism has been rehabilitated, two other ideas have also been dangerously revitalized: the bourgeois state and Stalinist political practice. Left-leaning liberals within academic circles have sought to rationalize and politicize nationalism by confidently asserting the necessity of the nation-state and its sovereignty within the context of globalized neoliberalism. These thinkers contend that because transnational capital and financial institutions have become so powerful and Anglo-American imperial ambitions have grown so wild, the nation-state is the last, best hope of those who would seek to thwart the expansion of imperialism and capitalism. In the revitalization of nationalism, in this school of thought, comes a defense of the state, which has been properly critiqued before. Similarly, erstwhile radicals in Anglo-American academic circles have sought to defend nationalism by lionizing the radical contributions of the Communist Party and its intellectuals in national liberation struggles. This is the product of a Soviet nostalgia, in which the existence of mutual antagonists during the Cold War was supposed to have slowed the pace of imperial expansion, despite the fact that it produced the dangerous situations in Afghanistan, Iran, Nicaragua, El Salvador, Korea and the like. Neither of these approaches really resolves the problem, since their revisionism is a product of a different kind of presentism, one in which globalization is seen as a worse problem than sectarian or ethnic conflict. The cumulative effect of these maneuvers has been to turn back the clock to the earlier triumphalist narrative without re-evaluating the real dangers inherent in nationalism.

The aim of this book has been to articulate a rationale for the study of anticolonial literature to be added to studies of nationalism in a different way: instead of the reading for complicity, in which all utterances of nationalist slogans or episodes with nationalist figures damn a book as guilty of the crimes of nation-states, the argument here has been for a conscious readerly suspension of historical outcomes so that the multivalent, ambiguous, contradictory and open aspects of nationalist imagination can be brought to the fore, without falling into romantic nostalgia or the invective of the disillusioned. Since the postcolonial reading of this literature is identical to the nationalist reading, only with the ethical conclusions reversed, this procedure also has the benefit of critiquing the nationalist as well as the postcolonialist reading of nationalist teleologies. Part of the animating impulse of this study has been the belief that nationalism is not only relevant today, it is important as the primary way that imperialism and neocolonialism are combated, and that if we re-examine the debates that made up nationalist discourse we can find alternative trajectories to the movements for national liberation that did not end up in the nation-state. At the same time, such a reading also opens up explanations for why these radical gestures did not come to fruition, thereby holding out the possibility of a socially redistributive and egalitarian fight against empires and states simultaneously. From there, the question can become tactical–political rather than philosophical–ethical, and it necessarily dilates beyond the written word or the novelistic form.

Nationalism ends in the state primarily because alternative actualizations of nationalist aspirations either fail to differentiate themselves adequately or fail to see the pitfalls of the state form for the realization of their aims. Either way, the problems are contingent rather than inevitable.

As this book has argued, nationalism moves in two opposite directions simultaneously, avoiding the inevitable breach between its democratic and its majoritarian poles through, on the one hand, an ideological divide papered over and even avoided by a careful slippage in vocabularies (democratic and majoritarian, after all, resemble each other) and, on the other hand, a political crisis between the more radical and reactionary views of nationalism that can never come to a resolution, since both poles need each other in order to win independence. The ideological problem presents itself thus: nationalism both intends to include the histories of all indigenous identities into its fold with greater or lesser mythological success and relegates minorities who refuse to identify with anticolonial politics as necessarily agents of colonialism. If the first operation is best represented by the enormous historical and geographical vistas represented in Nehru's *The Discovery of India*, then the latter is indexed by Nehru's simultaneous reference to the problems of "divide and rule" politics as the primary method of understanding the organizing efforts of Jinnah and Ambedkar. It is in fact the figure of Nehru who most successfully embodies the contradictory logics of nationalism, since his career from the Congress Socialists to the head of the independent Indian state maps cleanly onto the twin tracks on which nationalism simultaneously runs. This ideological problem also manifested itself at the level of political organization where the relative weakness of the Left in India compared to Congress meant that Congress nationalism continued to remain flexible and durable. Not only did most left-wing breaks fare poorly, the Communist Party of India, arguably one of the largest left-wing challengers to the Congress, folded itself entirely into the Congress when this fit the needs of the Soviet Union's aims in the Second World War. The consequence was a kind of pragmatic politics of unity at all costs, which delivered more radical elements into the Congress and offered them no alternatives when they were disillusioned or troubled by the policies of state-led growth in the newly independent nation. At the same time, the more conservative elements in the Congress, both its industrial financiers as well as the more orthodox elements of the Hindu Right, needed the more radical and democratic elements to be able to mobilize millions of people with the hope of social transformation on a more egalitarian pattern and to discipline them with the logic of a controlled, patient politics of pragmatism.

This internal map of nationalism – cynical and Machiavellian as it is – bears little or no resemblance to the euphoric, triumphalist and ultimately radical structure of feeling that marks the nationalist literary output of the 1930s and 1940s. In fact, it is only by reading very hard against the grain, as the postcolonialist readings of these novels do, that one can believe that novels about untouchable freedom are actually about the persistence of Brahminical prerogatives, that novels about the self-activity of peasant women are in fact narratives that capitulate to sexism, and that novels about the nationalism of the sharif denizens of Delhi are putatively apolitical. Perhaps worse still, it is only by ignoring the radical project of these novels, as the nationalist readings of these novels do, that one can come to the conclusion that the necessary and complete horizon of these novels rested in the postindependence Indian nation-state. At a minimum, the novels were far more democratic and socially redistributive than any reform ever accomplished by the Indian government; at a maximum, the novels were nascent expressions of a literary internationalism, which had lingering suspicions that nationalism could not accomplish the aims it had set out for itself and still lacked a vocabulary in which to express that discomfort. And yet, there is still something compelling about both the postcolonial and the nationalist readings of these novels, especially since nationalism has simultaneously failed to deliver on its promises and maintained that those same promises are still part of its program. As a result, nationalist literature bears within it traces of the unresolved tensions in nationalist politics as a formal contradiction. It is this contradiction that this book has charted, a contradiction that should allow us to recover nationalism from its postindependence deterioration into crass statism and to see in nationalism and nationalist movements the possibility of different outcomes that ultimately failed to come to fruition for political rather than ontological reasons.

Implicit in this reorganization of the genealogy of nationalist thought is the claim that there are substantive differences between the leadership of the Congress and the middle-class intellectuals who proselytized in its name, who knowingly or unwittingly used the banner of Gandhi to advance ideas that could only troublingly be reincorporated into later, mature Gandhian thought (usually affiliated with an aversion to technology and science, a reformist-democratic impulse towards religion, an idealization of Indian village life, nonviolence in political methods and a limited program of social redistribution). There is a story that remains to be told about the relationship between the radical intelligentsia and the nationalist movement, in which radicals were solicited and invited into the nationalist orbit in order to do the work of providing a nationalist image with which the downtrodden could identify, only then to find themselves hemmed in when they attempted to expand the leftward potential of bourgeois nationalism. There were, of course, limits to what the Indian bourgeoisie that ran the Congress was willing and able to deliver, but there was no limit on what the middle class was willing and able to imagine, and the sheer opposition between those two ideological and political structures finally came to a head in the postcolonial dissatisfaction with the nationalist project. The Indian bourgeoisie needed freedom from British taxation and tariff policies in order to develop its own industry; but in order to set up a state complete with its protections for domestic production they needed the masses of Indians to be mobilized against the British, as their own economic and political strength paled in comparison to the Crown's. In this project, the middle-class radicals were invaluable, since they felt deeply the problems of colonialism in their own alienation but were also relatively free to engage in some of the most radical organizing experiments. At the same time, there was a limit to what the Indian bourgeoisie (landed and industrial) was willing to accept in terms of an organized opposition to the British, especially since peasant organizations threatened landlord interests and unions limited the powers of manufacturers to extract surplus efficiently. But if the radicals were good at moving peasants and workers into action, they were quite ineffective at and uninterested in disciplining them. The grammar of their radicalism was composed of principled declarations, unable to accommodate the flexible and knotted realpolitik of the pragmatic subjunctive. If in this story radical intellectuals come off as dupes of more Machiavellian moneyed interests, then this is the result of the novelty of national liberation in the Indian case, by which time the betrayal of the bourgeoisie was not a well-established pattern. Indian Mazzinis still could not recognize Cavours.

But then, somewhere between the 1920s and 1930s, this began to change. By the time of the Salt March, young nationalists were discovering that Gandhi was not only openly discussed but even worshipped, that nationalist ideas had not only audiences but admirers, and Gandhian uplift programs were not only taken up but enthusiastically spread. This was not a linear development; it had fits and starts and evolved along different patterns in different places. But something was beginning to change in the experience of this section of the radical middle class, which now saw an increasing openness to reform and change in a Gandhian manner. Moreover, Gandhi became an entry point for discussions of ideas beyond *sarvodaya* and noncooperation: women's organizations that picketed liquor shops began to talk about real emancipation for women; intercaste association was increasingly common; poverty and taxation were critiqued and people who benefited from them were excoriated; education was seen as a virtue; indigenous models of progress and technology were unearthed and lionized. It was not inconsistent to be a Gandhian and believe that caste abolition, technological progress, social redistribution of land and wealth, gender equality and an end to religious orthodoxy were on the horizon. Individuals who had never shown signs of political courage suddenly became leaders; untouchables demanded temples to be opened; women courted arrest; peasants resisted soldiers. And in many instances, rather than abandoning Gandhi for more radical leaders, the newly radical classes of Indians found themselves happily marrying Gandhi and their own demands for change. This was all the more complicated for the radical middle class, since most students held on to Gandhian ideals begrudgingly and had learned from the experience of the 1920s that they might need to look elsewhere for sources of radical inspiration. Independence from the British was one thing, but organizing a new society on the hidebound ideas of the sleepy hamlets from which they had escaped must have seemed sheer nonsense. Having seen the world that modernity had created, nationalism was for many of these young radicals the means by which peasant relatives could be won over to modernizing their worlds for themselves. They may have created Congress committees in the countryside but the aspirations were clearly urbane and cosmopolitan. And if, along with Benedict Anderson, we attempt to imagine the lifeworld of the individuals capable of imagining communities on a national scale (civil servants, journalists, novelists, and the like), we have to take seriously the ways they understood Gandhi in order to imagine the India that satisfied their aspirations.

This is, more or less, the contradictory milieu that gave rise to the first renaissance in Indian writing in English, often referred to as the "Gandhian Age," in which nationalist writers attempted to describe this new experience of Indians developing political muscles and exercising them in their own interests, through the baggage of the previous decade, for a Western audience. More should be said about this contradiction that can be experienced at the level of form, as it penetrates the novel to the level of the symbol. Anglophone nationalist literature was by and large written by a class of Indians who left their homes to be educated, mainly in England, but who returned to discover that there was a vast gulf that separated them from their families and their worldviews. This bears an important resemblance to the career of the nationalist civil servant tracked in Benedict Anderson's *Imagined Communities* (1983), where nationalism was only imaginable from the vantage point of the deracinated and mobile government employee and his coterie. The writers who produced this literature followed in Gandhi's footsteps, too, leaving India for a British education (though Rao went to France and Desani left for Africa, while Narayan famously never left) and then returning to India to participate in nationalist agitations. Their European education, though, had a profoundly different impact on them than did Gandhi's. After leaving England, Gandhi was convinced that the solution to the problems of colonial modernity lay in India's rural and therefore traditional values. Anglophone writers, though, were unable to resolve colonialism with a return to the village. Partly because they had chosen to write in English – a choice that necessarily allied them to cosmopolitanism rather than provincialism – and partly because they could not tolerate the kinds of values that the village seemed to represent – sexism, caste chauvinism, orthodoxy and superstition, ignorance – there was no easy route for them back to the villages that they had left, often on penalty of excommunication.

The consequence of this experience was a double alienation felt by a radical middle class. On the one hand, nationalism became coterminous with the structure of feeling that separated them from their families, since they had now discovered the joys of egalitarianism ruined by superstition, racism, chauvinism and orthodoxy. Their ability to sympathize with their social and economic inferiors stood in sharp contrast to the inability of the world around them to do the same. The goal was to demonstrate that not only was the radical middle-class intellectual capable of feeling for the untouchable, the peasant, women and the like, but also to show that at its core the alienation of the radical middle class from its families could only be understood from the perspective of its others, who were equally repulsed by the etiquette of the middle-class home. Nationalism was in fact oddly necessary to overcome domestic alienation, substituting as it did a more palatable fantastic family for the biological one. On the other hand, nationalism also came to organize their experience of racism in the metropolis, where the daily encounters with anti-Indian prejudices seemed to dovetail with the reluctance of the British to accept the legitimacy of Indian demands for independence. The response to this chauvinism was not only a compulsion for a humanist pedagogy – a ceaseless sociological impulse present in the fiction of the period designed to show the humanity of Indians against a baseline racism – but also a political internationalism, which sympathized with the struggles of working class and minorities in Europe. This book has attempted to explore this problem of the simultaneity of elite-led populism and middle-class social democracy through investigations of formal contradictions in the literature of the 1930s and 1940s. The pitfalls of Gandhian leadership were major blind spots for most radical intellectuals, who often found themselves standing behind Gandhi in order to make their own anticolonial arguments to British audiences and readers. Still, the relationship between their own democratic ambitions and Gandhi's was tenuous even if it wasn't openly tendentious. Insisting on a radical genealogy for this literature is not merely an act of defending Anand, Ali and Rao from legitimate criticisms of their blindness but a demonstration that nationalism was not merely an elite-driven movement. There were significant challenges that could have been made politically to the direction that the new national bourgeoisie was charting for the nation, but this would have required something that was missing in India and for which the authors of late-colonial fiction can only fractionally bear the responsibility for – independent political organization.

In the main, the decision to write in English came out of the long itinerary of the intelligentsia of which they were a section: unmoored from their homes and alienated from their communities, seeking education and openings in England but discovering simultaneously European prejudices and a circle of continental radicalism, and returning to India to find the nation on the brink of its independence but still divided along the lines of class, caste, gender and religion. In Benedict Anderson's famous formulation, the nation was imagined most importantly in the minds of these pilgrims who could only experience their Indian-ness in English universities, on English ships bound for the metropolis. As a result, the pull of English, which each of these writers describes in their own ways as "natural" (Anand argued that he could not write well in Punjabi; Rao said that English was the language of his emotional makeup; Ali wrote in both but wanted the audiences that English provided), was the product of an alienation that was both constitutive and perhaps traumatic for the literature they produced. The consequences of that decision are equally interesting, for unlike the British modernists (who sought to resolve their alienation formally through experiments in language that might allow the subject to reimagine their relationship to history and community), South Asian anglophone writers attempted to imagine a solution to their alienation not through a formal return to their class but through an immersion in the imagination of their social inferiors, by imagining their own alienation mirrored in the social and economic deprivation of peasants, women, untouchables and dispossessed Muslims. It is indeed the case that anglophone literature did some of the work of uniting the Indian intelligentsia to one another in the only language that they all spoke, but this necessarily had to take a detour through the lives of people who could not read the literature and who were not a part of the class that was imagining the nation. Nationalists could only relate to one another through their others, since the one thing they ironically shared was their common alienation.

The solution that they uncovered to their own alienation was a dangerous one: a compromise with political ideas and figures that they hoped they could surpass. But it was also a solution that allowed them the opportunity to explore the possibilities of real solidarity, to expand the bounds of their own ideological predispositions and to engage in the work of fighting for justice for another. Nationalism, then, must be understood in two ways: as the most capacious grammar of solidarity available to the middle class (in which the largest number of people can be brought into a common constituency to fight side by side), and as the most effective means to silence social conflict and enforce allegiance by way of posing common enemies. This dangerous solidarity in which expressions of statism and egalitarianism commingled freely allowed for the development of radical forces under the cover provided by the banner of the Mahatma. It indigenized radicalism (which otherwise carried the taint of being European) and provided it with a field of maneuver. It brought radicals into contact with far more people than they could have hoped otherwise. But it also left them vulnerable to an ideological offensive from their own countrymen, an offensive for which they were ultimately unprepared. Activist solidarity was replaced with justice in the courts; minority rights were corralled into the feeble politics of representation; economic redistribution was turned into a distant horizon; and the rights of women received meager lip service. Without the combination of colonialism–capitalism–chauvinism as a common enemy, the radicals found that they had not, in fact, built up sufficient political organization to challenge the new syndicate of Congress–capitalism–chauvinism. Here, the banner of the Mahatma after independence served to discipline the radicals rather than allow them freedom of maneuver.

The ambition of this book has been to explain both why this happened and why the novelists who participated in the movement for independence should be understood as casualties of the new nation-state after independence rather than its beneficiaries. But it should also offer all opponents of empire new tools in thinking about how to engage in projects of dangerous solidarity, a term preferable to its closest cousin – "strategic essentialism" – because it is both necessary and ingenuous. Solidarity is dangerous precisely because it always carries the possibility that an offer of real alliance is actually a bait-and-switch con game, perhaps even more so when the stakes are as high as independent nations. But it is a game that has to be played, insofar as empire has to be resisted and injustice deserves to be remedied. In the twentieth century, there have been few figures who have simultaneously been global symbols of solidarity and have politically ushered in some of the most authoritarian state practices; Gandhi is perhaps the tallest of a small class. Tracking his career through the eyes of his left-wing critics, though, explains both the promise and the danger inherent in nationalism. But it also shows that the outcomes of anticolonial nationalism were not given or isomorphic with the intentions of the Congress. The job in the present is to find ways of organizing resistance to empire while understanding the real dangers that come from a failure to recognize the perils of nationalist politics, of misunderstanding the Mahatma in his current incarnation.

NOTES

Introduction

1 For a full version of this criticism see: Benita Parry, *Postcolonial Studies: A Materialist Critique* (London: Routledge, 2004) and Neil Lazarus, *The Postcolonial Unconscious* (Cambridge: Cambridge University Press, 2011).

Chapter 1   The Mahatma as Proof: The Nationalist Origins of the Historiography of Indian Writing in English

1 See also: Dandapani Natarajan, *Indian Census Through a Hundred Years* (New Delhi: Office of the Registrar General, 1972) and N. Gerald Barrier, ed., *The Census in British India: New Perspectives* (New Delhi: Manohar, 1981).

2 As the Indian Constitution originally explained:

§1. The official language of the Union shall be Hindi in Devanagari script. The form of numerals to be used for the official purposes of the Union shall be the international form of Indian numerals.

§2. Notwithstanding anything in clause 1, for a period of fifteen years from the commencement of this Constitution, the English language shall continue to be used for all the official purposes of the Union for which it was being used immediately before such commencement:

> Provided that the President may, during the said period, by order authorise the use of the Hindi language in addition to the English language and of the Devanagari form of numerals in addition to the international form of Indian numerals for any of the official purposes of the Union.

3 Robert Desmond King, *Nehru and the Language Politics of India* (New York: Oxford University Press, 1997); Sajal Basu, *Regional Movements: Politics of Language, Ethnicity, Identity* (New Delhi: Manohar Publications, 1992); Y. D. Phadke, *Politics and Language* (Bombay: Himalaya Publishing House, 1979); Anil Baran Ray, *Students and Politics in India: The Role of Caste, Language, and Region in an Indian University* (New Delhi: R. C. Jain for Manhora Book Service, 1977); Paul Brass, *Language, Religion and Politics in North India* (New York: Cambridge University Press, 1974); and Prakash Karat, *Language and Nationality Politics in India* (Bombay: Orient Longman, 1974).

4 U. A. Asrani, *What Shall We Do About English* (Ahmedabad: Navjivan Publishing House, 1964) and R. S. Gupta and Kapil Kapoor, eds., *English in India* (Delhi: Academic Foundation, 1991).

5 As a consequence, a number of changes were taking place in the curriculum: "Two major moves mark the reorientation of English studies in these postindependence decades: the separation of the acquisition of the English language from the study of literature, and the shift from the definition of English literature as the literature of Britain to a broader characterization of English studies now concerned with all literatures in English." Susie Tharu, "Government, Binding and Unbinding: Alienation and the Teaching of Literature," in *Subject to Change: Teaching Literature in the Nineties* (Hyderabad: Orient Longman, 1997), 16.

6 Also of interest is the footnote on page 77: "What adds interest to a dry fact is that subsequently when the President of India honoured Raja Rao with the award of Padma Bhushan the newspaper

which had earlier published the letters of protest about *Kanthapura* announced him on its front page as 'Raja Rao, the author of the controversial *Kanthapura*.'" Also, Hemenway describes the content of the objections to *Kanthapura*: "It is something of a period piece in India today, but it was once the controversial center of a tempest in a teapot. Vested interests disapproved of *Kanthapura*'s negative portrait of Bhatta, the usurious Brahmin moneylender; of the crudity in actions and/ or words of the British coffee-planter and the Indian police constable; and of the non-Victorian English in which the book is written. Hence, they fought tooth and nail to get *Kanthapura* removed from the list of prescribed textbooks in schools in the Mysore area" (81).

Chapter 2 "The Mahatma didn't say so, but …": Mulk Raj Anand's *Untouchable* and the Sympathies of Middle-Class Nationalists

1 I continue to use "untouchable" instead of the modern "Dalit" only because it produces consistency with the vocabulary that both Anand and Gandhi deploy. In all other instances, I am in favor of using the term "Dalit" to represent members of castes formerly designated as "untouchable."
2 See: Arun P. Mukherjee, "The Exclusions of Postcolonial Theory and Mulk Raj Anand's 'Untouchable': A Case Study," *ARIEL: A Review of International English Literature*, 22 (3) (1991): 27–48; Saros Cowasjee, "Mulk Raj Anand's Untouchable: An Appraisal," *Literature East and West* 17 (1973): 199–211; Susheila Nasta, "Between Bloomsbury, Gandhi and Transcultural Modernities: The Publication and Reception of Mulk Raj Anand's *Untouchable*," *Books Without Borders* (New York: Palgrave Macmillan, 2008), 151–69.
3 Anand writes: "I have been in the study devouring the words of Gandhi in Young India. […] As I turned the pages, casually reading here and there, I came across the story of Uka. In simple direct words, the Mahatma had written about how this sweeper boy had been brought to the Sabarmati Ashram, how he was despised by everyone, until he had a bath, washed his clothes and was allowed to sit in the kitchen-dining room among other members of the house, and how this untouchable rose to be the equal of all the other Ashramites, specially because Gandhiji insisted on everyone, including himself, taking a vow that, like Uka, everyone would clean latrines in turn. The Mahatma adopted him as his son, and appealed to everyone not to call the outcastes untouchables, but Harijans, sons of God" (525).
4 *Untouchable* had been rejected, Anand claimed, by nineteen different publishers, a fact that had driven him to contemplate suicide before he found a publisher for the book.
5 Susie Tharu, "Reading against the Imperial Grain: Intertextuality, Narrative Structure and Liberal Humanism in Mulk Raj Anand's *Untouchable*," *Jadavpur Journal of Comparative Literature* 24 (1986): 60–71 and Teresa Hubel, *Whose India? The Independence Struggle in British and Indian Fiction and History* (Durham: Duke University Press, 1996). Recently some have argued that the influence of Gandhi was at least mediated in terms of form through Joyce (even though this does not seem to affect the political trajectory of the novel's Gandhian bent). See, for instance: Jessica Berman, "Comparative Colonialisms: Joyce, Anand, and the Question of Engagement," *Modernism/modernity* 13 (3) (2006): 465–85.
6 See also: Mahatma Gandhi, *Gandhiji in England, and the Proceedings of the Second Round Table Conference* (Madras: B.G. Paul, 1932) and Subhamani N. Busi, *Mahatma Gandhi and Babasaheb Ambedkar: Crusaders Against Caste and Untouchability* (Hyderabad: Saroja Publications, 1997).
7 See, among others: C. B. Agrawal, *The Harijans in Rebellion: Case for the Removal of Untouchability* (Bombay: D. B. Taraporevala sons & co., 1934); Shri Ram Bakshi, *Gandhi and Status of Harijans* (New Delhi: Deep & Deep Publications, 1987); and Marguerite Rose Dove, *Forfeited Future: The Conflict Over Congress Ministries, 1933–1937* (Delhi: Chanakya Publications, 1987).
8 Manmath Nath Das, *India Under Morley and Minto* (London: Allen and Unwin, 1964); Vinod Kumar Saxena, *Muslims and the Indian National Congress, 1885–1924* (Delhi: Discovery, 1985);

and Stanley Wolpert, *Morley and India, 1906–1910* (Berkeley: University of California Press, 1967).

9 See: S. K. Chahal, *Dalits Patronised: The Indian National Congress and Untouchables of India, 1921–1947* (Delhi: Shubhi Publications, 2002) and Periyar E. V. Ramasami, *Why Brahmins Hate Reservations?* (Madras: Periyar Self-Respect Propaganda Institution, 1983).

10 For an example of this, see: Mahatma Gandhi, *Caste Must Go and the Sin of Untouchability* (Ahmedabad: Navjivan Publishing House, 1964).

11 See: Nairanjana Raychaudhury Bhattacharya, *Caste, Reservation, and Electoral Politics, 1919–1937* (Calcutta: Progressive Publishers, 1992) and Vivek Kumar, *Dalit Leadership in India* (Delhi: Kalpaz Publications, 2002).

12 See, among others: N. Gerald Barrier, ed. *The Census in British India: New Perspectives* (New Delhi: Manohar, 1981); Nairanjana Raychaudhury Bhattacharya, *Caste, Reservation, and Electoral Politics, 1919–1937* (Calcutta: Progressive Publishers, 1992); Nicholas Dirks, *Castes of Mind: Colonialism and the Making of Modern India* (Princeton: Princeton University Press, 2001); Christophe Jaffrelot, "Sanskritization vs. Ethnicization in India: Changing Identities and Caste Politics Before Mandal," *Asian Survey* 40.5 (September–October 2000): 756–66; Dandapani Natarajan, *Indian Census Through a Hundred Years* (New Delhi: Office of the Registrar General, 1972); Oliver Mendelsohn and Marika Vicziany, *The Untouchables: Subordination, Poverty and the State in Modern India* (Cambridge: Cambridge University Press, 1998); and Susan Bayly, *Caste, Society and Politics in India from the Eighteenth Century to the Modern Age* (New York: Cambridge University Press, 1999).

13 See: Frederic Salmon Growse, *Bulandshahr, or Sketches of an Indian District* (Benares: Medical Hall Press, 1884); J. A. Turner, *Sanitation in India* (Bombay: The Times of India, 1914).

14 Mulk Raj Anand, *The Bubble*, 426: "Like a bird, my eyes were uplifted towards home. I saw Lakha, Bakha, Rakha, Chotta, Ram Charan and family, in worn-out military uniforms, smoking stubs of Red Lamp cigarettes dropped on the road by the Tommies in Lal Kurti. To be sure, the poorest of the poor accepted the world run by the upper people, the Sahibs, the Subedars and the babus. They were abject when they received anything from the well-off. Even a smile was a precious gift. They would be very surprised if I told them that I was their brother. Maybe, Allen Hutt's ideas could sway people ultimately, but the Harijans still believed in Gugga Pir and amulets against misfortune. I would have to be the mouth of all their silent mouths as I shall be 'England-returned.' They wanted crumbs and cigarettes and some country liquor, not words."

15 Misra quotes G. D. Birla's depiction of British racism towards Indian business elites: "When I was sixteen I started an independent business of my own as a broker, and thus began my association with Englishmen who were my patrons and clients. [...] Their racial arrogance could not be concealed. I was not allowed to use the lift up to their offices, nor their benches while waiting to see them. I smarted under these insults, and this created within me a political interest which from 1912 until this day I have fully maintained" (135).

Chapter 3   "The Mahatma may be all wrong about politics, but ...": Raja Rao's *Kanthapura* and the Religious Imagination of the Indian, Secular, Nationalist Middle Class

1 See: Ralph Russell, *The Pursuit of Urdu Literature: A Select History* (New Delhi: Seagull Books, 1992) and Ali Jawad Zaidi, *A History of Urdu Literature* (Delhi: Sahitya Akademi, 1993).

2 See also: Harish Trivedi, "Literary and Visual Portrayals of Gandhi," in *The Cambridge Companion to Gandhi*, ed. Judith Brown and Anthony Parel (New York: Cambridge University Press, 2011), 199–218.

3 See also: Richard Cashman, *The Myth of the Lokamanya: Tilak and Mass Politics in Maharashtra* (Berkeley: University of California Press, 1975).

4 Tabish Khair, "Raja Rao and Alien Universality," *Journal of Commonwealth Literature* 33 (1) (1998): 78.

5 See also: Radha Kumar, *The History of Doing, An Illustrated Account of Movements for Women's Rights and Feminism in India, 1800–1990* (London: Verso, 1993).
6 They write: "Women also played a key role in a similar campaign in the coastal district of North Kanara (in present-day Karnataka), garlanding and smearing ritual paste on men who went off to the forest to cut the valued sandal tree. There, too, the timber was loaded on to carts and stacked in front of a local temple. When the men were arrested, the women symbolically breached the rules themselves, invoking the god Sri Krishna who had gone into the forest."
7 See also: T. J. Abraham, "Flawed Gandhism or Hindu Fundamentalism? No Cheers for Kanthapura," *Indian Literature* 47 (4): 162–6.
8 As compared to the view of nationalism in Partha Chatterjee, *Nationalist Thought and the Colonial World, A Derivative Discourse* (Minneapolis: University of Minnesota Press, 1993).
9 Kesavan argues: "For example, Hindustani classical music is part of the metropolitan Indian's baggage, but Carnatic music is not. This is because words matter in Carnatic music in a way that they have long since ceased to do in the Hindustani tradition. Hindustani music has been secularized over time but an appreciation of vocal Carnatic music depends on an understanding of the devotional songs of Thyagaraja or Purandaradasa. In a linguistically diverse country like India, the Hindustani classical tradition was always likely to prevail because it allowed connoisseurship without the effort of learning a language."

Chapter 4   The Missing Mahatma: Ahmed Ali and the Aesthetics of Muslim Anticolonialism

1 The translations of all the passages in Urdu are my own.
2 Ali explains: "We were filled with a zeal to change the social order and right the wrongs done to man by man … we dreamed of winning for Urdu and the regional languages the same respect and for the Indian people the same dignity which other civilized languages and societies enjoyed" (Ali 1974, 36).
3 Translation mine.
4 Italics mine; the lines in italics are references to stories from the *Angare* collection.

Chapter 5   The Grammar of the Gandhians: Jayaprakash Narayan and the Figure of Gandhi

1 See: Satyabrata Rai Chowdhuri, *Leftism in India, 1917–1947* (New York: Palgrave Macmillan, 2007), 43–92, and Sanjay Seth, *Marxist Theory and Nationalist Politics: The Case of Colonial India* (New Delhi: Sage Publications, 1995), 154–7.
2 Harold Bloom continues: "The metalepsis leaps over the heads of other tropes and becomes a representation set against time, sacrificing the present to an idealized past or hoped-for future. As a figure of a figure, it ceases to be a reduction or a limitation and becomes instead a peculiar representation, either proleptic or 'preposterous,' in the root sense of making the later into the earlier. As a defense, this *apophrades* chooses between introjections and projection, between a kind of identification and a kind of dangerous jealousy" (103).

Chapter 6   The Mahatma Misunderstood: The Arrested Development of the Nationalist Dialectic

1 The phrase is taken from: Chris Harman, "Gramsci versus Eurocommunism," *International Socialism* 98 (1977): 23. For an understanding of the relationship between Gramsci and Eurocommunism, see also: Nigel Greaves, *Gramsci's Marxism: Reclaiming a Philosophy of History and*

Politics (Leicester: Matador, 2009); Marcus Green, ed. *Rethinking Gramsci* (New York: Routledge, 2011); and Jules Townshend, *The Politics of Marxism* (London: Leicester University Press, 1996). For a critique of Subaltern Studies see: Sumit Sarkar, *Beyond Nationalist Frames* (New Delhi: Permanent Black, 2002).

2 See also Sumit Sarkar: "The Decline of the Subaltern in Subaltern Studies," in *Reading Subaltern Studies*, ed. David Ludden (London: Anthem Press, 2002); Pheng Cheah, *Spectral Nationality* (New York: Columbia University Press, 2003); and Sunil Choudhary, "The 'Elitism' of Nationalist Discourse," *Social Scientist* 16 (3) (1988): 57–77.

3 See also: Timothy Brennan, *Wars of Position: The Cultural Politics of Left and Right* (New York: Columbia University Press, 2006), 233–72.

4 See: John Patrick Haithcox, *Communism and Nationalism in India* (Princeton: Princeton University Press, 1971); Sobhanlal Datta Gupta, *Comintern, India and the Colonial Question, 1920–37* (Calcutta: K. P. Baghci and Co., 1980); Sobhanlal Datta Gupta, *Comintern and the Destiny of Communism in India, 1919–43* (Kolata: Seribaan, 2006); D. N. Gupta, *Communism and Nationalism in Colonial India, 1939–45* (London: SAGE, 2008); and Kiran Maitra, *Roy, Comintern and Marxism in India* (Calcutta: Darbari Prokashan, 1991).

BIBLIOGRAPHY

Abbas, K. A. 1946. *Tomorrow is Ours!* Delhi: Rajkamal.
Abraham, T. J. 2003. "Flawed Gandhism or Hindu Fundamentalism? No Cheers for Kanthapura." *Indian Literature* 4: 162–67.
Agnihotri, G. N. 1993. *Indian Life and Problems in the Novels of Mulk Raj Anand, Raja Rao, and R. K. Narayan.* Meerut: Shalabh Prakashan.
Agnihotri, H. L. 1983. "Gandhian Ethos in Mulk Raj Anand." *Journal of Literature and Aesthetics* 3 (1): 43–53.
Agnihotri, R. K. and A. L. Khann. 1997. *Problematizing English in India.* New Delhi: SAGE.
Agrawal, C. 1934. *The Harijans in Rebellion: Case for the Removal of Untouchability.* Bombay: D. B. Taraporevala Sons.
Ahluwalia, B. K. and S. Ahluwalia. 1981. *Tagore and Gandhi.* New Delhi: Pankaj Publications.
Ahmad, A., trans. 1971. *The Ghazals of Ghalib.* New York: Columbia University Press.
_____. 1993. *In the Mirror of Urdu: Recompositions of Nation and Community, 1945–1967.* Shimla: Indian Institute of Advanced Study.
_____. 1994. *In Theory.* New York: Verso.
_____. 2002. *On Communalism and Globalization: Offensives of the Far Right.* Delhi: Three Essays.
Ahmad, D. N. 2003. *Fasana-i-mubtala.* Delhi: Kitabi Duniya.
Ahmad, M. N. 2001. *The Bride's Mirror.* Translated by G. E. Ward. Delhi: Sangam Books.
Ahmad, T. 2005. "Mulk Raj Anand: Novelist and Fighter." *International Socialism* 105: 40–63.
_____. 2009. *Literature and Politics in the Age of Nationalism: The Progressive Episode in South Asia, 1932–56.* London: Routledge.
Ahmed, N. 1967. *Shehrashob: mamuqadimah o havashi.* Dilli: Jamal Printing Press.
_____. 1979. *Shehrashob ka tahqiqi mutalah.* Aligarh: Adabi Akademi.
Ahsan, M. 1986. "The Muslim Aristocracy and the Birth of the All-India Muslim League." *Journal of the Asiatic Society of Bangladesh* 31 (2): 71–84.
Aiyar, S. 1968. "Language and Modernization." In *The Great Debate: Language Controversy and University Education*, edited by A. Shah, 54–72. Bombay: Lalvani Publishing House.
Ajneya. 1995. *Tar Saptak.* Nayi Dilli: Bharatiya Jnanpith Prakashan.
Ali, A. 1950. *The Falcon and the Hunted Bird.* Karachi: Kitab.
_____., ed. and trans. 1960. *The Bulbul and the Rose: An Anthology of Urdu Poetry.* Karachi: Maktaba Jamia Talim-i-Milli.
_____. 1964. *Ocean of Night.* London: Peter Owen.
_____. 1969. *Ghalib: Two Essays.* Roma: Istuto Italiano per il Medio ed Estremo Oriente.
_____. 1973. *The Golden Tradition: An Anthology of Urdu Poetry.* New York: Columbia University Press.
_____. 1974. "The Progressive Writers Movement and Creative Writers in Urdu." In *Marxist Influences and South Asian Literature*, edited by C. Coppola, 42–54. East Lansing: Asian Studies Center, Michigan State University.
_____. 1985a. *Of Rats and Diplomats.* Bombay: Orient Longman.
_____. 1985b. *Shole.* Karachi: Akrash.
_____. 1985c. *The Prison House.* Karachi: Akrash.
_____. 1986. *The Prison-House: Short Stories.* Karachi: Akrash.

———. 1994. *Twilight in Delhi*. New York: New Directions.
———. 2007. "A Night of Winter Rains." Translated by S. Shingavi. *Annual of Urdu Studies* 22: 240–46.
Ali, I. 2003. *The Punjab Under Imperialism, 1885–1947*. New York: Oxford University Press.
Ali, T. 1983. *Can Pakistan Survive?* New York: Penguin.
———. 1985. *The Nehrus and the Gandhis: An Indian Dynasty*. London: Pan Books.
Ambedkar, B. R. 1946. *What Congress and Gandhi Have Done to the Untouchables*. Bombay: Thacker.
———. 1969. *The Untouchables*. Uttar Pradesh: Bharatiya Baudha Shiksha Parishad.
———. 1990. *Annihilation of Caste: An Undelivered Speech*. New Delhi: Arnold.
Amin, S. 1996. *Event, Memory, Metaphor: Chauri Chaura 1922–1992*. New York: Oxford University Press.
Amur, G. 2001. *Essays on Modern Kannada Literature*. Bangalore: Karnataka Sahitya Akademi.
Amur, G. S. 1984. *Essays on Comparative Literature and Linguistics*. New Delhi: Sterling.
Anand, M. R. 1940. *Untouchable*. London: Penguin.
———. 1942. *Letters on India*. London: Routledge.
———. 1946. *Apology for Heroism*. New Delhi: Arnold-Heineman Publishers.
———. 1947. *On Education*. Bombay: Hind Kitabs.
———. 1967. *The Humanism of M. K. Gandhi*. Chandigarh: University of Punjab.
———. 1972. "Pigeon-Indian: Some Notes on Indian-English Writing." *Journal of the Karnatak University* 16: 69–90.
———. 1984. *The Bubble*. New Delhi: Arnold-Heinemann.
———. 1990. Preface. In B. R. Ambedkar, *Annihilation of Caste*. New Delhi: Arnold.
———. 1991. *Little Plays of Mahatma Gandhi*. New Delhi: Arnold.
———. 1992. "On the Genesis of Untouchable: A Note." In *The Novels of Mulk Raj Anand*, edited by R. Dhawan, 180–192. New Delhi: Prestige Books.
———. 1993. *Coolie*. New Delhi: Penguin Books.
———. 1995. "Why I Write." In *Creative Aspects of Indian Literature*, edited by S. K. Desai, 20–33. New Delhi: Sahitya Akadmie.
Anand, M. R. and I. Singh. 1946. *Indian Short Stories*. London: New India.
Ananthamurthy, U. R. 2010. *Bharathipura*. Translated by S. Punitha. New Delhi: Oxford University Press.
Anderson, B. 1983. *Imagined Communities: Reflections on the Origin and Spread of Nationalism*. London: Verso.
Anderson, K. B. 2010. *Marx at the Margins: On Nationalism, Ethnicity, and Non-Western Societies*. Chicago: University of Chicago Press.
Andrews, C. F. 2003. *Zakaullah of Delhi*. New York: Oxford University Press.
Arnold, D. 1993. *Colonizing the Body: State Medicine and Epidemic Disease in Nineteenth-Century India*. Berkeley: University of California Press.
———. 2001a. *Gandhi*. New York: Longman.
———. 2001b. *Gandhi: Profiles in Power*. New York: Longman.
Arnold, M. 2006. *Culture and Anarchy*. London: Oxford University Press.
Askari, M. H. 1994. "A Novel by Ahmed Ali." Edited by C. Coppola. *Annual of Urdu Studies* 9: 27–38.
Asrani, U. A. 1964. *What Shall We Do About English*. Ahmedabad: Navjivan Publishing House.
Bairathi, S. 1987. *Communism and Nationalism in India*. Delhi: Anamika Prakashan.
Bakshi, S. R. 1987. *Gandhi and Status of Harijans*. New Delhi: Deep & Deep.
Barrier, G. 1981. *The Census in British India: New Perspectives*. New Delhi: Manohar.
Baruah, S. 2005. *Durable Disorder: Understand the Politics of Northeast India*. Delhi: Oxford University Press.
Basu, S. 1992. *Regional Movements: Politics of Language, Ethnicity, Identity*. New Delhi: Manohar Publications.

Bayly, S. 1999. *Caste, Society and Politics in India from the Eighteenth Century to the Modern Age*. Cambridge: Cambridge University Press.
Benjamin, W. 1969. "The Work of Art in the Age of Mechanical Reproduction." In *Illuminations*, edited by W. Benjamin and H. Arendt, translated by H. Zohn, 217–52. New York: Schocken Books.
Berman, J. 2006. "Comparative Colonialisms: Joyce, Anand, and the Question of Engagement." *Modernism/modernity* 13 (3): 466–85.
Bharati, S. 1987. *Communism and Nationalism in India*. Delhi: Anamika Prakashan.
Bhatnagar, M. K. and M. Rajeshwar. 2000. *The Novels of Mulk Raj Anand*. New Delhi: Atlantic.
Bhattacharya, B. 1948. *Indian Cavalcade, Some Memorable Yesterdays*. Bombay: Nalanda Publications.
———. 1954. *He Who Rides a Tiger*. New Delhi: Arnold-Heinemann.
———. 1968. *Steel Hawk and Other Stories*. Delhi: Hind Pocket Books.
———. 1969. *Gandhi the Writer: The Image as it Grew*. New Delhi: National Book Trust.
———. 1976. *Glimpses of Indian History*. New Delhi: Sterling.
———. 1977. *Mahatma Gandhi*. New Delhi: Arnold-Heinemann.
———. 1978. *So Many Hungers!* New Delhi: Orient Paperbacks.
Bhattacharya, H. 1989. *Raj and Literature: Banned Bengali Books*. Calcutta: Firma KLM.
Bhattacharya, S., ed. 1997. *The Mahatma and the Poet: Letters and Debates Between Gandhi and Tagore 1915–1941*. New Delhi: National Book Trust.
Bilgrami, A. 2011. "Gandhi's Religion and Its Relation to His Politics." In *The Cambridge Companion to Gandhi*, edited by J. Brown and A. Parel, 93–116. New York: Cambridge University Press.
Blair, S. 2004. "Local Modernity Global Modernism: Bloomsbury and the Places of the Literary." *ELH* 21 (4): 813–38.
Bloom, H. 1975. *A Map of Misreading*. New York: Oxford University Press.
Bond, R. 1988. *The Night Train at Deoli and Other Stories*. New Delhi: Penguin.
Bottomore, S. 1997. "'Have You Seen the Gaekwar Bob?': Filming the 1911 Delhi Durbar." *Historic Journal of Film, Radio and Television* 17 (3): 309–45.
Bramford, P. C. 1985. *History of the Non-Cooperation and Khilafat Movement*. Delhi: K. K. Book Distributors.
Brass, P. 1974. *Language, Religion and Politics in North India*. New York: Cambridge University Press.
Brayne, F. L. 1937. *Better Villages*. New York: Oxford University Press.
Brennan, T. 2001. "Antonio Gramsci and Postcolonial Theory: 'Southernism'." *Diaspora* 10 (1): 143–87.
Brennan, T. 2006. *Wars of Position: The Cultural Politics of Left and Right*. New York: Columbia University Press.
Brians, P. 2003. *Modern South Asian Literature*. Westport: Greenwood.
Brijbhushan, J. 1976. *Kamaladevi Chattopadhyay: Portrait of a Rebel*. New Delhi: Abhinav.
Brock, R. 2011. "Framing Theory: Towards an Ekphrastic Postcolonial Methodoly." *Cultural Critique* 77: 102–45.
Brown, J. 1989. *Gandhi: Prisoner of Hope*. New Haven: Yale University Press.
———. 1994. *Modern India: The Origins of an Asian Democracy*. New York: Oxford.
———. 2003. *Nehru: A Political Life*. New Haven: Yale University Press.
Busi, S. N. 1997. *Mahatma Gandhi and Babasaheb Ambedkar: Crusaders Against Caste and Untouchability*. Hyderabad: Saroja.
Cammett, J. 1967. *Antonio Gramsci and the Origins of Italian Communism*. Stanford: Stanford University Press.
Cashman, R. 1975. *The Myth of the Lokamanya: Tilak and Mass Politics in Maharashtra*. Berkeley: University of California Press.
Chahal, S. K. 2002. *Dalits Patronised: The Indian National Congress and Untouchables of India, 1921–47*. Delhi: Shubhi Publications.
Chandra, B. 2003. *In the Name of Democracy: JP movement and the Emergency*. New Delhi: Penguin.

Chandra, B. 1979. *Nationalism and Colonialism in Modern India.* New Delhi: Orient Longman.
Chatterjee, M. 2000. "Khadi: The Fabric of the Nation in Raja Rao's Kanthapura." *New Literatures Review* 36: 105–13.
———. 2001. "1930: Turning Point in the Participation of Women in the Freedom Struggle." *Social Scientist* 29 (7/8): 39–47.
Chatterjee, P. 1986. *Nationalist Thought in the Colonial World: A Derivative Discourse?* Minneapolis: University of Minnesota Press.
Chattopadhyay, K. 1986. *Inner Recesses Outer Spaces.* New Delhi: Navrang.
Chaturvedi, V. 2007. *Peasant Pasts: History and Memory in Western India.* Berkeley: University of California Press.
Chaudhuri, A. 2004. *The Vintage Book of Modern Indian Literature.* New York: Vintage.
Chauhan, K. 1998. *Pragativadi andolan ka itihaas.* Nayi Dilli: Prakashan Samsthaan.
Cheah, P. 2003. *Spectral Nationality.* New York: Columbia University Press.
Choudhary, S. 1988. "The 'Elitism' of Nationalist Discourse." *Social Scientist* 16 (3): 57–77.
Chowdhuri, S. R. 2007. *Leftism in India, 1917–1947.* New York: Palgrave Macmillan.
Chrisman, L. 2003. *Postcolonial Contraventions: Cultural Readings of Race, Imperialism and Transnationalism.* New York: Manchester University Press.
———. 2004. "Nationalism and Postcolonial Studies." In *The Cambridge Companion to Postcolonial Studies,* edited by N. Lazarus. New York: Cambridge University Press.
Coppola, C. 1981. "The Angare Group: The Enfants Terrible of Urdu Literature." *Annual of Urdu Studies* 1: 57–69.
Cowasjee, S. 1973. "Mulk Raj Anand's Untouchable: An Appraisal." *Literature East and West* 17: 199–211.
Das, M. N. 1964. *India Under Morley and Minto.* London: Allen and Unwin.
Das, S. K. 2006. *A History of Indian Literature.* New Delhi: Sahitya Akademi.
Davis, M. 1985. Urban Renaissance and the Spirit of Postmodernism. *New Left Review* 151: 106–13.
Dayal, P. 1991. *Raja Rao: A Study of His Novels.* New Delhi: Atlantic.
Deva, A. N. 1987. *Socialism and the Nationalist Movement.* Delhi: Anupama.
Dey, E. 1992. *The Novels of Raja Rao: The Theme of Quest.* New Delhi: Prestige Books.
Dove, M. R. 1987. *Forfeited Future: The Conflict Over Congress Ministries, 1933–1937.* Delhi: Chanakya.
Dumbell, P. H. 1930. *Loyal India: A Survey of Seventy Years 1858–1928.* London: Constable.
Dwivedi, A. N. 1991. *Indian Writing in English.* Delhi: Amar Prakashan.
Eagleton, T. 1976. *Marxism and Literary Criticism.* Berkeley: University of California Press.
———. 1976. *Criticism and Ideology.* London: New Left Books.
———. 1986. *Against the Grain: Essays 1975–1985.* London: Verso.
———. 1990. *The Significance of Theory.* Oxford: Basil Blackwell.
———. 1996. *Literary Theory: An Introduction.* Minneapolis: University of Minnesota Press.
Effendi, S. 1982. *Story of Hir and Ranjha.* Lahore: Panjabi Adab Lahir.
Elwin, V. 1932. *The Truth About India: Can We Get It?* London: George Allen & Unwin.
Embree, A. T. 1989. *Imagining India: Essays on Indian History.* New York: Oxford University Press.
Famine Commission. 1976. "Report on Bengal." New Delhi: Usha Publications.
Fanon, F. 1968. *The Wretched of the Earth.* New York: Grove Press.
Faruqi, S. R. 1999. *Early Urdu Literary Culture and History.* New York: Oxford University Press.
Faulkner, P., ed. 1986. *The English Modernist Reader, 1910–1930.* Iowa City: University of Iowa Press.
Fisher, M. 1973. "Interview with Mulk Raj Anand." *WLWE* 22: 109–22.
———. 1980. *The Wisdom of the Heart: A Study of the Works of Mulk Raj Anand.* New Delhi: Sterling.
Forrester, D. B. 1966. "The Madras Anti-Hindi Agitation, 1965: Political Protest and its Effects on Language Policy in India." *Pacific Affairs* 39 (1/2): 19–36.

Frankel, F. 1978. *India's Political Economy, 1947–77*. Princeton: Princeton University Press.
Gandhi, L. 2003. "Novelists of the 1930s and 1940s." In *Illustrated History of Indian Literature in English*, edited by A. K. Mehrotra. New Delhi: Permanent Black.
Gandhi, M. 1969. "Speech at Gandhi Seva Sangh Meeting – III." In *The Collected Works of Mahatma Gandhi* 77. New Delhi: Government of India.
———. 1997. *Hind Swaraj and Other Writings*. Cambridge: Cambridge University Press.
Gangopadhyay, S. 2010. *Days and Nights in the Forest*. Translated by R. Ray. New York: Penguin.
Ganguly, S. M. 1984. *Leftism in India*. Calcutta: Minerva Associates.
Gopal, P. 2009. *The Indian English Novel: Nation, History, and Narration*. New York: Oxford University Press.
Gramsci, A. 1971. *Selections from the Prison Notebooks*. New York: International Publishers.
———. 1977. *Selections from Political Writings, 1910–1920*. Edited by Q. Hoare, translated by J. Mathews. New York: International Publishers.
Greaves, N. 2009. *Gramsci's Marxism: Reclaiming a Philosophy of History and Politics*. Leicester: Matador.
Green, M. 2011. *Rethinking Gramsci*. New York: Routledge.
Growse, F. S. 1884. *Bulandshahr, or Sketches of an Indian District*. Benares: Medical Hall Press.
Guha, R. 1988. "The Prose of Counter-Insurgency." In *Selected Subaltern Studies*, edited by R. Guha and G. C. Spivak. New York: Oxford University Press.
Guha, R. and M. Gadgil. 1989. "State Forestry and Social Conflict in British India." *Past and Present* 123 (1): 141–77.
Gupta, D. 2008. *Communism and Nationalism in Colonial India*, 1939–45. London: SAGE.
Gupta, N. 1981. *Delhi Between Two Empires*. New York: Oxford University Press.
Gupta, R. D. 1990. "Plantation Labour in Colonial India." *Working Paper Series* 140.
Gupta, R. S. 1991. *English in India*. Delhi: Academic Foundation.
Gupta, S. D. 1980. *Comintern, India and the Colonial Question*. Calcutta: K. P. Bagchi.
———. 2006. *Comintern and the Destiny of Communism in India*. Kolkata: Seribaan.
Haithcox, J. P. 1971. *Communism and Nationalism in India*. Princeton: Princeton University Press.
Halappa, G. S. and M. V. Krishna Rao, eds. 1964. *History of Freedom Movement in Karnataka*. Bangalore: Government of Mysore.
Handa, M. 1985. "The Elements of a Gandhian Social Theory." In *In Theory and in Practice: Essays on the Politics of Jayaprakash Narayan*, edited by D. Selbourne, 33–58. Delhi: Oxford University Press.
Haque, Md. R. 2011. "The Nation and One of Its Fragments in Kanthapura." *Transnational Literature* 4 (1): n.a.
Hardiman, D. 2003. *Gandhi in His Time and Ours*. New York: Columbia University Press.
Harman, C. 1977. "Gramsci Versus Eurocommunism." *International Socialism* 98: 30–54.
Hasan, M. 1992. *Nationalism and Communal Politics in India, 1885–1930*. Delhi: South Asia Books.
———. 2005. *A Moral Reckoning: Muslim Intellectuals in Nineteenth-century Delhi*. New York: Oxford University Press.
Hashmi, A. 1994. "Professor Ahmed Ali." *Annual of Urdu Studies* 9: 44–8.
———. 1996. "Literature in English." In *English Postcoloniality: Literatures from around the World*, edited by R. Mohanram and G. Rajan. Westport: Greenwood.
Hemenway, S. I. 1975. *The Novel of India 2*. Calcutta: Writers Workshop.
Hosagrahar, J. 2001. "Mansions to Margins: Modernity and the Domestic Landscapes of Historic Delhi, 1847–1910." *Journal of the Society of Architectural Historians* 60 (1): 26–45.
Hubel, T. 1996. *Whose India? The Independence Struggle in British and Indian Fiction and History*. Durham: Duke University Press.
University Grants Commission. 1965. "Report of the English Review Committee." New Delhi: Government of India.
Iyengar, K. R. S. 1945. *The Indian Contribution to English Literature*. Bombay: Karnatak.

———. 1962a. *Indian Writing in English*. Bombay: Asia Publishing House.
———. 1962b. *The Adventure of Criticism*. London: Asia Publishing House.
———. 1968. "Messing up the Medium." In *Retain English for Unity and Progress*, edited by K. P. K. Menon. Calicut: The Powra Sangham.
———. 1970. *Two Cheers for the Commonwealth*. London: Asia Publishing House.
J. K. Institute of Survey. 1955. "Survey of Living Conditions of Harijans in Uttar Pradesh." Lucknow: The Director, Harijan Welfare Department, Uttar Pradesh.
Jaffrelot, C. 2000. "Sanskritization vs. Ethnicization in India: Changing Identities and Caste Politics before Mandal." *Asian Survey* 40 (5): 756–66.
———. 2005. *Dr. Ambedkar and Untouchability*. New York: Columbia University Press.
Jahan, R. "In the Women's Quarters." In *Angare*, translated by S. Shingavi. Unpublished manuscript.
Jain, J. 2007. "A Phoenix Called Resistance: Aesthetics vs Meaning." *Journal of Postcolonial Writing* 43 (2): 172–82.
Jain, J. and V. Singh, eds. 2000. *Contesting Postcolonialisms*. Jaipur: Rawat.
Jain, R. K. 1968. *Essentials of English Teaching: Covering the Syllabi of Indian Universities*. Agra: Vinod Pustak Mandir.
Jalal, A. 1985. *Jinnah, the Muslim League, and the Demand for Pakistan*. New York: Cambridge University Press.
———. 1990. *The State of Martial Rule: The Origins of Pakistan's Political Economy of Defence*. New York: Cambridge University Press.
———. 2001. *Self and Soveriegnty: Individual and Community in South Asian Islam since 1850*. New Delhi: Oxford University Press.
———. 2008. *Partisans of Allah: Jihad in South Asia*. Cambridge: Harvard University Press.
Jalal, A. and A. Seal. 1981. "Alternative to Partition: Muslim Politics Between the Wars." *Modern Asian Studies* 15 (3): 415–54.
Jani, P. 2010. *Decentering Rushdie: Cosmopolitanism and the Indian Novel in English*. Columbus: Ohio State University Press.
Jatava, D. R. 1997. *The Critics of Dr. Ambedkar*. Jaipur: Surabhi.
Jha, R. 1981. "The Influence of Gandhian Thought on Indo-Anglian Novelists of the Thirties and Forties." *Journal of South Asian Literature* 16 (2): 163–72.
———. 1983. *Gandhian Thought and Indo-Anglian Novelists*. Delhi: Chanakya.
Jones, O. B. 2002. *Pakistan: Eye of the Storm*. New Haven: Yale University Press.
Joshi, C. 2003. *Lost Worlds: Indian Labour and its Forgotten Histories*. New Delhi: Permanent Black.
Joshi, K. and B. S. Rao. 1972. *Studies in Indo-Anglian Literature*. Bareilly: Prakash Book Depot.
Joshi, P. 2002. *In Another Country*. New York: Columbia University Press.
Joshi, S. 1991. *Rethinking English: Essays in Literature*. New Delhi: Trianka.
Jusdanis, G. 2001. *The Necessary Nation*. Princeton: Princeton University Press.
Jussawalla, F. 1985. *Family Quarrels: Towards a Criticism of Indian Writing in English*. New York: Peter Lang.
Kachru, B. 1983. *The Indianization of English: The English Language in India*. Delhi: Oxford.
———. 1988. "Toward Expanding the English Canon: Raja Rao's 1938 Credo for Creativity." *World Literature Today* 62 (4): 582–6.
Kamran, M. 2010. *Profaisar Ahmad Ali, 1910–1004: hayat aur adabi khidmat*. Karachi: Anjuman Taraqqi-i Urdu Pakistan.
Karat, P. 1974. *Language and Nationality Politics in India*. Bombay: Orient Longman.
Kesavan, M. 2001. *Secular Common Sense*. New York: Penguin.
Khair, T. 2001. *Babu Fictions: Alienation in Contemporary Indian English Novels*. Delhi: Oxford University Press.
Khan, S. A. 2000. *The Causes of the Indian Revolt*. London: Oxford University Press.
King, R. D. 1997. *Nehru and the Language Politics of India*. New York: Oxford University Press.

Lazarus, N. 1999. *Nationalism and Cultural Practice in the Postcolonial World.* New York: Cambridge University Press.
———. 2011. *The Postcolonial Unconscious.* Cambridge: Cambridge University Press.
Lazarus, N. and C. Bartolovich, eds. 2002. *Marxism, Modernity and Postcolonial Studies.* Cambridge: Cambridge University Press.
Leenerts, C. 2003. "'How Can We Be Like We Used to Be?': The Collective Sita and the Collective Draupadi in Raja Rao's Kanthapura and Jyotirmoyee Devi's The River Churning." *South Asian Review* 24 (2): 84–105.
Lelyveld, D. 2004. *Aligarh's First Generation: Musilm Solidarity in British India.* New York: Oxford University Press.
Lenin, V. 1965. "Draft Theses on the National and Colonial Questions." In *Collected Works*, 144–51. Moscow: Progress.
Low, A. D. 1958. *Lenin on the Question of Nationality.* New York: Bookman Associates.
Lukacs, G. 1978. *Hegel's False and His Genuine Ontology.* Translated by D. Fernbach. London: Merlin.
Mahmud, S. 1996. "Angare and the Founding of the Progressive Writers' Association." *Modern Asian Studies* 30 (2): 447–67.
Maitra, K. 1991. *Comintern and Marxism in India.* Calcutta: Darbari Prokashan.
Malik, A. 2004. *Muslim Narratives and the Discourse of English.* New York: SUNY.
Malina, D. 2002. *Breaking the Frame: Metalepsis and the Construction of the Subject.* Columbus: Ohio State University Press.
Mandala, J. C. 1999. *Poona Pact and Depressed Classes.* Calcutta: Sujan.
Markovits, C. 2004. *The Un-Gandhian Gandhi: The Life and Afterlife of the Mahatma.* London: Anthem Press.
Marris, W. S. 1928. *The Speeches of Sir William Marris as Governor of the United Provinces of Agra and Oudh, December 1922–January 1928.* Mysore: Wesleyan Mission Press.
Marshik, C. 2006. *British Modernism and Censorship.* New York: Oxford University Press.
Mathew, T. 1991. *Ambedkar, Reform or Revolution.* New Delhi: Segment Books.
Mathur, O. P. 1993. *The Modern Indian English Fiction.* New Delhi: Abhinav.
———. 1995. *Indian Political Novel and Other Essays.* Allahabad: Kitab Mahal.
McCutchion, D. 1969. *Indian Writing in English.* Calcutta: Writers Workshop.
Mehan, U. S. 2001. "Transgressing Bodies in Postcolonial Fiction." *Journal of Comparative Literature and Aesthetics* 24 (1–2): 1–13.
Mehrotra, N. C. 1995. *The Socialist Movement in India.* Delhi: Radiant.
Mehrotra, R. R. 1987. "The Language of Indian Writing in English: Some Sociolinguistic Evidence." *Journal of South Asian Literature* 22 (2): 103–12.
Mehta, B. 2002. *Widows, Pariahs, and Bayaderes: India as Spectacle.* Lewisburg: Bucknell University Press.
Mehta, G. 1991. *Bhabhani Bhattacharya as a Novelist of Social Conscience.* Meerut: Shalabh Prakashan.
Mehta, V. 1976. *Mahatma Gandhi and His Apostles.* New York: Viking.
Memmi, A. 1991. *The Colonizer and the Colonized.* Boston: Beacon.
Mendelsohn, O. and M. Vicziany. 1998. *The Untouchables: Subordination, Poverty and the State in Modern India.* New York: Cambridge University Press.
Menon, D. M. 1994. *Caste, Nationalism and Communism in South India.* New York: Cambridge University Press.
Menon, K. P. K. 1968. *Retain English for Unity and Progress.* Calicut: The Powra Sangham.
Menon, M. 2004. *Wanton Works: Rhetoric and Sexuality in English Renaissance Drama.* Buffalo: University of Toronto Press.
Menon, V. P. 1995. *Transfer of Power in India.* New York: Sangam Books.
Mercanti, S. 2007. "The Village and Its Story: Indigenization of the 'Alien' Language in Raja Rao's Kanthapura and Ignazio Silone's Fontamara." *Quaderni del '900* 7: 53–63.
Metcalf, T. R. 1994. *Ideologies of the Raj.* New York: Cambridge University Press.

Mezey, J. 2002. "'My Heart It Beat Like a Drum': Transference as Therapeutic Performance in Raja Rao's Kanthapura." *Journal of Commonwealth and Postcolonial Studies* 9 (2): 73–94.
Minault, G. 1982. *The Khilafat Movement: Religious Symbolism and Political Mobilization in India.* New York: Columbia University Press.
Misra, M. 1999. *Business, Race, and Politics in British India, c. 1850–1960.* New York: Oxford University Press.
———. 2003. "Lessons of Empire: Britain and India." *SAIS Review* 23 (2): 133–53.
Mitra, R. 1992. *Caste Polarization and Politics.* Patna: Syndicate Publications.
Mitter, P. 2007. *The Triumph of Modernism, India's Artists and the Avant-garde, 1922–47.* New York: Reaktion Books.
Mondal, A. 1999. "The Ideology of Space in Raja Rao's Kanthapura." *Journal of Commonwealth Literature* 34: 103.
———. 2002. "The Emblematics of Gender and Sexuality in Indian Nationalist Discourse." *Modern Asian Studies* 36 (4): 913–36.
Moorty, S. S. 1996. "Narrative Technique in Raja Rao's Kanthapura." *Commonwealth Essays and Studies* 19 (1): 111–15.
Morton, A. D. 2007. *Unravelling Gramsci: Hegemony and Passive Revolution in the Global Economy.* London: Pluto.
Mufti, A. 2004. "Towards a Lyric History of India." *Boundary 2* 31 (2): 245–74.
Mugali, R. S. 1975. *History of Kannada Literature.* New Delhi: Sahitya Akademi.
Mukherjee, A. P. 1991. "The Exclusions of Postcolonial Theory and Mulk Raj Anand's 'Untouchable': A Case Study." *ARIEL: A Review of International English Literature* 22 (3): 27–48.
Naik, M. K. 1966. "The Cow of the Barricades and Other Stories: Raja Rao as a Short Story Writer." *Books Abroad* 40 (4): 392–6.
———. 1982a. *A History of Indian English Literature.* New Delhi: Sakitya Akademi.
———. 1982b. *Raja Rao.* Bombay: Blackie.
———. 1984. *Dimensions of Indian English Literature.* New Delhi: Streling Publishers.
Nanda, B. R. 1972. *Socialism in India.* Delhi: Vikas Publications.
———. 2002. *Mahatma Gandhi: A Biography.* New York: Oxford University Press.
Nandkumar, P. 2003. "Tracing History Accurately, the Literary Way." *The Hindu.* Online: http://www.hindu.com/thehindu/fr/2003/05/09/stories/2003050901130500.htm (accessed August 20, 2005).
Naoroji, D. 1901. *Poverty and Un-British Rule in India.* London: S. Sonnenschein.
Narang, H. 1997. "Lord Shiva or the Prince of Pornographers: Ideology, Aesthetics, and Architectonics of Manto." In *Life and Works of Saadat Hasan Manto*, edited by A. Bhalla, 69–89. Shimla: Indian Institute of Advanced Study.
Narasimhaiah, C. D. 1967. *The Writer's Gandhi.* Patiala: Punjabi University.
———. 1973. *Raja Rao.* New Delhi: Arnold-Heinemann.
Narasimhan, S. 1999. *Kamaladevi Chattopadhyay, the Romantic Rebel.* New Delhi: Sterling.
Narayan, J. 1936. "Issues Before and After Lucknow." *Congress Socialist*: 2–6.
———. 1946. "Gandhiji's Leadership and the CSP 1940." In *Towards Struggle: Selected Manifestoes, Speeches and Writings*, edited by Y. Meherally, 30–45. Bombay: Padma Publications.
———. 1964a. *Socialism, Sarvodaya, and Democracy.* Edited by B. Prasad. Bombay: Asia Publishing House.
———. 1964b. "The Transition to Socialism." In *Socialism, Sarvodaya, and Democracy*, edited by B. Prasad, 1–90. Bombay: Asia Publishing House.
———. 1977a. *JP's Jail Life.* Edited by R. K. Pandey, translated by G. S. Bhargava. New Delhi: Arnold-Heinemann.
———. 1977b. *Prison Diary, 1975.* Edited by A. B. Shah. Bombay: Popular Prakashan.
———. 1980a. "My Picture of Socialism." In *A Revolutionary's Quest: Selected Writings of Jayaprakash Narayan*, edited by B. Prasad, 119–26. Delhi: Oxford University Press.

———. 1980b. "The Socialists and the Congress." In *A Revolutionary's Quest: Selected Writings of Jayaprakash Narayan*, edited by B. Prasad, 134–8. Delhi: Oxford University Press.
———. 1980c. "To All Fighters for Freedom II." In *A Revolutionary's Quest: Selected Writings of Jayaprakash Narayan*, edited by B. Prasad, 80–98. Delhi: Oxford University Press.
———. 2001a. "Comment on Gandhi's article entitled, 'The Dissentients,' Harijan 26 and 30 January 1940." In *Jayaprakash Narayan: Selected Works Vol. 3*, edited by B. Prasad, 25–7. Delhi: Manohar.
———. 2001b. "Political Earthquake in Bihar, Article in the Congress Socialist, 6, February 1937." In *Jayaprakash Narayan: Selected Works Vol. 2*, edited by B. Prasad, 152–6. Delhi: Manohar.
———. 2001c. "Speech while Moving the Resolution on Socialist Unity at the Congress Socialist Party Conference, Lahore, 13 April 1938." In *Jayaprakash Narayan: Selected Works Vol. 2*, edited by B. Prasad, 214–8. Delhi: Manohar.
———. 2001d. "Why Socialism?" In *Jayaprakash Narayan: Selected Works Vol. 2*, edited by B. Prasad, 1–89. Delhi: Manohar.
———. 2002. "Ends and Means." In *Jayaprakash Narayan: Essential Writings 1929–1979*, edited by B. Prasad, 107–17. New Delhi: Konark.
Narayan, R. S. 1988. *Gangadharrao Deshpande*. New Delhi: Publications Division, Ministry of Information and Broadcasting, Government of India.
Nasta, S. 2008. "Between Bloomsbury, Gandhi, and Transcultural Modernities: The Publication and Reception of Mulk Raj Anand's Untouchable." In *Books Without Borders: Perspectives from South Asia*, edited by R. Fraser and M. Hammond, 151–69. New York: Palgrave Macmillan.
Natarajan, D. 1972. *Indian Census Through a Hundred Years*. New Delhi: Office of the Registrar General.
National Council of Educational Research and Training Directorate of Extension Programmes for Secondary Education. "The Teaching of English in India." 1963. Report of the Conference on the Teaching of English in Schools, Delhi, April 15–20. New Delhi: Government of India.
Nehru, J. 1948. *The Unity of India: Collected Writings, 1937–1940*. New York: J. Day.
———. 1958. *An Autobiography*. London: The Bodley Head.
———. 1981. *The Discovery of Indai*. New Delhi: Oxford University Press.
———. 1989. *An Autobiography, Centenary Edition*. New York: Oxford University Press.
Niblett, H. 1957. *The Congress Rebellion in Azamgarh, August and September, 1942*. Allahabad: Superintendent of Printing and Stationary.
Nikam, S. 1998. *Destiny of Untouchables in India: Divergent Approaches and Strategies of Mahatma Gandhi and Dr. B. R. Ambedkar*. New Delhi: Deep & Deep.
Nilekani, N. 2009. *Imagining India: The Idea of a Renewed Nation*. New York: Penguin.
Niranjan, S. 1979. "The Nature and Extent of Gandhi's Impact on the Early Novels of Mulk Raj Anand and Raja Rao." *Commonwealth Quarterly* 11 (3): 36–46.
———. 1985. *Raja Rao, Novelist as Sadhaka*. Ghaziabad: Vimal Prakashan.
Niranjana, T. 1992. *Siting Translation: History, Post-Structuralism, and the Colonial Context*. Berkeley: University of California Press.
———. 1993. *Interrogating Modernity*. Calcutta: Seagull.
Niven, A. 1978. *The Yoke of Pity: A Study in the Fictional Writings of Mulk Raj Anand*. New Delhi: Arnold-Heinemann.
Nizami, M. Y. 1995. *Pakistan se Inglistan tak: Bartaniyah men abad eshiyai tarikin-i-vatan ki tarikh 1700 se 1995 tak*. Gujranvalah: Ismail.
O'Hanlon, R. 1988. "Recovering the Subject: Subaltern Studies and Histories of Resistance in Colonial South Asia." *Modern Asian Studies* 22 (1): 189–224.
Omvedt, G. 1990. "Hinduism and Politics." *Economic and Political Weekly* 25 (14): 723–9.
———. 1994. *Dalits and the Democratic Revolution: Dr. Ambedkar and the Dalit Movement in Colonial India*. New Delhi: SAGE.

Page, D. 1982. *Prelude to Partition: The Indian Muslims and the Imperial System of Control, 1920–1932*. New York: Oxford University Press.
Pandey, B. N., ed. 1977. *Leadership in South Asia*. New Delhi: Vikas.
Pandey, G. 2002. *Ascendancy of the Congress in Uttar Pradesh: Class, Community and Nation in Northern India*. London: Anthem Press.
Pandey, G. 1978. *The Ascendancy of Congress in Uttar Pradesh, 1926–1934: A Study in Imperfect Mobilization*. New York: Oxford University Press.
Paniker, K. A., ed. 1991. *Indian English Literature Since Independence*. New Delhi: The Indian Association for English Studies.
Parel, A. 2011. "Gandhi in Independent India." In *The Cambridge Companion to Gandhi*, edited by J. Brown and A. Parel, 219–38. New York: Cambridge University Press.
Parry, B. 2004. *Postcolonial Studies: A Materialist Critique*. London: Verso.
Pathan, B. A. 1987. *Gandhian Myth in English Literature in India*. New Delhi: Deep & Deep.
Patil, V. T. 1997. *Gandhism and Indian English Fiction*. Delhi: Devika.
Petievich, C. 1992. *Assembly of Rivals: Delhi, Lucknow and the Urdu Ghazal*. New Delhi: Manohar.
Phadke, Y. D. 1979. *Politics and Language*. Bombay: Himalaya Publishing House.
Pousse, M. 1989. "So Many Freedoms." *Commonwealth* 12 (1): 30–38.
Prakash, J. P. 2002. "Ends and Means." In *Jayaprakash Narayan: Essential Writings 1929–1979*, edited by B. Prasad. New Delhi: Konark.
Prasad, L. 2006. *Poetics of Conduct: Oral Narrative and Moral Being in a South Indian Town*. New York: Columbia University Press.
Prasad, M. M. 1998. *Ideology of the Hindi Film: A Historical Construction*. New York: Oxford University Press.
Prashad, V. 1995. "Between Economism and Emancipation: Untouchables and Indian Nationalism." *Left History* 3 (1): 1–30.
———. 2000. *Untouchable Freedom*. New Delhi: Oxford University Press.
———. 2001. "The Technology of Sanitation in Colonial India." *Modern Asian Studies* 35 (1): 113–55.
Premchand, M. 2005. *Sevasadan*. Translated by S. Shingavi. New Delhi: Oxford University Press.
Pritchett, F. 1994. *Nets of Awareness*. Berkeley: University of California Press.
Rahman, T. 1991. *A History of Pakistani Literature in English*. Lahore: Vanguard Press.
Rai, A. 2000. *Hindi Nationalism*. Hyderabad: Orient Longman.
Rajagopalachari, C. 1960. "Five Fallacies About Hindi." In *India Demands English Language*, edited by I. Mathai, 26–32. Bombay: Mathai's Publications.
Ram, A. 1983. *Interviews with Indian-English Writers*. Calcutta: Writers Workshop.
Ram, T. 1983. *Trading in Language: The Story of English in India*. Delhi: GDK Publications.
Ramasami, P. E. V. 1983. *Why Brahmins Hate Reservation?* Madras: Periyar Self-Respect Propaganda Institution.
Ramaswamy, M. 1956. "Constitutional Developments in India, 1600–1955." *Stanford Law Review* 8 (3): 326–87.
Ramaswamy, S. 1999. "Sanskrit for the Nation." *Modern Asian Studies* 33 (2): 339–81.
Ramssey-Kurtz, H. 2007. *The Non-Literate Other: Readings of Illiteracy in Twentieth-Century Novels in English*. New York: Rodopi.
Ranadive, B. T. 1982. *Caste, Class and Property Relations*. Calcutta: National Book Agency.
———. 1986. "India's Freedom Struggle." *Social Scientist* 14 (8/9): 3–32.
Rao, R. 1947. *The Cow of the Barricades and Other Stories*. London: Oxford University Press.
———. 1963. *Kanthapura*. London: Allen & Unwin.
Ray, A. B. 1977. *Students and Politics in India: The Role of Caste, Language, and Region in an Indian University*. New Delhi: RC Jain for Manohar Book Service.
Ray, B. 1996. *Gandhi's Campaign Against Untouchability, 1931–34: An Account From the Raj's Secret Official Reports*. New Delhi: Gandhi Peace Foundation.

Riemenschneider, D. 2005. *The Indian Novel in English: its Critical Discourse, 1934–2000*. New Delhi: Rawat.
Robinson, F. 1998. "The British Empire and Muslim Identity in South Asia." *Transactions of the Royal Historical Society* 6 (8): 271–89
———. 2004. *Islam and Muslim History in South Asia*. New York: Oxford University Press.
Rosenbaum, S. P. 1981. "Preface to a Literary History of the Bloomsbury Group." *New Literary History* 12 (2): 329–44.
Rothermund, D. 1993. *An Economic History of India, from pre-colonial times to 1991*. New York: Routledge.
Roy, M. N. 1920. *Minutes of the Second Congress of the Communist International*. Online: http://www.marxists.org/history/international/comintern/2nd-congress/ch04.htm (accessed October 15, 2011).
Roy, M. N. 1923. "Anti-Imperialist Struggle in India." *The Communist International* 6.
———. 1924. *Political Letters*. Zurich: Vanguard Workshop.
———. 1964. *M. N. Roy's Memoirs*. New York: Allied Publishers.
———. 1971a. *India in Transition*. Bombay: Indian Renaissance Institute.
———. 1971b. *The Future of Indian Politics*. Calcutta: The Minerva Associates.
———. 1997. "Manifesto of RPIWC." In *Selected Works of M. N. Roy Vol. 4*, edited by S. Ray, 189–269. Delhi: Oxford University Press.
Roy, S. 1987. *M. N. Roy and Mahatma Gandhi*. Calcutta: Minerva Associates.
Roy, S. C. 1962. *Caste, Race, and Religion in India*. Ranchi: Man in India Office.
Russell, P. and K. Singh. 1952. *G. V. Desani: A Consideration of His All About H. Hatter and Hali*. London: Karel Szeben.
Russell, R. 1992. *The Pursuit of Urdu Literature*. New Delhi: Seagull Books.
———. 1995. *Hidden in the Lute*. New York: Penguin.
Said, E. 2004. *Humanism and Democratic Criticism*. New York: Columbia University Press.
Saklatvala, S. 1930. "Who is this Gandhi?" *Labour Monthly* 12 (7): 1–49.
Sankaran, C. 1993. *The Myth Connection: The Use of Hindu Mythology in Some Novels of Raja Rao and RK Narayan*. Ahmedabad: Allied Publishers.
Santucci, A. 2010. *Antonio Gramsci*. Translated by G. Di Mauro. New York: Monthly Review Press.
Sarachchandra, E. 1981. "Illusion and Reality: Raja Rao as Novelist." In *Oly Connect: Literary Perspectives East and West*, edited by G. Amirthanayagam. Honolulu: Center for Research in the New Literatures in English & East-West Center.
Sarkar, J. 2006. "Power, Hegemony, and Politics: Leadership Struggle in Congress in the 1930s." *Modern Asian Studies* 40 (2): 333–70.
Sarkar, S. 1973. *The Swadeshi Movement in Bengal, 1903–1908*. New Delhi: People's Publishing House.
———. 1983. "'Popular' Movement and 'Middle Class' Leadership in Late Colonial India: Perspectives and Problems of a 'History from Below'." Calcutta: KP Bagchi.
———. 1985. *A Critique of Colonial India*. Calcutta: Papyrus.
———. 1989. *Modern India, 1885–1947*. New York: St. Martin's Press.
———. 1997. *Writing Social History*. New York: Oxford University Press.
———. 2002a. *Beyond Nationalist Frames*. New Delhi: Permanent Black.
———. 2002b. "The Decline of the Subaltern in Subaltern Studies." In *Reading Subaltern Studies*, edited by D. Ludden. London: Anthem Press.
Sarkar, T. 1987. *Bengal, 1928–1934: The Politics of Protest*. Delhi: Oxford University Press.
———. 2000. *Hindu Wife, Hindu Nation: Community, Religion, and Cultural Nationalism*. Delhi: Permanent Black.
Sarker, S. 2001. "Locating a Native Englishness in Virginia Woolf's The London Scene." *National Women's Studies Association Journal* 13 (2): 1–30.
Sarma, G. P. 1990. *Nationalism in Indo-Anglian Fiction*. New Delhi: Sterling.

Sathyamurthy, T. V. 1998. *Region, Religion, Caste, Gender and Culture in Contemporary India*. Delhi: Oxford University Press.
Saxena, V. K. 1985. *Muslims and the Indian National Congress, 1885–1924*. Delhi: Discovery.
Schultz, A. 2002. "Hindu Nationalism, Music, and Embodiment in Marathi Rashtriya Kirtan." *Ethnomusicology* 46 (2): 307–22.
Selliot, E. 1992. *From Untouchable to Dalit: Essays on the Ambedkar Movement*. Delhi: Manohar.
Seth, S. 1995. *Marxist Theory and Nationalist Politics: The Case of Colonial India*. New Delhi: SAGE.
Sethi, R. 1999. *Myths of the Nation, National Identity and Literary Representation*. Oxford: Clarendon.
———. 2003. "The Other Side of History: The Politics of Representation in Nationalist Fiction." *South Asian Review* 24 (1): 76–94.
Shah, A. B., ed. 1968. *The Great Debate: Language Controversy and University Education*. Bombay: Lalvani.
Shah, N. and A. Sinroja, eds. 2006. *English in India: Issues and Approaches*. New Delhi: Creative Books.
Shingavi, S. 2010. "Developing the Nationalist Canon." In *Literature and Nationalist Ideology*, edited by H. Harder, 353–75. New Delhi: Social Science.
Singh, I. and R. Rao, eds. 1984. *Wither India?* Baroda: Padma.
Sircar, A. 1992. "Production of Authenticity: The Indo-Anglian Critical Tradition." *Economic and Political Weekly* 27 (36): 1921–6.
Smith, J. 1999. *The Bolsheviks and the National Question, 1917–23*. London: Macmillan.
Sobhanlal, D. G. 2006. *Comintern and the Destiny of Communism in India, 1941–43*. Kolkata: Seribaan.
Sonntag, S. 2003. *The Local Politics of Global English*. New York: Lexington.
Sreenivas, M. 2008. *Widows, Wives and Concubines: The Conjugal Family Ideal in Colonial India*. Bloomington: Indiana University Press.
Stilz, G. 1990. "'Live in Fragments No Longer': A Conciliatory Analysis of Ahmed Ali's Twilight in Delhi." In *Crisis and Creativity in the New Literatures in English*, edited by G. Davis, 369–88. Atlanta: Rodopi.
Suhrasrabudhey, S. 1990. *Science and Politics: Essays in Gandhian Perspective*. Varanasi: Gandhian Institute of Studies.
Suri, K. C. 1987. "The Agrarian Question in India During the National Movement, 1885–1947." *Social Scientist* 15 (10): 25–50.
Symonds, R. 1951. *The Making of Pakistan*. London: Faber & Faber.
Tagore, R. 1950. *Three Plays: Mukta-Dhara, Natir-Puja, Chandalika*. Translated by M. Sykes. New York: Oxford University Press.
Talwar, A. 2003. *Congressism: The Ideology of the Indian National Congress*. New Delhi: Frank Bros.
Tarinayya, M., ed. 1992. *English Language Teaching: Theory and Practice*. Madras: T. R. Publications.
Thanawi, M. A. A. 1990. *Perfecting Women*. Translated by B. Metcalf. Berkeley: University of California Press.
Thapar-Bjokert, S. 1988. "Gender, Nationalism, and the Colonial Jail: A Study of Women Activists in Uttar Pradesh." *Women's History Review* 7 (4): 583–615.
Tharu, S. 1986. "Reading Against the Imperial Grain: Intertextuality, Narrative Structure and Liberal Humanism in Mulk Raj Anand's Untouchable." *Jadavpur Journal of Comparative Literature* 24: 60–71.
———. 1997. "Government, Binding and Unbinding: Alienation and the Teaching of Literature." In *Subject to Change: Teaching Literature in the Nineties*, edited by S. Tharu, 1–29. Hyderabad: Orient Longman.
Thekaekara, M. M. 1999. *Endless Filth: The Saga of the Bhangis*. Bangalore: Books for Change.
Tivari, P. N. 1998. *Chand: Achhut Ank*. Nai Dilli: Radhakrishna Prakashan.
Tomlinson, B. R. 1976. *The Indian National Congress and the Raj, 1929–1942: The Penultimate Phase*. London: Macmillan.

———. 1979. *The Political Economy of the Raj, 1919–1947: The Economics of Decolonization in India*. London: Macmillan.
———. 1993. *The Economy of Modern India, 1860–1970*. New York: Cambridge University Press.
Townshend, J. 1996. *The Politics of Marxism*. London: Leicester University Press.
Tripathi, J. P. 2003. *Raja Rao: The Fictionist*. Delhi: B. R. Publishing Corporation.
Trivedi, H. 1986. "Ahmed Ali, Twilight in Delhi." In *Major Indian Novels: An Evaluation*, edited by N. S. Pradhan. Atlantic Highlands: Humanities Press.
———. 1995. *Colonial Transactions: English Literature and India*. New York: Manchester University Press.
———. 2000. "Gandhian Nationalism: Kanthapura." In *Literature and Nation: Britain and India, 1800–1990*, edited by R. Allen, 107–20. London: Routledge.
———. 2011. "Literary and visual portrayals of Gandhi." In *The Cambridge Companion to Gandhi*, edited by J. Brown and A. Parel, 199–218. New York: Cambridge University Press.
Trivedi, H. and M. Mukherjee. 1996. *Interrogating Post-Colonialism: Theory, Text, and Context*. Shimla: Indian Institute of Advanced Study.
Trivedi, L. 2003. "Visually Mapping the 'Nation': Swadeshi Politics and Nationalist India, 1920–1930." *Journal of Asian Studies* 62 (1): 11–41.
Turner, J. A. 1914. *Sanitation in India*. Bombay: The Times of India.
Uniyal, R. 1993. "The Women of Kanthapura: From Slumber to Awakening." *Journal of the School of Languages* 3: 1035–60.
Vadgama, K. 1984. *India in Britain: The Indian Contribution to the British Way of Life*. London: R. Royce.
Veerathappa, K. 1986. *Studies in Karnataka History and Culture*. Bangalore: Karnataka History Congress.
Vijaya-Tunga, J. 1935. *Grass for My Feet*. London: Edward Arnold.
Visram, R. 1986. *Ayahs, Lascars and Princes: Indians in Britain, 1700–1847*. London: Pluto.
———. 2002. *Asians in Britain: 400 Years of History*. London: Pluto.
Viswanathan, G. 1989. *Masks of Conquest: Literary Study and British Rule in India*. New York: Oxford University Press.
———. 1998. *Outside the Fold: Conversion, Modernity, and Belief*. Princeton: Princeton University Press.
Vohra, A. 1997. "Manto's Philosophy: An Explication." In *Life and Works of Saadat Hasan Manto*, edited by A. Bhalla, 129–42. Shimla: Indian Institute of Advanced Study.
Wadhawan, J. C. 1998. *Manto Naama: The Life of Saadat Hasan Manto*. New Delhi: Roli Books.
Wadia, A. R. 1954. *The Future of English in India*. Bombay: Asia Publishing House.
Washbrook, D. A. 1988. "Progress and Problems: South Asian Economic and Social History." *Modern Asian Studies* 22 (1): 57–96.
Weeks, T. R. 1996. *Nation and State in Late Imperial Russia: Nationalism and Russification on the Western Frontier, 1863–1914*. DeKalb: Northern Illinois University Press.
Weir, L. M. 1938. *The Tragedy of Ramsay MacDonald: A Political Biography*. London: Secker & Warburg.
Wexler, J. P. 1997. *Who Paid for Modernism? Art, Money, and the Fiction of Conrad, Joyce, and Lawrence*. Fayetteville: University of Arkansas Press.
Williams, H. M. 1973. *Studies in Modern Indian Fiction in English*. Calcutta: Writers Workshop.
———. 1976. *Indo-Anglian Literature, 1800–1970: A Survey*. Madras: Orient Longman.
Williams, R. 1962. *Culture and Society, 1780–1950*. New York: Harper & Row.
Windmiller, M. 1954. "Linguistic Regionalism in India." *Pacific Affairs* 27 (4): 291–318.
Wolpert, S. 2001. *Gandhi's Passion: The Life and Legacy of Mahatma Gandhi*. New York: Oxford University Press.
Wolpert, S. 1967. *Morley and India, 1906–1910*. Berkeley: University of California Press.
Woodcock, G. 1967. *Kerala: A Portrait of the Malabar Coast*. London: Faber & Faber.

Yashpal. 2008. *The Second Nose and Other Stories*. Translated by A. Anand. New Delhi: Rupa.
Zaheer, S. "Can't Sleep." In *Angare*, translated by S. Shingavi. Unpublished manuscript.
———. 2006. *The Light: A History of the Movement for Progressive Literature in the Indo-Pak Subcontinent*. Translated by A. Azfar. Karachi: Oxford University Press.
Zaidi, A. J. 1993. *A History of Urdu Literature*. Delhi: Sahitya Akademi.
Zaman, M. Q. 2008. *Ashraf Ali Thanawi: Islam in Modern South Asia*. Oxford: One World.

INDEX

Ab-e-hayat (Azad) 137, 142
Action Party (Gramsci) 179–81, 191
Afghanistan 179, 196–7
Africa: education in 201; Socialism in 195
Ahmad, Aijaz 9
Ahmad, Nazir 115, 119–20, 133, 142–3
Ahmad, Sayyid 114, 141–3
Ahmed, Naeem 146
Ahmedabad 65
"Akkaya" (Rao) 70
Algeria 182
Ali, Ahmed, 4, 6–7, 9–10, 27, 105, 107, 201–2; break with *Angare* group 115–18; anticolonialism of 132; loyalty to cultural past 112–13, 132–3, 135, 154; affection for Delhi 113–14, 144–5; and Gandhian politics 154; as modernist 152–3; as nationalist writer 124, 152–3; novelistic politics of 145–54; break with Progressive Writers' Association 121–4; use of *shehrashob* by 147–51, 154; *see also Twilight in Delhi*
Ali, Mohammad 105, 140–41, 154
Ali, Shaukat 105, 140–41, 154
Ali brothers 105, 140–41, 154
Aligarh Muslim University 65, 115, 118, 141–3, 146
All About H. Hatterr (Desani) 27
All India Congress Committee 65
allegory 2, 6, 32–3, 36, 43, 60, 114, 128: religious 61–4, 77, 85
All-India Depressed Classes Association 39
All-India Khadi Board 88
Ambedkar, Bhimrao Ramji 10, 30–31, 36–9, 198; *Annihilation of Caste* 41–3; and electoral reform 41; identity politics of 45; and the untouchable debate 32
Anand, Mulk Raj 3–4, 6–7, 9–10, 13–17, 27, 31, 201–2; anticolonialism of 46; preface to *Annihilation of Caste* 41–2; on caste 34–6, 39–45; distaste for Indian feudal life 46; influence of Gandhi on 34–41, 205n3; views on religion 64; on solidarity 45–58; and untouchables 205n1; *see also Untouchable*
Anandanaphoras 72
Anderson, Benedict 3, 5, 200–202
Andhra 19–20
Andhra State Bill 20
Andhra University 17
Angare project 4, 64–5, 107, 110, 115–19, 121–3, 125–6, 133, 139, 152
Anglophilia 10
Angrezi Hatao Andolan 21
animal sacrifice 68
Ankola 88, 92
Annihilation of Caste (Ambedkar) 41–3
anticolonialism 40, 43, 46, 50, 58, 66, 102, 112–14, 125, 129, 134–5, 169–71, 175, 177, 186–7, 190–91; of Ali 132; and Islam 106; and literature 193–4, 197; Muslim 107–9, 140, 142, 150; and nationalism 191, 197–8, 203; in *Twilight in Delhi* 145; *see also* colonialism
anti-imperialism 165–6, 187, 194
anti-intellectualism 98–9
Anti-Untouchability League 38
Apology for Heroism (Anand) 46, 49
Arnold, David 95
Arthur Road jail 92
Arya Samaj 132
ashraf elite 110–12, 127–8, 134, 140, 144, 152, 154
Asia and the Americas 1
Asia, Socialism in 195
Assam 196
atomic bombs 49
Aurobindo, Sri (Aurobindo Ghosh) 24
Austen, Jane 25
authenticity: and democracy in *Kanthapura* 100–103; in *Kanthapura* 70–79, 85–6; in *Untouchable* 32, 36, 52

Autobiography, An (Nehru) 43
Azad, Maulana Abul Kalam 105, 140, 159–60
Azad, Muhammad Husain 118, 137, 142
Azamgarh 44

"Baadal nahin aate" (The clouds aren't coming) (Ali) 122–3
Bahadur Shah: *see* Zafar, Bahadur Shah
Balbo, Italo 179
Balochistan 179, 196
Bankim (Rishi Bankim Chandra Chattopadhyay) 176
Bannerjee, G. C. 18
Bapu Gokhalyachi Pagadi 81
Bardoli Satyagraha 87, 89, 92
Basava Jayanti 81
Behishti Zewar (Celestial ornaments) (Thanawi) 115, 121
Belgaum 88, 92
Bendre, D. R. 67
Bengal 37
Bengali 18
Benjamin, Walter 75–6
Bhagini Mandal Parishat 88
Bharatiya Hindu Shuddhi Sabha 132
Bhattacharya, Bhabhani 13–14, 27
Bhavani Talwar 81
Bhave, Vinoba 20, 155, 157, 160
Bhoodan campaign 160
Bihar 101, 160
Bildungsroman 52, 55, 57, 81
Birla, G. D. 206n15
Bloom, Harold 169, 207n2
Bolshevism 160
Bombay Presidency 87, 92; *see also* Karnataka
Borivli 92
Bose, Subhas Chandra 166
bourgeois state 178, 197; *see also* bourgeoisie
bourgeoisie, 5–6, 10–11, 33, 49, 157–8, 161, 163, 167–9, 176–79, 182; betrayal of 200; and boycotts 190; and consolidation of power 182; in Indian National Congress 199; Italian 179, 181; liberation movements of 187–9; and nationalism 186–7, 202; and revolution 192; Russian 188; *see also* bourgeois state
Brahmins 61, 63–4, 66–7, 69–70, 72, 86–7, 91, 102; authority of 100; and Gandhi 103; privilege of 8, 198

Brennan, Timothy 7, 178
British imperialism 26, 43, 45–6, 48, 144, 188, 195; criticized by Ali 113; Communist support for 158; compromise with 178; conflict with 47; independence from 162 (*see also* India, liberation of); in *Kanthapura* 81; opposition to 125, 158, 175, 197; and religious conservatism 40; untouchable revolt against 51; *see also* anti-imperialism; British Raj; colonialism
British Raj 21; abolition of 161; and caste identity 43; decline of 152; demonstrations against 2, 65, 73; in Delhi 129–30; and minorities 10; negotiations with 2, 19, 175; *see also* British imperialism; colonialism
Bubble, The (Anand) 34, 206n14
Buddhism 137
Bundelkhand 89

Calcutta 127, 130, 152
Cammett, John 181
capitalism 159, 161, 168, 178, 189, 192, 195; critique of 179; establishment of 176; global 197; resistance to 176–8, 197, 203
caste system 10; abolition of 2, 7, 32, 38–9, 47–8, 51, 200; and colonial modernity 41–5; exploitation of by British 37; Gandhi's view of 29–30, 32, 36, 40; intercaste association 200; low-castes 7; politicization of 43–4; reform of 43; *see also* untouchables
caste-based organizations 88
Cavour (Camillo Paolo Filippo Giulio Benso) 179–81, 185, 200
Central Asia, American military presence in 196
Champaran 87
charkhas 31, 65, 89
Chatrath, Dhani Ram 35
Chatterjee, Partha 10, 175–7, 179–84, 190, 192
Chatterjee, Sarat Chandra 35
Chattopadhyay, Kamaladevi 4, 10, 76, 92, 99; nationalist writings of 92–5
Chaturvedi, Vinayak 6–7
Chauri Chaura 188
chauvinism: caste 7–8, 31–2, 38, 48, 52–4, 56, 58, 67, 201; literary 15; national 10;

and nationalism 195–6; religious 10; resistance to 203; *see also* racism; sexism
Cheah, P. 177
Chhatarpur 89
Chinese Revolution 186
Chipko movement 155
Choudhary, S. 177
Chrisman, Laura 7, 177, 195
Christianity 30, 62, 69; conversion of untouchables to 38
Christians 19; in Congress 39
Civil Disobedience movement 2, 17, 36, 48, 65, 70, 76, 87, 89–91, 140, 181; Muslim distance from 110; participants jailed 92; among the peasantry 93; women's participation in 103; *see also* nonviolence; protests; *satyagrahas*
class stratification 116, 121
"Client, A" (Rao) 70
Cold War 160, 195
colleges, nationalist 65; *see also* education; universities
Colonial Bureau (of Comintern) 158
colonial modernity 114, 125, 134–5, 177, 187, 201; and caste 41–5; and Islam 105; *see also* modernity
colonialism 28, 64, 112–14, 137, 152; and the Cold War 195; consequences of 193; critique of 60; and decay 152; in Delhi 128, 139; and Muslims 106, 138–9, 149; and nationalism 196; neocolonialism 197; postcolonialism 9, 15, 113–14, 193, 196–7; protests against 87; repression under 1–2; resistance to 75, 199, 203; *see also* anticolonialism; British imperialism; British Raj
Comintern 158, 165, 175, 186, 188–9, 190, 193
communalism 8, 96–100, 124, 132–3, 156, 167, 169
Communism: Eurocommunism 177–8; in India 175 (*see also* Communist Party of India); and national liberation struggles 197; and nationalism 178, 190; Soviet 162
Communist International: *see* Comintern
Communist Manifesto (Marx/Engels) 98
Communist Party of Great Britain 190
Communist Party of India 2, 4, 51, 105, 132, 163–4, 168, 171, 186–90, 192, 198; criticized by Gandhi 184; and nationalism 188; and the Progressive Writers' Association 121, 124–5, 132
Communist Party of Mexico 186
Comrade Kirilov (Rao) 4
Confession (Anand) 4, 46
Congress: *see* Indian National Congress
Congress Left 32, 38, 43, 48, 106; *see also* Indian National Congress; Left
Congress Socialist Party 158, 160–68, 186, 189–90, 198; *see also* Indian National Congress; Socialists
Constitution: *see* Indian Constitution
Coomaraswamy, Ananda 31, 57
Coorg 88
Coronation Durbar 107–8, 115, 126, 131, 134, 138, 140–41, 150, 153
Cousins, Margaret 92
"Cow of the Barricades" (Rao) 1–2, 4
Crooke, William 44
Cuoco, Vincenzo 191

D'Azeglio, Massimo Taparelli 179
Dadabhoy, M. D. 44–5
Dakshina Kannada (Dakshin Kanara) 87, 92
Dalit: *see* untouchables
Dandi 76, 91
Dard, Khwaja Mir 136, 148–9
daridranarayan 159
Decentering Rushdie (Jani) 7
decolonization 192, 194–5
Dehlvi, Dagh 136
Dehlvi culture 127, 131–3, 145, 149
Delhi 108–9, 152; under British colonialism 115; sacking of by British 125–6; capital moved to 113, 130–32, 139, 152; communalism in 132; culture of 110, 113, 124, 127; decline of 127–34; description of 127; expansion of 139; feudal economy in 128; as representative of Hindustan 148–9; as representative of India 131–2, 136; monuments in 136–7; Muslims in 145, 151, 198; nationalist politics and 105–13; poetry in 137, 139 (*see also* Urdu poetry); post-Mutiny 10; invasion of by Punjabis 132
Delhi Durbar: *see* Coronation Durbar
Delhi Municipal Committee 44
democracy 56, 84, 97, 106, 138, 167–8, 170, 187, 189, 191, 201; and authenticity 100–103

Deoband 115
Derozio, Henry 16
Desai, Anita 136
Desani, G. V. 14, 27, 201
Deshpande, Gangadhar Rao 10, 59; arrest and trial of 60–63; influence of Gandhi on 60–63; use of religious imagery by 59–63, 66
Deva, Acharya Narendra 189–90
Devanagari script 22, 219
Dharwar 59, 81
Dharwar District Political Conference 59–60
Dharwar Provincial Congress Committee 89
Discovery of India, The (Nehru) 43, 137, 198
"Draft Theses on the National and Colonial Questions" 187
Dravida Munnetra Kazhagam (DMK) party 22
Dufferin, Lord (Frederick Hamilton-Temple-Blackwood) 44
Dutt, R. Palme 158
Dutt, Toru 16
Dutt-Bradley thesis 158, 164

economics: global depression 90; Nehruvian planning 4; reform of 43, 67, 72 (*see also* land redistribution; wealth, distribution of); rural 65
education: in Africa 201; debate concerning 22–3; encouragement of 200; English 17–19, 24–5, 200–201; and English instruction 18–19; in France 201; and modernization 64–5; nationalistic 81; and Westernization 64–5; *see also* colleges; universities
egalitarianism 21, 201–2
El Salvador 197
Ellis, Havelock 122
Emergency (of 1975) 155, 157
Engels, Friedrich 179
English language: advantages of 24–6; Ali's shift to 121, 124; move to banish 21–4; as court language 35; in education 17–19, 24–5, 204n5; as used by Gandhi 26–7, 162; Indian 25, 71; and nationalism 25; as official language 21; official uses of 204n2; politicization of 22; proponents of 143
English Review Committee 18–19
Enlightenment 183, 196
ethnic cleansing 177, 194–6
Eurocentrism 6, 10, 178

failed states 177, 194–5
Farsi 18
Faruqi, Shamsur Rahman 142
Fasana-i-mubtala (A story of one infatuated) (Ahmad) 143
fascism 75, 172, 178, 186
fatalism 134, 144, 178
feminism 15, 66–8, 93, 95, 99, 111
feudalism 64, 161
fiction: *see* literature
First World War 90
Five Year Plans 31
folk narratives 72
forest laws 88, 92
Forster, E. M. 121
France, education in 201
French Revolution 179, 182
Fugan-e-Dilli 151
functionalism 183

Gadgil, M. 93
Gandhi, Indira 155, 157
Gandhi, Mohandas Karamchand: Ali's sympathy for 109; and the Ali brothers 141; as anticolonialist 169, 176, 193; antimodernity of 31, 201; and the Brahmins 103; and caste identity 34–43; view of caste system 29–30, 32, 36, 40; Chatterjee's view of 183–5; and Civil Disobedience 2 (*see also* Civil Disobedience); criticized by Communists 184; and Congress 132; contradictions of 183; deification of 96, 200; and Delhi 152; influence on Deshpande 60–63; and use of English in literature 26–7; Epic Fast 36; on Gandhism 171–2; and democratic Hinduism 96; influence of 199–200; influence on *Kanthapura*, 71–4, 77, 79, 82–4; and the Left 157, 159, 186, 192; influence of on literature 4–5, 8–9, 16–17, 154–5, 201–3, 205n5; "the name of the Mahatma" 168–70; on intercommunal marriage 97; misunderstandings about 5–7; mobilization of the masses by 160–61, 178–9, 181–2, 184, 189–90; and Narayan 163–4, 166, 173; and nationalism 5, 97, 102, 183, 200; and Nehru 156, 159; philosophy of 156; political opposition to 10–11; political philosophy of 1–2, 100, 154, 158 (*see also*

INDEX

Gandhism); and popular initiative 177; as populist 176; public perception of 13–14, 156–62, 170; in Rao's writings 1–4; and religious imagery 100–101; and religious reform 45, 66; religious views of 100–101, 188; criticized by Roy 186; discussed by Roy and Lenin 188; and the Salt March (*see* Salt March); and Socialism 78, 160–61, 164–5, 169; and solidarity 203; and untouchables 34, 205n1, 205n3; influence on *Untouchable* 13, 55–7; utopian vision of 96; campaign against violence 106; and the role of women 92–5, 103; writings of 161–2; *see also* Gandhian; Gandhian Age; Gandhism; Mahatma, cult of
Gandhian, use of term 155–7, 165, 171–2
Gandhian age 16–17, 200
Gandhiji: *see* Gandhi, Mohandas Karamchand
Gandhism 15, 199; Deshpande's conversion to 60, 63; doctrine of 164; Gramsci's analysis of 185; common points with Marxism 99; post-Gandhism 3; problem of 184; as reactionary cult 188; twilight of 3; *see also* Gandhi, Mohandas Karamchand
Ganesha festival 81
Garibaldi, Giuseppe 179
genocide: *see* ethnic cleansing
George V (England) 125, 134; *see also* Coronation Durbar
Ghalib, Mirza 148
ghazal 10, 118, 128, 136, 139, 143, 145–6
Ghose, Aurobindo 18, 27
git (Hindi) 136
Gokak, V. K. 18
Golden Tradition, The (Ali) 136
Gopal, Priyamvada 7
Gramsci, Antonio 183; on India 185; on passive revolution 176–82, 185; on transformism 4, 10, 190–92
Guha, Ranajit 93, 97–8
Gujarat, conflict in 7
Gujarat Vidyapith 65
Gurkhas 196

Hali, Altaf Husain 118, 142–3; *shehrashobs* by 147–8
"Hamari galli" (Our lane) (Ali) 132
Hardikar, N. S. 88

Hardiman, David 156, 171, 177
Harijan Sevak Sangh 38
harikathas 10, 72, 76–8, 82, 100
Hasan, Mushirul 142
Hazare, Anna 155
Hazlitt, William 27
Hemenway, S. I. 100, 204–5n6
Hind Swaraj (Gandhi) 183
Hindalga jail 92
Hindi cinema 136
Hindi language 20–21, 60; as official language 219; limitations of 23–4; Sanskritized 21, 43
Hindi-vadis 23
Hindu, The 73
Hindu Mahasabha 38–9, 106, 132
Hinduism 62, 72, 106; Anand's quarrel with 42; Brahminical 64, 66 (*see also* Brahmins); Hindus, caste 58 (*see also* Hinduism); in Congress 37–8; democratization of 86, 96; as Indians 137–8; and Indian nationalism 132; and Muslims 96–7, 107, 114, 124, 132; orthodox 46–7, 57; and peasant ideology 64; reformist version of 66, 69, 72; and religious reform 66; and Socialism 163; superstitious 68; and the untouchables 36–7, 51; *see also* Hindus
Hindus: relationship with Congress 40; in Delhi 137; as new Indian identity 113; in North India 136; position of majority of 37; punishment of 101; reform organizations 106; right-wing 156, 166, 198; *see also* Hinduism
Hindustan, Delhi as representative of 148–9
Hindustani Seva Dal 88, 92
Hiroshima 49
Hitler, Adolf 158
Hizbollah 196
Home Rule Movement 124, 134
homoeroticism, in poetry 146
Hosagrahar, J. 127
Hubel, Teresa 49
humanism 7, 31–2, 40, 48, 68–9, 102, 114, 201; radical 195; Socialist 58
Humayun's tomb 136–7
Hunter, William Wilson 143

Ibn ul-Vaqt (Ahmed) 141
Imagined Communities (Anderson) 201
imperialism: *see* British Imperialism

In Custody (Desai) 136
"In Defence of Angare, Shall We Submit to Gagging?" (uz-Zafar) 116
In Theory (Ahmad) 9
India in Transition (Roy) 188
India: classical tradition of 100–101; division into linguistic states 30, 39; Gandhian vision of 3; liberation of 2, 4–5, 37, 47, 50, 86–7, 107, 158, 160, 162, 167, 171–3, 175, 179, 182, 192; postcolonial 5, 136; postindependence 142; unification of 17–19, 37, 71, 137–8
Indian Constitution 24, 219: British constitutional reform 36–7, 39; and the language question 9, 19–20, 22, 24, 204n2; provision for separate electorates in 36; and the Socialist Party 165; removal of untouchability 38
Indian Contribution to English Literature in English, The (Iyengar) 25
Indian English: *see* English; Indian literature, in English
Indian Forest Act 88, 92
Indian independence: *see* India, liberation of
Indian literature: *see* literature
Indian National Army 182
Indian National Congress: analysis of 100; Anand's defense of 39–40, 48; and anti-imperialist struggle 171; Belgaum meeting of 88; Calcutta Congress 60; character of 157; and civil disobedience 89–90; and the Communist Party 2, 158, 164, 189; compromise for independence 48, 175; conservatives in 198; evolution of 90; relationship with Gandhi 101; and Gandhism 184–5; as Hindu outfit 106; ideology of 102; and independence 34, 39; and the Karnataka incident 59–63; in Karnataka 86–95; and the language issue 21–2, 24; leaders of 199; and the Left 186; influence on literature 8, 13, 15–16; Meerut session 167–8; and the question of minorities 37; Muslims in 105, 132; and Muslims 154; and national unity 38; nationalism in 5, 7, 49, 65–6, 70, 159, 189; and the peasantry 78, 80, 88–90, 96, 182; problems of 10; resistance to 203; and the Salt March 76; separate electorates in 19, 36–7, 40–42; Socialism in 2,
99–100, 106, 160–61, 163, 167–8; student membership in 91; session in Tripuri 186; and the question of caste (untouchability) 31–4, 37–41, 43, 48; vision of independence by 3; women in 76, 88, 91, 103; *see also* Congress Left; Congress Socialist Party; Left; Right
Indian nationalism: *see* nationalism
Indian Writing in English (Iyengar) 26
Indian Writing in English (revised) (Iyengar), 26–8
Indo-Anglian Literature (Iyengar) 25
Indraprastha 113
industrialization 31, 156, 173
Insha, Ibn-e 148
intelligentsia: bilingual 67; colonized 193; Muslim 106; nationalist 64, 176; relationship with peasantry 97; radical 47, 50, 181, 199; unification of 202; urban 64–5; view of Gandhi by 62
International Monetary Fund 197
internationalism 199, 201
Iqbal, Muhammad 18, 35
Iran 197
Iraq 196
Iron Pillar 137
Islam 65, 69, 105–6, 143; and British colonialism 107–8, 152; decadence in 142–3; as Indian 137; Indian nationalism and 111, 135, 139, 154; and peasant ideology 64; reform movements in 105; in Turkey 142; Unitarian 143; conversion of untouchables to 38; *see also* Mughal culture; Muslims; Pakistan
Israel 196
Iyengar, K. R. S. 17–20, 22–3, 25
Iyer, Ranga 39

Jacobins 178–9, 186, 191
Jahan, Rashid 107, 116–17, 120
Jahan, Shah 137
Jalal, Ayesha 141
Jama Masjid (Mosque) 107–8, 136, 138, 144
Jamaat-e-Islami 105
Jamaat-e-Ulema-e-Hind 105
Jamia Millia Islamiya: *see* Aligarh Muslim University
Jammu Kashmir Liberation Front 196
Jana Sangh 21
Janata Party 160

INDEX

Jani, Pranev 7
"Jannat ki basharat" (A vision of heaven) (Zaheer) 117, 123
"Javanmardi" (Virility) (uz-Zafar) 123
"Javni" (Rao) 67–70
Jinnah, Muhammad Ali 31, 39, 105–6, 198
Jite ji maut ke tum munh mein, na jana hargiz (Hali) 147
Joshi, Priya 124, 132, 147
Joyce, James 35, 52, 55, 205n5
Judeo-Christian religion 72; *see also* Christianity
Jusdanis, Gregory 193

kaliyug ("end of days," "age of Kali") 64
Kanara: *see* Kannada
Kannada 60, 66–7, 72, 76, 80, 87; Dakshina Kannada 87, 92
Kanpur conspiracy 186, 189
Kanthapura (Rao) 1, 3–4, 6, 13, 16, 204–5n6; authenticity in 70–79; and postindependence communalism 96–100; controversy over 25; democracy and authenticity in 100–103; Gandhi's influence in 71–4, 77, 79, 82–4, 96; nationalist reading of 67; Nehruvian ideology in 97; religious ideology in 97
Karanth, Shivaram 67
Karnataka 19, 59–60, 63, 89, 91–2, 207n6
Karnataka Gatha Vaibhava (A. V. Rao) 82
Karnataka Khilafat Parishat 88
Karnataka Non-Brahmin Conference 89
Karnataka Parishat 88
Karnataka Vidyavardhaka Sangha 81
Kashmir 179, 196
Kashmiris 20
Kerala 19
Kesavan, Mukul 100
khadi 65, 89
Khadi Association 88
Khair, Tabish 79
Khan, Syed Ahmed 114, 141–3
Kheda 87
Khilafat 88, 140
Khilafat Maidan 59
Khilafat party 59
Khilafatist boycott 144
Khooni Darwaza 137
King, Martin Luther, Jr. 155
kirtan movement, 76
kisan sabhas 90

Korea 197
Krishnasharma, Betgeri 67

labor unions 51, 199
land redistribution 2, 31, 87, 90, 106, 163, 200; *see also* Bhoodan campaign
language: Biblical 72; controversy over 19–21; Indian official 9, 20–22; official 219; regional 22–3; religious, 60–63, 96–7; vernacular (*bhasha*) 3, 35, 66–7, 72; *see also* English language; Farsi; Hindi language; Tamil language; Telugu language; Urdu language
Latin America, Socialism in 195
Lawrence, D. H. 122–3
Lazarus, Neil 7–8
Lebanon 196
Left 6, 38, 89, 102, 157–9, 168, 173, 175, 185–6, 189–90, 195, 203; academic 115, 192, 197; activist 191–2; challenge to capitalism by 179; collapse of 194; Communist 157, 164, 175, 179, 198; assimilation into Congress of 10–11, 186, 192; collaboration with Congress 189; demoralization of 194; and Gandhi 159, 186, 192; role in national liberation 179; and nationalism 157–8, 179; official 167, 191; call for revolution by 157; Socialist 157, 164, 175, 179; study of 190–92; ultra 186; weakness of 198; *see also* Congress Left
Lenin, Vladimir 178–9, 187–9
Leninism 100
Letters on India (Anand) 39
liberalism 160, 191; neoliberalism 192, 197; vs. religion 64
Lingayats 88
Linguistic Provinces Commission 19
literature: anticolonial 193–4, 197; British models of 67; Gandhian 5–6, 13, 26, 96, 155; Indian, in English 3–4, 14–19, 23–7, 200–202; late-colonial Indian 3; literary forms 3, 10; Muslim 114–16; nationalist 3, 5, 17, 82, 193–4, 199–200, 202; Old and New Light 135; Persian 142, 145–7; postcolonial 193–4, 196–9; South Asian 9; role of in unification 20; Turkish 145–6; vernacular 14, 16, 18, 67; vernacular (*bhasha*), in translation 3, 71; *see also* Urdu literature

Little Plays of Mahatma Gandhi (Anand) 35
Lohia, Rammanohar 21
Lutyens 132

MacDonald, Ramsay 37
Madras Presidency 20, 22, 37, 87–8
Madras State Anti-Hindi Conference 22
Mahabharat, Battle of 129
Mahabharata 74, 76
Maharashtra 19, 43, 66, 81, 87, 89
Mahatma, cult of 6, 13, 83, 171;
    see also Gandhi, "the name of
    the Mahatma"
Malaviya, Madan Mohan 38, 106
*Manifesto for the Revolutionary Party of the Indian
    Working Class, The* (Roy) 184
Maoists 11, 156
Markovits, Claude 14, 155–6
Marx, Karl 157, 170, 179
Marxism 9, 48–9, 99, 156, 160, 178–9,
    182–3, 185, 191–2
masnavi 145
Mathai, S. 18
Mazzini, Giuseppe 179–82, 185, 200
Memoirs (Roy) 188
Menon, Madhavi 169
metalepsis 11, 169–70, 207n2
Metcalfe, Thomas 138
metonyms 26, 169
middle class: alienation of 52, 55, 201–2;
    anti-imperialism of 140; intellectuals
    91; use of literary forms by 100; loyalist
    143; and nationalism 10, 56, 64–5,
    201–2; political use of 79; radical 58,
    200–201; role of 102; solidarity with
    untouchables 58
militarism 195
minorities 6–7, 10, 15, 19, 22; and
    colonialism 198; in Congress 39–40;
    discrimination against 177; and
    ethnic violence 194–5; in Europe 201;
    exploitation of 195; freedom for 2; in
    late-colonial India 107; portrayals of
    8; problem of 37; demand for reform
    by 38; rights of 203; sensitivity toward
    101; uplift for 106
Mir, Mir Taqi 136, 148
Mirat ul-Urus (The bride's mirror) (Ahmad)
    115, 119–20, 141
Misra, Maria 54, 206n15
Moderates (Gramsci) 179, 182, 191

modernism 102, 117, 139, 144, 152; in
    Kanthapura 97; resistance to 176–7;
    secular 106; *see also* modernity;
    modernization
modernity 135, 141, 175, 179, 183, 196, 200;
    see also colonial modernity; modernism;
    modernization
modernization 66–7, 111, 200; *see also*
    modernism; modernity
Mondal, Anshuman 80, 96
Montagu–Chelmsford reforms 37
Morely–Minto reforms 37
Motilal Nehru Report 21
Mughal culture 113–14, 125, 133, 135–6,
    138, 145, 147, 152
Muhammadans: *see* Muslims
"Muhavaton ki ed raat" (A night of winter
    rains) (Ali) 122
Muqaddama-e-shair-o-shairi (The introduction to
    poetry and poetics) (Hali) 118, 142
musaddas 145
Mushaira 151
music, Hindustani 207n9
Muslim League 37, 39, 50, 98, 105–7, 132,
    140–42, 175
Muslims 5, 7, 10, 19; aesthetics of 132;
    and British rule 134, 140–41; and
    colonialism 138–9, 149; confiscation of
    homes of 127; and Congress 106, 154;
    in Congress 39–40, 105, 141; criticism
    of by Ali 139; culture of 113–14,
    118–19, 139, 145; in Delhi 137, 145,
    151; attempt to convert to Hinduism
    132; and Hindus 96–7, 107, 114, 124;
    ideology of 112; as Indians 138; of
    Indian middle ages 101; in late-colonial
    India 124; in literature 202; loyalist 143;
    as minority 106; in North India 107,
    135–6, 141; Muslim identity 114–16,
    133, 141; Muslim weddings 114–16,
    119–23; nationalism and 111, 113,
    124–5, 134–5, 140–41, 152, 154; politics
    of 132; separate electorates for 37;
    see also Islam; Mughal culture; Pakistan
Mussaddas (Hali) 143
Mussolini, Benito 178
mutinies, 182; *see also* Mutiny (of 1857)
Mutiny (of 1857) 44, 107–9, 118, 126–7, 132,
    138–40, 143, 145, 150–51
Mysore 87–9, 204–5n6
Myths of the Nation (Sethi) 96

Nadwat-al Ulema 141
Nagarajan, K. 27
Nagasaki 49
Naidu, Sarojini 24
Naik, M. K. 15–16
Naji, Mahmud Shakir 146
Narasimhaiah, C. D. 18, 25
Narayan, Jayaprakash ("J. P.") 4, 10–11, 14–17, 27, 31, 201; and Communism 171; in Congress 159–70; demands for Congress 162–3; and Emergency (1975) 155, 157, 160; and Gandhi 163–4, 166, 173; as Gandhian 155, 171; emphasizing his Indian-ness 163–4; and nationalism 159; political capriciousness of 160; disillusionment with Socialism 170–71; as Socialist 155, 159–71; vision for India 173
Narayan, R. K. 13
nationalism 5–7, 15, 22, 152, 168–9; anticolonial 50, 171, 177, 195–8, 203; bourgeois 178; and chauvinism 195–6; and colonialism 196; and the Communists 178, 188, 190; criticism of 124, 178; and Delhi 105–13; derivativeness of 98–9; different faces of 31; disarticulation of 10; disillusionment with 177, 194; economic 38, 54; encouraging 19; and English language, 24–5; and English language novels 14, 26–8; and Gandhi 183, 200; Gandhian 9, 17, 30, 70, 73–4, 97, 100, 102; idealist 50; Indian 173; intellectual view of 102; and Karnataka 93; and the Left, 157–8, 179; and liberal imperialism 48; literary 3, 8, 17, 20, 119, 193, 199, 202; middle-class 10, 56, 64–5, 201; and minorities 10; and modernity 175; and modernization 200; and Muslims 109, 111, 113, 124–5, 134–5, 140–41, 152, 154; modified by novelists 7–8; opportunist 50; pan-Indian 140; problems of 137, 179, 183, 197–8; and religion 66, 97; rural focus of 65, 67, 77–9, 86–7, 90–91, 98; secular 166; and social reform 107; and Socialism 170, 178, 186, 189, 192; and the untouchable debate 32–3; urban-rural 71; and women 91–5, 103
"Nationalism in Indo Anglian Fiction" (Sarma) 26

Nationalist Thought and the Colonial World: A Derivative Discourse (Chatterjee) 10, 175
nationalization of industry 163, 173
Navalgund 60
navodaya 67; *see also* Kannada
Naxalites 15
Nayi Roshni 135
nazm 145
"Neend nahin aati" (I can't sleep) (Zaheer) 118–19, 123
Nehru, Pandit Jawaharlal 10, 22, 31, 48, 64, 102, 106, 137, 159–60, 162, 179, 198; on caste 43; and Congress 132; as Congress president 186; and Gandhi 101, 156, 159; on the peasantry 91; as populist 176; secular vision of 99; and Socialism 78
New Delhi 127; *see also* Delhi
New Light literature 135, 141
Nicaragua 197
nihilism 133
No Tax Satyagraha 65, 89, 91–2
Non-Aligned Movement 194–5
Noncooperation movement 17, 59–60, 63, 89, 158, 169, 181, 185, 188, 200; all-India 65; rural agitation during 87
nonviolence 1–2, 4, 60, 155–6, 158, 173, 181, 183, 196, 199; *see also* noncooperation movement; protests; *satyagrahas*
no-rent campaign 87, 89–91, 162
no-revenue campaign 65
Northern India, Muslims in 140–41, 152
Northwest Provinces 37, 132, 141
no-tax campaign 65, 89, 91–2
"Notes on Italian History" (Gramsci) 179, 185
Numani, Shibli 105, 141–2

Official Languages Act 22
Old Fort (Delhi) 136–7
Old Light literature 135
Orientalism (Said) 57

Padma Bhushan award 204n6
Pakistan 13, 19–20, 22, 39, 98, 107, 125, 132, 196
Palestine 196
panchayati raj 99
Pandey, Gyanendra 90
Pan-Slavism 188
Parde ke picche (In the women's quarters) (Jahan) 120–21

Parel, Anthony 155–6
Parry, Benita 7
Parsis, in Congress 39
Pashtun separatists 196
passive revolution 185, 191–2
paternalism 8, 35, 67, 70, 103, 165
Patidar–Dharala conflict 7
patriotic dramas, 81
Peasant Pasts (Chaturvedi), 6
peasantry: and Communism 175; consciousness of 176; dissatisfaction of 90; economic pressure on 90; financial pressures on 88; Gandhi's peasant past 10; historical struggles of 96; ideology of 64–6, 81, 98; and the intelligentsia 97; in Italy 181; in late-colonial India 7, 70; in literature 202; mobilization of 86–7, 199; reluctance of to modernize 101; and nationalism 7, 91, 98; paternalistic attitudes toward 67; and religion 68; secularization of 102; sociology of 101; in Uttar Pradesh 66; voting by 165; worldviews of 67–70, 80, 102, 194; *see also* proletariat
People's Union for Civil Liberties 160
Persian literature 142, 145–7: *see also* Urdu literature
Philip, P. J. 18
Piedmont (Italy) 180
Pisacane, Carlo 180
"Plea for Gandhianism, A" (Narayan) 171
poetry: *see* literature; Urdu poetry
polysyndetons 71–2, 80, 84–5
Poona Pact 31, 36, 39, 42
Portrait of the Artist as a Young Man, A (Joyce) 55
Postcolonial Unconscious, The (Lazarus) 8
postcolonialism 5–9, 15, 136
postmodernism 178, 183, 195
Prabhat Pheris 95
pragativadi 64; *see also* progressivism; Progressive Writers' Association
Praja Socialist Party 160
Prashad, Vijay 48
Premchand: *see* Srivastav, Dhanpat Rai (Premchand)
presentism 177, 197
Pride and Prejudice (Austen) 25
Princely State of Mysore 87–9, 204–5n6
Prison House, The (Ali) 121
Prison Notebooks, The (Gramsci) 185
Progressive Writers' Association 106–7, 109, 115, 125, 132–3; Ali's break with 121–4

Progressive Writers' Movement 4, 64, 67
progressive writing 121, 125
progressivism 4, 64, 67
proletariat 175; proletarian parties, in colonial countries 187; *see also* peasantry
protests 91, 109; boycotts 65, 88, 144, 185, 190; against British Raj 2, 65, 73; against colonialism 87; fasts 20, 36; of jail conditions 92; mass 106; pickets 59–60, 200; strikes 51, 162, 190; against taxation 87, 89; women and 207n6; *see also* noncooperation; nonviolence; *satyagrahas*
public sanitation 44–5, 48, 50–51
Punjab 37, 86, 131–3
Punjab Municipalities Act 51
Punjabi language 35, 202
Puranas 74, 76, 86

qasida 145
qawwali 128
Quit India movement 2, 167, 170, 181
Qutab Minar 136–7

racism 54–5, 58, 201, 206n15; *see also* chauvinism
Radhakrishnan 24
radicalism 112, 202–3
Rajagopalachari, C. (Rajaji) 23
Ram Rajya 72
Ramaswamy, Sumathi 20–21, 177
Ramayana 63, 74, 76, 165
Ramsey-Kurtz, Helga 58
Rana Bheemadeva 81
Rao, Alur Venkata 82
Rao, Raja 1–6, 8–10, 13–17, 25, 27, 201–2, 204–5n6; concerns of 67; literary style of 71, 74–6, 84, 100; on nationalism 98–9; translation of Hindu epics by 72; *see also Kanthapura*
Rashid, Abdul 132
Ravana Rajya 60–62
Ray, Suprakash 98
realism 32, 73, 121–2, 128; in the *shehrashob* 146; social 133; Socialist 117, 121; Soviet 64, 117, 121; Stalinist 121
Reddy, C. R. 18
religion: and authenticity 100–101; and colonial enslavement 64; conservative 103; and nationalism 97; and peasant ideology 81, 98; and politics 100; linked

INDEX

to progressive mobilization 65–6; religious reform 66; *see also* Buddhism; Christianity; Hinduism; Hindus; Islam; Muslims; religious orthodoxy; Sikhism
religious imagery 100–101
religious orthodoxy 8, 78, 86, 139, 153, 193, 200–201
Revision Settlement 88
revisionism 197
revolution 175, 182; passive 177–8, 185, 191–2
Revolutionary Party of the Indian Working Class 189
Right: Brahminical 38; in Congress 38, 158, 167; and "failed states" 194–5; and Gandhi's legacy 173; Hindu 156, 166, 198; modernists and 102
Risorgimento, Italian 176–8, 179–82, 191
Round Table Conferences 36, 40, 42, 44, 49, 106
Rowlatt Act 60, 109
Roy, Arundhati 9
Roy, Manabendranath (M. N.) 4, 10–11, 158, 167; on Gandhi 184–5; in India 186–90
Roy, Raha Rammohan 16
Royal Indian Air Force 182
Royal Indian Navy 182
Rushdie, Salman 9, 15–16
Russell, Ralph 140
Russian Revolution 175
Ruswa, Muhammad Hadi 114

Sabarmati 76
Sahitya Akademi 15, 25
Said, Edward 3, 57
Saklatvala, Shapurji 190
Salt Law 190
Salt March 4, 65, 76, 87, 91, 190, 200
Salt Police 190
Salt Satyagraha: *see* Salt March
Sanatani Hindu 40
sangathan (consolidation) projects 132
sanitation reform 51; *see also* public sanitation
Sanskritic tradition 17–18
Sanskritization 21, 43
Sarfaroshi ki tamanna 144
Sarkar, Sumit 88, 177
Sarma, Gobinda 26, 124
sarvodaya 200
satyagrahas 39, 87, 92, 100, 158, 162; Bardoli Satyagraha 87, 89, 92; No Tax Satyagraha 65, 89, 91–2; no-rent campaign, 87, 89–91; no-revenue campaign 65; Salt March 4, 65, 76, 87, 91; *see also* noncooperation; nonviolence; protests
Sauda 148–9
Scott, Helen 7
Second World 192, 195
Second World War 140, 186, 198
secularism 72, 106; literary 64–70
Serpent and the Rope, The (Rao) 25
Sethi, Rumina 96
Seva Dal 88, 92
Sevika Sangh 76
sexism 8, 10, 67, 103, 111, 115–17, 125–7, 152, 198, 201; *see also* chauvinism; women
sexual repression 115, 117–18, 122–3, 126, 141
"Shaadi" (Wedding) (Ali) 122–4
Shah, Bahadur: *see* Zafar, Bahadur Shah
Shankaracharya 63
sharia 114
sharif culture 112–13, 127–8, 134–5, 139–40, 151, 198
Shauq, Mirza 136
shehrashob 10, 124, 145–50, 154
Shivaji festival 81
Shole (Flames) (Ali) 109–10, 121–2
Shraddhanand, Swami 132
shuddhi (reconversion) projects 132
Siddapur 88
Sikhism, conversion of untouchables to 38
Sikhs 19; in Congress 39
Simhagad 81
Simon Commission 41
Singh, Bhagat 102
Singh, Bhai Vir 35
Singh, Iqbal 98–9
Singh, Khushwant 14, 27
Singh, Mangal 89
Singh, Nanak 35
Sirsi 88
Sirsri-Siddhapur 92
Sitaram, Swami 20
So Many Hungers (Bhattacharya) 13
Socialism 4, 8, 48, 67, 72, 78–9, 103, 106, 157, 159–61, 163, 165–6, 168; and anticolonialism 187, 191; and anti-imperialism 194–5; in Congress 99–100, 106; democratic 160;

disenchantment with 195; feminist 99; Gandhi and 160–61; and Hinduism 163; humanist 58; in India 167, 170–71, 175; indigenous 164; international 175; in *Kanthapura* 97; and nationalism 170, 178, 186, 189, 192–3; Socialist realism 117, 121; as statist authoritarianism 194; Western 163
"Socialism and Sarvodaya" (Narayan) 171
Socialists: *see* Socialism
sociologism 183
solidarity 8, 10; dangerous 203; Indian 101; intelligentsia with untouchables 47, 50; intercaste 46; middle class with untouchables 58; urban-rural 71
Soviet realism 64, 117, 121
Soviet Union 4, 192, 198; collapse of 194
soz 145
spinning wheels (*charkhas*) 31, 65, 89
Spivak, Gayatri Chakravorty 196
Sri Lanka 196
Sri Sivaji Arya Samaj 81
Srikanthaiah, B. M. 67
Sriramulu, Potti 20
Srivastav, Dhanpat Rai (Premchand) 35, 64
Stalin, Joseph 186, 189
Stalinism 191, 197
Stalinist realism 121
States Reorganization Act 22
States Reorganization Commission 20
statism 168, 199, 202
sthalapuranas 10, 72, 74, 79, 82, 84–6
Stock, A. G. 18
Strachey, Sir John 37
strategic essentialism 203
stream-of-consciousness writing 53–4, 122
Stridharma 92
Subaltern studies 5, 7, 98, 177, 182
Subbarayan, Paramasiva 39
Sunni orthodox elite 152
swadeshi campaigns 1, 31, 36, 46, 65, 88, 95, 99
Swami and Friends (Narayan) 13, 16, 25
symbols: expressionist 128; novelistic 112; *see also* allegory, religious
synecdoche 30

tabahi o barbadi 146
Tagore, Rabindranath 18, 31, 101
Tamil Eelam 179, 196
Tamil language 20, 22

Tamil Nadu 43, 88
Tamils, genocide against 196
taraqqi pasandi 64, 125; *see also* progressivism; Progressive Writers' Association
"Tasveer ke do Rukh" (The picture has two faces) 109–10
Tata, J. R. D. 102
taxation 2, 65, 70, 74, 84–5, 92; British 199; criticism of 200; protests against 87, 89
technological development 57, 200; and art 75–6; and social revolution 48–50; *see also* public sanitation
Telangana 20
Telugu language 20
temples, access to 38–9, 200
Thanawi, Maulana Ashraf Ali 114–15, 121
Tharu, Susie 47–8
Third Period (Comintern) 186, 189–90
Third World 195
three-language formula 22
Tilak, Bal Gangadhar "Lokamanya" 63, 76, 88
Tolstoyism 185
trade unions 171
transformism 4, 10, 190–92
"Transition to Socialism, The" (Narayan) 167
Trilling, Lionel 27
Trivedi, Harish 124
Tughlaq, Feroz Shah 137
Turkey, Islamic caliphate in 142
Twilight in Delhi (Ali) 4, 6, 7, 27, 105, 107, 124; anticommunal vision of 114; contradictions in 153; culture of Delhi in 126–34; Gandhi represented in 110; introduction to 113–14; marriage in 115–16, 124–7, 133–4; politics of Delhi in 134–45; tensions in 139–40; Urdu literary antecedents to 116–21; Urdu poetry in 128, 130–31, 142, 147–51
two-nations theory 105, 142

ulama, Muslim 105
Ullah, Zaka 142–3
Umrao Jan Ada (Ruswa) 114
underconfidence: and the Congress in Karnataka 86–95; in narration 79–85
Union Public Services Commission 22
United Provinces 105–6, 116, 132, 154
United Provinces Municipalities Act 51
universities, Indian writing in English at 15, 18–19, 24–5; nationalist 65

INDEX 235

Untouchable (Anand) 3, 6, 16, 25, 205n4; Anand's description of writing process, 46–7; examination of untouchables in 29–33; Gandhi's influence on 13, 29, 34–6, 55–7; nationalism in 30–33; race-consciousness in 32; theme of solidarity in 51–8
untouchables 5, 10, 19, 27, 205n1; abolition of untouchability 36–9, 99, 101, 200; abuse of 29; accurate depiction of 35–6; freedom for 198; Hinduism and 36–7; in literature 202; political debate over 31–3; revolt of 51; separate electorates for 36–7, 41; solidarity with middle class 58; voice of 49, 52–4, 57–8
urban restructuring projects 44–5
urbanization, Nehruvian 71
Urdu culture 133, 135; *see also* Urdu literature; Urdu poetry
Urdu language 35, 60, 140, 207n2; Ali's shift away from 121, 124; as literary language 145; proponents of 143; *see also* Urdu literature; Urdu poetry
Urdu literature 4, 64, 112–13, 116–21, 125, 132, 140, 142, 154; weddings in 125; *see also* Urdu language; Urdu poetry
Urdu poetry 118, 131, 133, 136–7, 139, 142–3, 145; *ghazal*, 10, 118, 128, 136, 143, 145–6, 149; *shehrashob* 10, 124, 145–51, 154; in *Twilight in Delhi* 128, 130–31, 142, 147–51; *see also* Urdu language; Urdu literature
utopianism 125, 153, 189, 193
Uttar Kanara 1, 70, 87–9, 91–3
Uttar Pradesh 66, 87, 90
uz-Zafar, Mahmud 107, 116–17, 123

Vana Dukha Navrana Sabha 92
varnashrama 38, 42
varnashrama dharma 29
Veerasaiva Mahasabha 88
Venkataramani, K. S. 27
Victoria High School 81
Vietnam 182, 194
Vietnam War 196
violence: caste-based 29, 53; communal 97, 106; ethnic 177, 194–6; in Russia 170; against women 97; *see also* nonviolence
Vishnupurana 63
Vivekananda, Swami 24
Vokkaligara Sangha 88
Vokkaligas 88

War of Independence (1857) 140
Waterfield, E. H. 63
wealth, distribution of 8, 106, 193, 200, 203
weddings, Muslim 114–16, 119–27, 133–4
Western imperialism: *see* imperialism
"Why Socialism?" (Narayan) 162, 164
women 5–7, 10, 19; and Brahminical Hinduism 66; and civil disobedience 103; in Congress 88, 91, 103; in *Kanthapura* 77–81, 85–6; liberation of 2, 64, 93, 95, 111, 118, 200; in literature 202; Muslim 111; and the nationalist movement 91–5, 103; peasant 93–5, 19; and political leadership 76; understanding of politics by 79–80; and poverty 92–4, 117, 122; and protest 207n6; reform for 67–8; rights of 203; self-activity of 198; self-emancipation of 103; and sexuality 122 (*see also* sexual repression); stereotype of 103; uplift for 106, 150; viewpoint of 72; violence against 97; *see also* sexual repression
"Work of Art in the Era of Mechanical Reproduction, The" (Benjamin) 75
World Bank 197

Yama rajya 60–62
yarn, homespun (*khadi*) 65, 89
Yeravda Jail 36
yoga 99
Young India 34, 36
Youth League 189
Yudhishtra, Raja 129

Zafar, Bahadur Shah 131, 136–7, 152
Zaheer, Sajjad 107, 112, 116–19, 121, 123–5, 132–3
Zauq, Muhammad Ibrahim 148–9
zenana 111–12, 115, 126
Zetli, Mir Jafir 146

www.ingramcontent.com/pod-product-compliance
Lightning Source LLC
Chambersburg PA
CBHW021825300426
44114CB00009BA/321